AN INTRODUCTION TO
ANGLO-SAXON ENGLAND

AN INTRODUCTION TO ANGLO-SAXON ENGLAND

BY

PETER HUNTER BLAIR

Fellow of Emmanuel College, Cambridge

CAMBRIDGE

AT THE UNIVERSITY PRESS

1956

PUBLISHED BY
THE SYNDICS OF THE CAMBRIDGE UNIVERSITY PRESS
London Office: Bentley House, N.W. 1
American Branch: New York
Agents for Canada, India, and Pakistan: Macmillan

Printed in Great Britain at the University Press, Cambridge
(Brooke Crutchley, University Printer)

TO MY FATHER

PREFACE

THIS book has been written at the suggestion of the Syndics of the Cambridge University Press. Its purpose is to give a general introduction to the history of England from the latter part of the Roman occupation until the beginning of the Norman Age. Within this period of about seven centuries Britain ceased to be part of the Roman Empire and was three times invaded, first by Anglo-Saxons, then by Scandinavians and finally by Normans. Such events are without parallel in Britain's later history and in the changes which they worked lie the origin and early growth of many elements which are at the roots of English history. The establishment of Germanic peoples in an island whose earlier population had been Celtic, the creation of the kingdom of England as a political unit, the development of English as a spoken and written language, the death of heathenism and the growth of a vigorous Christian Church—these are matters which belong in some ways as much to the present as to the past.

The novice whose schooling has taught him at least something about the history of more recent times may well find himself bewildered on his first approach to the Anglo-Saxon period. In these pages I have sought to smooth his path by offering him a guide to what seem to me at least to be its most interesting and important features. The study of this period is at heart a study of sources and because this ought to be understood even by the novice, I have tried to tell him something about the evidence on which the narrative is based, about its weakness as well as its strength. In particular the plates have been chosen mainly to illustrate objects which are in themselves important historical documents, whether the material of which they are made is vellum, stone, whalebone or needlework. Footnotes have been used sparingly, perhaps too sparingly, to refer the reader to the source of a passage quoted in the text, to adduce support for an opinion on a controversial topic, or to cite a source of information which may not be familiar even to those who are no longer novices. The book is based at almost every point upon a first-hand study of the evidence, but I am not so foolish as to pretend that its foundations are everywhere of equal strength. The period is too long and the evidence too diverse for any one person to be able to take a firm grasp of the whole. Nor am I so ungracious as to be unmindful of my debt to others, to my first teacher, H. M. Chadwick, to Mrs Chadwick who has helped me both by her comments on the proofs and by her unfailing enthusiasm, and, through their writings, to many other scholars, especially Sir Frank Stenton and Dr Whitelock. There remain two others, my wife whose help has been greater than she can know or I can tell, and Professor Bruce Dickins who has read the whole book in typescript and again in proof. There are many other authors who have watched (not without trembling) while his eagle eye has scanned their pages and pounced on error. They will understand how much I owe him.

For help in obtaining photographs and for permission to reproduce them my thanks are given to the Trustees of the British Museum, to the Cambridge University Library Syndicate, to the librarians of Bodley and the Bibliothèque Nationale in Paris, to the Master and Fellows of Corpus Christi College, Cambridge, the Air Ministry, the National Buildings Record, the Society of Antiquaries of Newcastle-upon-Tyne and the Hampshire and Dorset Field Club; also to the Rev. T. Romans, Dr J. K. St Joseph, Mr L. P. Morley and Mr R. H. Hayes. My particular thanks are due to Lieut.-Col. C. F. Battiscombe for his help in obtaining for me one of the photographs of Ælfflæd's stole which have been taken for the Friends of Durham Cathedral for use in their forthcoming work on the relics of St Cuthbert. I must also thank the Society of Antiquaries of London and Oxford University Press for per-

Preface

mission to reproduce church plans drawn by C. R. Peers, A. W. Clapham and W. H. Knowles, as well as the Gyldendalske Boghandel Nordisk Forlag, Copenhagen, for allowing me to reproduce the plan of Trelleborg drawn by P. Nørlund. For permission to reproduce some passages of Anglo-Saxon verse in translations by Professor C. W. Kennedy I am grateful to Messrs Hollis and Carter and to Oxford University Press. Finally I owe much to the kindly help ungrudgingly given by the staff of the Cambridge University Press, especially in the drawing of the maps.

P. H. B.

Emmanuel College
Cambridge

CONTENTS

Contents

LIST OF PLATES

List of Plates

LIST OF MAPS

LIST OF TEXT-FIGURES

CHAPTER I

THE FOUNDATIONS OF ENGLAND

I. THE LAST DAYS OF ROMAN BRITAIN

BRITAIN was part of the Roman Empire for about four centuries. At first a single province, then, in the time of Severus, two provinces, it was later subdivided into four which together formed one of the twelve dioceses which then constituted the empire. The diocese of Britain was united with transalpine Gaul and Spain to form a prefecture. In 350, to make an arbitrary choice of a date, the Hadrianic frontier from Tyne to Solway was garrisoned in strength and formed the effective northern boundary of Roman civil and military rule in Britain. South of this line the whole of what are now England and Wales was under Roman rule, but the country was threatened from the north and west by the Celtic peoples of Scotland and Ireland, as well as from the east and south by Germanic seafarers against whom it had become necessary to erect strong coastal defences, but who had not yet established any permanent foothold. Three hundred years later Roman political and military authority in Britain had long since vanished, and Germanic peoples possessed most of what now forms England and the lowlands of Scotland. South of Forth and Clyde, Celtic peoples maintained their independence only in three more or less isolated groups, in the south-western peninsula, in Wales and in an ill-defined part of south-western Scotland between Clyde and Solway. North of Clyde, the Scots, formerly natives of Ireland, had established a kingdom which was not yet extensive, and the remainder of northern Scotland formed the kingdom of the Picts. The Hadrianic Wall which had marked the north-western frontier of the Roman Empire for close on three centuries, had completely lost all significance as a boundary.

These changes, whose magnitude is unsurpassed in the later history of Britain, were accompanied by a breakdown in those processes of recording history which are the normal accompaniment of literate civilizations in less turbulent ages. The difficulties of assembling, and even more of interpreting, the evidence of their progress are so great that some may think the attempt ought not to be made, yet by the critical study of traditions embodied in the records of later times and by the use of archaeological and place-name evidence it seems possible to reach at least some tentative conclusions. Those who interest themselves in this period should understand that from about 409, the year in which the Emperor Honorius wrote to Britain bidding the *civitates* defend themselves as best they could, until 597, when Augustine landed in Thanet, there are few events in the history of Britain so firmly established that they can be regarded as incontrovertible historical facts. In these circumstances history must give place to conjecture.

During the first half of the fourth century Roman Britain enjoyed peace and prosperity behind her frontier defences, but in 360 bands of Picts and Scots ravaged the northern frontier districts and a field army was sent to Britain to assist the garrison forces in suppressing these disturbances. In 367 a combined assault was made by Picts, Scots and Saxons, who overwhelmed the Hadrianic Wall, defeated its garrisons, killed one of the two commanders-in-chief in Britain and overran a large part of the country. For two years the civil and military government ceased to function, but in 369 Theodosius, a distinguished soldier, reached Britain with large forces and began to rid the country of bands of marauders who were roaming at will and had reduced even London to a state of siege. By vigorous action he re-established Roman authority as far north as the Wall, whose buildings he repaired. Outpost forts beyond the Wall were left abandoned, but it seems likely, in the light of later events in the north, that he reached some understanding with the rulers of native states beyond the Tyne-Solway line.

In 383 Magnus Maximus, a Spaniard who then held a high command in the army in Britain, determined upon an attempt to seize the western empire from Gratian, and to achieve this end he crossed the Channel to Gaul, taking with him many of the troops stationed in Britain. It is at present the most widely accepted view that this episode left the Hadrianic Wall either entirely abandoned, or at best held only by skeleton forces, and that it marked the end of the Wall's history as a military frontier. Yet since the evidence for this view is almost wholly negative it may not be acceptable to all. Magnus Maximus was killed in 388 and some years passed before Britain was again brought under Roman control, but at some time between 395 and 399 measures were taken for its defence by Stilicho, one of the generals of Theodosius. There is much uncertainty about the nature of these measures. In 401 or 402 Stilicho himself withdrew troops from Britain for warfare against the Goths. During the next few years, the remainder of the armies in Britain set up a succession of usurpers in the hope that they would provide a more effective defence for the country. Two of these, Marcus and Gratian, were soon murdered, and the third, Constantine, seeking to justify his loyalty to the emperor, crossed over to Gaul, taking with him troops for his support. The Britons, thus deserted by Constantine, expelled his governors, made what arrangements they could for their own defence and appealed to Honorius for help. In his reply, sent in 409, Honorius told the British *civitates* that they must take care of themselves. There are some who hold that the letter sent by Honorius marks the final abandonment of Britain as part of the Roman Empire, but others believe that a subsequent attempt to recover Britain led to a re-occupation of a part of the country for a few years from *c.* 417 till *c.* 429. Much turns upon the evidence contained in a document called the *Notitia Dignitatum* and upon the significance attached to the distribution of late Roman coins in south-eastern Britain. Many scholars have given close attention to the problems raised by these materials, but no general agreement has been reached.

2. THE ENEMIES OF ROMAN BRITAIN

For the first two centuries of the Romano-British period the defences of Britain were designed in part to restrain the upland peoples of Wales and northern England whose lands fell within the boundaries of the province and in part to prevent an irruption of the more northerly peoples whose lands lay beyond the frontier. It was not until after the middle of the third century that the growth of piracy in the Narrow Seas led to the building of fortifications along the eastern and southern shores of Britain. These took the form of a series of large, defensive fortresses which guarded the principal harbours from the Wash to the Isle of Wight, and at the end of the Roman period they were commanded by an officer called the Count of the Saxon Shore.[1] It is important not to lose sight of the dual nature of the attack upon Roman Britain in its later years, the Celtic from the north and west and the Germanic from the east and south.

The two peoples mainly concerned in the northern attack were the Picts and the Scots. The Roman historian Ammianus Marcellinus, writing of the events of 367–8, states that the Picts were then divided into two peoples, the *Dicalydonae* and the *Verturiones*. The former name is to be associated with the *Kalēdonioi* of Ptolemy and with *Caledonia*, the name applied by Tacitus to the northern part of Britain. The name *Verturiones* survived as Fortrenn, that part of the Pictish kingdom which lay immediately to the north of the Antonine Wall. It appears that by the end of the fourth century the Picts enjoyed supremacy over virtually the whole of Scotland north of the Forth-Clyde isthmus. The principal centre of their power seems generally to have lain near the eastern coastal areas between Tay and Dee, the district known as Circinn, though there was a time in the sixth century when it lay as far north as Inverness (see Map 4). Bede, writing in the eighth century, also describes the Picts as being separated into two groups. He calls them the northern and southern Picts and states that they were separated from one another by a great range of

---

[1] The name 'Saxon Shore' (*litus Saxonicum*) refers to those parts of the shores of Britain and Gaul which were subjected to attack by Germanic seafarers. After the fall of Roman power in Britain, small groups of Germanic settlers, offshoots from the larger groups then crossing to Britain itself, established themselves at one or two points on the Gaulish coast, mainly near Boulogne and Bayeux. Near the latter lay a district called *Otlinga Saxonia* and perhaps also another called *Otlinga Harduini*. On these and on the *Saxones Bajocassini*, mentioned by Gregory of Tours, see H. Prentout, *Essai sur les Origines et la Fondation du Duché de Normandie* (Paris, 1911), pp. 51–76, 280–1, a reference for which I am indebted to Professor B. Dickins.

4

mountains. The Irish missionary Columba established himself in Iona in *c.* 563, whence he led a successful mission to the northern Picts, securing the conversion of the Pictish King Brude, son of Mailcon, near Inverness. According to Bede the southern Picts had been converted long since by Ninian. The earliest recorded contact between the Picts and the English took place *c.* 620 when members of a Northumbrian royal family sought refuge among them as exiles, but by this time the supremacy of the Picts in northern Britain had been effectively challenged by another of the peoples named by Ammianus Marcellinus, the Scots.

At the time of the great attack on Roman Britain in 367 the Scots were an overseas people whose home was in Ireland. It is difficult to say when they first established settlements on the mainland of Britain, but a variety of evidence, some of it legendary, some archaeological and some historical, suggests that the western coasts of Britain from the southern shores of the Bristol Channel northwards to the Clyde, were exposed to attack from at least the fourth century and in some instances such attacks were followed by enduring settlements. Archaeological discoveries at Lydney in Gloucestershire have revealed the existence there of a prosperous community in the late fourth century which worshipped a god with close Irish affinities. Irish records indicate that the royal house of the kingdom of Dyfed in south-west Wales was believed to be descended from people who had been expelled from Meath in the third century. The construction of a fortress at Cardiff of a type similar to those found along the Saxon shore, the building of a new fort at Carnarvon and the fortification of the harbour at Holyhead represent some of the measures taken to meet the danger of attack from Ireland during the latter part of the Roman occupation. Something will be said later of the evidence which seems to indicate a successful attempt to evict Scottish settlers from north-west Wales after the end of the Roman occupation. St Patrick's account of how he was carried off to Ireland by a band of marauding Scots is an indication of the conditions prevailing in western Britain late in the fourth and early in the fifth centuries. After he had become a bishop St Patrick experienced a raid in the opposite direction when some of his newly-baptized Irish converts were carried off by marauders from the Clyde area.

The Scottish attacks against the western shores of what are now England and Wales had no lasting consequences for the political geography of Britain, but a little after the middle of the fifth century a Scottish settlement was established farther north, in Argyll and the islands to the west of the mainland. This settlement was an offshoot from the kingdom of Dalriada in northern Ireland and is said to have been established by three princes, Fergus, the son of Erc, and his two brothers, Loarn and Angus. It too came to be called the kingdom of Dalriada and care must be taken to distinguish the Dalriada of Ireland from its offshoot the Dalriada of Scotland. It has been suggested that the Dalriada of Scotland came into being through a colonizing movement carried out with the co-operation of the northern Welsh people who lived near the western end of the Antonine Wall and whose capital was at Dumbarton on the Clyde. According to this conjecture, the purpose of the move was to interrupt the western sea-communications of the Picts, and by confining them to their mountain territories, to reduce the menace which they offered to the security of the northern Welsh. The principal strongholds of the new kingdom were at Dunolly Castle, Oban, and at Dunadd in the Moss of Crinan. It grew steadily in power and towards the end of the sixth century one of its kings, Aedan, son of Gabran (*c.* 574–608), was strong enough to overrun the Pictish provinces between Forth and Tay. Meanwhile the English in Northumbria were growing in strength and in the year 603 their king Æthelfrith inflicted a defeat on Aedan which proved a severe setback to the power of the Scots in northern Britain. Throughout the seventh and eighth centuries the kingdom of Dalriada continued to exist alongside the kingdom of the Picts, but *c.* 850 Kenneth MacAlpin, king of Dalriada, secured possession of the kingdom of the Picts and the kingdom of Scotland began to take shape.

Roman writers usually refer to the raiders who periodically attacked the eastern and southern shores of Britain from the third century onwards as Saxons, a generic term which may be supposed to have embraced a variety of different Germanic peoples. Later writers distinguish four such peoples as taking part in the invasion and settlement of Britain. Both Bede and Alfred were interested in their remote ancestry and left a record of what they had learned about it. Bede's record is the most detailed. He believed that the invaders of Britain had come from three of the more powerful peoples of *Germania*, that is from the Saxons, the Angles and the Jutes. From the Saxons, that is from the district which in his day was called the land of the Old Saxons, had come the East Saxons, the South Saxons and the West Saxons. From the Angles, that is from the country called *Angulus* which lay between the land of the Saxons and the Jutes and which had lain deserted ever since, came the East Anglians, the Middle Anglians, the Mercians and the Northumbrians. And from the Jutes came the people of Kent, the Isle of Wight and the coastal area of Wessex opposite Wight.

Alfred's information about the peoples and geography of northwestern Europe was mainly derived from two sea-captains who visited his court after much sailing in northern waters. One of these, Ohthere (O.N. Óttarr), a native of Norway, described to Alfred the course of a five-day journey by sea from a port near Oslo southwards to Hedeby near Slesvig. As he sailed south for the first three days open sea lay to starboard and land which was then controlled by the Danes, but which is now part of Sweden, to port. For the last two days a number of islands lay to starboard and among these islands the English (*Engle*) formerly lived. Hedeby, his objective, he described as lying between the lands of the Wends, the Saxons and the English (see Map 1). Alfred made a lasting record of this valuable information by inserting it in his translation of the *History* written by Orosius in the fifth century. The evidence of Bede and Alfred can be supplemented by information derived from the *History of the Wars* which was written at Byzantium by Procopius soon after the middle of the sixth century. Procopius records that among the peoples living in Britain at that time were the English and the Frisians. Procopius also believed that Britain was inhabited by the souls of the dead who were ferried thither across the Channel and that the climate north of the Roman Wall was so pestilential that only serpents could live there, but his information about the human races of Britain was probably derived from a small group of Englishmen who are known to have visited Byzantium as part of a Frankish embassy to the Emperor Justinian. His reference to the English in Britain is earlier than Bede's by nearly two centuries and his statement about the Frisians is supported by linguistic evidence of a close connexion between the English and Frisian languages which a cautious scholar has called 'the first certain fact in English history'.[1]

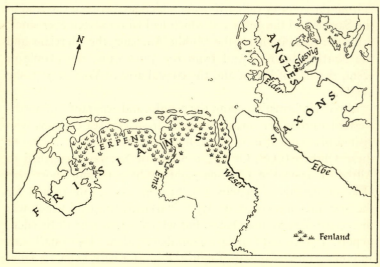

Map 1. The Continental homelands of the Germanic invaders.

The earliest reference to the English is in the *Germania* of Tacitus where, under the name *Anglii*, they are described as being one of a group of seven tribes who worshipped a goddess called Nerthus at an island sanctuary. It may be inferred from this passage that the *Anglii* were a seaboard people, though the passage itself does not reveal whether the island on which the sanctuary of Nerthus lay was in the North Sea or the Baltic. There is a conflict of evidence between Tacitus and the geo-

[1] F. M. Stenton, *Anglo-Saxon England* (Oxford, 2nd ed. 1947), p. 6.

grapher Ptolemy who regarded the Angles as an inland people and located them to the west of the middle Elbe. Most scholars are, however, agreed that Ptolemy was here in error. A fragment of tradition preserved in the Old English poem *Widsið* refers to Offa, a king of *Angel*, establishing the boundary of his kingdom by a river called *Fifeldor*. This is thought to be a name by which the River Eider was once known. The evidence of *Widsið*, combined with that of Tacitus, Bede and Alfred, justifies the belief that the English lived in the southern part of the Jutland peninsula before they migrated to Britain. The name of their homeland, which Bede calls *Angulus*, seems to be preserved in the provincial name Angeln applied to the area north-east of Slesvig. According to Bede the northern neighbours of the *Angli* were the Jutes (*Iutae*), but the difficulties in the way of accepting this location are so great that many scholars reject it. Wherever the original home of the Jutes may have been, there are indications that they had been in close contact with the Frankish Rhineland before migrating to Britain.

Tacitus makes no reference to the Saxons, but Ptolemy places them on the neck of the Cimbric peninsula, that is in the modern Holstein. At the time of which Tacitus was writing, the first century A.D., the dominant people in this part of the European mainland were the *Chauci* whose home according to Ptolemy lay along the coast between the Elbe and the Ems. Beyond the Ems and as far down the coast as the Rhine mouths Ptolemy placed the Frisians. In the course of time the *Chauci* lost their pre-eminence and the Saxons began to spread southwards. By the middle of the third century they seem to have been in possession of all the country between the Elbe and the Weser, and soon afterwards the Romans found it necessary to strengthen their Channel fleet as a protection against Saxon piracy. The excavation of large numbers of cremation cemeteries has shown that the area between the Elbe and the Weser came to be heavily populated.

Westwards from the Weser to the Zuyder Zee, then as now, geographical conditions presented formidable difficulties to those who sought to earn their livelihood in this part of the North Sea littoral. Dutch archaeologists estimate that at some period about

500 B.C. or a little later the North Sea which had receded during the last glaciation, broke down the low-lying barriers protecting the Frisian coast and rendered it entirely uninhabitable. Shortly after 300 B.C. silting had proceeded so far that habitation again became possible on mounds artificially raised above the natural ground level as a protection against flooding. Such mounds, called *terpen*, at first small and subsequently growing to a great size, continued to be inhabited for many centuries, providing the only sure defence against the sea until the construction of dykes was begun about the year A.D. 1000. The mounds themselves were carefully built of successive layers of vegetable material, cattle dung, sods and clay and in time they became able to support substantial farming communities. Several of these *terpen* and their associated cemeteries have now been excavated and it has been demonstrated with almost startling clarity that in the period A.D. 400–450 a strong Saxon element intruded itself upon the native civilization of the Frisian *terpen*. This intrusive element is distinguishable not merely by characteristic forms of Saxon and Frisian pottery, but even more strikingly by the strong contrast offered between the types of dwelling-houses and other buildings erected by the two peoples. The evidence seems to justify the conclusion of a Dutch archaeologist that in the first half of the fifth century the northern part of the Netherlands suffered an Anglo-Saxon invasion similar to that which Britain experienced soon afterwards.[1] No vestige of any Continental Frisian tradition about such an invasion has been preserved, but the Anglo-Saxons themselves may have remembered something of it into historical times.

Although several authorities recognize the separate existence in early times of Angles, Saxons and Frisians, and in some degree also of Jutes, it is probable that the great movement of peoples which historians know as the Migration Period, did much to lessen racial distinctions, particularly when the crossing of a sea was involved. Bede's evidence on racial distribution in England is not to be lightly set aside, but there are many grounds for thinking

---

[1] P. C. J. A. Boeles, *Friesland tot de Elfde Eeuw* (2e dr., 's-Gravenhage, 1951), especially pp. 109–258, English summary, pp. 566–82.

PLATE I

JEWELLERY FROM SUTTON HOO

that his threefold division reflects the orderliness of his own mind rather than the realities of the settlements. The evidence of language, social and agrarian custom, archaeology and place-names reveals a general measure of uniformity throughout most of the country which argues strongly against the existence of sharp racial differences. Philologists recognize linguistic dialects which they call West-Saxon, Kentish, Anglian and so forth, but most of the distinguishing criteria can first be observed long after the invasion period and seem to have been determined more by political and geographical boundaries within England itself than by distinctions of racial origin. Bede himself occasionally uses *Angli* and *Saxones* as alternative names for the same people, and Alfred, though a native of Saxon territory, as Bede would have it, regularly called his language English. Similarly, archaeologists recognize certain kinds of jewellery as characteristic of Anglian, Saxon and Jutish areas, but it is doubtful whether their distinguishing features represent anything more than local differences of fashion. Some brooches from Kent are of types common in East and Middle Anglia, and East Anglia has recently yielded jewellery of a 'Kentish' type which is of greater excellence than the Kentish material itself (Pl. I). Although there are some features, mainly of social and agrarian organization, which are peculiar to Kent and part of East Sussex, the general uniformity in the remainder of the country is of greater significance than the occasional variations.

It is not apparent why the people called *Engle* in Old English and *Angli* by Latin writers gave their name to the country which they came to inhabit. There is no evidence to suggest that they were more numerous than the other immigrants or that they took a particularly prominent part in the invasions. In the vernacular chronicles the territorial name, in the form *Englaland* from which 'England' developed, first comes into regular use in the eleventh century. Despite sporadic occurrences in these and other sources at an earlier date, it still seems something of a novelty when Cnut became king (1016), though it was well established before the middle of the eleventh century. It was not, however, the only vernacular name in use at this time. Alongside it occurs the term

Angelcynn, which meant literally 'the English nation', but which was used territorially of the country itself. This latter name represents an earlier phase of nomenclature in which reference was commonly made to peoples rather than to the geographical areas in which they lived. It was used regularly by Alfred, both in his translation of Bede's *Ecclesiastical History* and in the preface to his translation of Gregory's *Pastoral Care*, works which are generally attributed to the closing years of the ninth century. The vernacular usages of the time of Bede are not known because of the lack of records in the native language. Bede himself, writing of course in Latin, knew from Pliny the old name *Albion*, but whenever he wished to refer to the island which now comprises England, Wales and Scotland he used the name *Brittania* or *Britannia*. Of the country as a whole he never used any territorial name derived either from *Engle* or from the Latin form *Angli*.

The adjective *Englisc* was in regular use from the time of Alfred onwards, both in the sense of 'Englishman' and as meaning 'the English language'. Thus an entry for the year 897 in the *Anglo-Saxon Chronicle* records that sixty-two Frisians and Englishmen (*Engliscra*) fell in a sea-fight in that year. The same source records that among those who recognized the authority of Edward the Elder in 920 were all who lived in Northumbria, whether Englishmen (*Englisce*), Danes, Norwegians or others. For the linguistic sense of the word *Englisc* we cannot do better than refer to the words of Alfred's complaint about the decay of scholarship in his day, when, so he wrote, there were very few south of Humber who could understand their service-books in English (*on Englisc*) or even translate a letter from Latin into English (*of Lædene on Englisc*). It was partly because of the growing ignorance of Latin that he set himself to translate into English the book called in Latin *Pastoralis* and in English *Hirdeboc* (*þa boc...þe is genemned on Læden Pastoralis ond on Englisc Hirdeboc*).[1] The practice of designating this earliest phase of English history by the term 'Anglo-Saxon' has become established by long use. The term was first used in Continental Latin sources, to

[1] Alfred's *Preface* to his translation of Gregory's *Pastoral Care*, ed. H. Sweet, E.E.T.S. 45 (1871), p. 6.

distinguish the Saxons who lived in England, the English Saxons, from those who lived on the Continent and who were known to Bede as the Old Saxons. It was never very common in England though it was used of Alfred by Asser, and it is also found in the charters of his successors, Edward the Elder and Athelstan.

3. TRADITIONS ABOUT THE INVASIONS

The written traditions about the Anglo-Saxon invasions of Britain can best be considered under two heads, the Welsh and the English. In addition to these two groups of material there are some isolated pieces of information contained in Continental sources. The Welsh tradition is most fully represented in a work called *De Excidio et Conquestu Britanniae* which is ascribed to Gildas, a native of Britain, who is believed to have composed it shortly before 548. Gildas was prophet and preacher rather than historian and most of his *De Excidio* was devoted to a vituperative attack upon backsliding Christians of his own times. Although he was capable of gross error, believing, for example, that the two Roman walls in Britain were built after the time of Magnus Maximus, it would be a great mistake to dismiss out of hand the work of the earliest writer to attempt a narrative of events in Britain from the latter part of the Roman period until the latter part of the Anglo-Saxon invasion period.

This narrative contains several points of great difficulty and is not easily summarized without distortion. It seems, however, to imply that the native British were in some way able by their own efforts to overcome the difficulties in which they had been placed by the Roman withdrawal and to prevent any repetition of the disaster of 367. This achievement, it is said, introduced a period of prosperity to which Gildas and his contemporaries looked back as to a golden age. But in time there was a renewed threat of invasion to meet which a certain man who is called 'a proud tyrant' (*superbus tyrannus*), but who is not otherwise named, decided to call in the Saxons in order that they might help the British to repel invaders from the north. Three shiploads of Saxons arrived and were given lands on which to settle in the eastern part of the island. They were later followed by further contingents who agreed to fight for the British in return for lands. All went well for a time, but a dispute about the supply of provisions led the Saxons to revolt against the British and in the course of their revolt they caused great destruction throughout the country. Later some of the Saxons went home and the British, led by Ambrosius Aurelianus, won a victory over the remainder. A long period of warfare followed in which now one side and now the other was victorious until the British won a great victory at a place called *Mons Badonicus.* This victory was followed by a period of peace which still endured when Gildas was writing his account. The points about this story which deserve particular attention are that the Saxons originally came to Britain as hired mercenaries, not as invaders, to fight against northern enemies, that the locality of their earliest settlements is described only in the most general terms as being in the eastern part of the island, that the only name mentioned in the whole story is that of Ambrosius Aurelianus and that no dates are given. It should further be noted that in describing the period of peace which followed the British victory at *Mons Badonicus,* Gildas was writing of what he himself witnessed and his evidence on this point is that of a contemporary authority.

English traditions about the invasion period are found in a variety of sources. One, and perhaps two, of these traditions relate to times before the English reached Britain. It is now generally accepted that certain stories which are told in a twelfth-century St Albans work called *Vitae Duorum Offarum* and in the work of the twelfth-century Danish historian Saxo Grammaticus, are to be connected with brief passages in two Old English poems, *Widsið* and *Beowulf,* and that these various sources establish the historical existence of a line of English kings who were ruling near Slesvig at the end of the fourth century. One of these kings was called Offa and from him was descended the dynasty which ruled in Mercia and which included a second Offa (757–96) as its most famous member.

The other tradition is found in a fragment of an Old English poem called *The Fight at Finnsburg* and in what is called *The Finn*

Episode in *Beowulf*. There are many obscure points in the story told in this tradition, but in its general outline it runs as follows. A company of warriors from Denmark led by their King Hnæf visited Finn, a king of Frisia. One night a band of Finn's men attacked these warriors in the hall in which they were living and there was a fierce fight lasting five days. None of the warriors from Denmark fell during these five days, and it seems that the attackers were about to turn away, but at this point the fragmentary poem breaks off. From *Beowulf* we learn that Hnæf was eventually killed and that the men from Denmark, now led by Hengest, made a truce with Finn whereby they were to receive a separate hall of their own in which to live and to be treated equally with the men of Finn. Hengest and his companions remained in Frisia during the winter which followed, but some of them eventually returned to Denmark where they gathered reinforcements to make a further attack upon Finn whom they eventually killed. Nothing is said of what happened to Hengest. The only other Hengest known to tradition is the man of that name who is associated with the familiar story of the Jutish settlement in Kent. H. M. Chadwick's consideration of the evidence led him to think it more probable than not that the two Hengests were identical.[1] It may perhaps be further suggested that the story of Hengest and Finn preserves the memory of an episode in that Anglo-Saxon invasion of Frisia whose occurrence in the first half of the fifth century has been demonstrated by excavations in the Frisian *terpen* and their associated cemeteries. If this interpretation could be accepted, we should be able to see in Hengest the progress of one chieftain from Denmark, through Frisia to south-eastern Britain within the period *c*. 400–450.

Before turning to the more familiar aspects of Hengest's story, it may be remarked that Bede incorporated in his *Ecclesiastical History* almost the whole of the tradition told by Gildas, but with certain important modifications. He gave the name Vortigern to the man whom Gildas called simply *superbus tyrannus* and he said also that the leaders of the Saxons whose help Vortigern enlisted, were two brothers called Hengest and Horsa, and that

[1] *The Origin of the English Nation* (Cambridge, 1907), pp. 44–50.

Horsa was buried in Kent.[1] In addition, where Gildas left everything vague, he fitted the whole story into the chronological framework upon which his *History* was based. The principal result of
Bede's modifications was to give locality, definition and chronological rigidity to a tradition which, in the form recorded by
Gildas, was singularly lacking in all these characteristics, and it
must not be forgotten that Bede was writing nearly two hundred
years later than Gildas. The most detailed story about Hengest is
found in a later work called the *Historia Brittonum*, sometimes
known by the name of one of its editors, Nennius. In this work
Hengest and his brother Horsa are represented as exiles who were
given land in Thanet against a promise to fight Vortigern's
enemies. Later they sent for reinforcements which arrived in
sixteen ships bringing with them Rowena, Hengest's daughter,
who married the British king. Some of Hengest's followers made
an expedition to the north, but in Kent hostilities broke out
between Hengest and the son of the British king. The Saxons
were worsted in four battles, but were able to restore their fortunes
by a treacherous attack upon the British whom they had met for
a conference. It will be observed that romance has established a
footing in this version of the story of Hengest. But more serious
than this is the fact that its superficial resemblance to the story
told by Gildas has so obscured the fundamental differences
between the two that it is now extremely difficult to contemplate
the story told by Gildas without thinking of the settlements in the
eastern part of the island (to which he referred) in terms of the
settlement of Hengest and Horsa in Kent (to which Bede and the
Historia Brittonum refer).

Further English tradition about the invasions is preserved in
the A text of the *Chronicle*. Five successive entries placed under
dates ranging from 449 to 473 tell of the establishment of a kingdom in Kent by Hengest, his brother Horsa and his son Æsc
(Pl. III, p. 34). These entries are followed by three others under
477, 485 and 491 telling of the landing of Ælle and his three sons

---

[1] It is possible that *superbus tyrannus* is a Latinization of the name Vortigern.
Bede, *H.E.* 1, 15, refers to a tomb in Kent believed to bear Horsa's name. See
B. Dickins in *Beiträge zur Runenkunde und nordischen Sprachwissenschaft. Gustav
Neckel zum 60. Geburtstag* (Leipzig, 1938), pp. 83–5.

at a place which has now disappeared beneath the sea off Selsey Bill, and of battles against the Welsh, including one in which the Saxon shore fort at Pevensey was captured, incidents which led to the establishment of a kingdom in Sussex. These entries in turn are followed by a longer series which begins under 495 and extends through the first half of the sixth century. They tell of the arrival of various chieftains near the Isle of Wight and the Solent. One of these chieftains who is called Cerdic and who is alleged to have landed in 495 came to be regarded as the ancestor from whom the kings of Wessex were descended. These various entries relating to Kent, Sussex and Wessex reflect the traditions current in Wessex in the eighth and ninth centuries, some three centuries or more after the events which they profess to record. Because they are in the form of annals referring particular events to particular years they have sometimes been accorded authority greater than that accorded to other traditions about the invasions. Anyone who is able to examine the manuscript, or a facsimile of it, in which they are contained and who observes the careful way in which the ninth-century scribe wrote down the left-hand side of the page a list of year numbers, one line for each year, irrespective of whether or not there was any event to record in any particular year, will at once perceive that the dates which are there attached to events are little more than conventional. On the other hand, though the dates cannot be regarded as more than approximations, there is no adequate reason for supposing the entries themselves to be other than reflections of genuine traditions about some episodes in the invasion period.

In addition to these Welsh and English traditions which, though valuable as traditions, contain little to which the authority of contemporary opinion can be accorded, there are some references to fifth-century Britain in Continental sources which are more nearly contemporary with the events to which they refer. The historian Zosimus records that during the reign of the usurper Constantine, the people of Britain seceded from the Roman Empire, took up arms on their own behalf and freed themselves from the attacks of the barbarians. The work from which this information is derived is thought to have been written *c*. 500, but it is believed that Zosimus was here drawing upon a lost work by the Greek historian Olympiodorus, who was contemporary with the events here described. Prosper Tiro, a native of Aquitaine who was living in Marseilles early in the fifth century, preserves contemporary evidence of a visit to Britain in 429 by Germanus, bishop of Auxerre. The purpose of this visit, according to Prosper, was to combat the propagation of the Pelagian heresy by which the British Church was being corrupted, and the fact of its occurrence may be accepted on Prosper's testimony.[1] In the works of later writers the relations of Germanus with Britain were embroidered with much legendary matter.

Another Gaulish source, an anonymous chronicle, records that in the nineteenth year of Theodosius (441–2), the provinces of Britain, after having been long harassed with various disasters, were reduced to subjection by the Saxons. It has been held that this chronicle is a contemporary authority, but it is not certain that this is the case. To these three—Zosimus, Prosper Tiro and the anonymous Gaulish chronicle—may be added a further passage from Procopius in which it is alleged that the English and the Frisians in Britain were so numerous that each year they sent large numbers of their men, women and children to the Franks who gave them lands on which to settle. The significance of this tradition, which is supported by an independent Germanic tradition testifying to the movement of Germanic peoples from Britain to the Continent, will be discussed later.

4. THE EVIDENCE OF ARCHAEOLOGY AND PLACE-NAMES

Written traditions about the Anglo-Saxon invasions can be supplemented by evidence derived from two other branches of study, archaeology and place-names. Since most of the narrative of Romano-British history is based upon archaeological evidence, supported by a sparse framework of written material, it may well be asked why the application of those archaeological methods which have solved so many problems of the Romano-British period should not be equally successful in solving problems

---

[1] See N. K. Chadwick, *Poetry and Letters in Early Christian Gaul* (London, 1955), pp. 248 ff.

of the fifth and sixth centuries. The answer lies in certain fundamental differences between the archaeological materials of the two periods. Most of the Romano-British evidence is derived from dwelling-sites, whether military stations, towns or farms, where the medium used for building was generally stone. Many of these sites remain to this day undisturbed by the imposition of later buildings. By contrast, the Anglo-Saxons normally built of wood or similarly less durable material, next to nothing is known of their dwelling-places and many of these, it may be surmised, lie beneath the farms and villages of medieval and modern England.

The evidence of inscriptions, coins and stratified sites is the very foundation of Romano-British archaeology. The heathen Anglo-Saxons left virtually no inscriptions, no coins at all of their own manufacture and no stratified sites, not at least as a student of Roman Britain would understand that term. Objects placed in the graves of the dead have added little to the narrative of Romano-British history, but it is of such material as this that almost the whole body of Anglo-Saxon archaeological material consists in the heathen period. Moreover, the greater part of this material was recovered by haphazard digging in the eighteenth and nineteenth centuries, whereas the major advances in knowledge about Roman Britain have been achieved through the careful excavation within the last generation of sites chosen particularly for the light they might be expected to throw on specific problems. The chief consequence of these and other distinctions is that the student of Anglo-Saxon archaeology can rarely extract from his evidence a contribution to the narrative of events based upon an absolute chronology.

No Anglo-Saxon site has yet been made to reveal so accurate and detailed a story as has been recovered from great numbers of Romano-British sites. Fundamental differences in the nature of the evidence yielded by the two periods make it unlikely that this will ever be the case, yet there are several grounds for thinking that archaeology can make a substantially greater contribution to knowledge about the Anglo-Saxon invasions than it has yet done, particularly if greater attention be paid to dwelling-sites and cemeteries whose use can be related to the closing stages of the previous period. Meanwhile, the objects already recovered from the cemeteries tell much about the standards of material civilization within the general limits of the pagan period and the cemeteries themselves provide a valuable indication of the strength and direction of the early settlements.

The Anglo-Saxons commonly buried their dead in shallow graves without raising any mound to mark the site of individual burials. For this reason most of the recorded cemeteries have been discovered accidentally, through the working of the plough or through building operations. Within the last few years large cremation cemeteries have been discovered at Lackford in Suffolk and at South Elkington in Lincolnshire, both of them first exposed by the plough, and a smaller inhumation cemetery has come to light at Petersfinger near Salisbury, the agency in this instance being a mechanical excavator digging chalk. The corpus of material is being steadily increased over the years by similar discoveries. The pattern of recorded cemeteries when plotted on a map corresponds very largely with what geographers know as the Lowland Zone of Britain.[1]

Almost all the known sites lie to the east of an area bounded by a line drawn from Flamborough Head to York, from York to the Peak district in Derbyshire and thence to Portland Bill on the south coast (Map 2). It is a striking fact that scarcely any Anglo-Saxon burials of the pagan period have been discovered north of the Yorkshire Wolds and none at all west of the Pennines. Such evidence, negative though it is, implies that the Anglo-Saxon invasions in the north amounted to little more than the imposition of foreign rule and a foreign language upon a basically Celtic

---

[1] The distribution is shown in detail on the *Map of Britain in the Dark Ages* prepared by O. G. S. Crawford and published by the Ordnance Survey (South Sheet 1935, North Sheet 1938). The pattern has not been significantly altered by cemeteries which have been discovered since. For Wessex see E. T. Leeds and H. de S. Shortt, *An Anglo-Saxon Cemetery at Petersfinger, near Salisbury, Wilts* (Salisbury, 1953) and G. J. Copley, *The Conquest of Wessex in the Sixth Century* (London, 1954), app. B, pp. 217–27; for Suffolk see R. L. S. Bruce-Mitford, *Archaeological Journ.* CVIII (1951), pp. 132–3; for Norfolk, R. R. Clarke, *ibid.* CVI (1949), p. 71; for Lincolnshire, G. Webster and J. N. L. Myres, *ibid.* CVIII (1951), pp. 25–99; see also T. C. Lethbridge, *A Cemetery at Lackford, Suffolk*, Cambs. Antiq. Soc., 4to publ. n.s., VI (1951).

population. South of Flamborough Head cemeteries are found in relatively small numbers on the Yorkshire and Lincolnshire Wolds, but they show a marked increase along the middle and upper reaches of the Trent and of the several rivers which drain into the Wash. In particular, well-marked concentrations are to be observed in Northamptonshire between the Welland and the Nene, and also in Cambridgeshire and west Suffolk. They are totally absent from the belt of low-lying and formerly marshy land which lies between the Pennines and the Humber estuary, as also from the East Anglian fens. In addition to the east midland concentrations, there are two other areas in which cemeteries are thickly grouped, one in Kent, as might well have been expected from its geographical position, and the other, somewhat surprisingly, along the valleys of the upper Thames and its tributaries in an area whose centre is roughly marked by Oxford. A smaller and rather sharply defined group is found on the slopes of the Sussex Downs between Pevensey and Brighton. Apart from these concentrations, cemeteries have been found in considerable numbers, but more widely scattered, in Norfolk and Surrey. In contrast there are some areas, in addition to those already mentioned, from which they are conspicuously absent. These are the Breckland of Norfolk, almost the whole of Essex and Hertfordshire and the Weald of Kent and Sussex.

The evidence afforded by place-names touches almost every aspect of English history from its beginnings to the present day, but we are for the moment concerned only with its contribution towards a better understanding of the Anglo-Saxon settlements. Place-name evidence shares in some degree the weakness of archaeological evidence in that it is difficult to establish the chronology of place-names. When an English place-name is recorded by Bede we know that it is at least as old as the eighth century and we may reasonably infer that it came into being when the place in question was first settled by the English. Although there are several instances of prominent places changing their name over the centuries—Derby, Peterborough and St Albans may be cited—there is abundant evidence of extreme conservatism. Only when a new language has been introduced by invasion from overseas has there been any major change of place-names in any given area of Britain. In these circumstances it may well be that a given name which is first recorded in writing as late as the eighteenth or even the nineteenth century can be confidently ascribed to the Anglo-Saxon period and even to its earlier part. By studying the earliest recorded forms of place-names and by examining the various elements of which they are constructed it has proved possible to establish the existence of certain archaic types. The most important of these are the names which originally ended in Old English *-ingas*. Hastings, which derives from O.E. *Hæstingas*, is an example of the type. In this case, as in many others of this type, the termination *-ingas* is compounded with a personal name. The name should probably be interpreted as meaning 'the followers of Hæsta'. A name such as this was not in origin a place-name at all, but the name of a group of people who may have been spread over a considerable area. In the course of time the group-name was transferred to the district in which they lived and finally, though not always, to a particular place within that district. Hastings is now the name only of a town, but the *Hæstingas* were a group of people who lived near the coast between Dungeness and Eastbourne. Their name could be translated into Latin in the eighth century by *gens Hestingorum*. In some instances names of this type still refer to districts, as with the Roothings or Rodings of Essex, from O.E. *Hroðingas*, a people whose lands covered a large area. Names of this type are very numerous in England. In so far as they are group or folk names they point to times near the original English settlement of newly won territory when groups of settlers were more prominent than the places at which they lived. Many of the personal names with which they are compounded seem already to have gone out of current use before written records began to be kept by the English, that is before the seventh century. On these and other grounds there is general agreement among place-name students that names of the *-ingas* type are of such high antiquity that they may be used alongside the cemeteries as evidence indicating the progress of the English settlements during the fifth and sixth centuries.

There is a general correspondence in the easterly and southerly

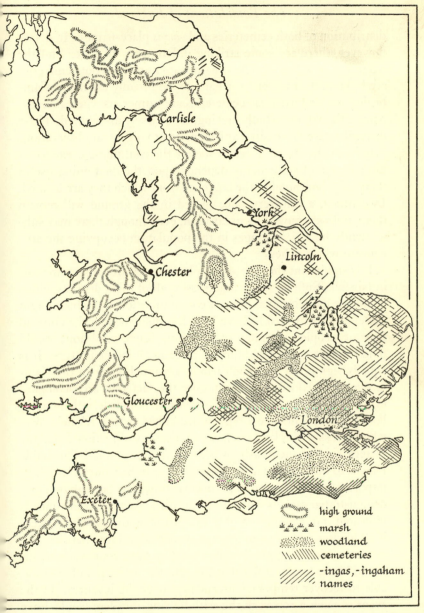

Legend:

- high ground
- marsh
- woodland
- cemeteries
- -ingas, -ingaham names

Map labels: Carlisle, York, Chester, Lincoln, Gloucester, London, Exeter

2. Distribution of the early Anglo-Saxon settlements. Based mainly on the Ordnance Survey of *Britain in the Dark Ages* (south sheet, Southampton 1935) and E. Ekwall, *English Places in -ing* (Lund, 1923).

distribution of both cemeteries and *-ingas* place-names. In detail, however, there are some striking differences. In Essex and the western part of Sussex, *-ingas* names are numerous but cemeteries are lacking. Conversely in what may be broadly called the Cambridge and Oxford areas cemeteries are numerous whereas *-ingas* names, though not wholly lacking, are sparsely distributed. These disparities are not easily explained, but two general observations may be made. In an illiterate society the continuing existence of most names of settlements depends upon the continuing use in their neighbourhood of the language from which they are formed. In contrast, a cemetery once placed in the ground will remain there, unless removed by excavation, even though there may subsequently be racial changes in the population occupying the area beneath which it lies.

It is significant that the *-ingas* place-names are most numerous in Norfolk, Suffolk, Essex and Sussex, all of them districts which lie off the main internal lines of communication and which might therefore be expected to have been less disturbed by the ebb and flow of peoples in times of invasion. Such conditions would tend towards greater stability of place-name nomenclature. It is equally significant that such names are much rarer in the Cambridge and Oxford regions, despite the fact that archaeological evidence testifies to early and concentrated English settlements in both regions. These two regions are linked by the Icknield Way which crosses England in a south-westerly direction from the eastern side of the Wash by way of the Luton and Dunstable Downs to the Thames near Goring and so to Salisbury Plain. The importance of this route in prehistoric times has been abundantly demonstrated and its importance in early Anglo-Saxon times is indicated no less clearly by the massive dykes which were built to interrupt its passage across Cambridgeshire. Settlers who penetrated to the upper Thames along an open route such as this would be the first to suffer if at any time the native population was able to recover temporary ascendancy over the invaders. In the event of such a recovery the withdrawing invaders would leave their dead behind them for archaeologists to discover, but the names which they had given to their settlements might well perish.

5. GEOGRAPHICAL FACTORS

In his narrative of events in Britain Gildas quotes from what purports to be a letter addressed to Aetius during his third consulship (446–50). The letter began with the words 'the groans of the Britons' and a later passage stated 'the barbarians drive us to the sea, the sea throws us back on the barbarians and so two modes of death await us, we are either slain or drowned'. These words, which are all that we have of the letter, have been quoted many times to illustrate the situation in Britain during the Anglo-Saxon invasions. They may perhaps have been applicable to particular times and places, but it is becoming increasingly evident that the general impression which they give of a harassed people being driven back and forth in hopeless confusion from shore to shore is false. There is much evidence, some of it deriving from Gildas himself, to suggest that, despite their ultimate defeat, the people of Britain offered a prolonged, skilled and at times successful resistance to the Anglo-Saxon invaders. The nature of this resistance and the degree of success which it attained were very largely determined by the opportunities for defence which were offered by the physical geography of the country itself. Apart from mere administrative boundaries, of whose course we are largely ignorant, the provinces of Roman Britain were fundamentally divided into civil and military zones of occupation. For most of the Roman occupation the northern boundary of the military zone rested on the Tyne-Solway isthmus, but for a short while in the second century it was advanced to the Forth-Clyde isthmus. A corresponding division between groups of peoples who were known to contemporaries as the northern and southern English is clearly marked in the political geography of seventh-century England. The seventh-century boundary between the northern and southern English corresponded broadly with the boundary between the civil and military zones of Roman Britain, for the good reason that both followed the fundamental geographical division between the highland and lowland zones of Britain. The northern boundary of the northern English lay, not on the Tyne-Solway line, but on the Forth, though it never extended the full width of the northern zone to the Clyde.

As a general rule river valleys throughout the Anglo-Saxon period served to unite rather than to divide the peoples through whose territories they flowed. Their use as boundaries is a device of administrative convenience belonging to times of settled government. But there was an exception to this rule in the Humber estuary whose width combined with its treacherous currents and swift-flowing tides to form an effective barrier which no seventh-century army could have crossed in the face of even moderate opposition. The numerous rivers which unite in the Humber previously flowed across a wide expanse of flat land which even now is subject to heavy flooding and which in Anglo-Saxon times would certainly be waterlogged for much of the year. These rivers find their sources in the Pennines from which they make a steep descent, and between the Pennines on the west and the marshes on the east there is a belt of open country scarcely more than 15 miles wide. The Romans used this belt as one of their main lines of communication with the north, placing the military capital of the province at York, near its northern end where any southerly movement of invaders could be checked if the frontier defences were overrun. The interruption of this route by the construction of a fortification running transversely from east to west would create a continuous barrier between north and south from the North Sea to the western slopes of the Pennines. It is possible that the so-called Roman Rig represents the remains of such a fortification which was in use after the end of the Roman occupation and there is abundant evidence to show that the Humber estuary 'and the boundaries adjacent thereto', as Bede expressed it, represent a frontier of fundamental importance in seventh-century England. This was the frontier between the northern and southern English and it seems probable that this was the March from which Mercia took its name.[1]

There are certain deep-rooted and long-lasting differences which distinguish the history of the northern peoples from the history of the southern kingdoms. The fundamental distinction

[1] The O.E. name of the Mercians was *Mierce*, meaning 'the borderers'. It is usually held that they took this name from their position in relation to Wales. The case for the alternative view expressed here is argued by P. Hunter Blair, *Archaeologia Aeliana*, 4th ser., XXVI (1948), pp. 98–126.

is the one imposed by physical geography, the distinction between the highland and lowland zones, between a land difficult of access, of hills and moors from which indigenous elements could never be wholly rooted out, and an open, spreading plain upon which a new civilization could be more easily imposed. South of Humber, once invasion was successfully begun, the ultimate defeat of the natives could never be in doubt save within the security of the remote hills which form a westerly extension of the highland zone itself. The question here was not whether British or English would ultimately triumph, but which of the various English kingdoms would finally establish supremacy over the others. That supremacy was achieved by Mercia in the eighth century. It passed to Wessex in consequence of the great changes wrought by the Scandinavian invasions in the ninth. North of Humber there was no English rival to the kingdom of Northumbria and the issue here was not fought primarily between different elements of the same race, but between English, Welsh, Scots and Picts. The northern Welsh remained a powerful force in south-western Scotland until the eleventh century and the war against the Scots continued intermittently until the seventeenth. If the great achievements of Northumbrian civilization in the eighth century were a product of the fusion of widely differing peoples, the greater political stability of the southern kingdoms was no less a product of their greater racial homogeneity.

6. THE KINGDOMS OF THE SOUTHERN ENGLISH

The existence of ten independent states can be recognized in England south of Humber in the year 600 (see Map 3). Along the eastern seaboard lay the kingdoms of Lindsey, embracing the upland parts of Lincolnshire; East Anglia, comprising the counties of Norfolk and Suffolk; Essex which included not only the modern county but also much of Hertfordshire, as well as Middlesex and Surrey; and Kent. On the south coast lay the kingdom of Sussex, bounded on the north by the Weald. The north midlands were divided between Mercia extending westwards towards the Welsh border, and Middle Anglia reaching eastwards to the Cambridgeshire fens. Southwards along the Welsh border from

Shropshire to the estuary of the Severn lay the kingdoms of the *Magonsætan* and the *Hwicce*.[1] In the valleys of the upper Thames and its tributaries and reaching southwards to Salisbury Plain lay the kingdom of Wessex. This distribution represents the outcome of about a century and a half of history which is unknown in its details and obscure in its outlines.

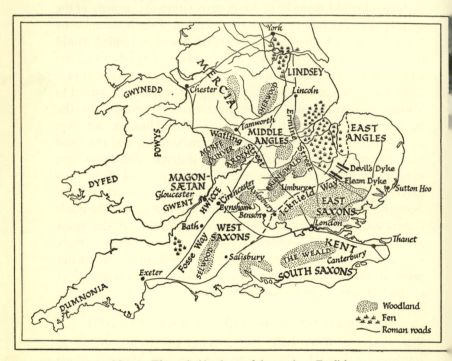

Map 3. The early kingdoms of the southern English.

Although it is a likely conjecture that the English settlements in Britain resulted in many areas from largely haphazard movements of people extending over a long period, it is difficult to avoid the belief that a movement so large in scope and so successful in outcome would involve at some stage in its course a considerable degree of military organization. It is nevertheless a fact that there

---

[1] The name *Magonsætan* seems to have vanished but *Hwicce* survives in the Oxfordshire Wychwood, E.P.N.S. xxiv, p. 386.

is no record of any single episode comparable with the landing of the Roman legions in 43, with the arrival of the great Danish army in 865 or with the Norman victory at Hastings in 1066. We do not know whether the Gaulish chronicler who recorded that in the nineteenth year of the Emperor Theodosius (441–2) Britain was reduced to subjection by the Saxons, was aware of some particularly significant event in that year or whether he was merely commenting in general terms upon what he believed to be the existing situation. More than once Bede referred to particular events of later times as having occurred so many years after the *aduentus Saxonum*, and although it is evident from these references that he was calculating from *c.* 445, he was always careful to indicate that the date implied by these reckonings for the *aduentus Saxonum* was no more than an approximation. In his only reference to the *aduentus* as an event in itself he referred it to some unspecified year in the joint reign of Marcian and Valentinian whose beginning he placed in 449.

The tradition recorded by Gildas about the course of the Anglo-Saxon invasions is sufficiently convincing in its broad outlines to justify the belief that it contains some truth. Time and time again a country driven by desperate need to seek external help has later been conquered by those whose help it sought, and we may well think that this was what befell Britain in the fifth century. To anyone with the least knowledge of the means by which Rome defended her frontiers in the fourth century, it may well have seemed that the employment of foreign mercenaries was the obvious way of extricating Britain from the difficulties in which she had been left by the withdrawal of the legions. Gildas himself makes no attempt to give a date for the rebellion of these mercenaries against their employers, but there are some who think that the appeal for help which was addressed to Aetius during his third consulship (446–50) was dispatched in consequence of this rebellion. According to Gildas the rebellion was followed by a long period of warfare in which the British were led by Ambrosius Aurelianus and which culminated in a great British victory at a place called *Mons Badonicus*. Ambrosius Aurelianus is described by Gildas as the last of the Romans then still living in Britain. His parents who had held some position of authority were killed in the wars which followed the Saxon revolt and his descendants were still known in the days of Gildas himself. Both the date and the site of the battle, or as Gildas calls it, the siege, of *Mons Badonicus* are unknown save within wide limits. Gildas attempted to give a date and Bede thought that he meant *c.* 493, but the *Annales Cambriae* place it in 517. Many guesses have been made at the site, but none of them is well founded.[1] Despite these obscurities we may accept as historical fact the winning of a major British victory over the invaders and the consequent enjoyment by the victors of a respite which lasted for half a century or more, for on this latter point the testimony of Gildas is that of a contemporary witness. A much later tradition ascribed a prominent part in this victory to Arthur. This we must treat with caution, though not with caution so extreme as to deny all historical existence to that same Arthur, for Arthur's fame was great in the sixth century, though we do not know why.

The traditions about the invasions, and particularly the narrative of Gildas, seem to suggest that there were three distinct phases leading to the Anglo-Saxon conquest of Britain. The first of these included a period of largely successful adaptation to the conditions resulting from the reduction of the armed forces in Britain by transfer of many units to Gaul. Later it became necessary to increase the armed strength of the country and this was done by the employment of Germanic mercenaries, a step which was at first successful, but in the end fatal. The hirelings rebelled and with the support of reinforcements from home overran much of the country. They were met with organized resistance from the British who eventually won a great victory over them and with this victory which we may place *c.* 500, admitting a possible error of a decade on either side, the first phase comes to an end. The second phase, introduced by the British victory at *Mons Badonicus*, was one of equilibrium, if not of British supremacy over the attackers. It endured during the lifetime of Gildas, that is at least

[1] Many years ago H. M. Chadwick drew my attention to an entry in the *Annales Cambriae* (R.S., *s.a.* 665)—*Bellum Badonis secundo*. This clue to the whereabouts of *Mons Badonicus* seems generally to have been overlooked.

till 548, and perhaps it endured over much of midland and southern England until *c.* 571. The third phase begins with what has the appearance of a major English victory in that year 571 and the renewal of the advance which marked the final defeat of the British. This third phase cannot be said to have ended at any precise time.

It is to be hoped that more widespread examination of the upper levels of Roman military sites and more detailed study of the relations between Roman military sites and pagan Saxon cemeteries may yet throw considerable light on the problems of the earliest of these three phases. This is a matter which concerns the north and east and, perhaps in particular, East Anglia as much as the south, for on the evidence of Gildas the Saxons were first brought in to assist the British in the defence of their northern frontier and they were settled in the eastern part of Britain. The accidental survival of a detailed tradition about the settlement of a prominent Germanic chieftain in Kent should not be allowed to obscure the wider view, even though that tradition may be trustworthy in itself. Of the Saxon rebellion and the period of warfare which culminated at *Mons Badonicus* it may be difficult to discover more than has been recorded by Gildas. If, however, it should prove possible to establish a more accurate chronology for the objects recovered from Anglo-Saxon graves, this would enable some estimate to be made of the depth to which the invaders penetrated in the first phase of the invasions. The evidence at present available suggests that before 500 they had established settlements in Kent, Sussex, East Anglia and the east midlands and further that they had penetrated as far west as the upper Thames in the region of Oxford. It does not follow, however, that they retained permanent hold of all these settlements.

An entry in the *Chronicle* records that in the year 571 the English won a victory over the British in consequence of which they captured four towns, Limbury in Bedfordshire, Aylesbury in Buckinghamshire, and Benson and Eynsham in Oxfordshire. This entry implies that the whole stretch of country which is traversed by the Icknield Way from near the southern extremity of the East Anglian fens along the Chilterns to the upper Thames was in British occupation before 571. Many attempts have been made to explain this puzzling entry which appears to conflict so strongly with the belief that the invaders had reached the upper Thames before 500. Some have suggested that the entry is misplaced nearly a century late and others have argued that the Oxford region was first reached by invaders who passed along the Thames from the river mouth, thus leaving a British enclave in the Chiltern area. The most reasonable suggestion, however, is to see in this entry the beginnings of a movement by the Anglo-Saxons to recover territory which they had first penetrated in the fifth century but from which they had been expelled as a result of their defeat at *Mons Badonicus*. About twenty miles to the north-east of Limbury is found the first of a series of earthworks which cut across the Icknield Way and also across the full width of the open country which is traversed by this route. The three largest of these earthworks face towards the south-west and are clearly intended to interrupt the progress of an enemy approaching along the Icknield Way from that direction. Two of them, the Fleam Dyke and the Devil's Dyke (see Pl. II), are still of extremely massive proportions. It has been demonstrated by excavation that in part at least they are of post-Roman date, but they are not likely to be as late as the seventh century since they are not in accord with what is known of the political geography of that or any later century.[1] It may be conjectured that they represent defences erected by invaders who had been compelled to abandon the upper Thames valley in the face of defeat at the hands of the British and to seek security within the natural protection afforded by the Fens on the one hand and the sea on the other. Such a conjecture, and it is certainly no more, is in accord with the distribution of *-ingas* place-names. When these various points are considered in conjunction with the tradition recorded by Procopius and an independent Germanic source of the movement of Germanic peoples from Britain to the Continent, it begins to appear

---

[1] The Cambridgeshire dykes are described by Sir Cyril Fox, *The Archaeology of the Cambridge Region* (Cambridge, 1948), pp. 123–34. The author there expresses views about their date which he held in 1923 when the book was first published. A modification of these views in the light of subsequent excavation will be found on pp. A 20–1 in Appendix IV to the 1948 reissue.

PLATE II

THE DEVIL'S DYKE, CAMBRIDGESHIRE

The Dyke is seen running south-eastwards from the village of Reach on the edge of the Fen across a belt of open chalkland bordered on its far side by heavier forest-bearing soils. The ditch is on the south-western side. The course of the Newmarket–London road, shown by arrows, marks the approximate line of the Icknield Way in its progress from the Wash to Salisbury Plain.

that British opposition to the Anglo-Saxon invasions was conducted with greater skill and effectiveness than has often been
supposed.

This interpretation of the evidence does not, however, explain
all the difficulties connected with the origin of the kingdom of
Wessex. West Saxon tradition persistently traced the descent of
the kings of Wessex from chieftains who landed near the head of
Southampton Water and made their way inland towards Salisbury
Plain late in the fifth and early in the sixth centuries. The situation
is complicated by the evidence of Bede who ascribes the first
Germanic occupation of the Isle of Wight and of the mainland
opposite to the Jutes. The contents of cemeteries in the island, as
well as the late survival of a place-name related to Bede's *Iutae* in
the New Forest area, demonstrate that Bede was right at least in
supposing the settlers in these areas to have been closely connected with the settlers in Kent. Yet the West Saxon tradition
preserved in the *Chronicle* makes no reference to the Jutes, but
alleges that the ancestors of later West Saxon kings entered the
country through what was, on Bede's evidence, Jutish territory.
Evidence deriving from Alfred's biographer, Asser, indicates that
there was still some memory in ninth-century Wessex of Jutish
settlers in what was then West Saxon territory, and it may well be
that the absence of any reference to the Jutes in the *Chronicle* was
due to a deliberate attempt to avoid perpetuating a tradition which
did not agree with the incipient nationalist spirit behind the West
Saxon annals.

This conflict between the evidence of Bede and the *Chronicle* is
of greater moment than the apparent conflict between the literary
and the archaeological evidence of which too much has sometimes
been made. The West Saxon annals relating to Cerdic and Cynric,
the two chieftains from whom Alfred and his line claimed descent,
have been dismissed by some as worthless fabrications because, in
strong contrast with the upper Thames area, there is very little
archaeological evidence indicating early settlement in Hampshire
and Wiltshire. But this is to misunderstand the nature of the
annals which were concerned with the exploits of individuals who
achieved posthumous fame as the ancestors of the royal house of

PLATE III

THE PARKER CHRONICLE, A.D. 455–90
Corpus Christi College, Cambridge, MS 173, f. 5a.

This manuscript belonged to Winchester, the entry for 1001 being the last to be written there. After being neglected during the eleventh century, it was sent, probably after the Norman Conquest, to Canterbury. The hand shown opposite is that of the scribe who in about the year 900 copied the work from its beginning till the end of the entry for 891. The year numbers on this page run from 455 to 490, but there are only seven entries. The omission and subsequent insertion of the year number 468 shows one way in which chronological error could arise. The text and G. N. Garmonsway's translation of the first four entries on the page are given below. The fifth and sixth entries refer to events leading to the foundation of the kingdom of Sussex, and the last to a change of king in Kent.

455   Her Hengest and Horsa fuhton wiþ Wyrtgeorne þam cyning*e* in / þære stowe þe is *ge*cueden Agǫlesþrep and his broþur Horsan / man ofslog, and æf*ter* þ*am* Hengest feng (to) rice and Æsc his sunu.

In this year Hengest and Horsa fought against king Vortigern at a place which is called *Agǫlesþrep* (*possibly* Aylesford, Kent), and his brother Horsa was slain. And after that Hengest succeeded to the kingdom and Æsc his son.

457   Her Hengest and Æsc fuhton wiþ Brettas in þære stowe þe is / gecueden Crecganford and þær ofslogon .iiii. wera and þa / Brettas þa forleton Centlond and mid micle ege flugon to / Lundenbyrg.

In this year Hengest and Æsc fought against the Britons at a place which is called *Crecganford* (*possibly* Crayford, Kent) and there slew four thousand men; and the Britons then forsook Kent and fled to London in great terror.

465   Her Hengest and Æsc gefuhton uuiþ (wiþ) Walas neah Wippedes fleo/te and þær .xii. Wilisce aldormenn ofslogon and hiera þegn / án þær wearþ ofslægen þam wæs noma Wipped.

In this year Hengest and Æsc fought against the Welsh near *Wippedesfleot* (*identity unknown*) and there slew twelve Welsh nobles; and one of their thegns, whose name was Wipped, was slain there.

473   Her Hengest and Æsc gefuhton wiþ Walas and genamon unarimed/lico herereaf and þa Walas flugon þa Englan swa fýr.

In this year Hengest and Æsc fought against the Welsh and captured innumerable spoils, and the Welsh fled from the English like fire.

PLATE III

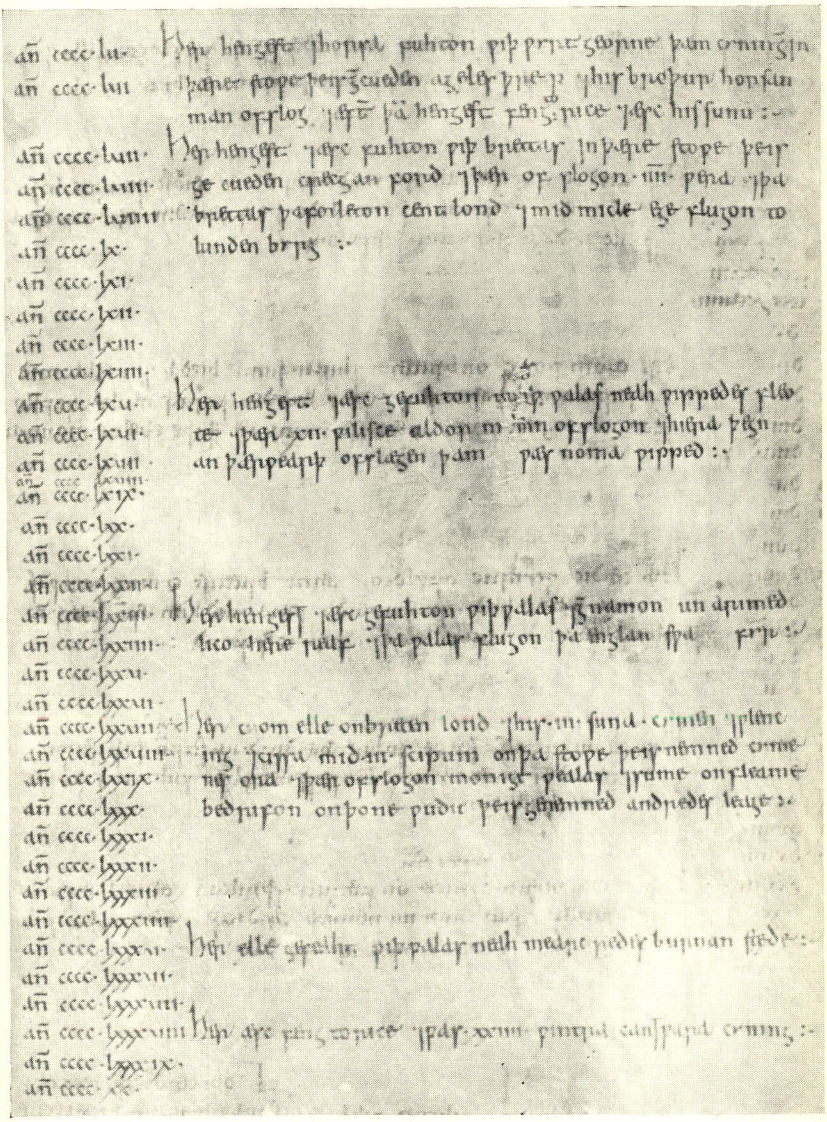

Wessex and England, not with the wider movements of the invasion period as a whole. The first West Saxon bishopric was at Dorchester-on-Thames and there is other evidence to suggest that the nucleus of the West Saxon kingdom lay in this area, but this is no ground for rejecting the persistent tradition that the particular family which finally established its supremacy in Wessex made its approach from the south coast.

That the invaders had already begun to make further progress in the south before the victory of 571 is suggested by an entry in the *Chronicle* which records an English victory at Old Sarum in 552. This was followed by a second victory in 556 at Barbury Castle, a prehistoric fortification on the Marlborough Downs south of Swindon, and a third at Dyrham, north of Bath, in 577. With these events we are able to move from conjecture towards history. The victor at Dyrham was Ceawlin, king of Wessex, and his victory resulted in the conquest by the English of Gloucester and Cirencester, as well as Bath itself. It forms a notable landmark in the history of the invasions, since it brought English rule to the western sea for the first time and thereby cut the land communications between the Welsh of Wales and the midlands and their kinsmen of the south-western peninsula. The western edge of Salisbury Plain was formerly marked by a wide belt of forest-land running north and south approximately along the present boundary between Wiltshire and Somerset. This belt of woodland which still formed part of the royal forests in the thirteenth century, played an important role in the history of Wessex. The Welsh knew it as the Great Forest (*Coit Maur*— Asser, ch. 55) and the English as Selwood (*Sealwudu*). In the eighth century it marked the boundary between the two West Saxon bishoprics, Winchester and Sherborne, and in the ninth it gave protection to Alfred while he reorganized his forces against the Danes. At the end of Ceawlin's reign, late in the sixth century, it marked the western limit of the English advance and it continued so to do for upwards of half a century.

So far as can be determined, the kingdom of Wessex at the end of Ceawlin's reign comprised Berkshire, Hampshire, Wiltshire and a large part of Gloucestershire. The westerly advance was resumed soon after the middle of the seventh century and its progress is marked by a series of English victories. The British were defeated at Bradford-on-Avon in 652 and again in 658 at Penselwood in Somerset. They suffered a further defeat in 682 when they were driven in flight as far as the sea, presumably somewhere on the north coast of Somerset or Devon. Nothing is recorded of the advance across Dorset and south Devon, but it is not likely to have lagged far behind progress on the northern side of the peninsula. Exeter was certainly in English hands before 700, since Boniface, the great West-Saxon missionary who was born *c.* 675, received his education in an English monastery there. Ine, king of Wessex 688–726, founded a bishopric at Sherborne in 705 to serve Wessex west of Selwood and he is also credited with the establishment of a town at Taunton. In 710 he fought against Geraint, king of Dumnonia, all that remained of British territory in the south-west, and in 722 he was as far west as the River Hayle in Cornwall, but the people of Cornwall continued to enjoy some degree of independence for another century. They were active against the English of Devon early in the ninth century, at the height of the Danish wars, and they did not suffer final defeat until the victory won by Egbert of Wessex in the battle of Hingston Down near the Tamar in 838.

The stages by which English authority spread westwards across the midland plain have not been recorded and they cannot now be traced in detail. The history of Mercia first emerges from obscurity during the reign of Penda (*c.* 632–55) who is represented by Bede as one of Northumbria's most formidable enemies in the first half of the seventh century. In the thirteenth century the royal forests of Cannock, Morfe, Kinver and Feckenham formed a continuous belt stretching for some fifty miles from the headwaters of the Trent to the Warwickshire Avon. It is unlikely that the extent of this forest-land was any less in the seventh century and it may well have put a temporary limit to the westerly advance of the English in much the same way as did Selwood. At the northern end of the modern Welsh border a Northumbrian force penetrated as far as Chester *c.* 613, but this exploit seems to represent no more than a passing raid into Welsh territory. It is probable that the isolation of the British in Wales, the Welsh as we now know them, had been completed by the end of the seventh century and that the boundary between them then followed much the same course as the great dyke which bears the name of Offa. This work was not a fortification, or even a continuous barrier, intended to be manned as Hadrian's Wall had been. Its surviving remains, which now form the most impressive monument of Anglo-Saxon antiquity, show that it was constructed as a series of separate lengths wherever open country provided an easy way of crossing the boundary which it was intended to mark. There is no direct evidence that it was built by Offa, but both English and Welsh knew it by his name (O.E. *Offan dic*, W. *Clawdd Offa*) and there is no reason to doubt the tradition, even though the work may not be all of the same period. It is probable that the greater part of it was built between *c.* 784, when Offa's position in Mercia became thoroughly secure, and his death in 796.[1]

7. THE NORTHERN ENGLISH

Anyone familiar with the history of the military zone of Roman Britain might well have expected the abandonment of this heavily fortified area by the forces under Roman command to have been swiftly followed by southerly onslaughts as devastating as those which achieved the overthrow of the Hadrianic frontier in 367. It is one of the most surprising facts in the history of northern Britain in the late fourth and in the fifth centuries that no such movements occurred. All the available evidence indicates that the wide stretch of country which lies between Humber and Mersey to the south and Forth and Clyde to the north passed under the control of native British rulers who established themselves in a position of such strength that they were able not only to resist attack from the north but also to offer strong opposition to the English attack when it came from the east. At present it is not possible to do more than conjecture how this surprising situation came about. That the Hadrianic frontier was restored and

---

[1] A detailed survey of Offa's Dyke will be found in *Archaeologia Cambrensis*, (1926–31), also in Sir Cyril Fox, *Offa's Dyke* (London, 1955). For a summary account see C. Fox, 'The Western Frontier of Mercia in the Eighth Century', *Yorkshire Celtic Studies*, 1 (1937–8), pp. 3–10.

garrisoned afresh after the disaster of 367 is well established, but so far no evidence has been recovered which might suggest that it was the object of any later attack on the scale of 367. The most widely held view, though one not shared by all, is that the frontier was abandoned by peaceful evacuation in or soon after 383 through the withdrawal of its garrisons by Magnus Maximus to assist him in his continental adventures.[1] Even if this is true, it does not fully account for the way in which this great barrier, for long the most formidable of its kind in the whole of the Roman Empire, seems suddenly to have lost all significance as a military or political boundary.

The causes of so great a change are not to be found in the mere movements of a few regiments of auxiliary troops, but must rather be sought in fundamental shifts of power which removed the very *raison d'être* of this whole frontier zone. Between the restoration of the Hadrianic frontier after the disaster of 367 and the defeat of Ecgfrith, king of Northumbria, at Dunnichen Moss about three hundred years later (685) such fundamental shifts were occasioned by three events—a powerful resurgence of native British authority over most of what had formerly been the military zone of Roman Britain, the establishment of a Scottish kingdom in Argyll and the creation of an English kingdom out of settlements near the east coast between Humber and Tweed. So far as can be seen the original settlements from which the kingdoms of England and Scotland eventually grew both took place at about the same time. This may have been no more than a coincidence arising from the exposure of Britain to attack by the withdrawal of Roman forces under a central command, but it is by no means impossible that both were deliberate measures intended to serve the same purpose —the defence of Britain.

Such evidence as there is about the political geography of northern Britain in the fifth and sixth centuries indicates that when the English menace first became serious, in the second half

---

[1] From 383 till *c.* 600 the history of Britain south of Forth and Clyde and north of Humber and Mersey is almost unknown. The account which follows is conjecture, not history. It summarizes a paper by P. Hunter Blair, in *Archaeologia Aeliana*, 4th ser., XXV (1947), pp. 1–51. But see more recently K. Jackson, 'The Britons in Southern Scotland', *Antiquity*, XXIX (1955), pp. 77–88.

of the sixth century, the territory which had once been bisected by the Hadrianic Wall was divided between a considerable number of small, independent kingdoms ruled by native British dynasties. The genealogies of about a dozen of these dynasties have been preserved and the names of some of the kingdoms over which they ruled are known, but only in two or three instances has it proved possible to locate the geographical position of the kingdoms themselves. Despite these obscurities, it is certain that the English did not achieve supremacy in northern Britain until the very end of the sixth century, that they had first to overcome formidable opposition and that the kingdom which they created was carved out of British, not Pictish or Scottish, territory. In the light of these facts it would be difficult to escape the belief, even though there were no other evidence to support it, that a renaissance of British military strength occurred at some period after the overthrow of the Hadrianic Wall by the Picts and Scots in 367.

How or when this renaissance was achieved cannot now be told even in the barest outline, though again the Arthurian tradition, with its testimony of great military achievements, is not irrelevant to the scene as a whole. There is more than guesswork behind the view held by some that steps were taken by the establishment of client states far to the north to anticipate some of the possible consequences of evacuating the Roman military command which had been responsible for frontier defence. The most powerful of the Welsh kingdoms in the north in the seventh century was the kingdom of Strathclyde whose main stronghold was at Dumbarton. Its territories lay in south-western Scotland and no doubt they varied considerably with the changing fortunes of the kingdom. Its history can be traced with fair continuity from the seventh century until the beginning of the eleventh and throughout this long period it retained its independence for all but one or two brief intervals, playing a very important part in the history of what is now Scotland. The history of this kingdom did not, however, begin in the seventh century. There is evidence that the kingdom was not a new foundation even in the middle of the fifth. One invaluable document, a letter addressed by Patrick from

Ireland to the soldiers of a king called Coroticus, momentarily enlightens the general obscurity of this time. There is general agreement that this letter is a genuine work written by Patrick himself at about the middle of the fifth century and several scholars accept the identification of Coroticus with a member of the Strathclyde dynasty who is known from other sources as Ceredig. The writing of the letter was brought about by a raid against Ireland in which the soldiers of Coroticus killed or captured a number of Christians who had recently been baptized by Patrick himself. Patrick knew that the captives were to be sold as slaves, he denounced the soldiers as men with whom no Christians should associate and he asked that his letter of rebuke should be read as widely as possible, even in the presence of Coroticus himself.

At the very least the contents of this letter may be taken to imply that Coroticus was a man of eminence who commanded the services of a professional army strong enough to undertake expeditions across the sea to Ireland. The existence of such an army may further suggest that the kingdom to which it belonged was both powerful and well established at the time in question, a time probably not more than half a century after the withdrawal of the Roman military command from Britain. According to the genealogies the grandfather and great-grandfather of that Ceredig who is commonly identified with Coroticus, were called respectively *Cinhil* and *Cluim* which may perhaps be derived from the Roman names Quintilius and Clemens. Whatever may be thought about the bearing of these names upon the origin of the kingdom of Strathclyde, it is evident that the kingdom itself acquired and long maintained a firm hold upon the western end of the old Antonine line and that in this position it was able to oppose a strong front against any danger of attack from the north. It is an indication of the continuing strength of the kingdom that in the opening chapter of his *History* which he devoted to a survey of the physical and political geography of Britain as a whole, Bede thought fit to describe its capital, Dumbarton, as *ciuitas Brettonum munitissima usque hodie*. It should be noted that this stronghold lies on the north side of the Clyde, a fact which lends some support

40

to the hypothesis noticed above that the Scottish settlements in Argyll arose from a deliberate act of policy designed to restrain the activities of the Picts against the British.

Bede knew that the Firth of Clyde was matched on the east by a similarly deep penetration of the sea, the Firth of Forth. Somewhere along this latter, there lay a place which he called *Urbs Giudi*.[1] It may be seen from other passages in which he used the word *urbs* that he meant by it 'a fortified stronghold', but the site itself has never been identified. Before English authority reached the Firth of Forth, near the middle of the seventh century, its southern shores were controlled by a kingdom called *Manaw Gododdin* (Manau of the *Votadini*). Both the extent and the history of this kingdom are very obscure, but there are some indications that it was in existence in the fifth century and that it may then have been serving to protect the eastern end of the Antonine line in much the same way as Strathclyde protected the west. It was later believed that the kings of Gwynedd, a Welsh kingdom which lay in north-west Wales, were descended from a king of Manaw Gododdin called Cunedda who migrated to Wales in order to repel bands of Scots from Ireland who were seeking to establish settlements in Wales. The date of this migration is disputed, but the evidence suggests a time towards the middle of the fifth century as the most probable. The possibly Roman nomenclature found in the genealogy of Coroticus is paralleled in the genealogy of Cunedda whose father, grandfather and great-grandfather are called respectively Aetern, Patern and Tacit (Aeternus, Paternus, and Tacitus). South of Strathclyde and Manaw Gododdin other north Welsh kingdoms came into being, but very little of their history can yet be told. The most important among them seems to have been the kingdom of Rheged. Carlisle and the northern shores of Solway lay within its boundaries but its further extent is uncertain. One of its rulers, Urien, played a prominent part in leading Welsh opposition to the English

[1] Bede uses the words *in medio* to describe the position of *Urbs Giudi* in relation to the Firth of Forth. These are commonly taken to mean 'in the middle of', but 'half-way along' seems to be a better translation. For the possible connexion of *Giudi* with *Evidensca*, see I. A. Richmond and O. G. S. Crawford, *Archaeologia*, XCIII (1949), p. 34.

invaders in the second half of the sixth century. One of the more southerly of these kingdoms, Elmet, which lay between the Vale of York and the Pennine watershed, maintained its independence until the seventh century.

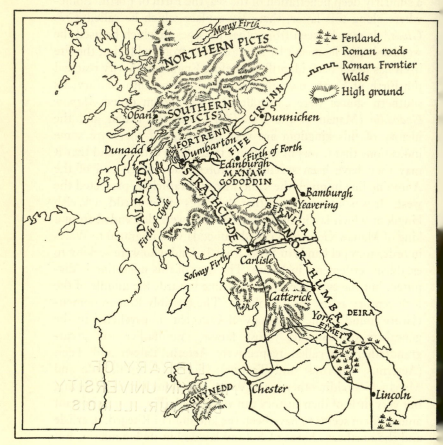

Map 4. Northern Britain in the sixth century.

English Northumbria grew from two originally distinct kingdoms, Deira to the south and Bernicia to the north. These territorial names are based on O.E. *Dere* and *Bernice* whose meaning is uncertain, but which seem to be based ultimately on Welsh names.[1] The nucleus of Deira lay on the Yorkshire Wolds. Its first historical king was Ælle who was reigning in the second half of the sixth century. It is, however, certain that there were Germanic settlements in the eastern parts of Yorkshire at least a hundred years before this date. A considerable quantity of material has been found in Germanic cemeteries in eastern Yorkshire, but the great bulk of it was recovered haphazardly in the nineteenth century, much of it has since been lost, and what remains has not yet received sufficiently close study. This is particularly unfortunate, because it is a strange circumstance that the one area north of Humber which has yielded evidence of even moderately intense settlement in the pagan Saxon period should be that very area in which an organized Roman military command is known to have survived longest. In addition there is a tantalizingly inadequate record of what seems to have been a large and early cremation cemetery almost at the gates of the Roman legionary fortress at York. This fortress was set on low-lying ground virtually surrounded by wood or marsh, a most unexpected situation in which to find evidence of early Anglo-Saxon settlement. These and other indications may well be taken to suggest that the earliest settlements in Yorkshire were not those of hostile invaders, but of Germanic mercenaries employed by the British to fight against their northern enemies in the manner recorded by Gildas.

Evidence of Germanic settlement north of Tyne in the fifth century is wholly lacking. Both English and Welsh tradition suggests that Bernicia originated in little more than the establishment of a band of pirates on the rock of Bamburgh at the middle of the sixth century. Bede believed that the kingdom was founded by Ida in 547 and it is probable that this date is correct to within a year or so. A considerable body of Welsh poetry which tells of wars between the English and the north Welsh in the second half of the sixth century may be accepted as evidence that such wars did in fact take place, though only a small part of this material can yet be used to illumine any particular incident in their progress.

[1] A new etymology of the name 'Bernicia' is suggested by K. Jackson, *Language and History in Early Britain* (Edinburgh, 1953), pp. 701–5.

Four Welsh rulers are known to have taken part in this warfare and one of them, Urien of Rheged, is said to have besieged the English invaders in the island of Lindisfarne late in the sixth century.

At this date the kingdom of Bernicia seems scarcely to have had any territorial existence, but a sudden change of fortune occurred during the reign of Æthelfrith (*c.* 593–616), the first of the Bernician kings about whom English sources tell something more than the mere number of years he reigned. Bede said of Æthelfrith that he conquered more British territory than any other English king. A Welsh elegiac poem called the *Gododdin* seems to tell part of the story of a major, but in the issue disastrous, attempt by the North Welsh to halt the progress of the invaders at about this time. The poem is now preserved only in a thirteenth-century manuscript but Welsh scholars believe that most of it is a genuine composition of the sixth. It is in the form of a lament for the many Welshmen who died in a great battle at a place which is thought to have been Catterick. The poem contains no reference to Æthelfrith, but it seems probable that the battle was fought, if not in Æthelfrith's reign, at least towards the end of the sixth century. Where the evidence is so slight the results of the battle cannot be precisely assessed, but the Welsh themselves regarded its outcome as an overwhelming disaster such as is likely to have marked an important stage in the consolidation of English power in the north.

The most important event of Æthelfrith's reign in the eyes of Bede was a victory which he won over the Scots of Dalriada at an unidentified place called *Degsastan* in 603. The Scottish leader in this battle was their king Aedan, son of Gabran. During his reign Dalriada became a powerful kingdom and Aedan himself won some measure of control over Pictish lands north of the Forth. Looking back over more than a century of past events Bede was able to appreciate the full significance of this English victory which eliminated the Scots from the claimants to supremacy in northern Britain. From that day to this, he wrote, no king of the Scots ever dared to make war against the English in Britain. It is not until late in the ninth century when the kingdoms of the Scots and the Picts had been amalgamated and Northumbria virtually destroyed by the Danish invasions that we can observe the beginnings of renewed Scottish pressure towards the south which lasted over several centuries and which at times threatened to bring the Scottish border as far south as the Tees.

Soon after his victory at *Degsastan* Æthelfrith was able to win control over Deira and so to create the kingdom of Northumbria. For most of its history the kingdom of Northumbria was ruled by members of the Bernician dynasty, but on the death of Æthelfrith (616), the kingdom was secured by Edwin of Deira (616–32).[1] During Edwin's reign the Bernician royal family, with many of the nobility, found refuge in the remoter north, some with the Picts and some with the Scots. After the death of Edwin, the Bernician line was restored in the person of Oswald (633–41) and this restoration was accompanied by a considerable influx of Scots, many of them monks, into Northumbria. The great importance of this movement for the history of Christianity in England will be noticed in its proper place. Here it may be remarked that the friendly relations which were established with the Picts and Scots while the Bernician rulers were in exile is likely to have played an important part in enabling the English to secure control of the Welsh lands in the south-eastern lowlands between Tweed and Forth. There is no certain record of any warfare between the English and the Welsh in these areas and it is possible that they were gradually absorbed rather than conquered in battle.[2]

As the seventh century advances the recordings of history become fuller and more certain. Cuthbert, who was born *c.* 634, spent part of his childhood in an English village which has not been identified but which probably lay near the hills above Leader Water where he later worked as a shepherd. In about 651 he entered a monastery at Melrose which was then ruled by an

---

[1] The use in different sources of different starting-points for the year of grace has caused uncertainty about the exact date of several events in Northumbria in the seventh century. For the sake of consistency with the most authoritative current work I have followed the chronology adopted in F. M. Stenton, *Anglo-Saxon England*.

[2] Professor Kenneth Jackson, however, draws my attention to an entry in the *Annals of Ulster, s.a.* 637, *recte* 638, recording 'the siege of Etin', that is of Edinburgh. The combatants are not named, but a conflict between Welsh and English forces at Edinburgh is not unlikely at about this date.

English abbot and while a monk there he visited the English abbess of a double house at Coldingham. The background of Cuthbert's early life suggests that by the middle of the seventh century all the land bounded on the north by Lammermuir and on the west by Ettrick Forest was firmly in English hands. The degree of security implied by the existence of monasteries at Melrose and Coldingham may well be thought to indicate that the authority of the Northumbrian king reached as far as the Firth of Forth by *c.* 650. Before the reign of Ecgfrith (670–85) it had crossed the Forth and the beginning of that reign was marked by an unsuccessful attempt by the Picts to free themselves from the English domination which had been imposed upon them by Ecgfrith's predecessor. In or soon after 680 Abercorn became the seat of an English bishopric and at about the same time Dunbar was the seat of an English earl. The attempts of the Northumbrian kings to dominate the southern Picts ended in a disaster which put an enduring halt to the northerly advance of English rule. In 685 Ecgfrith crossed the Tay, as Agricola had done six hundred years before. He met a Pictish army at Dunnichen Moss near Forfar. In the battle which followed Ecgfrith himself was killed and his army destroyed. No other English army penetrated so far to the north until the expedition led by Athelstan in 934.

After the defeat at Dunnichen Moss the English frontier fell back to the line of the Antonine Wall and for some twenty years sporadic warfare continued in its neighbourhood between the Picts and the English. An important part in ending this warfare and bringing peace to the northern frontier was played by Bede. In about 710 Nechtan IV, king of the Picts, sent envoys to the abbot of Monkwearmouth and Jarrow asking for advice on various matters concerning the church. They took back with them a long letter which may well have been written by Bede, and the friendly relations which were established in this way remained unbroken when Bede finished his *History* in 731. The frontier between the Picts and the English then rested on the Forth.

It is difficult to determine the rate of English progress towards the western sea between Clyde and Mersey. The wide expanse of central moorland which forms the catchment area of the various rivers which flow to the North Sea and the Firths of Clyde and Solway is likely to have formed an extensive no-man's-land. The Tyne Gap offered the easiest approach to the western sea and the earliest recorded crossing of this gap by an Englishman was made by Cuthbert who was in Carlisle when Ecgfrith was killed at Dunnichen Moss in 685. It is likely, however, that the English had reached Carlisle long before this. Among Cuthbert's friends was an English anchorite who lived on an island in Derwentwater. Shortly before 731 Whithorn, on the northern shore of Solway, became the seat of an English bishopric which Bede regarded as forming part of Bernicia, a sufficient indication that English influence had long been dominant in this area. Shortly after the middle of the eighth century a Northumbrian king made conquests in Ayrshire, even capturing Dumbarton, the Strathclyde capital, but these conquests were short-lived and at a later period Strathclyde seems to have recovered much land formerly lost to the English.

Contact between the eastern and western sides of the Pennines had been maintained in Roman times by three main routes whose course was dictated by physical geography, the Tyne Gap in the north, the Aire Gap in the south and the crossing of Stainmore by Bowes and Brough midway between. The eastern ends of the Tyne and Aire Gaps came to be controlled by Bernicia and Deira respectively. In about 613 Æthelfrith of Bernicia won a victory over the Welsh near Chester, but it is not known whether he made his approach westwards from York or southwards from Carlisle and the consequences of his victory are not easy to estimate. On several occasions in the seventh century the various armies engaged in the struggle for supremacy in the north operated at great distances from their homelands, and it would be unwise to assume that Æthelfrith's victory near Chester was part of a war of conquest followed by settlement in the area of the victory. In later times Chester belonged to Mercia, not to Northumbria. The boundary between these two kingdoms was not so sharply defined on the western side of the Pennines as it was on the east. Political control over the lands between Mersey and Ribble tended to fluctuate between the two kingdoms, but the linguistic boundary between the south Northumbrian and north-west midland dialects of Old English lay along the Ribble. The kingdom of Elmet survived as a solitary Welsh outpost on the eastern side of the Pennines until its conquest by Edwin.

Both Welsh and English sources indicate that Edwin conducted a vigorous warfare against the Welsh. He is said to have besieged Cadwallon, king of Gwynedd, in the island of Priestholm off the coast of Anglesey and to have conquered both Anglesey and Man. It is difficult to judge the significance of these conquests, but Gwynedd seems not to have suffered any lasting consequences from Edwin's attacks. In 632 Cadwallon himself, the most vigorous opponent of the northern English at this date, crossed the Pennines and defeated and killed Edwin in Hatfield Chase on the borderland between Mercia and Northumbria. In these times, and indeed till much later, the supremacy of one kingdom over others depended upon the military prowess of the individual ruler, and it may well be that the death of Edwin resulted temporarily in the loss of all English authority west of the Pennines. Cadwallon himself was killed a year later after being defeated by Oswald near the Roman Wall north of Hexham.

The earliest direct literary evidence of permanent English settlements west of the Pennines is to be found in an account of the dedication of Wilfrid's new church at Ripon between 671 and 678. The occasion was marked by a ceremony at which Wilfrid read to the assembled company a list of estates with which the church had been endowed by various benefactors. The names of some of these estates were recorded by Wilfrid's biographer and among them were lands near the Ribble. Particular interest attaches to the remark of Eddius that the endowments of Ripon also included 'consecrated places in various parts which the British clergy had deserted when fleeing from the hostile sword wielded by the warriors of our nation'.[1] The passage seems to suggest that the flight of the British clergy before an English invasion was an event of the recent past at the time when the church at Ripon was dedicated. Eddius was probably present at the ceremony and his testimony is not to be doubted. It is more

---

[1] *Life of Wilfrid*, c. xvii, ed. B. Colgrave, pp. 36–7.

difficult to know what value can be attributed to a late Durham tradition that the district of Cartmel, now part of Lancashire north of the sands, was given to the church of Lindisfarne at about the same time. The literary evidence by itself might be taken to suggest that, although raiding armies crossed the Pennines early in the seventh century, the effective English occupation of Cumberland, Westmorland and Lancashire did not take place much before *c*. 650. Yet this evidence is too slight to allow sure conclusions. It has been maintained that 'there are enough ancient place-names in Cumberland and Lancashire to suggest that Æthelfrith could have ridden from the Solway to the Mersey through territory in the occupation of his own people'.[1]

8. MOVEMENTS TOWARDS UNITY

Hitherto we have been mainly concerned with the general movement whereby the English took possession of the greater part of the mainland of Britain. During this period there was only one recorded attack by the English against Ireland. It was made by a Northumbrian army in the year 684. Before the landing of the Danish army of invasion in 865 considerable advance was made towards internal political unity through the establishment of dominion by two or three of the more powerful kingdoms over their smaller neighbours. The establishment of the English monarchy was a long process which was not completed until the tenth century, but from early times certain kings were recognized as having supremacy over other kings who were ruling at the same time. Bede gives a list of seven kings who were regarded as having been pre-eminent in their days. The first four of these—Ælle of Sussex (reigned *c*. 477–*c*. 514), Ceawlin of Wessex (*c*. 560–*c*. 591), Æthelberht of Kent (*c*. 560–616) and Rædwald of East Anglia (late sixth century to 616 or a little later)—all belonged to the kingdoms of the southern English. It will be observed that whereas the reigns of the last three of these kings overlapped, those of the first two were separated from one another by more

---

[1] Stenton, *Anglo-Saxon England*, p. 78. See further E. Ekwall, *The Place-Names of Lancashire* (Manchester, 1922), pp. 227–41, F. T. Wainwright, *Trans. Hist. Soc. Lancs. and Chesh.* 93 (1941), pp. 1–44 and E.P.N.S. XXII, pp. xxi–xxii.

than half a century, an interval which may be thought to reflect the phase of British recovery between their victory at *Mons Badonicus* and their defeat by the English in 571. The reasons which prompted Bede to distinguish these four rulers as pre-eminent are obscure, particularly in the case of Ælle of Sussex, but whatever the nature of their supremacy there is no evidence that any of them exercised any great influence north of Humber.

The expansion of Northumbria during the reign of Æthelfrith led to a conflict between the northern and the southern English peoples. As the sons of Æthelfrith sought refuge with the Picts and Scots during the reign of Edwin, so also Edwin himself had previously undergone a long period of exile during the ascendancy of Æthelfrith. He passed the latter part of this period at the court of Rædwald, king of East Anglia. Refusing Æthelfrith's demand that Edwin should be either killed or surrendered, Rædwald led an army to the northern frontier of Mercia and defeated the Northumbrians in a battle fought near the River Idle in 616. Æthelfrith himself was killed and Edwin restored to his kingdom. Edwin is named by Bede as the fifth of the pre-eminent English kings and he was the first of the northern English rulers to be so distinguished. He was followed in this distinction by two other Northumbrians, Oswald and Osuiu. The reigns of these three kings covered a large part of the seventh century (616–670) and they mark the only stage in the Anglo-Saxon period when the northern English dominated the southern kingdoms. Their supremacy was not undisputed. The years 633 and 634 witnessed two battles from which important consequences flowed.

Despite the rapid growth of Northumbria during Æthelfrith's reign, Welsh opposition to English expansion in the north remained strong and the common interest which was shared by the Welsh and the Mercians in resisting Northumbrian domination led to an alliance between Cadwallon, Christian king of Gwynedd, and Penda of Mercia. It was at the hands of these two that Edwin met his death in 632 in the battle in Hatfield Chase, that same borderland between the northern and southern English in which Rædwald had defeated Æthelfrith. Edwin's death was followed by the momentary disintegration of Northumbria into its two component parts and the succession of apostate kings in Bernicia and Deira. Both were killed within a year and Cadwallon himself was killed near Hexham in 633 after his defeat by Oswald in the battle near the Roman Wall. The victory of the Welsh and the Mercians in the battle of Hatfield Chase established Penda on the Mercian throne, the death of Edwin in the same battle extinguished the main line of the Deiran royal family and the death of Cadwallon a year later removed the most formidable Welsh opponent of English rule in the north.

For the next twenty years Mercia, ruled by Penda, remained a constant source of trouble to the northern English. Northumbria was repeatedly invaded and on at least one occasion Penda reached as far north as Bamburgh. Oswald himself was defeated and killed by Penda in 641. The presence of this powerful neighbour to the south encouraged separatism in Deira which for a while became a dependent province of Mercia. The conflict came to a head in 654 in the greatest of all the battles between the northern and the southern English. Penda sought allies from both East Anglia and Wales and led his forces, 'thirty legions strong' as Bede wrote, against the Northumbrian King Osuiu, successor of Oswald, and the two armies met by the banks of a river called *Winwæd*. This river is unidentified, but it was probably one of the many which drain into the Humber. In the battle which followed, the Northumbrians won a decisive victory. The king of East Anglia was killed and Penda also was killed either then or very soon afterwards.

This victory confirmed Osuiu in the possession of his Northumbrian kingdom and also established his supremacy over the southern English kingdoms, but the Northumbrians were not able to maintain this position for more than a few years and when Osuiu died in 670 Mercia was again a strong and independent kingdom. The end of Northumbrian attempts to dominate the southern English was marked by the defeat of Osuiu's successor, Ecgfrith, in a battle fought against the Mercians near the Trent in 678. For the remainder of his reign Ecgfrith was mainly concerned with the security of his own kingdom in the north and it was while he was engaged in this way that he was killed in 685. The constant danger of attack from Picts, Scots or Strathclyde Welsh was one of the main reasons which led to the passing of Northumbrian influence in the south. After the death of Ecgfrith the character of Northumbrian history begins to change. Boundaries had been roughly shaped and the age of conquest was largely complete. Interest shifts from narrative history to the great works of learning and art which have long been recognized as being among the great achievements of the early Middle Ages. Through most of the seventh century Northumbria had enjoyed a succession of strong rulers—Æthelfrith, Edwin, Oswald, Osuiu and Ecgfrith. All save Osuiu died in battle. Æthelfrith was the last of the heathens, and his four successors are known to us almost solely from the pages of Bede's *History* where they are portrayed first and foremost as Christian warriors whose achievements in war gave security to the Church within their kingdom. The picture is perhaps a little idealized and is certainly tinged with hagiography, but we can only see it now as Bede painted it.

It is well to remember that the written evidence for the history of Northumbria in the seventh century is very largely the product of a single mind. That no Mercian was found to do for eighth-century Mercia what Bede did for seventh-century Northumbria is a misfortune. The loss both to history and literature is great, yet Mercian history seems to gain something in reality from the very fact that it must now be reconstructed from scattered and fragmentary sources widely diverse in kind and mainly free from didactic purpose. For some fifty years after the Mercian victory over the Northumbrians in 678 the scene of English history is confused with no one kingdom long able to sustain a dominant position. The beginning of a new and important phase is marked by the accession of Æthelbald to the kingdom of Mercia in 716. Perhaps the most important fact of English political history in the eighth century is that two successive kings, Æthelbald and Offa, between them ruled the great block of midland territory for eighty years (716–96). Such length of reign is surprising at this early date, but the mere fact that the government of the midlands was exercised for so long by two strong and able rulers was a factor of great importance, both as tending towards greater political stability and as marking a long step towards the ultimate political unity of the country. During the same eighty years there were eleven kings in Northumbria. Two of them resigned their office to become monks and most of the others met violent deaths.

In the survey of the state of Britain in the year 731 with which Bede brought his *History* to its end, he wrote that all the kingdoms of the southern English were then subject to Æthelbald. The ordering of government was not yet so firmly established that a supremacy of this kind could survive the death of the king who exercised it. Æthelbald himself was murdered in 757, seemingly the victim of some internal conspiracy whose details are unknown, and some years passed before Offa was able to establish himself in a position as strong as that which had been held by his predecessor. It is a significant indication of the degree of supremacy exercised by Offa later in his reign that several of the once independent kingdoms neighbouring Mercia became either wholly extinct or so greatly reduced in authority that the representatives of their dynasties might be styled *subreguli* or even *duces* in the documents of the time. In this way the kingdoms of East Anglia, Lindsey and Essex lost what little political importance they had ever had and became, as the kingdoms of Middle Anglia, the *Hwicce* and the *Magonsætan* had long since become, no more than dependent provinces within the kingdom of Mercia itself. Kent, Sussex and even Wessex similarly came under strong Mercian influence.

There is little known of Æthelbald himself and that little is not to his credit. In a letter which was addressed to him by the West Saxon missionary, Boniface, and his fellow bishops in Germany, he was sharply rebuked both for his own immoral behaviour and for the violent and extortionate practices followed by himself and his underlings in their dealings with the Church in England. The saintly world of Edwin and Oswald as pictured by Bede seems very remote from the world of Æthelbald as contemporaries saw it and yet more remote when it is contrasted with the reign of Offa, perhaps the greatest of all the Anglo-Saxon kings, save only Alfred.

The changing conditions are perhaps most strikingly marked

by the increasing importance which England now began to assume in the eyes of the leading Continental powers. Charlemagne saw in Offa a man of sufficient importance to be the father-in-law of one of his own sons, even though he quarrelled with the suggestion that he in turn should become the father-in-law of one of Offa's sons. It was much that Offa should even be able to claim that he was Charlemagne's equal. In 786 the pope sent legates to England for the first time since the arrival of Augustine nearly two centuries before. Ostensibly this papal mission was concerned with renewing the ancient ties of friendship between Rome and England which Augustine had first established, but in the background it was closely concerned with Offa's wish, which he achieved for a time, to establish an independent archbishopric at Lichfield within the boundaries of his own kingdom.

Apart from the great Dyke which defined the English border with Wales, and which remains the most enduring monument of his strength, Offa was also concerned in the issue of a new type of currency, a silver penny which continued to form the basis of English currency until long after the Norman Conquest. It has recently been claimed that a number of illuminated manuscripts which were formerly held to have been Canterbury work were produced in Mercia at this time.[1] During the latter years of Offa's reign Tamworth and Lichfield seem almost to be established as the civil and religious capitals of England, but his death in 796 was soon followed by a further southerly shift of political power and by 829 Egbert of Wessex, the representative of an ancient dynasty which had passed through a century of obscurity, had established himself in a position which was hardly less secure than Offa's had been. But already before the death of Offa there had occurred an event which foreshadowed fundamental changes in the course of English history. This event was the sack of Lindisfarne by sea raiders in 793.

[1] S. M. Kuhn, *Speculum*, XXIII (1948), pp. 591–629.

CHAPTER II

BRITAIN AND THE VIKINGS

I. THE SCANDINAVIAN BACKGROUND

THE attack on Cuthbert's monastery on Lindisfarne in 793 marks the end of a period of about two centuries during which the shores of Britain seem to have been wholly free from attack. Bede's church at Jarrow was sacked in the following year and in 795 Columba's monastery on Iona was plundered. It is small wonder that later writers should have had difficulty in finding words fit to describe the men whose arrival was heralded by the destruction of three of the most venerable centres of Christendom in Britain. Writing to the community at Lindisfarne after he had heard the news of the attack, Alcuin said that there had never been such a disaster while the English had been living in Britain and that no one had believed that such a voyage was possible. It is easy to understand the impression which the news would make upon Alcuin, himself a Northumbrian who had inherited much from Cuthbert and Bede and something even from Columba. It is also easy to understand the feelings of the monks in Britain as one after another their monasteries were attacked and their treasures dispersed. Better than any others they knew the full meaning of the fury of the Northmen from which they prayed for deliverance. No one who has considered the evidence can well deny that the Viking attack on Britain was accompanied by great violence and widespread destruction, yet the evidence for such a judgement comes largely from the people who suffered most, and it should not be forgotten that the Vikings, whose very name is synonymous with piracy, themselves introduced the word 'law' into the English language.

It is a common mistake to suppose that before the Viking Age the various Scandinavian peoples lived in complete isolation both from Britain in particular and from western Europe in general. There is now abundant archaeological evidence to show that mere geographical remoteness was a much less potent factor in preventing intercourse with foreign lands than might have been expected. The ignorance of classical writers about Scandinavia was due less to its remoteness than to the great expansion of the Celtic peoples westwards across central Europe in the last five centuries before the Christian era, a movement which interrupted the old lines of communication between the Mediterranean world and the remote north in still earlier times. The disruption of Celtic power in central and western Europe under a double attack from the Germanic peoples and from the rapidly expanding Roman Empire led to a renewal of contact between north and south soon after the time of Augustus when Roman products began to reach Scandinavia in considerable quantities. Denmark, as might be expected, received these products in greater numbers than either Sweden or Norway. Several sets of scales and weights which have been recovered from Norwegian graves show that the system of weights used in Norway was based at one time upon the early imperial system of Rome and later upon the reformed system of Constantine the Great.

Early in the Christian era movements of peoples from Scandinavia southwards and eastwards, particularly of the Goths, some of whose settlements eventually reached as far east as the Black Sea, brought Scandinavia into close contact with central and eastern Europe. In consequence of these movements Roman *denarii* reached the island of Gotland in the Baltic in such numbers as to suggest that they were for a time used as currency not only in Gotland itself, but also on the southern Swedish mainland. For a while Sweden enjoyed close contact with central Europe by way of Gotland and the Vistula. The subsequent movements of Slavonic peoples along the southern shores of the Baltic and as far west as the Elbe deflected the course of Swedish trade with the European mainland into more westerly channels, but there was no isolation comparable with that caused by the earlier expansion of the Celts. Large quantities of gold reached Sweden, and to a lesser degree Norway, late in the fifth century and much of it is thought to have come by way of Germany and the Rhine. During the time of Theodoric, when much of Italy came under Germanic control, conditions for trade between Scandinavia and the Mediterranean were particularly favourable. With the subsequent rise of Frankish power in western Europe a wide variety of west European products reached Scandinavia. In short, it may be said that throughout the first eight centuries of the Christian era and despite fluctuating political conditions, Scandinavia experienced a steadily growing intercourse with the more southerly peoples of Europe. A variety of evidence, among which some of the objects from Sutton Hoo hold a prominent place, indicates that England lay well within the range of Scandinavia's foreign contacts before the Viking attacks began.

It is impossible to say how many of the foreign products which have been recovered from Scandinavian graves found their way to the north by trade and how many as the spoils of war. The distinction is perhaps an over-fine one to be applied to the conditions of those times. There are several references in *Beowulf* to a military expedition from southern Sweden against the lands between the Zuider Zee and the lower Rhine early in the sixth century and there may well have been other expeditions like it. In the sixth century, as in the first half of the ninth, the purpose of such expeditions was mainly the acquisition of wealth and the degree of success which they achieved depended largely upon the degree of opposition which they met. The expedition recorded in *Beowulf* ended in disaster because it was strongly opposed. The invaders were routed and the booty recovered. Swedish colonies were established on the island of Gotland before Augustine reached England, a full two centuries before Lindisfarne was attacked, and by the middle of the seventh century the Swedes had established settlements on the eastern shores of the Baltic whence they slowly expanded across the Polish and Russian plains. During the eighth and ninth centuries parts of Sweden, mainly in the area of the great lakes west of Stockholm, began to enjoy a degree of prosperity comparable with that of the Hanseatic merchants in later times. One site in particular, the town of Birka (Mod. Swedish Björkö) which lies in a small island in lake

Mälar and which was visited in 829 by Anskar, the first Christian missionary in Sweden, has yielded objects gathered from almost every part of the known world, including Britain.

As merchants the Swedes had strong contacts with both east and west, but as colonists they moved mainly towards the south-east in directions dictated partly by the geographical situation of their country and partly by the lines of communication offered by the great rivers of the Russian plains. Striking evidence of their oriental contacts is provided by the numbers of Arabic coins which reached the countries lying on the eastern and southern shores of the Baltic as well as Scandinavia itself. The flow began at about the middle of the ninth century and reached its peak *c.* 980–1000 after which it dwindled rapidly. Gotland alone has yielded more than 25,000 coins of the eastern Caliphate. Close on 12,000 have been found in Sweden and Denmark, whereas, in contrast, only three or four hundred are known from Norway.[1]

In the later stages of the Viking Age a number of Swedes took part in military expeditions against England, as Swedish runic inscriptions testify, and the English in their turn played an important part in Swedish ecclesiastical affairs and as coiners of Swedish money, but the initial attacks against Britain and the permanent settlements which were later established there were mainly the work of Danes and Norwegians. The Danes, traditionally believed to have come from Sweden, were probably established in Denmark shortly before the end of the fifth century, but it was not until near the end of the eighth that they became prominent in European affairs. In campaigns extending over the last thirty years of the eighth century the Franks, under Charlemagne, conquered both the Frisians and the Saxons, their northern neighbours, and more than once during these years Saxon leaders sought refuge at the court of Danish kings. At the end of his Saxon wars Charlemagne found himself confronted by a powerful Danish ruler, Godfred, whose kingdom embraced not only Jutland

---

[1] The figures are derived from R. Skovmand, 'De danske Skattefund fra Vikinge-tiden og den ældste Middelalder indtil omkring 1150', *Aarbøger for nordisk Old-kyndighed og Historie* (København, 1942), pp. 13–17, 201–8.

and the Danish islands, but also parts of southern Sweden. Like his contemporary, Offa of Mercia, Godfred regarded himself as Charlemagne's equal and for a short while his power was a serious menace to Frankish supremacy over the Frisians and the Saxons, but it was a rare occurrence in the history of Denmark in these times for any king to establish himself in a position of such strength as that achieved by Godfred. The lack of any strong central authority, such as might have exercised a restraining influence within Denmark itself, was one of the factors tending to encourage the growth of piracy in the Narrow Seas. The Frankish conquest of the Frisians who had long been the leading seafarers of north-western Europe, and the later dissolution of the Frankish kingdom after the death of Louis the Pious, created the conditions in which piratical attacks could be made without the likelihood of their being effectively opposed.

Although many such descents were made, it would be a mistake to regard the Danes of this time as no more than pirates. Godfred fortified the southern frontier of his kingdom with an earthen bank topped by a wooden palisade and with a ditch on its southern side. It is believed that this fortification is now represented by the earthen bank known as the Kograb or Kurvirke which runs some miles westwards across the neck of the Jutland peninsula from the Schlei upon whose northern shore Slesvig now stands. In addition, Godfred established on the southern shore of the Schlei a trading centre which was either then or subsequently enclosed by a massive semicircular rampart. Alfred, who had learnt something about it from the Norwegian sea-captain Ohthere, knew it by the name *æt Hæðum*. It is now called Hedeby. The importance of this site was due to its peculiar geographical position. The Schlei upon which it stood cuts so deeply into the eastern side of the Jutland peninsula as to reach almost half-way across. A short way from its innermost shores rises the River Treene whose waters reach the North Sea by way of the Eider. It was formerly possible to navigate small craft up these rivers from the North Sea at least as far as Hollingstedt and the distance from that point to the headwaters of the Schlei was so small that merchandise, or even boats, could have been carried across. At the beginning of the Viking Age this route from the North Sea to the Baltic was no less important than, for more recent times, the Kiel Canal, of which it was in a sense the predecessor. Such was the importance of Hedeby as a clearing-house for Baltic and North Sea trade that there was considerable rivalry for its possession between the Danes themselves and the Swedes during the ninth and tenth centuries.

The Danish Hedeby and the Swedish Birka represent an aspect of Scandinavian civilization in the Viking Age which is not reflected in the English and Irish monastic chronicles. At these two sites there existed large and prosperous communities having remarkably wide contacts with both the Eastern and the Western worlds. They are to be regarded not so much as the haunts of freebooting pirates, but rather as ninth-century predecessors of the Hanseatic towns, and they are part of the evidence which suggests that the beginning of the Viking Age was less the sudden eruption of previously isolated peoples than the culmination of several centuries of steadily widening intercourse with foreign lands. No site has yet been discovered in Norway comparable with Birka and Hedeby.[1] Norway possessed considerable potential sources of wealth both in its fisheries and in its furs, but lying at the extreme end of the European trade routes it did not receive the benefits reaching countries which included any of their main points of intersection. The more powerful of the Danish kings were able to control both the eastern and the western shores of the Oslo fjord which now belong to Sweden and Norway respectively and any movement which markedly affected Denmark was likely to have repercussions in Norway. Similarly, despite the long range of mountains which marks the common boundary between Norway and Sweden, Swedish influence made itself strongly felt both in the north through the gap leading to Trondhjem and in the south along the Kongsvinger route to Oslo. Scandinavian tradition attributed the original settlement of the Trondelag to Swedish immigrants and also ascribed a Swedish origin to the

---

[1] The name of the Norwegian port from which Ohthere sailed to Hedeby is called *Sciringesheal* by Alfred in his account of Ohthere's voyage which he inserted in his translation of *Orosius*. Excavations begun in 1953 near Larvik on the western side of the Oslo fjord are believed to have revealed the site of this place.

Yngling dynasty from whom the kings of Norway in the Viking Age claimed descent.

Apart from the reaction upon Norway of events in Sweden and Denmark, there were other factors which influenced the part played by the Norwegians in the Viking Age. Norway's physical geography was such as to make it difficult for any one tribe or king to establish supremacy over the whole. The political organization of the country was closely affected by these physical conditions. The long and narrow strip of land which extends into the remote north was never of any importance politically, though it had great economic importance both for its fisheries and for its trade in skins, a trade which was old when the Viking Age began. The remainder of the country fell into four main divisions, each of them with clearly marked characteristics. Of these four, the Trondelag which embraced the comparatively flat and low-lying plains neighbouring the Trondhjem fjord, was traditionally believed to have been settled from Sweden. Within its narrow confines it developed an advanced degree of political organization. South of it lay the great fjords stretching from near Ålesund in the north to Stavanger in the south. Here there were neither plains nor river valleys, but only narrow strips of cultivable land between the deep waters of the fjords and the towering cliffs. Communication between one fjord and another was often impossible except by water and it was from this training ground of seamanship, far more exacting than the sheltered waters of the Baltic, that Norse Vikings came to Britain in large numbers. The western fjords are backed by wide stretches of mountainous country, the modern Jotunheimen and Hardangervidda. To the east of these mountains lay the two remaining districts, the one comprising the two sides of the Oslo fjord around which the earliest attempts were made to establish a united kingdom of Norway, and the other round Mjösa, Norway's largest inland lake. In these two latter districts both internal and external communications were considerably easier than in other parts of the country.

When the Icelandic historians of the twelfth and thirteenth centuries wrote the history of the country from which their ancestors had come to Iceland in the ninth, they attributed the migration of the Norwegians to their spirit of independence which made them unwilling to submit to the domination of Harold Fairhair. This was true in a number of individual cases, but the movement overseas had probably begun before the times at which Harold is believed to have been reigning, and its attribution to political events in Norway may in part reflect the conditions of later times when Norwegian kings were seeking to establish their sovereignty over Norse settlements across the sea. Such claims could well be met by propagating the view that these settlements had come into being as part of a movement of independence against that king, Harold Fairhair, who was later regarded as the first king of a united Norway. It seems likely that the influence of changing conditions in Sweden and Denmark and the difficulty in many parts of Norway of earning a living by any means other than seafaring were at least as important as internal developments in leading to overseas migration. It is significant that one member of an expedition which set sail for Iceland from the western fjords of Norway was reported to have said that every blade of grass in Iceland dripped with butter, though others told both the good and the bad of the land.

2. THE NORSE APPROACH TO BRITAIN

The English possessed about half the mainland of Britain by the middle of the seventh century. The Scandinavian settlements in Britain were not greatly smaller in extent, but they were more widely scattered and lacked the solid core which had enabled the English to create a new country out of the old. There were two distinct approaches to Britain from Scandinavia. The more northerly led from the western fjords of Norway to Shetland and Orkney and thence by the Western Isles to the Isle of Man and Ireland. The Vikings who followed this route were mainly Norwegians. The more southerly route which was followed mainly by Danes, led from southern Jutland along the Frisian coast to the Rhine mouths and thence down Channel to the opposing shores of England and France. This route likewise, by the rounding of Land's End, led ultimately to Ireland. For some fifty years from *c.* 800 the raiders came across the North Sea with the easterly winds of spring and returned home with their loot before the westerly gales of autumn. Soon after the middle of the ninth century some of them began to pass the winter at convenient coastal bases such as Sheppey or Thanet.

The success of these expeditions was mainly due to the complete unpreparedness of Britain to meet such attacks and it was this factor more than any other which led to the ultimate conquest of large parts of the British Isles. Once the most vigorous phase of the Germanic migrations was over, western Europe seems to have been so fully engaged in adapting itself to the resultant changes that the seas and their opposing shores were left undisturbed for a long time. On the Continent, as in Britain, new states were being shaped and although there was much internal strife between one state and another, there were no hostile movements overseas.

The English themselves seem largely to have abandoned seafaring once they had become established in Britain and there is no evidence that English kings of the seventh or eighth centuries normally kept a fleet of warships. The most striking evidence of Britain's unpreparedness to meet attack from the sea is to be found in the location of those three ancient centres of Christendom which were the first places to suffer—Lindisfarne, Jarrow and Iona—two of them islands and the other close by a river mouth. To these could be added a long list of similar monastic communities, such as Coldingham, Monkwearmouth, Whitby and Hartlepool, all of them famous in the eighth century and all of them situated on exposed coasts. Further afield there were religious communities in Iceland and Orkney, and near the coasts of Ireland, Wales and France, many of them on small islands. Such places had been chosen because they offered secluded sanctuaries where monastic life could be followed with the least danger of external interference and in themselves they afford strong evidence that their occupants had no reason to think that they would be in any danger from attack by sea. We may well believe that the astonishment with which Alcuin received the news of the sack of Lindisfarne was matched by the astonishment of the attackers themselves at finding so many communities which housed considerable wealth and whose inhabitants carried no arms.

The detail with which the progress of the different Scandinavian settlements can be traced in Britain as a whole varies greatly in different areas. In general terms the evidence falls into one or other of three categories—native Scandinavian records, objects recovered from Scandinavian burials, and the English and Irish monastic chronicles. The first of the Icelandic historians to write in the vernacular was Ari Thorgilsson who was born *c.* 1067. It is a measure of the differing levels of English and Scandinavian civilization that Ari's birth almost coincided with the battle of Hastings, four hundred years after the birth of Bede and two hundred years after the destruction by the Vikings themselves of the library at York which was famed in the eighth century as one of the greatest libraries of its day in western Europe. The surviving written records about Scandinavia in the Viking Age are mainly the work of Icelandic historians living in the twelfth and thirteenth centuries, although some of the material which they used can be shown to have been composed at much earlier dates and to have been handed down orally for several generations. Such records must be used with great care, particularly in their chronology.

The archaeological evidence is very slight compared with the corresponding evidence for the Anglo-Saxon invasions. It consists mainly of objects recovered from Viking burials in Shetland, Orkney, the Western Isles, Man, Ireland and the north-western counties of England, and as an indication of its quantity it may be noted that the most recent survey of the material records only some thirty-five burials from the whole group of Orkney islands. It has long been recognized that the Irish annals provide a highly accurate chronology for ninth- and tenth-century events. It frequently happened both in Ireland and in England that monasteries where history was being written were themselves destroyed, a disaster which involved not only the destruction of existing libraries, but also the dispersal of the monks who might have continued to add to them. Such was the case with most of the monasteries near the eastern coast of England. In Wessex and in parts of Ireland the disturbance was not always so great as to interrupt the keeping of records. In more remote areas, such as

Shetland and Orkney, where there is no evidence that historical records were being kept at the time, the progress of the Viking settlements can be inferred from the chronology established for other parts of Britain where the evidence is more detailed.

The Scandinavian traditions about the Norse conquest of Orkney are confused and inconsistent, but it is probable that Norsemen had settled in Orkney well before the middle of the ninth century and perhaps before the end of the eighth. If Viking fleets had penetrated as far west as Iona by 795, it is difficult to believe that the islands off the north coast of Scotland could have escaped their attentions previously. An Irish monk, called Dicuil, who wrote a geographical treatise in 825, recorded how a priest had told him that certain islands, possibly the Faeroes, which had previously been occupied by Irish hermits for a hundred years had now become uninhabitable owing to the attacks of the Norsemen. In time the Faeroes, Shetland and Orkney became, and for centuries remained, wholly Scandinavian in race, language and custom. Orkney came to be governed by earls who were nominally subjects of the kings of Norway and whose authority at times extended over much of Caithness and Sutherland. A detachment of their fleet played a part in the affairs of England in 1066. The earldom remained with descendants of the first earl until the thirteenth century when it passed successively to various Scottish families who still in theory held it of the king of Norway. The islands themselves were pledged to the Scottish Crown in 1468 and formally annexed in 1472.

All the islands to the west of the Scottish mainland were known to the Norsemen as *Suðreyjar*, 'the southern islands', and some of them were known to Irish chroniclers as *Innsi Gall*, 'the islands of the foreigners'. The settlement of these 'southern', or as we should now call them western, islands, took place during the first half of the ninth century. For some thirty years from the attack on Iona in 795 there are numerous references in the Irish annals to Viking raids both against the islands and against the mainland of Scotland. The archaeological evidence of Viking settlement in the Outer Hebrides is very slight, but a number of richly-equipped Viking graves of the ninth century, including some ship-burials, have been found on Colonsay, Islay and Arran. The names of some of the early settlers have been preserved in Icelandic tradition because they were believed to be the ancestors from whom some prominent Icelandic families were descended. At times the islands were controlled by the Orkney earls, but there are indications of a close dependence upon a Norse kingdom whose headquarters lay in the Isle of Man.

There are no written records about the earliest Norse settlements on Man, but other evidence suggests that a Norse population imposed itself upon the Celtic inhabitants of the island at about the middle of the ninth century. From *c*. 950 there are references in Irish and English sources to Norse 'kings of the isles' who seem to have been closely connected with the Norse rulers in Dublin. For much of the eleventh century Man and the Western Isles came under the influence of the Orkney earls who were then at the height of their power. Shortly after the defeat of the Norwegians at Stamford Bridge in 1066, Godred Crovan, who had shared in that defeat, found his way to Man and established there a dynasty whose successive members continued to rule for two centuries, despite attempts by both Norwegian and Scottish kings to possess themselves of the kingdom. The last of Godred Crovan's line died at Rushen in 1265 and in the following year the king of Norway surrendered in perpetuity all Norwegian claims to sovereignty over Man and the Hebrides to Alexander III of Scotland, thereby bringing to an end some four centuries of Norse domination. Man itself was secured for England by Edward III, but for long afterwards the island continued to be regarded as a kingdom and its English governors as kings.

Viking attacks against the coastal districts of Ireland began in the first decade of the ninth century. A backward people politically and militarily, the Irish were seldom able to offer effective opposition to the attackers. In about 832 a prominent chieftain whom the Irish called Turges made his appearance in Ireland and sought to establish his sovereignty over several groups of foreign settlers. He expelled the abbot of Armagh and usurped the abbacy for himself, but in 845 he was captured and put to death by Mael Shechlainn, king of Meath. Most of the earliest Viking settlers in Ireland were Norsemen, but *c.* 850 a large Danish host arrived and soon began to dispute the claims of the Norsemen to the possession of their Irish lands. The Danes, often fighting in alliance with Irish chieftains, were at first successful, but in 853 a Norse chieftain called Olaf reached Ireland with a large fleet and soon established himself as ruler of a kingdom whose capital was Dublin. The conflict between the Norsemen and the Danes in Ireland had important consequences for the history of northern England in later times. While Olaf was ruling in Dublin, the great Danish army of invasion landed in East Anglia and in 876 part of it settled in what is now Yorkshire. Early in the tenth century Olaf's successors at Dublin sought to gain control over the Danish settlements in northern England and for about half a century a succession of Norse kings who had close contacts with Dublin ruled at York. The Viking settlers in Ireland intermarried with the Irish and in time many men of mixed Irish-Norse origin crossed the Irish Sea to establish new settlements from the Wirral northwards to the Scottish side of the Solway Firth.

3. THE DANISH INVASIONS

Offa was still king of Mercia when the Vikings first attacked Lindisfarne. One of his daughters was married to Beorhtric, king of Wessex (reigned 786–802), and 'in his days came for the first time three ships: and then the reeve rode thither and tried to compel them to go to the royal manor, for he did not know what they were, and they slew him. These were the first ships of the Danes to come to England'.[1] It is not known whether this attack occurred before or after the attack on Lindisfarne. A later writer believed that the raiders were Norwegians from Hörthaland and from another source we learn that the reeve was in Dorchester when he first heard the news. The attack itself was evidently made against the Dorset coast near Portland. There is no record of any further attack against southern England for more than thirty

[1] *A.S.C.* 787 A. The narrative which follows is based on the A text of the *A.S.C.* whose evidence is in the main contemporary with the events which it describes. Care must be taken with its chronology which is frequently in error, sometimes as much as four years. See further R. Vaughan, 'The Chronology of the Parker Chronicle, 890–970', *E.H.R.* LXIX (1954), pp. 59–66.

years and during this time important political changes occurred within England itself.

Offa died in 796, but his two successors were able to maintain the supremacy of their kingdom and even to extend it by vigorous warfare to the west of Offa's Dyke. In 825 the Mercians were heavily defeated by Egbert of Wessex who rapidly exploited his victory. In the next four years he annexed to Wessex all other English lands south of Thames and conquered Mercia and its dependencies, including Lindsey and East Anglia. He also led an army to Dore near Sheffield on the northern border of Mercia and there he received the submission of all the Northumbrians. The events of these years mark the end of Mercian supremacy and the final southerly shift of the centre of political power in England. In its detail much of the history of England in the ninth and tenth centuries presents an appearance of great confusion, but amid this confusion it is possible to discern five major developments between 825 and 975: first the destruction of the old order of petty states and the emergence of the English monarchy in its place, second the establishment of a large Danish element in an area bounded roughly by Thames on the south, Watling Street on the west and Tees on the north, third the reconquest of this area by the descendants of Egbert of Wessex, fourth the settlement of a substantial Norse population, with some admixture of Irish, in the north-west from the northern side of Solway to the Wirral, and fifth the growth of a united kingdom of Scotland and the subsequent abandonment to Scotland of formerly English lands between Tweed and Forth (see Map 6, p. 86).

The landing on the Dorset coast during the reign of Beorhtric was a minor episode, perhaps brought about by the chances of wind and weather. The first major attack against southern England took place a generation later, in 835, and was directed against Sheppey. It marks the beginning of a series of raids which were of almost annual occurrence during the next thirty years and which ranged along the south coast from Cornwall and Somerset to Portland, Southampton, Winchester, Sandwich, Canterbury, Rochester and London. Their scale varied, according to contemporary English estimates, from about 30 to as many as 350 ships.

It is not to be supposed that the West Saxon annals have preserved a complete record of the Viking raids on Britain during the first half of the ninth century. There are likely to have been many unrecorded attacks, particularly along the east coast. Occasionally during this period Viking forces passed the winter in England, but their normal practice was to return home after harrying the countryside lying within easy reach of their coastal bases. They seldom penetrated more than ten to fifteen miles inland. The situation in the Narrow Seas at this time was in some respects much the same as had prevailed late in the third century when Saxon pirates, heralding the Anglo-Saxon invasions, first became a menace to seaboard life, with the great difference that whereas Roman Britain enjoyed the protection of a power which was strong enough to fortify its exposed shores and to meet seaborne attack upon the seas themselves, the English had no fleet and no organized system of coastal defence. It is a measure of this difference that whereas close on two centuries elapsed between the earliest recorded appearance of Saxon raiders in the Narrow Seas and the ultimate conquest of Britain by the English, only thirty years separated the first Viking attack on Sheppey and the landing of the Danish army of invasion in 865.

The Great Army (*micel here*), as a contemporary called it, landed in East Anglia in the autumn of 865. Its leaders included Ivar the Boneless and Halfdan, sons of a Viking, famous in Scandinavian legend, called Ragnar Lothbrok, and in a series of campaigns extending over the next fifteen years, during which it displayed remarkable powers of cohesion and discipline, it took possession of most of eastern England. After making its landing, the army came to terms with the men of East Anglia in whose country it remained for the next twelve months, equipping itself with horses in preparation for its campaigns of the coming year. The Vikings in England never fought as cavalry, but by using horses for transport they gained a great tactical advantage in the speed with which they were able to move about the country. In the autumn of 866 the army left its East Anglian base, made a circuit of the Fens and struck north to York. Contemporary documents do not explain this surprising move which involved a march of more than 200 miles and which is strongly suggestive of deliberate purpose. According to later Scandinavian legend, the purpose of its leaders was to avenge their father, Ragnar Lothbrok, who was said to have been put to death in a snake pit in York by Ælla, a Northumbrian usurper, but this is little more than a fairy tale. The attack on York coincided with an attack on Dumbarton, the capital of Strathclyde, by a large force of Norse Vikings gathered from the Western Isles, Man and Dublin, but it is perhaps straining the evidence too far to suggest that these two simultaneous assaults were part of a co-ordinated plan to conquer the whole of northern Britain. It is more probable that the choice of York as the army's first objective depended on some now forgotten episode in Northumbrian history earlier in the century. Owing to the destruction of so many Northumbrian records, the history of that kingdom during the first half of the ninth century is almost wholly unknown.

The Danish army entered York on 1 November 866, using the old Roman fortifications for their protection. The capacity of the Northumbrians to resist the invaders was weakened by a state of civil war, but the contending English rulers joined in an attack on the Danish army in the spring of 867. A battle was fought partly inside and partly outside the Roman defences, both Northumbrian rulers were killed and with their defeat the English kingdom of Northumbria ceased to exist as a political force, though it still covered much territory. In the autumn of 867 the Danish army left York for Mercia, establishing itself in winter quarters at Nottingham. Burgred, king of Mercia, who was married to a sister of Æthelred of Wessex, elder brother of Alfred the Great, appealed to the West Saxons for help. A force was sent from Wessex, but the Danes remained within their entrenchments and no major battle took place. This campaign is of interest both as an instance of the disciplined restraint whereby the Danes often sought to avoid open fighting when conditions seemed un-favourable and as marking the beginning of a collaboration between Mercia and Wessex which led to important results in the early years of the tenth century. Checked at least for the moment, the Danes moved back to York where they remained for the winter of 868–9. Moving again in the autumn, as was their custom, they returned to East Anglia and set up winter quarters at Thetford. Soon afterwards they met and defeated an East Anglian army led by Edmund in a battle traditionally believed to have been fought near Hoxne in Suffolk. The contemporary West Saxon annals give scarcely a dozen words to this campaign, but whatever may be the truth of the well-known tradition that Edmund met his death by being bound to a tree, then pierced with arrows and finally beheaded, it is certain that within half a century of his death he had come to be honoured in East Anglia as a saint. Later writers allege that on this its second visit to East Anglia the Danish army devastated the countryside and behaved with great brutality to its inhabitants. The almost complete lack of written records relating to the earlier history of East Anglia is confirmation that the monasteries suffered severely from this visitation which marked the destruction of the second of the English kingdoms.

Late in 870 the Danes left Thetford to make their first attack upon Wessex, choosing as their base a site at Reading where the junction of Thames and Kennet offered a position which required little fortification to make it secure. Partly because of the repeated coastal attacks during the previous generation and partly because of the military exploits which had brought Wessex to the fore during Egbert's reign, there was a greater state of military preparedness in Wessex than there had been in Northumbria, Mercia and East Anglia. Within three days the invading force was engaged by the Berkshire levies led by the ealdorman of the shire and four days later by a larger force led by king Æthelred and his brother Alfred. In the first engagement a small Danish raiding party was routed, but in the second the main English force, unwisely attempting a direct assault upon the Danish positions, suffered a sharp defeat. The Danes thereupon advanced from their base at Reading westwards to the Berkshire Downs, then known as Ashdown. Somewhere in this open country the main bodies of the West Saxon and Danish armies met and after a long and hard-fought battle the Danes were driven back in flight to their base at Reading. This was the first pitched battle on open ground against the Danish army, but although the victory went to the West Saxons, its influence upon the course of the war was smaller than the contemporary accounts of it might have led us to expect. Within a fortnight Æthelred and Alfred were defeated south of Reading. Æthelred died in April 871 and was immediately succeeded by his brother Alfred who was hard pressed for the remainder of the year. Summarizing the year's fighting, a West Saxon annalist wrote 'in the course of the year nine general engagements were fought against the host in the kingdom to the south of the Thames, besides those innumerable forays which Alfred, the king's brother, and a single ealdorman and king's thegns rode on, which were never counted. And in the course of this year were slain nine jarls and one king; and this year the West Saxons made peace with the host'.[1] With his forces exhausted by the year's fighting there was little else that Alfred could do except pay the price which he might hope would bring a respite to his kingdom. His hope was justified. The Danes left Reading for London and did not come back to Wessex for five years.

The campaigns of 870–1 were naturally of particular interest to the West Saxon annalist of the time and for this reason they can now be followed in close detail. For the next few years, while Wessex was left in peace, the movements of the Danish army can only be traced in broad outline. It passed the winter of 871–2 in London and after making a brief incursion into Northumbria during the following campaigning season, it moved to Torksey on the Trent for the winter of 872–3. The next year witnessed the destruction of the third of the English kingdoms. Moving from Torksey to Repton in the heart of Mercia, the Danes expelled Burgred who went overseas to end his life in Rome, and handed over his kingdom to 'a foolish king's thegn' who undertook to hold himself and his followers at the disposal of the Danes. For nine years, 865–74, the army had moved up and down the country as a single fighting force, travelling by horseback and living on the lands through which it passed, but late in 874 it broke into two parts and began to turn from military conquest towards the per-

[1] *A.S.C.* 871A, tr. G. N. Garmonsway.

manent settlement of the lands which it had conquered. One part, led by Halfdan, moved north from Repton to the Tyne and after a year spent in harrying attacks against the Picts and the Strathclyde Welsh, it returned to southern Northumbria and settled down to permanent homes in what, as later evidence shows, corresponded broadly with modern Yorkshire. The West Saxon annalist thus briefly describes this settlement of 876, the first large-scale Danish settlement in the country—'in this year Halfdan shared out the lands of Northumbria, and they were engaged in ploughing and in making a living for themselves'.[1] Halfdan himself apparently left Northumbria and died fighting in Ireland a year or two later. While Halfdan's forces were possessing themselves of southern Northumbria, the remainder of the Danish army moved southwards from Repton to Cambridge where they stayed for twelve months and thence, in 875–6, they turned to make a fresh attack on Wessex.

The situation for Wessex was a grave one, the more so as no help could now be expected from other parts of the country, but five years had passed since the first attack and there is an indication of at least one way in which the interval had been profitably spent in the record that in the summer of 875 Alfred's own ships had been able to engage and rout a small force of Vikings at sea. Leaving Cambridge in the autumn of 875 the Danes made straight for Wareham, at the inner end of Poole harbour, apparently expecting to make contact with reinforcements which, according to one authority, were making their way up Channel from the west, perhaps from Ireland. If this was the plan, its later stages miscarried owing to a storm which destroyed a large number of Viking ships off Swanage. The land force found itself in no position to risk an open battle and was compelled to submit to terms whereby hostages were given in guarantee of a pledge to leave Wessex, but the pledge was broken and the Danes slipped away to Exeter by night, eluding the pursuit of Alfred's army which was unable to overtake them before they reached the security of Exeter's defences. It is evident from the willingness with which the Danes gave further hostages that Alfred remained in command

[1] *Ibid.* 876A.

of the situation and in the summer of 877 the invaders left Wessex and crossed to Gloucester in Mercian territory.

Their failure in this second attempt to conquer Wessex was followed by the detachment of another large part of their army. While some of it remained at Gloucester under the leadership of Guthrum, another part turned back towards the east and took possession of much of eastern Mercia. The extent of this settlement cannot be exactly determined but it probably included what later came to be known as the territory of the Five Boroughs, that is of the shires of Lincoln, Nottingham, Derby and Leicester and the land formerly dependent on Stamford. Thus by 877 much of eastern England from Tees to Welland had been settled by the greater part of the army which had landed in East Anglia in 865. There may have been some further settlement, though on a less thorough scale, in the eastern midlands south of Welland. Mercia west of Watling Street remained in English hands, so also did East Anglia and Essex, though the former had been ravaged in the campaign of 869–70.

Early in January 878 that part of the Danish army which had remained at Gloucester under Guthrum turned south again to make a third and last attempt to conquer Wessex. Guthrum's forces must have been considerably smaller than those which had assaulted Wessex on the two previous occasions, yet something like panic was caused among the West Saxons by this third visitation. Some of them fled overseas and others submitted to the Danes, but Alfred himself, accompanied by a small force, fell back to the inner fastnesses of his kingdom west of Selwood. Early in the year his position, which had already seemed hopeless to many, was yet more gravely threatened by the descent of another Danish force upon the coast of Devonshire, but the new invaders suffered a sharp defeat while attempting to besiege an English force on Countisbury Hill.

At Easter of 878 Alfred built a small fortification at Athelney in the Somerset marshes and with this as his base he organized a series of harassing raids against the enemy in preparation for warfare on a large scale when the time was ripe. Early in May he was strong enough to leave the security of the marshes and to cross back to the eastern side of Selwood where the men of Somerset joined forces with those of Wiltshire and the nearer part of Hampshire. The combined levies advanced north-eastwards along the western scarp of Salisbury Plain towards Guthrum's camp at Chippenham. At Edington, fifteen miles south of Chippenham, Alfred won a decisive victory. A fortnight later the Danes again undertook to leave Wessex and after another week Guthrum and thirty of his army leaders were received by Alfred at Aller, close by Alfred's stronghold at Athelney. Guthrum was baptized at Aller and then led his army back to Chippenham whence it moved to Gloucester and finally, in 879, to East Anglia whose lands it proceeded to occupy (see Map 5, p. 77).

4. CONSOLIDATION IN WESSEX

Alfred had reigned for only eight years when Guthrum's followers left Wessex to establish their homes in East Anglia and there yet remained to him a further twenty before his death. His victory at Edington had put an end to the conquests of the great army of invasion but not before it had almost entirely destroyed the old basis of political organization in England. Two urgent tasks now faced Alfred, first to secure his hold on England south of Thames and second to seek some understanding with both his English and his Danish neighbours in the midlands. The urgency of the first task was demonstrated by the arrival of another Viking fleet in the Thames even as Guthrum's army was still taking possession of East Anglia. To the old danger of external attack was now added the further danger that such attackers might find support from their own countrymen in England. The only certain way of securing the country against such fresh attacks would have been by the organization of naval forces strong enough to destroy the ships of the attackers, the method which Carausius had successfully used against Saxon pirates in the third century, but unlike Carausius, Alfred commanded only one side of the Channel and moreover he was faced in the Vikings by enemies who had centuries of seafaring experience behind them. That Alfred was alive to the importance of warships for the defence of his kingdom is evident from several references to minor naval engagements against small flotillas of Viking ships, as well as from his attempts to build ships much larger and faster than the normal Viking ship, although his sailors soon learnt that in the tidal estuaries of southern and eastern England greater size, with an accompanying increase in draught, was not always an advantage. The lack of experienced English sailors and shipwrights was a handicap which could not be overcome quickly, though it was lessened by the use of Frisian sailors.

The English seaboard was too long for its effective defence by any ruler with less than the whole resources of the country at his disposal as well as the skill to organize them, but if the Vikings could not be prevented from landing, their movements after landing could be controlled by methods which their own habits in land warfare may have suggested. During the fourteen years from 865 to 879 the Danes had several times shown reluctance to engage in open battle. So long as they were protected by fortifications there was little that the English could do, but once they could be caught in the open they could be beaten, as Ashdown and Edington had shown. The campaigns of 875–7, when the Danes skilfully avoided battle by using the defences first of Wareham, then of Exeter and finally of Gloucester, must have fully persuaded Alfred of the great value of fortified strongholds both as providing bases for resistance in times of invasion and as giving a means of controlling the nearby countryside.

Where so many records have been lost it is fortunate that there should survive one which contains valuable evidence about the defensive system used by Alfred and his successors. This document, known as the *Burghal Hidage*, dates from the reign of Alfred's successor, Edward the Elder, but it discloses the system as then in being and there are several indications that its early development belongs to Alfred's reign, not the least interesting among them being a reference in the *Anglo-Saxon Chronicle* to an occasion when a Viking army surprised a group of peasants occupying a half-built fortification four miles from the mouth of the River Lymne. The easterly location of this particular fortification suggests that much of Wessex had already been similarly fortified. The *Burghal Hidage* itself names thirty centres, all of

Map 5. The Danish settlements in the ninth century.

them save Buckingham on or south of the Thames and stretching from Pilton and Lydford in the west to Hastings and Southwark in the east. They include several Roman sites, such as Bath, Exeter, Porchester, Winchester and Chichester, where it may be presumed that the old Roman walls formed the basis of defence. Elsewhere, as at Christchurch, a promontory site requiring little additional fortification was used, or, as at Wareham and Walling-ford, an enclosure consisting of an earthen bank and ditch served for defence. The duties of construction, maintenance and garrisoning were laid on the neighbouring district according to a system whereby each hide of land assigned to a fortress should supply one man and each pole of the defence work should be held by four men in time of need.

The fortification of southern England placed Alfred in a posi-tion to meet fresh attack and as the work proceeded he turned to his second urgent task, the seeking of some understanding with his English and Danish neighbours north of Thames. In 886 he occupied London, an event which was followed by the recognition of his sovereignty by those of the English who were not in subjec-tion to the Danes and by an agreement with Guthrum, king of the East Anglian Danes. For more than a century and a half before its occupation by the Danes London had been a Mercian town and Alfred now wisely entrusted its defence to a Mercian ealdor-man, Æthelred, who for some two or three years previously had been the effective governor of English Mercia. Alfred saw that the best hope of eventually achieving the reconquest of the Danish-occupied lands lay in the establishment of a firm alliance with English Mercia. The basis of such an alliance had been created by the marriage of Burgred, the last legitimate king of Mercia, to one of Alfred's sisters, and by the sending of West Saxon forces to help Burgred in the campaign of 867-8.

After the death of Edmund of East Anglia and the flight of Burgred overseas, Alfred remained the sole representative of English sovereignty south of Tees. By entrusting the defence of London to a Mercian, he avoided the danger of giving offence and within a few years he strengthened the alliance by giving his daughter Æthelflæd in marriage to Æthelred. The terms of the agreement which Alfred reached with Guthrum are embodied in a document commonly called the *Treaty of Alfred and Guthrum*. This treaty, which represents an agreement between equals rather than the imposition of terms by one side upon the other, left Alfred in possession of London but recognized the sovereignty of Guthrum over the north shore of the Thames as far west as the Lea which forms the modern boundary between Essex and Middlesex. The western boundary of Guthrum's kingdom followed the Lea to its source on the downs near Luton. From there it ran in a straight line to Bedford and thence westwards up the Ouse to its meeting with Watling Street at Fenny Stratford. So defined, Guthrum's kingdom included the whole of Essex, Norfolk, Suffolk and Cambridgeshire as well as part of the shires of Bedford and Hertford. How much farther to the north it extended is uncertain.

There was no major change in the general situation in England during the thirteen years of Alfred's reign which remained after the occupation of London in 886. Wessex had been secured for the English and there was good prospect that the alliance with Mercia would at least allow the Danes to be confined within the area which they had occupied between Thames and Tees. As yet the danger of attack against north-western England from the already powerful Norse kingdom of Dublin had not begun to make itself apparent, but the threat, and more than the threat, of renewed invasion from the opposite quarter remained with Alfred for the rest of his reign. Powerful Danish forces continued to rove the Narrow Seas at will and were liable to turn against south-eastern England if they were checked elsewhere, knowing that in much of England they would find friendly territory. One such force after several years of successful campaigning in France suffered a severe defeat there in 891 and in the following year it sailed from Boulogne to make successful landings in two detachments, the one on the southern and the other on the northern shores of Kent.

These new invaders severely tested the defences of Wessex, but they were the remains of a beaten army, encumbered with their horses which they had brought with them in their ships and also with their wives and children. They received some support from the Danes in England, but there was never any likelihood of their being able to succeed in the conquest of Wessex where their predecessors had failed in much more favourable circumstances. In their one attempt to penetrate deeply into West Saxon territory they were sharply defeated by Alfred's son, Edward the Elder, but they remained in being as an army for four years, camping in Danish territory and making periodical excursions across Watling Street into English Mercia. Conditions such as these made it impossible for Alfred to do more than retain his hold upon what had been recognized as his by the treaty with Guthrum, more, that is, in the sphere of military achievement. In the year after his occupation of London, then a man approaching forty, Alfred began to learn Latin and so to prepare himself for those translations of various Latin works into Old English which now mark the foundations of English prose literature. Either of his two great achievements, the military or the literary, would by itself alone have been ample justification for the verdict which posterity has passed upon this remarkable man.

5. THE CREATION OF THE KINGDOM OF ENGLAND

The date of Alfred's death is not established with certainty, but the evidence points to 26 October 899. He was succeeded in turn by his son, Edward the Elder, and by his grandsons Athelstan, Edmund and Eadred. Their reigns extended from 899 to 955, a half century which is marked by the reconquest of the Danish settlements east of Watling Street, by the beginnings of the Irish-Norse assault against north-western England and by steadily growing pressure from the Scots in the north. The recovery of the Danish-held lands between Thames and Humber was achieved in a series of campaigns conducted jointly by Edward the Elder and his sister Æthelflæd, widow of Æthelred, the Mercian ealdorman who had been entrusted with the defence of London in 886. A preliminary English attack towards the north, followed by a Danish expedition towards the Bristol Avon, resembled the pattern of earlier wars which had been marked by swift movements over large distances, but this episode which ended in an English victory in 910 over the retreating Danish force at Tettenhall in

Staffordshire, was not characteristic of the methods by which Edward and his sister achieved their successes. Confronted by opponents who had by then abandoned regular warfare for almost a generation and who lacked any unified system of government, they chose rather to reduce individual communities by slow and steady stages and to secure what they had won at each stage by extending north of Thames the system of fortification which Alfred had used in Wessex.

Æthelflæd's chief task was to fortify the frontier of English Mercia and to maintain a constant threat of attack against the Danes east of Watling Street, while Edward moved northwards at first into Essex and Hertfordshire and later into the shires of Oxford, Cambridge and Huntingdon. These preliminaries were completed in 916 and in the next year a general assault was delivered with the result that by the end of 917 the whole of eastern England as far north as the Welland had been recovered (see Map 6). At the beginning of 918 there remained four Danish strongholds between Welland and Humber which were still outside English control. Two of them, Stamford and Leicester, were occupied by Edward and Æthelflæd respectively during the first half of the year, but on 12 June Æthelflæd died and Edward moved promptly to Tamworth to secure Mercian recognition of his sovereignty. Before the end of the year Lincoln and Nottingham, the other two Danish strongholds, had surrendered to Edward whose authority now reached from the Channel to the Humber, the ancient northern boundary of the southern English. The climax of Edward's military achievements came two years later, in 920, when at Bakewell in Derbyshire he received the 'submission' of Constantine, king of Scots, Rægnald the Scandinavian ruler of York, Ealdred of Bamborough, ruler of all that remained of English Northumbria, and the submission also of all the people of Northumbria, whether English, Danes, Norsemen or others, and of the king of the Strathclyde Welsh and all his people. Edward had now established himself as the most powerful ruler in the whole of Britain, although little more than forty years before his father's kingdom had scarcely extended beyond the Somerset marshes.

The striking changes which mark the political history of the midlands and south between 878 and 920 are paralleled by no less striking changes in the north, changes which are reflected in the names of those who submitted to Edward at Bakewell. The collapse of Northumbria, as a result of the Danish occupation of York in 866 and of the subsequent settlement of Halfdan's army in Yorkshire, marks the beginning of a period of great political confusion in the north which lasted throughout the Middle Ages and which indeed was resolved only with the union of the English and Scottish crowns in the seventeenth century. In Bede's time the authority of the Northumbrian king ran from Humber to Forth on the east and from Ribble to Ayrshire on the west. The break-up of this great kingdom had consequences in proportion to its size with, as their most enduring feature, the southerly shift of the no-man's-land from the Antonine line back towards the Hadrianic line across the Tyne-Solway gap.

The Danish settlement in Yorkshire, Northumbria's south-eastern quarter, was the immediate cause which brought the kingdom to collapse, but the settlers had been established for little more than a generation before the south-western quarter of Northumbria began to be threatened by other Scandinavian intruders, Norsemen in the main who had reached Ireland by the north-western circuit of Britain. Though closely akin, Norsemen and Danes were by no means necessarily well disposed to one another. They had come into conflict in Ireland and during the first half of the tenth century the Dublin Norse sought to gain control of the Danish settlements in Yorkshire. They succeeded as we may see from the extremely confused succession of Norse kings who came to rule in York over a mixed Anglo-Danish population until 955 when Eric Bloodaxe, the last of their number, was finally driven out and killed. These Norse rulers were hostile not only to the English rulers of the house of Wessex, but also to the Danish settlers in the confederacy of the Five Boroughs between Humber and Welland.

The situation in northern Northumbria was hardly less confused. After the formation of the kingdom of Scotland through the amalgamation, *c*. 850, of the formerly distinct kingdoms of the

Picts and Scots, Lothian, Northumbria's north-eastern quarter, came under increasing Scottish pressure until it was finally absorbed into Scotland. A similar process affected Northumbria's north-western quarter, but the situation here was complicated both by the continuing existence of the old kingdom of Strathclyde and by the infiltration of Norse settlers into the lands on the northern side of Solway. The course of events cannot be followed in detail, but there is some evidence that the kings of Strathclyde, like those of the Scots, were able to take advantage of Northumbria's weakened position after the Danish invasions and to expand their authority towards the south over formerly English lands. Strathclyde retained its independence until the beginning of the eleventh century, but thereafter it passed increasingly under Scottish control. It is against this confused background that we should view the campaigns of Edward the Elder and his successors in the tenth century.

The caution with which Edward moved in the early stages of his wars against the Danish areas in the east midlands was largely due to the danger of invasion in the north-west by Norsemen from Ireland. The danger was twofold, first that English Mercia, already faced with a hostile population east of Watling Street, might be assaulted in the rear by invaders entering the Dee and Mersey estuaries and be so greatly weakened as to deprive the alliance between Mercia and Wessex of all efficacy, and secondly that the arrival of such invaders might result in collaboration with the Scandinavian element in Yorkshire and the subsequent establishment of a block of Scandinavian territory across the full width of northern England from Mersey to Humber. Both Edward and Æthelflæd were fully alive to these dangers and they made their dispositions accordingly. A confused but, as it seems, basically reliable account, now preserved only in an Irish source, testifies to an invasion of the Wirral by Norsemen from Ireland in the early years of the tenth century. To meet this threat Æthelflæd repaired the walls of Roman Chester in 907 to such good effect that its people were able to meet and overcome a powerful assault which was later made upon it. Chester was the terminal point of Watling Street and so long as it was securely held the danger of

Norse penetration into the midlands was correspondingly reduced, but to hold Chester was not enough. The Cheshire plain offered an easy line of approach to Tamworth, the political centre of English Mercia, and to meet this threat Æthelflæd built fortifications at Runcorn, near the inner end of the Mersey estuary, and at Eddisbury, half-way between Runcorn and Chester. It was only after the north-western frontier of Mercia had been thus secured that Æthelflæd was able to play her part in the decisive campaign of 917 which brought Edward's armies north to the Welland.

After Æthelflæd's death early in the summer of 918 English Mercia, including the whole of Cheshire, was incorporated in Edward's kingdom. By the end of 918 the northern boundary of this kingdom rested on Humber in the east and Mersey in the west, but the danger of a breach of the north-western frontier still remained and in 919 Edward built a new fortress at Thelwall on the Mersey some miles upstream from Runcorn, and occupied Manchester, repairing its Roman defences. Manchester, like Chester, was the meeting-place of several Roman roads and its occupation by Edward interrupted the most direct line of communication between the Wirral and York. The reality of the danger in this area was emphasized in the following year, 920, when a Norse army from Dublin came to land and broke through the defences as far as Davenport in Cheshire. No details are known about the course of this attack, but that it was met and overcome is evident from the strong position in which Edward found himself established before the year was out. Despite Edward's successes, the Norsemen who had occupied the Wirral early in the century remained in possession of their lands and they have left abundant signs of their continuing presence in the place-names of the present day. They came too into the coastal areas of Lancashire, as well as into Westmorland, Cumberland and the northern shore of the Solway Firth, but the evidence of their presence in these more northerly areas is mainly derived from place-names and there is very little direct record either of the date or of the manner of their arrival. Carlisle was still a safe area of Northumbria *c*. 875, but records relating to St Cuthbert's see indicate that by *c.* 920 there was little security in Cumberland or Westmorland and that the westerly move, exemplified by the flight of the monks from Lindisfarne in 875 with the body of Cuthbert, to escape the Danish attacks from the east was giving way to a return move to the east to escape the Norse attacks from the west (see Map 6 overleaf.)

Edward the Elder died in 924 and was succeeded by his son, Athelstan, who was crowned at Kingston on 4 September 925. His upbringing in the household of Æthelred and Æthelflæd of Mercia ensured Athelstan the loyal support of the Mercian nobility and thereby placed him in a strong position to carry the war against Scandinavian Northumbria. Early in 926 he gave one of his sisters in marriage to Sihtric, the Norse ruler of York, but this attempt to secure control of York by peaceful means ended with Sihtric's death in the following year. Sihtric's son, Olaf, supported by a force of Norsemen from Dublin, attempted to claim his inheritance by force whereupon Athelstan invaded Northumbria and expelled Olaf together with his Irish-Norse supporters. A second attempt by the Norsemen was similarly defeated, York itself was occupied by Athelstan and its defences razed. Athelstan's triumph was marked by a gathering held on 12 July 927 near the Eamont, a little to the south-west of Penrith, at which he received the submission of the kings of Scotland and Strathclyde and of the ruler of English Northumbria north of Tees. The River Eamont forms part of the modern boundary between Westmorland and Cumberland and it is probable that it was chosen as the scene of the gathering because it then marked the extreme north-western limit of Athelstan's kingdom. Within the first three years of his reign Athelstan had thus advanced in the north-west some eighty miles beyond the frontier marked at the end of Edward the Elder's reign by the fortifications at Chester, Runcorn and Eddisbury, and he had, for the time being at least, incorporated the whole of Lancashire and Westmorland within the kingdom of England (see Map 6).

The settlement which was reached at the meeting by the Eamont in 927 endured for some years, but in 934 Athelstan moved northwards through Yorkshire and Durham to invade Scotland. His

Map 6. England in the Tenth Century.

army penetrated as far north as Kincardine and a naval force simultaneously harried the Scottish coast as far as Caithness. The appearance of powerful English forces in Scotland was a grave threat to all the diverse elements which had been fighting for supremacy in the north ever since the Danes reached York in 866 and in the face of this threat they made common cause. Olaf Guthfrithson, then ruler of the Norse kingdom of Dublin, sailed from Ireland in 937 with a large fleet and joined forces with Constantine, king of Scots, and with the king of Strathclyde. These combined forces invaded English territory in the same year and were engaged by Athelstan and his brother, Edmund, at the head of the Mercian and West-Saxon levies. The opposing sides met at a place which the English called *Brunanburh*, a place whose identity is now unknown, although there have been many ill-founded guesses, and in the battle which followed the English won a decisive victory.

The battle of *Brunanburh* was celebrated in verse by a contemporary English poet and it is an indication of the importance which the event assumed in the eyes of other contemporaries that the poem itself was incorporated in the *Anglo-Saxon Chronicle* (see Pl. IV). To posterity Athelstan's victory over the combined Scandinavian, British and Scottish forces seems to mark the climax, if not quite the end, of an epoch in English history. During a period of about three-quarters of a century (865–937) the older political system had perished through the disintegration or destruction of the several once independent kingdoms upon which that system had rested and its place had been taken by the single kingdom of England. Both disputed succession and foreign conquest lay in the future, but when the latter came early in the eleventh century, the conqueror set out to represent himself as successor to the kingdom created by the house of Wessex and to use its machinery of government rather than to subject the country to some wholly alien form of rule. The death of Athelstan in 939 showed how much the kingdom of England yet depended upon the person of its ruler. Olaf Guthfrithson who had fled to Ireland after his defeat at *Brunanburh*, returned to York in the year of Athelstan's death, invaded the midlands as far south as Northamp-

PLATE IV

THE PARKER CHRONICLE, A.D. 925–37
Corpus Christi College, Cambridge, MS 173, f. 26a.

The first hand (see Pl. III, p. 34) extends as far as the recto of F. 16, but in the remainder of this MS the changes of hand are frequent. The plate opposite shows work done by the eighth scribe who began with the entry for 925 and continued to 955 at the bottom of F. 27b. It should be compared with the eighth-century work shown on Pl. XVI, p. 324. The last seven words of the entry for 925 are in the hands of a later Canterbury scribe.

The five prose entries on the page include references to Athelstan's accession (*s.a.* 925, *recte* 924) and his invasion of Scotland (*s.a.* 933, *recte* 934). Beginning opposite the year number 937 and occupying the remainder of the page are the opening lines of the poem *The Battle of Brunanburh*. The poem is written, as was customary, in continuous lines as though it were prose, but with a point marking the end of each half line. The remainder of the poem extends over the whole of F. 26b and part of F. 27a. The text of the opening lines follows below with G. N. Garmonsway's translation. It should be noted that the word *Her* is the regular introduction to a new annal and that the poem properly begins with the word Æþelstan.

937   Her Æþelstan cyning,   eorla dryhten,
beorna beahgifa,   and his broþor eác,
Eadmund æþeling,   ealdorlangne tír
geslogon æt sæcce   sweorda écgum
ymbe Brun(n)an burh;   bordweal clufan,
heowan heaþolinde   hamora lafan
afaran Eadweardes;   swa him geæþele wæs
from cneomægum,   þæt he æt campe oft
wiþ laþra gehwæne   land ealgodon,
hord and hámas.

In this year king Athelstan, lord of warriors,
Ring-giver of men, with his brother prince Edmund,
Won undying glory with the edges of swords,
In warfare around *Brunanburh* .
With their hammered blades, the sons of Edward
Clove the shield-wall and hacked the linden bucklers,
As was instinctive in them, from their ancestry,
To defend their land, their treasures and their homes,
In frequent battle against each enemy.

88

PLATE IV

AN DCCCC · XXV   Her. eadpeard cyng forþ ferde 7 æþelstan his sunu ricsode

AN DCCCC · XXVI   to rice 7 sce dunstan geapd akenned. 7 polf holm

AN DCCCC · XXVII   feng to þan arcebiscopprice on cantparebyri.

AN DCCCC · XXVIII

AN DCCCC · XXVIIII

AN DCCCC · XXX

AN DCCCC · XXXI   Her monþadode wynstan biscop to pintanceastre
·IIII· kl iunii · 7 þe hpolo hpide healfgan biþ dom.

AN DCCCC · XXXII   Her forþ ferde fryþestan biscop

AN DCCCC · XXXIII   Her for æþelstan cyning in on peort land 7 þis gemid
land hine gemid scyp hhie 7 hiy micel ofh
heþ gade 7 byrnstan biff forþ ferde on pin
tanceastre to comnium forpan

AN DCCCC · XXXIIII   Her cyng ælfhach biscp to biscedpoome

AN DCCCC · XXXV

AN DCCCC · XXXVI

AN DCCCC · XXXVII   Her æþel stan cyning ton la opryh cun bropina
bah gipa 7 hisbhopop eac eadmuid æþeling eal dop langnecip.
geplogon æt pecce scop þa ægum. ymbe bjunanbupþ bopsd
peal clufan hiopan heaþolinde. ha mopa lapatrapapan ead
peap dþ. spati geæþele pecp. fpisenteo magū þ hiæt campe oft
rislaþpa geþcne. lcondeal godon hoþ 7 humar hæt cipo
cpungun pct ta leo da 7 iip plotan gage plollan peloocheo

ton and secured an agreement with Edmund, brother and successor of Athelstan, whereby he was recognized as ruler not only of York and its dependent territories, but also of the Five Boroughs, that is of the north-eastern midlands between Humber and Welland.

Olaf Guthfrithson died in 941 and within the next three years Edmund was able to recover both the Five Boroughs and York itself. In 945 he invaded Strathclyde and after ravaging its lands, as though intent upon destroying the ancient kingdom, he handed it over to Malcolm, king of Scots, evidently with the dual purpose of setting a limit to English rule in the north-west and of preventing the recurrence of an alliance such as had led to the battle of *Brunanburh* by securing the friendship of the Scots. Edmund's short reign came to an end in May 946 when he was killed in a brawl at Pucklechurch in Gloucestershire. Little has been recorded about the reign of his brother and successor Eadred (946–55), but the reign witnessed the last episode in the epoch which had opened in 865. This was the final expulsion in 954 of the last of the Scandinavian kings of York, Eric Bloodaxe, son of Harold Fairhair, king of Norway. The expulsion and subsequent death of Eric Bloodaxe marked the end of the Scandinavian attempt to establish an independent kingdom based upon Dublin and York, and Northumbria was thenceforward governed by a succession of earls ruling nominally as deputies of the kings of England.

Before the Norman Conquest England enjoyed only two periods of comparative freedom both from internal war and from the threat of external invasion. The earlier and longer belonged mainly to the late seventh and to the eighth centuries when the several kingdoms of early England had reached a rough state of equilibrium and the main impetus of the European migrations had spent its force. Its civilization was predominantly northern and is best represented in the works of Bede and in the school at York which produced Alcuin. The later belongs to the second half of the tenth century when the first and most far-reaching stage of the Viking attack had been met and overcome. Its civilization belonged predominantly to the south and to the east midlands and is best represented in the great revival of Benedictine monasticism which was set on foot by Dunstan, Æthelwold and Oswald. Politically it coincides with the reigns of Eadwig (955–9) and Edgar (959–75). The dominant interest of this period is in its ecclesiastical history.

In the sphere of political history there seem to be only two events of major significance, both of them in the reign of Edgar. The first, which is recorded only in a thirteenth-century source, though the account seems to be trustworthy, was an agreement between Edgar of England and Kenneth of Scotland, at a meeting held at Chester-le-Street in Durham, whereby Edgar made to Kenneth a formal cession of all the lands between Tweed and Forth. With this event, reminiscent of the earlier attempt by Edmund to secure the friendship of the Scots by the grant of Strathclyde, the Tweed first appears as a formally recognized boundary between England and Scotland. Centuries passed before this boundary became permanently established, but after the meeting between Edgar and Kenneth, the question at issue was not whether the lowlands of south-eastern Scotland should again become part of England, but whether Northumberland and Durham should become part of Scotland. The second event was the coronation of Edgar which took place at Bath in 973, only two years before his death. With this ceremony which included not only the act of crowning, but also solemn anointing and a form of coronation oath, the continuous history of the English coronation service may be said to begin. Prominent churchmen played the major part in the ceremony and, by thus investing a corporate body which would survive the deaths of individual kings with certain rights and privileges, their action was not without importance in securing the continuity of the monarchy (see below, pp. 207–8).

6. ÆTHELRED THE UNREADY

Edgar died in 975 and was succeeded by his son Edward who was murdered in 978 at Corfe, in circumstances which prompted a contemporary chronicler to describe the crime as the worst which had been committed in England since first the English settled in the island. Edward was followed by Æthelred the Unready whose reign ended thirty-eight years later in the subjection of England to the rule of a foreign king, Cnut of Denmark. Within two years of Æthelred's accession the Vikings resumed their attacks against England, coming at first as small bands of adventurers who sought to escape from the control which Harold Gormsson had established over Denmark, but later as organized professional armies led by the kings of Denmark themselves. It is unnecessary to follow the course of these attacks in detail, and attention may rather be drawn to certain general features which distinguish this second phase of the Viking attack from the earlier. Superficially the most striking contrast is that between the prompt resolution with which Alfred and his successors met and overcame the earlier attacks and the feeble hesitancy and treachery which seemed to contemporaries to characterize the handling of military affairs by Æthelred and his counsellors, a contrast epitomized in the nickname by which Æthelred came to be known.[1]

The comments of a contemporary Abingdon chronicler who seems at times to have been a greatly exasperated man, illumine this aspect of the period. In 992 land and sea forces were assembled at Æthelred's command in the hope that a Danish invading force might be engaged, but the ealdorman to whom they were entrusted sent word of the impending attack to the Danes and himself 'absconded from our army during the night before the battle should have been fought—to his great shame' (992 C). In 1003 when the levies of Wiltshire and Hampshire were assembled to oppose a Danish army led by Swein Forkbeard this same ealdorman 'began to play at his old tricks. As soon as the armies were near enough to see one another, he pretended to feel ill and began to retch and vomit, saying that he was a sick man, and thus he deceived the men whom he ought to have been leading' (1003 C). The attacks of Swein continued without pause and in 1010 the Abingdon chronicler wrote—'when the enemy were to the east, our army was kept to the west, and when the enemy were to the south, then was our army kept in the north. Then all the counsellors were summoned to the king to advise him how this land ought to

---

[1] 'Æthelred the Unready' corresponds with O.E. *Æðelræd Unræd* which could be literally rendered 'Noble-Counsel No-Counsel'.

be defended, but even though some decision was taken, it stood not even for a month, and at last there was not a leader who was willing to assemble an army, but each fled as best he could.'

The characteristics of a generation cannot be drawn from the remarks of one man, but the Abingdon chronicler is not alone in depicting the reign of Æthelred as an age of degeneracy marked by feebleness and treachery among its leaders. In a famous sermon which was probably composed in 1014, two years before Cnut's accession, Wulfstan, archbishop of York, denounced the evils of the age in similar terms, comparing as he did so the disasters which had befallen his own generation at the hands of the Vikings with those which had befallen the British at the time of the Anglo-Saxon invasions. The Church and its servants were deprived of all reverence and of all their just dues. The rights of free men were destroyed. Innocent men and young children were sold into slavery. Treachery was rife and the social order was so loosened that noblemen and slaves took each other's places. Wulfstan was certainly using the language of the sermon in which such denunciation is not uncommon, but even though, like Gildas, he may have hoped to make his call to better ways the more effective by denouncing the greatest evils of his time, he, like Gildas, was describing the age in which he lived and his evidence must carry great weight.

Yet the evidence of Wulfstan and the Abingdon chronicler tells only part of the story, and that the least creditable. It ignores the stand of Byrhtnoth and his companions in the battle of Maldon in 991, the valour of Ulfkell Snilling of East Anglia, and the stubborn resistance of the Londoners against repeated attacks. It ignores not only the great scholars, Ælfric of Eynsham and Byrhtferth of Ramsey, who were able to work undisturbed in a society which seemed to Wulfstan to be in a state of complete disruption, but also the unknown monks who produced some of the most notable illuminated manuscripts which have survived from the whole of the Anglo-Saxon period. It is perhaps unwise to make comparisons between the resolution of Alfred and the feebleness of Æthelred without taking a somewhat wider view of the circumstances which enabled Swein and Cnut to succeed where the sons of Ragnar Lothbrok failed. The Danish army which landed in East Anglia in 865 achieved its early successes partly because it had undisputed command of the sea and partly because of its ability to move rapidly on horseback, but in open battle it showed no marked superiority as a fighting force over the West Saxon levies. This army was intent upon colonization, and victory in battle was merely a means to that end.

By the end of the tenth century, when the Scandinavian countries had two centuries of fighting experience behind them, something new and much more formidable appeared. This was the highly trained army of professional soldiers whose purpose was not to colonize but to spend their lives in fighting. Scandinavian traditions tell of the establishment of such a community of professional soldiers in a fortress called Jómsborg near the mouth of the Oder. The fortress itself has not been found, but the saga of the Jómsvikings, as its inhabitants were called, gives an account both of its general appearance and of the strict rules of military discipline to which its occupants subjected themselves. It comprised both a fortified harbour so large that 300 ships could ride at anchor at one time and a land fortress whose defences, partly of stone, were strong enough for catapults to be mounted on them. Membership of the community was limited to warriors of tried valour. No women were allowed to enter the fortress. Ties of kinship were to be of no avail against the interests of the community and all booty won in the expeditions made each summer was to be placed at the disposal of the commander. Although the manuscript evidence is late, the story of Jómsborg cannot be dismissed as unfounded legend. Two famous men associated with the Jómsvikings played leading parts in English affairs during the reign of Æthelred—Thorkell the Tall and Swein Forkbeard.

Any doubts which may have been felt about the reality behind the Jómsborg legend have been dispelled by the discovery in Denmark of the remains of a number of remarkable fortresses whose plan and construction suggest that they were built and occupied by military communities of the kind described in the saga of the Jómsvikings. Four such fortresses have now been discovered and excavated in whole or in part. The first of the four to be found, at Trelleborg in western Sjælland, consisted of a massive circular defence work 17 m. thick and with a radius of 68 m. (234 Roman feet) from its inner edge (Fig. 1). The rampart

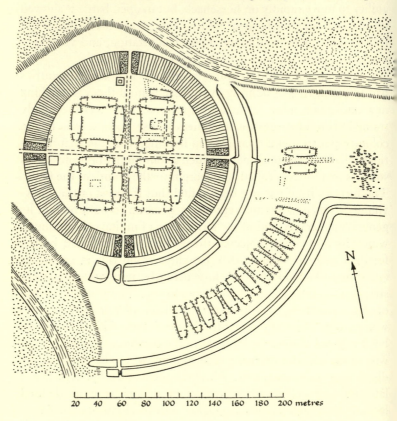

Fig. 1. Ground plan of the Viking fortress at Trelleborg, Denmark.

was pierced by four diametrically opposite gateways joined together by roads intersecting at the centre and in each of the four sectors so formed lay blocks of four houses placed end to end in such a way as to make a hollow square. All sixteen of these houses were of the same size and shape, 29·5 m. (100 Roman feet) long, with straight cut gable ends and slightly curved longitudinal sides. A fortified area outside the main stronghold enclosed another

94

fifteen houses of the same shape and construction, and also a cemetery. The large number of weapons among the many objects recovered by the excavators testified to the predominantly military nature of the settlement, although objects indicating the presence of women were not lacking. The period of occupation was established as lying within the limits 950–1050. The other three fortresses which have been discovered since were all of similar plan. Two of them, those at Fyrkat Mølle near Hobro and at 'Nun's Hill', Odense, were also of similar size and date. The last of the four, at Aggersborg, was considerably larger than the others and also rather later. Perhaps the most remarkable feature of these fortresses is the complexity of their construction and the geometrical precision of their plan which was based upon the Roman foot as the surveyor's unit of measurement. For military architecture of comparable excellence we must look either backward to the military forts of imperial Rome or forward to the more highly developed Norman castles. Estimates about the numbers which could be housed in these fortresses have varied, but it is thought that those at Trelleborg, Fyrkat Mølle and Odense could between them have provided permanent quarters for a force of not less than 3,000 men. All the fortresses lie on what were royal estates and there can be no doubt that they were built by royal command, the three earlier probably by Swein Forkbeard. Together they provide striking evidence for the existence in Denmark when Æthelred the Unready was reigning in England of a highly-skilled and well-disciplined professional army under royal command.[1]

A number of Swedish runic inscriptions dating from about the same period refer to Swedes who took service with such armies. One such records that it was set up by *Tóla* in memory of her son

---

[1] Short English accounts of Trelleborg will be found in *Antiquity*, XIV (1940), pp. 272–9, and in P. Nørlund, *Trelleborg* (Copenhagen, 1948), published in connexion with the exhibition of Danish art in London in 1948 and translated from Danish by J. R. B. Gosney. For the full account of Trelleborg see P. Nørlund, *Nordiske Fortidsminde*, IV Bind, 1 hefte, udg. af *Det Kgl. Nordiske Oldskriftsselskab* (København, 1948), also P. Lauring and A. Hoff-Møller, *Aarb. for Nord. Oldkyndighed 1952* (København, 1953), pp. 108–65. For Aggersborg see C. G. Schultz, 'Aggersborg, Vikingelejren ved Limfjorden' in *Fra Nationalmuseets Arbejdsmark 1949* (København, 1949). For information about Fyrkat Mølle and 'Nun's Hill', Odense, I am indebted to Mr C. G. Schultz of the Copenhagen National Museum who has been in charge of the excavations.

Geirr who died in a Viking expedition to the west.[1] Another was set up by *Rái* in memory of his brother *Gunni* who was killed in England.[2] A third commemorated *Þiálfi* of whom it was said that 'he was with *Knútr*'.[3] A fourth was to the memory of *Úlfr* of whom it was said—'he received geld three times in England. The first was paid by *Tósti*, the second by *Þorketill* and the third by *Knútr*'.[4] The first of these three leaders is probably to be identified with a famous Swedish Viking whose daughter married Swein Forkbeard, the second is Thorkell the Tall, the Jómsviking, and the third is that same Cnut who ruled England from 1016 to 1035.

The wages of such professional soldiers were paid out of the tribute which their leaders exacted from the countries in which they fought. In England this tribute was later known as Danegeld and the story of its exaction and distribution is revealed plainly enough by the English chroniclers, by the runic inscriptions and by the great quantities of silver which found their way to Scandinavia. Byrhtnoth, the heroic ealdorman of Essex, refused to pay the price of peace for which the Danes asked at Maldon in 991, but in that same year others less heroic handed over 10,000 pounds of silver. Even larger payments were made in later years, 16,000 pounds in 994, 24,000 in 1002 and 36,000 in 1007. Much of this silver was paid in coin as we may see from the numbers of Anglo-Saxon coins subsequently recovered from Scandinavian soil. A few such coins began to reach Scandinavia as early as the eighth century. A slight increase in the flow during the ninth and early tenth centuries was followed by nothing less than a flood during the reigns of Æthelred and Cnut (978–1035). Ten silver hoards recovered in Denmark and Skåne and belonging to the early part of the Viking Age contained only 33 Anglo-Saxon coins, but 23 such hoards from the same area and belonging to the times of Æthelred and Cnut contained no fewer than 5,000 Anglo-Saxon coins, a large number of them being Æthelred's. No exact figures are available for Scandinavia as a whole, but the total may

---

[1] *Nordisk Kultur*, VI, *Runorna*, utg. O. v. Friesen (Stockholm, 1933), p. 176.
[2] *Ibid.* p. 179.   [3] *Ibid.* p. 185.
[4] *Ibid.* pp. 207–8.

be near 35,000.[1] This figure, large though it is, cannot represent more than a very small fraction of the total number of silver coins which passed from England to Scandinavia at this time. The flow continued until near the end of the eleventh century, though on a gradually decreasing scale. In addition to coins, it is probable that part of the tribute was paid in silver bullion which could be carried on the person in the form of neck- or arm-rings. Such objects as these, together with silver ingots and coins, form the components of most of the silver hoards of the Viking Age found in Scandinavia. The greater part of this wealth found its way east to Gotland, as with the earlier westward flow of Arabic silver. Southern Sweden and Denmark also received large shares, but Norway lagged far behind. A small part of it found its way north to Orkney and the Hebrides.

England's whole order had been fundamentally changed by the events of 865 and later, and the country was in no position to offer sustained and united opposition to armies consisting largely of men who had submitted themselves to that kind of rigorous military discipline implied by the evidence of Jómsborg, Trelleborg, Fyrkat Mølle and 'Nun's Hill'. After some years of continuing attack, an unusually large Danish force arrived off the coast of Kent in 1009. It was led by two brothers, Thorkell the Tall, the famous Jómsviking, and Hemming. A third brother was himself the commander of the Jómsborg fortress. The invaders exacted tribute from Kent, but were strongly opposed by the men of London. After burning Oxford early in 1010, they turned to East Anglia where, in a hard-fought battle near Thetford, they defeated the East Anglian levies led by Ulfkell Snilling. In the autumn of 1011 they returned to Kent after making a series of raids into the heart of the country. They seized the archbishop of Canterbury, Ælfheah, whom they murdered with the utmost brutality in the following year. Their commander, Thorkell, tried to save the arcbishhop's life and it may have been his failure to do so which prompted him to transfer his services to the English

---

[1] R. Skovmand, *op. cit.* (p. 58, note 1 above), p. 213, gives the following: Gotland over 14,000; Sweden, excluding Skåne, 2,600; Bornholm 530; Øland 80; Finland 800; Skåne 7,200; Denmark, west of Øresund, 3,500; Norway over 2,000. These numbers are likely to have increased since 1942.

side when the greater part of his army left the country towards the end of 1012. Thorkell's desertion of the Jómsvikings, who owed allegiance to king Swein of Denmark, was one of the reasons which led Swein himself to invade England in the following year.

Swein Forkbeard, as he is commonly called, was the son of King Harold of Denmark, the reputed founder of Jómsborg and it is to Swein that Danish archaeologists attribute the building of Trelleborg. He had driven his father out of Denmark shortly before 988 and had twice campaigned in England, once in 994 in the company of Olaf Tryggvason who later became king of Norway, and a second time in 1003–5. Swein's army made its first landing at Sandwich in 1013, but it left again after a short stay and turned northwards, entering the Humber and passing up the Trent as far as Gainsborough where a base was established. Here Swein was at once accepted as king by the Northumbrians and by all the Danes of eastern England from Tees southwards to East Anglia and beyond. He then advanced into English Mercia and Wessex, receiving the surrender of Oxford and Winchester. After an unsuccessful attack on London, he marched west to Bath and finally returned to his base at Gainsborough. Towards the end of 1013 London surrendered, Æthelred fled to Normandy and Swein was recognized as king of England, but in February of 1014 he died. His elder son, Harold, succeeded to his father's Danish kingdom, but the Danish army at Gainsborough accepted his younger son, Cnut, as their leader. At the request of some of his subjects Æthelred returned from Normandy and led an expedition against the Danes in Lindsey, whereupon Cnut withdrew his army from the Trent and went back to Denmark. Cnut was back again in England in 1015 at the head of a powerful force which included Thorkell the Tall who had now left Æthelred's service. After some months of campaigning in which the chief opposition to Cnut came from Edmund Ironside, Æthelred's son, and from the people of London, Æthelred died in April 1016.

The Londoners acknowledged Edmund as their king, but many of the most distinguished men of Wessex gave their allegiance to Cnut. A successful campaign recovered Wessex for Edmund, but

PLATE V

CNUT AND ÆLFGYFU-EMMA AT THE NEW MINSTER,
WINCHESTER

left London exposed to close siege. Shortage of supplies eventually forced Cnut to withdraw from his siege lines, at first to East Anglia and Mercia where fresh supplies were secured and then to Kent where he was sharply defeated by Edmund and forced to withdraw to Sheppey. Edmund had achieved remarkable successes and it may have seemed that Cnut might yet be driven out, but so long as the Danish ships remained it was always open to Cnut to withdraw from one area where he was being hard pressed and to open a fresh campaign elsewhere. In the autumn of 1016 the Danes crossed into Essex and here, at Ashingdon on the Crouch, Edmund suffered a defeat in which the most powerful army he could assemble was overwhelmingly beaten. Edmund himself survived the battle and an agreement was made whereby Wessex was left to Edmund and the remainder of the country handed over to Cnut, but within a month of the battle of Ashingdon Edmund died, on 30 November 1016, and Cnut became king of England.

7. DANISH RULE

After the death of Edmund Ironside, England was ruled by Danish kings for rather more than twenty-five years, first by Cnut himself until 1035 and then successively by his two sons, Harold Harefoot and Harthacnut. On the death of the latter in June 1042, the old line of Wessex was restored in the person of Edward the Confessor. A well-known drawing in the *Liber Vitae* of Hyde Abbey, depicting Cnut and his wife, Emma of Normandy, presenting a gold cross to the New Minster at Winchester, epitomizes the kindly feelings with which the English Church came to regard this foreign conqueror (Pl. V). In longer retrospect the chief significance of his reign seems to be twofold, first that the very presence upon the English throne of a young man who was among the greatest warriors of a warlike Scandinavia was itself a guarantee that England would enjoy a respite from external attack, and second that the necessity of maintaining his position in Scandinavia led to the delegation of authority over domestic affairs in England and the resultant growth of powerful subjects. Towards the end of his reign interest begins to shift, for the first time in the

narrative of English history, from the king himself towards the
more ambitious of his noblemen.

Cnut's first acts were those of a soldier determined to secure his
hold upon what he and his father had won in battle. The change of
dynasty was made easier by the presence of a large Scandinavian
element in the population of England and by the absence of any
strong representative of the house of Wessex who might have
encouraged further opposition. Eadwig, the only surviving son
of Æthelred by his first wife, was quickly hunted down and killed
by Cnut's orders. By his second wife, Emma, sister of Richard II,
duke of Normandy, Æthelred left two sons who found refuge at
the Norman court. One of them, Alfred, visited England in 1036
where he was arrested and soon afterwards died of the brutal treatment which he received at his captors' hands. The other, Edward,
later known as the Confessor, became king of England in 1042.
There were also two sons of Edmund Ironside, but both were
infants at the time of their father's death. They were removed
from England and eventually found their way to the court of
Stephen, king of Hungary, by whom they were treated with great
honour. Children of one of these exiles were famous in later
days as Edgar the Ætheling and St Margaret of Scotland, Malcolm Canmore's wife. To meet the danger which might arise
if Richard of Normandy were to take up the cause of his nephews,
the children of Æthelred and Emma, Cnut put away Ælfgifu of
Northampton by whom he had become the father of children,
and married Emma herself who agreed to override the rights
of her children by Æthelred in favour of any which she might
bear to Cnut.

Whether Cnut realized it or not, the security of England was
less likely to be threatened from Normandy at this time than by
the arrival of other would-be conquerors from his own Scandinavia. One small Viking fleet which approached the coast of
England early in 1017 was swiftly destroyed. In the following
year Cnut's position in England, already strong, was more formally
recognized at a meeting of the national assembly held in Oxford,
and the magnates there assembled, looking back across the troubled
times of Æthelred's reign, agreed that the laws of Edgar, which

had recognized the right of Englishmen and Danes alike to keep their own customs, should once again be observed.

In 1019 Cnut embarked on the first of four expeditions to Scandinavia. This first expedition arose from the death of his brother Harold, king of Denmark, and the need for Cnut to secure that kingdom for himself. His second expedition, in 1023, was likewise concerned with Denmark. It arose from a quarrel between Cnut and Thorkell the Tall as a result of which Thorkell was outlawed and withdrew to Denmark. Possibly fearing that Thorkell might raise an army against England, Cnut sought him out in Denmark and the two came to terms. In his third and fourth expeditions, in 1026 and 1028 respectively, Cnut was engaged in forestalling attacks against Denmark from Norway and Sweden. His attempts to undermine the position of Olaf Haroldson, who had won control of most of Norway, led to an alliance between Olaf and Ånund, king of Sweden. These two determined to invade Denmark and thereupon Cnut, not a man who waited to be attacked, promptly sailed from England with a large fleet and engaged his enemies in a naval battle off the mouth of the Holy River in Sweden. The sources disagree over its outcome, but it seems that neither side won a decisive victory. After the battle Cnut left Denmark and went to Rome where he was present at the coronation of Conrad, the Holy Roman Emperor, in 1027.[1] In the following year he attacked Norway. After previously trying to win the support of disaffected Norwegians by bribery, he sailed from England at first to Denmark and then to Norway itself. Progressing northwards along the Norwegian coast, he landed at various points to secure the allegiance of local chieftains and finally, at Nidaros, he was proclaimed king of Norway. With this achievement he had reached the height of his power in Scandinavia, but he was not able to maintain his position and he had already lost the whole of Norway before his death in 1035.

Little has been recorded of the domestic events of Cnut's reign.

---

[1] Although it is certain that Cnut was in Rome in 1027, all the major English chronicles, including *A.S.C.* D, E and F, place his visit under the year 1031. The difficulty is discussed by O. Moberg, *Aarb. for nordisk Oldkyndighed og Historie* (København, 1945), pp. 6–25.

In 1017, the year after his accession, he divided the whole of England into four large areas. He retained Wessex under his own direct control for a short while, but within a few months he entrusted its administration to earls. Mercia he gave to Eadric Streona, East Anglia to Thorkell the Tall, and Northumbria to Eric of Hlaðir, but this arrangement was short-lived. Before the end of 1017 Eadric Streona and several other noblemen whom Cnut evidently distrusted were put to death. Towards the end of the same year he raised a large tax, with a particularly heavy contribution from London, and used the money to pay off the fleet which had brought him to power. Most of the crews were sent back to Denmark, but a few were retained to serve as the nucleus of a small standing army which was supported by a system of national taxation.

Before the Danish invasions the local government of much of England had been in the hands of ealdormen appointed by the king. In Wessex at least it appears then to have been normal for the sphere of authority exercised by each ealdorman to have been limited to a single shire. Prolonged warfare and the disappearance of the smaller kingdoms were among the factors which tended towards a decrease in the total numbers of ealdormen and an increase in the political stature of those who survived. This tendency, already apparent in the tenth century, became pronounced in the reign of Cnut by which time the ealdorman had been largely replaced by the sheriff on the one hand and the Anglo-Scandinavian earldoms on the other.[1]

Foremost among the new men who came to the front in Cnut's reign was Godwine. He seems not to have had any particular claim to high authority by birth, but he was holding an earldom in Wessex in 1018 and he established a close connexion with the court by his marriage. In later years his daughter, Edith, became the wife of Edward the Confessor and one of his sons was that Harold who became king in 1066 and died fighting against William of Normandy at Hastings. Another of the new men was Leofric whose father had held office as ealdorman in the west midlands during the reign of Æthelred. Leofric seems to have held some

[1] See below, pp. 228-9.

subordinate position in these parts from early in Cnut's reign. He later became earl of Mercia and, as the effective ruler of much of the midlands, a dominant figure in the reign of Edward the Confessor. The third of the earldoms which acquired great importance in the eleventh century was that of Northumbria. Its holders played a less prominent part in domestic affairs than did the earls of Wessex and Mercia, but it was they who were responsible for ruling and defending the remote borderland country which lay beyond the immediate control of the English kings.

After the fall of the old Northumbrian kingdom at the time of the Danish invasions, what remained of English Northumbria was governed by a succession of English earls whose authority was generally limited by the Tees but occasionally extended southwards into Yorkshire. Their province was an unruly one which suffered much from the incursions of successive Scottish kings. In 1017 Cnut appointed Eric of Hlaðir as earl, but the native line continued to hold office in a subordinate position. The settlement which had been reached between Edgar and Kenneth at Chester-le-Street seems to have endured for a generation, but in 1006 Kenneth's son, Malcolm, invaded Northumbria and besieged Durham. He was sharply defeated by a Northumbrian army, but in 1016, or a little later, in alliance with Owen the Bald of Strathclyde, Malcolm won a decisive victory over the Northumbrian earl at Carham on the Tweed. For some years Northumbria lay exposed, but in 1028, immediately after his return from Rome, Cnut himself invaded Scotland and secured his recognition by Malcolm. Towards the end of his reign Cnut appointed Siward, a vigorous Danish warrior, to the Northumbrian earldom. Though apparently not attempting to win back Lothian from the Scots, Siward established a firm hold upon the western parts of the border district and was strong enough to prevent any further resuscitation of Strathclyde. He married into the native line of the Northumbrian earls and his son, Waltheof, became an important figure in early Norman times.

Cnut died at Shaftesbury in November 1035 and his body was removed to Winchester for burial. At the time of his death Emma was alone in England. Harthacnut, her son by Cnut, was in

Denmark and Alfred and Edward, her sons by Æthelred, were in Normandy. Cnut himself had intended that Harthacnut should succeed him in both Denmark and England, but Denmark was then so greatly threatened by invasion from Norway that Harthacnut was unable to leave. At a meeting of the council at Oxford in 1036 it was agreed on the suggestion of Leofric of Mercia that Harold, Cnut's son by Ælfgifu of Northampton, should be made regent of England. Godwine opposed this suggestion without success, save that Emma was to be allowed to live in Winchester and hold Wessex until Harthacnut's arrival. The affairs of Denmark continued to delay Harthacnut and in England opinion moved rapidly towards electing Harold as king. Even Godwine seems not to have been strongly attached to the cause of Emma and Harthacnut. When Emma's son, Alfred, came from Normandy to visit his mother at Winchester in 1036, Godwine had him arrested and was rightly held responsible for his subsequent death. Harold, virtually king since 1035, was formally recognized as such in 1037 and Emma was then driven into exile. Harthacnut made his way to her at Bruges towards the end of 1039 and in March of the next year Harold died. Harthacnut was thereupon invited to England where he arrived in June 1040 to reign until June 1042.

8. EDWARD THE CONFESSOR AND THE END OF THE ANGLO-SAXON STATE

Edward, the only surviving son of Emma and Æthelred the Unready, had come to England in 1041 at the invitation of Harthacnut who received him into his own family. Although he had been living as an exile in Normandy for twenty-five years and must have returned to his country as a complete stranger, he was acclaimed king in London in 1042 even before Harthacnut had been buried. He was crowned at Winchester on Easter Day 1043 and in the autumn of that year, accompanied by the three most powerful of the earls, Godwine of Wessex, Leofric of Mercia and Siward of Northumbria, he went again to Winchester and possessed himself of all the wealth of his mother, Emma, and at the same time deprived her of her lands. Emma continued to live at

Winchester until her death on 6 March 1052, but in her later years she played little or no part in the affairs of the country. Edward's action towards his mother seems to accord ill with the saintly reputation which he was not long in acquiring, but perhaps it seemed no more than politic to the great earls upon whom he depended that he himself should control what was at one and the same time Emma's personal wealth and the national treasury. There were some who said that she had been less generous towards her son than she ought to have been, while others alleged that she was anxious for Magnus of Norway to invade England.

Cnut had brought security to England against attack from the north, but the restoration of the West Saxon line created a dangerous situation. The male line of the Danish royal family had become extinct with the death of Harthacnut, but there were two Danes who regarded themselves as claimants to Cnut's English kingdom. One of them, Harold, related to Cnut by marriage, was killed in 1043. The other, Swein son of Estrith, Cnut's sister, found himself fully occupied in seeking to maintain his position in Denmark against the attacks of Magnus, king of Norway, who claimed the kingdom of Denmark by the terms of an agreement with Harthacnut. There were men in England who well understood that if Magnus were once able to gain the mastery of Denmark, he was likely to turn against England. The struggle between Magnus and Swein Estrithson was watched with close attention by the English who for several years maintained a fleet in readiness at Sandwich, though they were not willing to meet Swein's requests for direct naval help. Before the end of 1046 Magnus had won most of Denmark. In 1047 Swein was driven out and the Danes received Magnus as their king, but Magnus died in the same year and Swein at once returned to Denmark. Magnus was succeeded in Norway by Harold Hardrada who at once made peace with England, biding his time for nineteen years. Soon after the threat of invasion had passed, Edward at first reduced and then wholly disbanded his fleet. In 1051 he abolished the heavy tax which had been levied annually for its maintenance for close on forty years.

Four years after the death of Magnus and the removal for the time being of the threat from Norway, England was brought to the verge of civil war. This affair, commonly called the English revolution of 1051, arose from an incident which occurred in Dover while Eustace, count of Boulogne, was on his way home with his retinue from a visit to Edward. According to a Canterbury writer, one of Eustace's men adopted a truculent manner in his demands for quarters of one of the men of Dover. The man of Dover was wounded and slew his attacker, whereupon a general mêlée broke out and some twenty men were killed on each side. Eustace and those of his followers who survived returned to Edward and told him, 'but only in part',[1] what had happened. Edward, it is alleged, accepted Eustace's version of the incident and ordered Godwine, in whose earldom Dover lay, to ravage the town, but Godwine refused to obey the order. At this time Godwine and his family seemed to be in an extremely powerful position in the country. His own earldom extended from Cornwall to Kent and his daughter, Edith, had been married to Edward for six years. His eldest son, Swein, who had twice contrived to win pardon for monstrous crimes, once after seducing an abbess and again after treacherously murdering his own cousin, then controlled the south-west midlands. His second son, Harold, held an earldom which reached from Thames to the Wash and inland to Cambridgeshire and Huntingdonshire.

Edward, who was at Gloucester at the time of the Dover incident, summoned an assembly to meet there on 8 September to deal with Godwine's refusal to obey his king's command. Before the assembly met Godwine called out the men of his own earldom and bade Swein and Harold do likewise. These three mustered a large army about fifteen miles from Gloucester and made ready to attack the king if he were not ready to hand over Eustace and his men. Edward, now in a dangerous situation, sent north to Leofric of Mercia and Siward of Northumbria. They came at once to his support with small forces and as soon as they realized the gravity of the situation they called out their men on a large scale. They were ready to attack Godwine if Edward so ordered

[1] *A.S.C.* 1048E.

'but some men thought that it would be great folly were they to come together in battle, because wellnigh all the noblest in England were in one or other of the two hosts'.[1] A compromise was reached whereby hostages were to be given by both sides and a further meeting of the assembly was to be held in London later the same month. Edward made the most of the interval to increase his military strength and by the time the assembly met, Godwine's supporters, though still numerous, were outnumbered and began to fall away before the growing strength of their opponents. In the upshot Godwine himself with his wife and three of his sons, Swein, Tostig and Gyrth, went to Bruges. Two other sons, Harold and Leofwine, went to Ireland and his daughter, the queen, was committed to the care of an abbess.

The exile of Godwine and his family was short-lived. Except for Swein who died while returning from a pilgrimage to Jerusalem, they were all restored within twelve months. Edward took advantage of their short absence to increase the Norman element about him. He had already, in 1049, appointed to the see of Dorchester a Norman priest whose conduct greatly shocked his contemporaries and early in 1051 he had secured the translation to Canterbury of Robert of Jumièges who had held the see of London since 1044. Later in 1051 he appointed another Norman to London in Robert's place and in the winter of 1051 or the spring of 1052 he is alleged to have received a visit from William of Normandy himself. Nothing was said about the purpose of this visit by the one contemporary English chronicler who recorded it, but most historians of that age as well as this have believed that it was concerned with the succession to the English throne and that William then received some promise of recognition as Edward's successor.[2] Early in the summer of 1052 Godwine reconnoitred the Sussex coast to test local feeling among the seafaring men. English ships had been held ready at Sandwich but they made no

[1] *Ibid.* 1052 D.
[2] But see D. Douglas, *E.H.R.* LXVIII (1953), pp. 526–45, who rejects the story of William's visit to England in 1051–2 and argues that Edward's promise of the English throne to William was conveyed to him by Robert of Jumièges early in 1051. On this interpretation, which Douglas regards as tentative, Edward's transactions with William preceded the revolution in the autumn of 1051.

contact with Godwine's which left for Bruges after only a short stay.

Measures were then taken to reorganize the king's fleet, but they were so ill managed that the crews began to desert and as soon as Godwine learnt how matters were faring he crossed the Channel again, this time making his way westwards to the Isle of Wight and Portland where he was joined by his son Harold who came up Channel from Ireland. The combined fleet turned eastwards to Pevensey and Dungeness, and thence to Romney, Hythe, Folkestone, Dover and Sandwich, gathering ships and supplies as they moved along the coast. Godwine's forces, now commanding much greater naval strength than could be brought against them by Edward, entered the Thames and made their way to London to lay their demands before the king. Through the mediation of Stigand, then bishop of Winchester, conflict was avoided and hostages were exchanged as a preliminary to a meeting of the assembly. Robert, the archbishop, and the Norman bishop of Dorchester at once took flight and were subsequently outlawed, together with all the Frenchmen who were alleged to have come between Godwine and the king. Godwine made his defence before the assembly and he himself, his family and his followers were restored to their possessions. Edith was brought back to court from the nunnery to which she had been sent. The vacant archbishopric was given to Stigand, but save for one short period his tenure of it was not recognized either by Rome or by the leading English churchmen.

Godwine began to sicken soon after his restoration and on 15 April 1053 he died suddenly while supping with the king at Winchester. His death removed the first of the three great earls who between them controlled most of England when Edward became king. The second of them, Siward, died in 1055 after stoutly defending the northern marches for many years, and the third, Leofric of Mercia, greatly honoured by all men, in 1057. When Godwine died Edward was about fifty years old, not a great age, but greater than that of any English king since Alfred. As the years passed he turned more and more away from matters of state and towards his own religious interests. The oft-told story of the last twelve months before the battle of Hastings is so familiar that it is difficult now to read what contemporary chroniclers recorded about the last decade of Edward's reign without the shadow of Hastings seeming to darken the pages. The record is confused and halting and it is sometimes hard to tell whether the silence of the chroniclers at what seem vital points of their narrative is due to discretion rather than ignorance or to stupidity rather than policy. In retrospect the second half of the reign seems to be dominated by two related factors, the rise of a formidable power west of Offa's Dyke and the ever-growing strength of the house of Godwine.

The first marked increase in the strength of Godwine's house followed upon the death of Siward in 1055. In the year before his death he had invaded Scotland in support of Malcolm, son of Duncan, against Macbeth. The invasion was successful but Siward's elder son was killed and when Siward himself died, his younger son, Waltheof, was little more than a child, no fitting successor to an earldom upon whose resolute tenure the security of much of England depended. The earldom might have been given to another Northumbrian but was in fact bestowed on Tostig, another of the sons of Godwine. By establishing friendly relations with Malcolm, Tostig was able to maintain the position won by Siward, but within his earldom he was regarded with hostility as a southern intruder and after ten years, almost on the eve of the Norman Conquest, the Northumbrians rebelled against his rule. Two other events of some importance occurred in 1055. One was the bringing of a charge of treason against Ælfgar, son of Leofric and holder at that time of the East Anglian earldom. The other was a victory won by Gruffydd ap Llywelyn, king of Gwynedd, over Gruffydd ap Rhydderch of southern Wales, a victory which marked the climax of a series of campaigns waged by Gruffydd ap Llywelyn over some fifteen years and which made him virtual master of the whole of Wales. We do not know why Ælfgar was charged with treason and there were some at the time who thought him innocent, but he was outlawed none the less and after going to Ireland, where he raised a fleet, he turned back to Wales and made common cause with Gruffydd in an attack against Hereford which had lately become the centre of a strong Norman settlement. In October 1055 the town was burned and its cathedral ravaged.

The attack on Hereford was the first incident in a series of campaigns between the Welsh and the English which ended only with the death of Gruffydd eight years later. The next incident occurred in June 1056 when the newly appointed bishop of Hereford himself led an army into Wales and was killed in battle, together with several of his priests and a number of other prominent men. An English army was assembled at Gloucester and under Harold's command it marched a short distance into Wales, but there was no decisive engagement and an agreement was reached whereby Ælfgar was restored to his earldom. Upon Leofric's death in the following year Ælfgar succeeded to his father's earldom of Mercia. By a consequential rearrangement of the East Anglian and south midland earldoms, the position of Godwine's house was greatly strengthened, but the alliance between Ælfgar and Gruffydd was similarly strengthened by the fact that their respective territories now marched with one another from Hawarden as far south as Ludlow. In 1058 Ælfgar was again outlawed and again restored with the help of his Welsh ally. Evidence which is by no means as detailed as might be wished, indicates that a powerful Norwegian fleet, commanded by Magnus, son of Harold Hardrada, was active in the Irish Sea at this time and played some part on the side of Gruffydd and Ælfgar.

Little is known about Ælfgar's activities after his second restoration. He married a daughter to Gruffydd, probably after 1058, and he himself seems to have died in 1062, to be succeeded in the Mercian earldom by his son, Edwin. Gruffydd's power was a serious threat to the midlands and in 1062 Harold made a determined effort to surprise him in one of his strongholds. Immediately after Christmas, when attack was least to be expected, he rode from Gloucester to Chester and thence westwards to Rhuddlan on the Clwyd. Gruffydd received timely warning of his approach and made a hasty escape, but his ships and houses were burnt. In the spring of 1063 a more elaborate campaign was organized. Tostig led a force down from Northumbria into north Wales and Harold embarked with another force at Bristol and made his way along the Welsh coast. The Welsh outside Gruffydd's hereditary lands were ready enough to throw off his rule and Gruffydd soon found himself being harried from one refuge to another by the combined English armies, until, in August 1063, he was killed by his own men.

Edward the king was growing old by 1063. He had provided no heir and the achievements of Harold the earl had now raised him to a position of such eminence that only his deficiency of royal blood seemed to stand between him and the throne. Edward, as most believe, had given some promise of the kingdom to William of Normandy in 1051 or 1052. In 1057 Edward the Ætheling, son of Edmund Ironside, had returned to England after living abroad since Cnut's accession in 1016. He would have been the natural heir to the throne if the succession were to remain in the royal family, but he died very soon after his arrival and his son, Edgar, was as yet too young to be considered as a possible successor. Away to the north Harold Hardrada who conceived himself to be the heir to Cnut's kingdom, was watching the situation closely and the part played by his fleet in the events of 1058 must have made the danger from this quarter abundantly clear to Harold of England. These were the circumstances in which occurred the famous visit of Harold to France. Contemporary English chroniclers make no reference to it and its date remains uncertain, though 1064 seems to be the most probable year. Later writers give conflicting accounts of the visit and exactly what befell will never be known, but most modern historians are more ready to accept the version represented pictorially in the Bayeux tapestry than any one of the written accounts.

The Bayeux tapestry is thought by some to have been worked in England for Odo, bishop of Bayeux, within twenty years of the battle of Hastings. Its opening scene shows Edward addressing Harold as though entrusting him with some mission. Harold and his men are then seen riding to Bosham whence they take ship to the land of Guy, count of Ponthieu. On disembarking Harold is arrested by Guy who takes him to Beaurain and holds him there. When news of this reaches William he sends messengers to Guy who brings Harold to William. Harold accompanies William on a campaign into Brittany and after the campaign William gives Harold arms. They then ride to Bayeux where Harold takes an oath to William. In this scene Harold is shown standing between two vested altars upon each of which is a reliquary. He has both his arms extended and one hand rests upon each of the reliquaries. Next he is seen returning to England and telling Edward how he had fared on his journey. What was the real object of that journey, whether he went to the land of Guy of set purpose or was carried there by a storm, what was the precise nature of his oath to William and whether he gave it voluntarily or upon Edward's instructions or under coercion, these are some of the points about this famous incident which have been discussed at great length, but with little profit.

While Harold's brother Tostig, earl of Northumbria, was visiting the king near Salisbury in the autumn of 1065, the situation in England was suddenly changed by a Northumbrian rebellion against the harsh rule of their earl. The rebels, only some 200 strong initially, marched upon York, killed Tostig's leading supporters there and seized his treasury and store of arms. They then outlawed Tostig and invited Morcar, brother of Edwin, earl of Mercia, to be their earl in his place. The rebellion developed on a much larger scale as a Northumbrian army marched southwards and was joined by a force of Mercians and Welshmen led by Edwin. Northampton was occupied and its neighbourhood harried. Negotiations between the king and the rebel leaders were opened at Oxford, with Harold acting as mediator, and in the upshot Morcar was confirmed as earl of Northumbria, and Tostig and his immediate followers went into exile. Meanwhile the king's health was failing. He was too ill to attend the consecration of Westminster Abbey on 28 December 1065 and on 5 January 1066 he died. He was buried in the abbey on the next day and on the day of his burial Harold was made king.

Harold governed England for nine months from 6 January until 14 October 1066. Early in the spring the affairs of Northumbria took him to the north, but at Easter he went south again from York to London. It was at this season that 'throughout all England there was seen in the heavens such a sign as men had never seen before'.[1] Halley's Comet, as we now call it, shone brilliantly for many nights and all over the land men must have gazed at 'the hairy star', as some called it, with the awestruck wonder of those who still watch it in the Bayeux tapestry. The comet first appeared on 24 April and early in May occurred the first episode in that swift succession of events which culminated at Hastings. Harold was in London when he heard the news that his brother, Tostig, had arrived with a fleet off the Isle of Wight. After provisioning there, Tostig coasted eastwards, harrying as he went, and occupied Sandwich where he was joined by a fleet which had come down from Orkney. Harold at once raised a large force and made his way to Sandwich, fearing that Tostig's arrival heralded invasion from Normandy. Tostig's force then left Sandwich and turned north, touching on the Norfolk coast and then entering the Humber where it disembarked. It did much damage in Lindsey, but was driven off by Edwin and Morcar and finally made its way to Scotland, greatly reduced in numbers.

The dispersal of Tostig's fleet was followed by an interval of some weeks while preparations for attack and defence were made on either side of the Channel. By the beginning of August William had assembled a great force, but contrary winds held it back and the continuing delay strained and finally broke the organization of the English defence. Provisions were almost exhausted by the second week in September and the decision was taken to disband the militia and to send the fleet from its station off the Isle of Wight to London. Many of its ships were lost in a storm on the way. In the midst of this confusion Harold Hardrada, accompanied by Tostig with a large force from Scotland, entered the Humber with a fleet of some 300 ships. They passed up the Ouse to an anchorage at Riccall and Harold of Norway prepared to advance to York, but two miles south of the city, at the village of Gate Fulford, he was engaged by Edwin and Morcar. At the end of a hard day's fighting the English forces were broken and the survivors came to terms with the invaders. The battle of Fulford was fought on 20 September. Four days later, Harold of England, making all speed from the south, reached Tadcaster and on the next day,

[1] *A.S.C.* 1066 C.

25 September, after covering the nine miles to York, passing through the city and marching another seven miles to the east, he attacked the enemy at Stamford Bridge on the Derwent. His assault took them by surprise and at its end 24 of the 300 ships were enough to carry the survivors away. Harold Hardrada and Tostig were both killed.

Two days after the battle of Stamford Bridge the wind shifted and William's host began to embark. It sailed on the evening of 27 September and on the morning of the next day disembarked at Pevensey, moving after a few days to Hastings. News of the landing probably did not reach Harold in the north until 1 October. With all speed he summoned additional levies and made his way south on the long journey of 250 miles. He left London on the last 60 miles of the journey through Sussex on 11 October and two days later news of his approach reached William who then began to move inland from his coastal base. The English army can scarcely have been in a condition to take the initiative against a force which, though numerically weaker, was well equipped with both archers and cavalry. Its best hope was to stand on a strong position from which it could meet the enemy's attack. The position chosen by Harold lay on the hill upon which the village of Battle now stands, some nine miles inland from Hastings. It was protected on either flank and in the rear by sharply falling ground, but to the front a gentler slope fell away to the valley below.

Battle was joined on 14 October. William had ordered his forces in three divisions, the Bretons to the left, the Normans in the centre and the French to the right. He set his archers in the forefront, his heavily armed infantry behind them and his cavalry in the rear. Harold held the English army which lacked both archers and cavalry, in close formation behind their 'shield wall'. The first assault delivered by the archers was effective so long as they remained outside the range of the English weapons, but at close quarters they were less effective against the English battle-axe. After a long struggle William's left wavered and finally gave way in confusion. Some of the English, thinking that the day was won, broke from their close order in pursuit, but William himself rallied his knights who, after cutting off many of the Englishmen, turned again to the attack. The success of this manoeuvre showed how the English ranks could be broken. Twice as the battle raged, groups of Norman knights turned as though in flight, twice the English too hastily pursued and twice the Normans turned and slaughtered their pursuers.[1] In spite of all, the English centre held firm until, late in the day, Harold himself fell, mortally wounded, as tradition tells, by an arrow which pierced him through the eye. His brothers, Gyrth and Leofwine, had already been killed and as darkness fell the remnants of the English army broke and fled. The decisive battle which marked the end of the Anglo-Saxon state and the beginning of the Norman Conquest, had been fought and lost.

[1] The story of the feigned flights is regarded with suspicion by R. Glover who also questions several other points in current views about the state of the English army in 1066, *E.H.R.* LXVII (1952), pp. 1–18.

CHAPTER III

THE CHURCH

I. ST AUGUSTINE'S MISSION

A TRADITION current among the faithful of Northumbria in the seventh century told that when Benedict I was pope, that is between 574 and 578, Gregory heard of the presence in Rome of some young strangers of light skin and fair hair. Some said that they were mere boys, others that they were handsome and cultured young men. Gregory questioned them about their homes and learnt that they were of English race from the kingdom of Deira which was then ruled by a king called Ælle. Greatly struck by their appearance and troubled that such men should be ignorant of the word of God, Gregory asked leave of Benedict to go and preach Christianity in their country. Permission was given and Gregory set out on his journey, but after he had travelled for three days he was overtaken by messengers who brought him back to Rome. A similar but slightly more dramatized version of the story in which the young Englishmen were represented as boys exposed for sale in the Roman slave market, was told by Bede.

Some twenty years after his encounter with the young English-men in Rome Gregory, then pope, wrote to a priest who was on his way to Gaul and told him that since Gaulish currency could not be spent in Italy some of the Church's revenue in Gaul was to be used in purchasing English boys of seventeen or eighteen who might then be placed in monasteries. No doubt he had already heard, as he wrote later to the rulers in Gaul, that there were men among the English who wished to hear the word of God but were prevented from doing so by the timidity of neighbouring priests, and by thus enlisting the help of a few young Englishmen who had found their way to Gaul, he may have hoped to ease the task of the missionary band which was soon to set out. As leader of this band he chose Augustine, then provost of the monastery of St Andrew which Gregory himself had founded in Rome. Accompanied by several others from the same monastery, Augustine set out early in 596, but when he and his companions reached southern Gaul they were overcome by fears of the formidable task which lay ahead and Augustine went back to Rome to ask for release from their mission. Encouraged by Gregory and bearing with him letters of commendation to the civil and ecclesiastical powers through whose territories they might be expected to pass, Augustine rejoined his companions and the mission went on its way to make a successful landing in the Isle of Thanet early in 597. Thanet, then separated from the mainland by a wide channel, lay within the territory of Æthelberht, king of Kent, and within a few days of their arrival Æthelberht went to meet them there, insisting, as Bede records, that the meeting should be held in the open air lest the strangers should practise sorcery upon him. Æthelberht, who must already have known something of Christianity since he was married to a Christian wife, listened to their preaching and gave them leave both to live and to preach in Canterbury itself. Before the year was out, and by later Canterbury tradition the date was 1 June, Æthelberht himself was converted and the first and most important stage of the mission was completed.

A second mission from Rome reached England in 601, bearing with it letters from the pope and a pallium for Augustine, who was consecrated archbishop and established his seat in Canterbury. Three years later another see was established at Rochester with Justus as its first bishop, and in the same year the king of Essex, a nephew of Æthelberht of Kent, was converted and Mellitus was consecrated bishop of the East Saxons with his seat in London, the East Saxon capital. The establishment of three bishoprics within less than a decade was an achievement which held out good hope of further rapid success, but this early promise was not fulfilled. Augustine himself died in some unknown year between 604 and 609, having previously consecrated Laurentius as his successor at Canterbury, and thereafter the mission seemed to lack the driving force necessary to overcome the formidable obstacles presented by districts less exposed to Continental influences than Kent. An attempt was made to convert the East Angles and Rædwald their king was indeed baptized, but he remained divided in his loyalties. All depended on the attitude of the royal families, and both in Essex and in Kent the following generation turned away from the example which had been set by their fathers. The relapse in Essex was so serious that Mellitus was driven out of London and no further headway was made there for more than a generation. Even in Kent the Church came near to extinction after the death of Æthelberht in 616.

These setbacks in the south-east were relieved by notable gains in the north, though in telling with such a wealth of detail a story which must have been dear to his heart it may be that Bede has exaggerated the importance of the Roman mission to Northumbria. The mission came about through the marriage of Edwin, king of Northumbria, to a daughter of Æthelberht of Kent. Edwin promised that his bride and her attendants should be free to practise their own religion and even that he himself would adopt it if his councillors thought fit that he should do so. Accordingly Paulinus, one of those who had come to England in 601, was consecrated bishop in 625 and travelled north with the Kentish princess. Paulinus laboured for a year to support his companions in their faith and strove, though without success, to convert others to their way of thinking. In the following year, at Eastertide, an emissary from Wessex made an unsuccessful attempt to assassinate Edwin and in gratitude for his escape Edwin allowed the infant daughter who had been born to his wife that same Eastertide, to be baptized. She and eleven others of the royal household received baptism at Pentecost in 626. Edwin himself promised that he would follow their example if his expedition to punish the West Saxons for their conspiracy against him was successful. On his return he still hesitated until Paulinus reminded him of a previous escape from death during a period of exile at the East Anglian court. He then declared his readiness to be baptized, but only after the whole matter had been submitted to general discussion by his councillors. Bede's account of the debate which followed still has power to stir the emotions of those who read it. In the upshot Edwin was baptized on the eve of Easter Day 627 in a wooden oratory in York, and many of his nobles followed him. From York Paulinus travelled north to a royal estate at Yeavering by the northern foothills of Cheviot and for thirty-six days, it was said, he never ceased instructing the people who came from the neighbouring villages to hear him, and baptizing them in the River Glen. Further south similar mass baptisms took place in the Swale near another royal estate at Catterick.

When even the very appearance of Paulinus was handed down to Bede's age, ultimately from a priest of Lindsey who had been baptized by him, it would be a mistake to discredit this account of the early days of Christianity in Northumbria simply because it is told in the form of popular traditions which contrast strongly with the documentary evidence from which Bede learnt of the conversion of Kent. The readiness with which paganism was abandoned accords with other evidence which suggests that its hold was much weaker in the north than it was in the south and it may be conjectured that many of those who came to hear Paulinus preach, particularly so far north as Yeavering, were men of Celtic race who were already Christians. During his mission to the north Paulinus turned aside to Lindsey where he baptized the *praefectus* of Lincoln and many others in the Trent at Littleborough. After his baptism Edwin persuaded Eorpwald, king of the East Angles, to follow his example, but Eorpwald died soon afterwards and the effective conversion of his people was not achieved till later. The rapid progress which had been made in the north seemed to justify the creation of a second archbishopric, and a pallium was sent by Pope Honorius with the intention that Paulinus should become archbishop in York, but before it arrived disaster overtook the northern mission. Edwin was defeated and killed in Hatfield Chase in 632 fighting against a coalition of Welsh and English forces led by Cadwallon, Christian king of Gwynedd, and the heathen Penda of Mercia. Paulinus and all but one of his companions, James the deacon, fled by sea to Kent, taking with them Edwin's widow, their infant daughter and others of the royal family. To the chronographers of Bede's time it seemed best that the unhappy year which followed Edwin's death should be expunged from their records, both because of the tyranny of Cadwallon and the apostasy of the English kings who followed Edwin in Deira and also in Bernicia.

At about the same time as the Church suffered this setback in Northumbria, a third, and this time successful attempt, was made to convert the East Angles. Sigeberht, the brother of Eorpwald, had been converted in Gaul, where he was living in exile during his brother's reign. On his return to England he sought help from Archbishop Honorius who sent him a Burgundian called Felix, already consecrated a bishop in Gaul. An episcopal seat was established for him at Dunwich on the Suffolk coast, and during his long episcopate of seventeen years the conversion of the East Angles was completed. Meanwhile, a certain Birinus reached Wessex. He appears to have worked in complete independence of Canterbury, but little is known about him, except that he came to England intending to preach in the midlands, but finding that the West Saxons on whose shores he landed were still heathen, he remained with them and after converting their king, Cynegils, in 635, he established a bishopric at Dorchester on Thames. With the introduction of Christianity into Wessex in this way, only Sussex and the Isle of Wight remained of the southern English lands which had not been visited by a missionary.

2. ANGLO-SAXON HEATHENISM

Mellitus, who reached England with the second mission in 601, brought with him a letter from Gregory giving instructions about the attitude which the missionaries were to adopt towards heathenism. He was to tell Augustine that heathen temples were not to be destroyed, but only the idols which they housed. The buildings themselves were to be purified and altered to make them fit for the service of God. Sacrifices of animals might be allowed to continue, but only as a means of providing good cheer for days of Christian festival with which they were to be associated. Thus supplied with outward comforts the people might the more readily be persuaded to accept spiritual teaching. But to the newly baptized Æthelberht, Gregory wrote more sternly, bidding him overthrow the temple buildings and set his face against the worship of idols. Such also was the bidding of Pope Boniface to Edwin of Northumbria a generation later. No structural remains of any Anglo-Saxon heathen temple have yet been discovered, but there are some indications that Augustine and his successors followed the policy of attempting to assimilate as much of the old ways as was consistent with the Christian faith. There was a Canterbury tradition that the church of St Pancras was built within the precincts of what had formerly been a heathen sanctuary, but perhaps the most remarkable application of this policy was the retention of the name of a heathen goddess, Eostre, and its use for the greatest of Christian festivals. Bede has left a vivid account of the destruction of a Northumbrian heathen temple at Goodmanham in the East Riding of Yorkshire. Coifi, the heathen high-priest, displayed his zeal for the new faith by remarking that none was more fitted than himself to initiate the overthrow of the old ways. Arming himself and mounting a stallion fitted with harness, actions which had been forbidden to the priestly caste, he rode away from the assembly which had been debating the matter and was the first to profane the old idols and altars which he himself had consecrated.

It was against the interests of the Church that knowledge of heathen ways should be perpetuated in writing and in consequence references to heathenism in the written records are generally to its suppression and only on rare occasions to the details of its practice. Even so these references are numerous enough to indicate that in parts of the country it continued to have a strong hold through much of the seventh century. In Kent itself, where Christian influences were strong, the people relapsed into idolatry under the rule of Æthelberht's son and the first formal edict ordering the destruction of idols throughout the Kentish realm was not issued until near the middle of the seventh century. In Essex, where the old ways seem to have had particularly deep roots, the three sons of Saberht, its first Christian king, returned to heathenism and gave free licence to all their subjects to worship idols. This ground, which had first been won by Mellitus, was not regained for more than forty years and even after the synod of

Whitby, under the stress of the great plague which visited England at that time and carried off many churchmen, the people of Essex began to repair their old temples and to resume worshipping the idols which they contained.

Rædwald, king of East Anglia, had first received Christian instruction from Kent, but he was later led astray by his wife and other false teachers and sought to secure the best of both worlds by housing in the same temple one altar for the service of Christ side by side with another for the service of 'devils'. Rædwald died soon after 617, but Bede had heard that a later king of East Anglia who did not die until 713 had witnessed this arrangement still continuing in his childhood. Wilfrid's biographer has left a vivid description of the pagan host which confronted Wilfrid and his companions when a storm cast them ashore on the coast of Sussex as they were returning from a visit to Gaul. The chief priest of the South Saxons 'took up his stand in front of the pagans, on a high mound, and like Balaam, attempted to curse the people of God, and to bind their hands by means of his magical arts'.[1] This episode occurred in 666 and almost a century later the Council of *Clofesho* (747) condemned those who practised divinations, auguries, incantations and the like. The *Dialogue* of archbishop Egbert named those who worshipped idols or gave themselves to the devil through others who took auspices or practised astrology or enchantment as men who should never be appointed to the priesthood.

These oblique references to Anglo-Saxon heathenism can be supplemented by a little information derived from the heathen calendar. The calendar which came into use in England during the early Christian period was of course the Roman ecclesiastical calendar. The names of all the months were of Roman origin and so also were the names of the days of the week, although this fact is now apparent only in three cases, namely the first, second and seventh days. The remaining four weekday names, deriving respectively from O.E. *Tiwesdæg*, *Wodnesdæg*, *Þunresdæg* (later influenced by O.N. *Þórsdagr*) and *Frigedæg*, embody the names of deities whose worship among the Anglo-Saxons is well attested,

[1] *Eddius, Life of Wilfrid*, ch. xiii, ed. B. Colgrave, pp. 26–9.

namely Tiw, Woden, Thunor and Frig, this last being a goddess associated with a fertility cult. But this association of heathen Saxon deities with the days of the week is nothing more than the consequence of a wholly artificial correlation of the four concerned with the four Roman deities from whom the corresponding days in the Roman week were called, namely Mars, Mercury, Jupiter and Venus. The equations are interesting as evidence for the attributes of the Anglo-Saxon deities concerned, but there is not the least ground for supposing that their association with weekdays is a reflexion of primitive custom. In one of his lesser works, however, Bede gives the old heathen names of the Anglo-Saxon months, seeking as he does so to interpret their meaning. Both the last and the first month of the year were called *Giuli*, a name which came to be used of Christmastide in the O.E. form *geol* and which survives in the modern Yule. Its meaning is unknown. The heathen year began, according to Bede, on 25 December and the night which followed this day was called *Modra Nect*, 'the night of the mothers'. The third and the fourth months were called, as Bede believed, after two goddesses, *Hretha* and *Eostre*. The ninth month which was called *Halegmonað*, 'holy month', interpreted by Bede as 'the month of offerings', evidently refers to some harvest festival and there is an implication of sacrificial ceremonies in the name of the eleventh month, called *Blotmonað*, 'month of sacrifice'.

The study of place-names has lately yielded a body of evidence which confirms the impression to be gained from the scanty literary sources, that heathenism was both widespread and deeply-rooted among the English when Augustine reached Canterbury in 597. In particular the names of Thunor and Woden are found as the first element in a considerable number of place-names, commonly combined with a second element such as *beorg*, *hlaw*, both meaning 'mound' either artificial or natural, *feld* 'open space' or *leah* 'wood' or 'clearing in a wood'. Such names as Thursley, Thunderfield, Thundersley, Thurstable and many others attest the worship of Thunor among the peoples of southern England from Kent and Essex in the east to near Southampton in the west. Names such as Woodnesborough, Wednesbury, Wednesfield,

Wodneslawe (now lost) and many others similarly attest the cult of Woden not only in the southern counties and the east midlands, but also as far to the north-west as Derbyshire and Staffordshire. Tiw is also widely, though less frequently, represented.

In addition to names denoting places associated with particular gods, there are others which contain terms denoting the places of worship themselves. A notable example is the hill-top, now occupied by a Christian church, at Harrow, once known as *Gumeninga hearh* 'the holy place of the *Gumeningas*'. *Hearh*, meaning 'hill sanctuary', is widely distributed in place-names and even commoner is *weoh*, 'idol' or 'shrine'. In two instances this element is combined with a personal name, seeming thereby to suggest that a heathen shrine might have a private owner. *Ealh*, 'temple', is also found in place-names. In addition to such names as these which refer to the gods themselves or to places at which they were worshipped, there is a host of others which embody references to the shadowy spectres of popular superstition.

The various types of place-name which attest the worship of heathen gods are widely distributed over the midland and southern counties, but they are notably absent from some areas, particularly the south-western counties, Lincolnshire and East Anglia and the whole country north of Humber. Their absence from the south-west and the north can perhaps be attributed to the continuing strength of British Christianity in these areas. It is significant that Goodmanham, the only place in Northumbria known to have been associated with Anglo-Saxon paganism, lies in the one part of that kingdom from which heathen burials have been recovered in substantial numbers.

3. THE CELTIC MISSION AND THE CONFLICT WITH ROME

While Edwin was reigning in Northumbria the sons of Æthelfrith and many of the Bernician nobility withdrew northwards to find a refuge with the Picts and Scots. Both of these peoples had long been Christian and several of the Northumbrian exiles, including Oswald, were baptized. For a year after Edwin's death Northumbria lay exposed to the attacks of Cadwallon and during that year the two apostate kings who had set up their rule in Bernicia and Deira were both killed. After the death of Cadwallon in 633, Oswald was accepted as king in both Bernicia and Deira, and he promptly turned to Iona for help in restoring Christianity to Northumbria. A small company of monks led by Aidan came from Iona and established a monastery on the island of Lindisfarne whence there was access to the mainland at low tide. As time went by many more Scottish monks came from Iona and elsewhere to build churches, establish monasteries and give instruction in the discipline and observance of monastic life. During the next twenty years Christianity was firmly established throughout Northumbria. Following their missionary work with the fervour characteristic of Celtic Christianity at this time, the monks of Lindisfarne soon began to extend their activities beyond Northumbria. In 653 Peada, the son of Penda who still ruled in Mercia, married into the Northumbrian royal family and received baptism at the hands of Finan, Aidan's successor at Lindisfarne. Penda himself remained heathen, but he allowed a small mission, part English, part Celtic, to work in Mercia, and soon after his death, one of this band, an Irishman called Diuma, was consecrated bishop among the Mercians. Shortly afterwards, another of the band, an Englishman named Cedd, was sent by the Northumbrian king to the East Saxons whose bishop he became. Despite his race the Christianity practised by Cedd was wholly Celtic in form.

It is impossible to say how much of the conversion was achieved by the Roman and how much by the Celtic missions. Bede blamed the Welsh Church for its failure to attempt the conversion of the English, but he is a hostile witness on this point and one who was not always correct in his statements about the Welsh Church. One Welsh source claimed that it was a Welshman who had baptized Edwin. Bede was less hostile to the Scottish and Pictish branches of the Celtic Church, but the efficacy of Aidan's mission was so apparent that he was in no position to deny its achievements. It should be recalled, moreover, that some twenty years before he wrote the *Ecclesiastical History*, envoys from the Pictish Church visited Jarrow and Bede's influence on the occasion of this visit was largely responsible for bringing the Pictish Church into conformity with Roman ways. There were also political factors which may have influenced him in what he wrote, for by his own account, although there was peace on the northern frontier when he finished the *History*, it was at best an uneasy peace which would not have been strengthened by a tactless display of hostility in a book which was not written that it might lie unread on a shelf. Yet when all allowances have been made, the work of the Irish missionaries, not merely in England but also on the Continent, must be recognized for the great achievement that it was. Their simpler, more ascetic way of living had a greater appeal for primitive peoples than the more flamboyant and highly organized ways of Rome. By contrast, it was just in these matters of organization and display that the real genius of the Roman Church lay and its triumph in England belonged less to the age of the conversion than to the succeeding age of Bede.

One of the questions which Augustine addressed to Gregory concerned his relations with the bishops of the Celtic Church in Britain. Gregory is alleged to have written in reply: 'We commit them all into your charge, that the unlearned may be taught, the weak strengthened by persuasion and the perverse corrected by authority.' Gregory was in no position to know about the condition of the Church among the Celtic people of Britain and if he had been better informed we may conjecture that his advice to Augustine would have been very different. As it was, if Augustine acted according to Gregory's instructions, there could be little likelihood of securing the co-operation of the Celtic Church in his missionary enterprise. Augustine himself showed no particular desire to secure the obedience of the Celtic bishops. He twice entered into conference with some of their number, but each time he failed in his attempts to secure their support.

Nothing certain is known of the beginnings of Christianity in Britain, nor is it likely that there ever will be. Among the legendary accounts perhaps the best known is the story told of Joseph of Arimathea and Glastonbury, but it is no more than a legend. Neither is there any truth in the account given by Bede of the conversion of a certain Lucius, king of the Britons, in the second century. The earliest clear evidence of the presence of Christians in Britain comes from the works of Tertullian and Origen, both of whom were writing in the first half of the third century. The earliest detailed story relating to Christianity in eastern Britain concerns the alleged martyrdom of Alban to whom the abbey at St Albans was later dedicated. The story is told by Bede and there are references to it in the works of Constantius and Gildas. Bede ascribes the episode to the persecutions of Diocletian early in the fourth century, but his date is probably wrong, even if the legend is well founded. Gildas refers to the destruction of churches in Britain during the persecution and to their subsequent re-building. Where so little remains of the churches of Roman Britain the evidence of Gildas on this point should not be overlooked.

Christianity became the official religion of the Roman Empire near the middle of the fourth century, and there are clear indications that the Christian community in Britain at this time was substantial. Three bishops from Britain, as well as a priest and a deacon, attended the council of Arles in 314, two of them seeming to have come from London and York. There were also three British bishops present at the council of Ariminum in 360 and the British Church was probably represented at other fourth-century councils. In about 380 Pelagius went from Britain to the Mediterranean where he preached against Augustine's doctrine of Divine Grace, thereby starting a controversy which raged hotly in the Mediterranean countries during the early years of the fifth century. Whether Pelagius ever preached his heresy in Britain we do not know, but after the heresy had been condemned and measures taken against those who continued to profess it, a number of Pelagians are said to have taken refuge in Britain. It is said to have been for the purpose of combating Pelagianism that Germanus visited Britain in 429. The spread of the Pelagian heresy in Britain is at least suggestive of a vigorous Christian community in the country at the time.

During the fifth and sixth centuries the Celtic Church grew from strength to strength in those parts of Britain which were not overrun by the English invaders. At about the middle of the fifth century or a little later, Patrick, then a bishop in Ireland, wrote a letter in which he rebuked the soldiers of a certain ruler of Strathclyde for their action in carrying off from Ireland some of his newly baptized converts. Although Patrick does not specifically state that either the soldiers or their king were Christian, it is abundantly plain from the whole tenor of his letter that Strathclyde was at that time a Christian kingdom and it was this very fact which made Patrick's position in Ireland so much the more difficult. Another phrase in this same letter has important implications. Patrick refers with great bitterness to certain 'apostate Picts'. It is possible that he was referring to Picts living in Ireland, but most scholars interpret the passage as referring to the Picts who lived in Scotland north of the Forth-Clyde isthmus.

If this interpretation is correct, it is possible that Christianity had reached at least the more southerly Picts before or very soon after the withdrawal of the Romans from Britain. The conversion of the northern Picts was achieved later by Columba. Born in Donegal *c*. 520, he crossed from Ireland to Britain *c*. 563 and established a base for his mission in Iona. Under his leadership Iona achieved a position of pre-eminence among the Scottish monasteries and it was from this community that Oswald sought help when he was restored to his kingdom in 634. In southwestern Scotland the Celtic monastery at Whithorn is alleged in late sources to have been visited by Irish saints in the sixth century. St Enda and St Finian of Moville are among those who are said to have been educated there. In that same quarter of Scotland lies Old Hoddam which is associated with the shadowy figure of Kentigern. It is not to be expected that there should be many traces of early Celtic Christianity in those parts of the country which were settled by the English, but from the north of England there is a passing reference by Eddius to the holy places which were deserted by the British clergy fleeing before the hostile sword of the invaders, and in the south it may be noted that Augustine's mission found two churches in Canterbury which were believed to have been built during the Roman period.

In Wales the sixth century has been fitly called 'the age of the saints'. Illtud, Samson who claimed Gildas among his pupils, and David himself are three of the more notable figures of this age. Unlearned, weak and perverse are perhaps not the epithets which Gregory would have used had he been better informed about this remote Western Church which numbered Patrick, Columba and David among its sons. It may well be that the Celtic bishops who rejected the advances of Augustine were prompted in part by a sense of what this Church had achieved during a century and a half in isolation from Rome.

Conflict between the Roman and Celtic Churches in Britain was inevitable. During its long period of isolation the Celtic Church had developed in complete independence and had diverged considerably from the paths followed by Rome, not merely in matters of form and ritual, but more fundamentally in its whole organization. Rome could not readily brook the continued existence of what it regarded as schismatic ways and still less could it contemplate that so large a Christian community which showed remarkable missionary zeal should not recognize the pope as its spiritual head. But on the other side, the Celtic Church, as some of its members realized, could not afford to ignore the benefits which Rome, representing by far the greater part of Christendom, had to offer. These were the deeper matters lying behind the seemingly arid and certainly bitter disputes about the right method of calculating the date of Easter and the outward forms of tonsure and baptism.

The Easter conflict is almost as old as Christianity itself. In the earliest Christian times when most Christians were Jews by origin, Passover and Resurrection were celebrated on the same day, but with the spread of Christianity among the Gentiles and the shifting of the Christian holy day from the Jewish Sabbath to the Christian Sunday Passover and Resurrection were separated and there arose a belief that no good Christian should celebrate the Resurrection on the same day as the Jews observed the Passover. In this and in the difficult mathematics involved in calculating a date which was based partly on the lunar and partly on the solar year there lay the root of a controversy which disturbed Western Christendom for several centuries. It was made the more difficult because the instructions of Rome might differ from the more exact calculations made by the mathematicians of Alexandria. The reconciliation of the solar and lunar years depended upon the adoption of a cycle of years and at different times cycles of 8, 11, 19 and 84 years were used. Of these the 19-year cycle was the most accurate and it was adopted at Alexandria at an early date. It seems likely, however, that Easter tables based on an 84-year cycle were carried back to Britain by the Celtic bishops who attended the council of Arles in 314. In 455 the Alexandrian tables indicated a date for Easter which fell outside the limits thought proper in Rome. After much discussion and correspondence Pope Leo decided to accept the Alexandrian date and he gave instructions accordingly to all the Western Churches. It is known that these instructions were received in Ireland and it is possible that they may also have reached Wales. The dispute about the date of Easter in 455 led to a detailed investigation of the whole matter by Victorius of Aquitaine and the acceptance by Rome of the 19-year cycle which he advocated. Although the tables compiled by Victorius on the 19-year cycle were apparently known in Ireland before the end of the sixth century, the older and less accurate tables based on the 84-year cycle remained in use. The question was discussed in a synod of the southern Irish Church in 631, and in 633, after the return of a mission which had been sent to Rome, this branch of the Celtic Church agreed to conform with Roman practice. This discussion, however, had no effect upon the northern Irish Church or upon Iona whence Aidan had come to Lindisfarne in 635.

Those parts of England which were controlled by Canterbury were naturally in conformity with Rome, but in Northumbria the presence of Aidan's mission led to a direct conflict between the Celtic and the Roman ways. James the deacon, who had remained in Northumbria after the flight of Paulinus, had taught the Roman practice and the Celtic mission also found itself opposed by a fellow Scot called Ronan who had spent some of his life in Gaul and Italy. The situation was made the more acute because Osuiu, the king, followed the Celtic practice, whereas his wife, that daughter of Edwin whom Paulinus had taken to Kent and who had now returned to the north as Osuiu's queen, followed the Roman ways she had learnt in Kent. The result, as Bede records, was that Easter was sometimes celebrated twice at the Northumbrian court, so that while the king was celebrating Easter, the queen was still observing the Lenten fast.

The dispute was referred to a synod which was held at Whitby in the autumn of 663.[1] Here the Celtic party represented by Osuiu, Cedd, bishop of the East Saxons, Hild, abbess of Whitby, and Colman, bishop at Lindisfarne who acted as spokesman, stated their case in opposition to the Roman party represented by Alchfrith, son of Osuiu, Agilberht, a bishop among the West Saxons who was then visiting Northumbria, James the deacon, and Wilfrid, then ruling a monastic community at Ripon. According to Bede's account of the synod, the only point debated was the date of celebrating Easter, but the wider issues involved are made clear in the speech attributed to Wilfrid, who stressed the folly of resisting the authority of St Peter and refusing to follow the example of all the rest of Christendom. How much of Wilfrid's speech was composed by Wilfrid and how much by Bede we cannot tell. Bede represents Osuiu as being convinced by Wilfrid's arguments and once he had given his decision the day was won for Rome. From the space alone which Bede devoted to his account of the synod, it may be inferred that the occasion was for him one whose importance might be compared even with the arrival of Augustine in 597 and in retrospect over a much longer period the synod may still seem to mark the beginning of an epoch in English Church history which ended only with the English Reformation of the sixteenth century. A decision had indeed been taken and Bede was not the man to lose such an opportunity of forwarding the interests of Rome, yet a mere decision in which only a small number of churchmen were involved could not of itself create an organized and united Church. That was a work which required more than two generations for its fulfilment and more than seventy years later Bede wrote to his pupil Egbert, then bishop of York, urging upon him a variety of reforms which were designed to bring the Church into greater conformity with the pattern designed for it by Gregory.

[1] The date 664 will be found in many standard works. See above, p. 45, n. 1.

4. THE ROMAN TRIUMPH

The mission from Rome which reached England in 601 brought with it a letter for Augustine in which Gregory set out his instructions on the organization of the English Church. There were to be two archbishoprics, the one in London and the other in York. During his own lifetime Augustine was to be supreme over both provinces, but thereafter the representatives of London and York were to take precedence according to the seniority of their appointment. Each of the two archbishops was to be authorized to consecrate twelve suffragans to be under his jurisdiction. Gregory's choice of the two chief cities of Roman Britain as the seats of the two archbishops suggests that he may have been thinking of the mission to England as initiating the recovery of what had once been part of the Roman Empire, with the old *civitates* forming the basis of its diocesan organization as they had done in Gaul, but his orderly scheme was wholly remote from the realities of the situation in England.

The mission depended for its success upon securing the support of the various royal families whose spheres of authority did not, except in the case of Kent, correspond with the boundaries of the *civitates* of Roman Britain. Canterbury, where Augustine enjoyed the support of a Christian ruler, offered much greater security than London, the capital of a kingdom in which heathenism was deeply rooted. The establishment of the second archbishopric at York came near to fulfilment, but was prevented by the death of Edwin and the subsequent flight of Paulinus. There was no established archbishop of York until 735, the year of Bede's death, and the difficulties which the mission met after its early successes prevented the creation of any regular diocesan organization outside the south-eastern area. It is noticeable that those of the early missionaries who acknowledged the supremacy of Rome concentrated their activities almost wholly upon what had been centres of population in Roman Britain and that monasticism played little or no part in their lives. A monastery was founded at Canterbury during Augustine's lifetime, but although Augustine and his companions had formerly been monks, they lived in Canterbury as a bishop and his household serving the cathedral church and no longer bound by any monastic rule. It is probable that the churches in Rochester and London were served in a similar way.

The arrival of Aidan's mission at Lindisfarne and the subsequent spread of Irish missionaries beyond Northumbria into the midlands and the eastern counties introduced into much of England a conception of episcopacy which was fundamentally different from that of the Roman Church. The Celtic Church in the seventh century was largely monastic in its organization and a bishop in the Irish or Scottish Church at this time was invariably a monk, subject as such to the authority of his abbot. He exercised the spiritual functions conferred upon him by his office, preaching, baptizing, confirming and ordaining, but he remained under his abbot's authority and was in no way territorially limited by fixed diocesan boundaries. No such boundaries existed.

It sometimes happened, and in Northumbria as often as not, that the abbot of a monastery was also a bishop and this fact assisted the later change to a regular diocesan organization, but it might also be that a single monastery would contain several monks in episcopal orders. Ecclesiastical jurisdiction and administrative responsibility rested with the abbots. Bede more than once comments upon the peculiarities of this system which had become unfamiliar to the age in which he was writing. The Columban community at Iona, he writes, was accustomed to have as its ruler an abbot and the bishops themselves were 'after an unaccustomed manner' (*ordine inusitato*)[1] subject to their abbot. His description of the Lindisfarne community, which is in greater detail, suggests that the monastery there was based very largely upon the Irish pattern.

And let no one be surprised that, though we have said above that in this island of Lindisfarne, small as it is, there is found the seat of a bishop, now we say also that it is the home of an abbot and monks; for it actually is so. For one and the same dwelling-place of the servants of God holds both; and indeed all are monks. Aidan, who was the first bishop of this place, was a monk and always lived according to monastic rule together with all his followers. Hence all the bishops of

[1] *H.E.* III, 4.

that place up to the present time exercise their episcopal functions in such a way that the abbot, whom they themselves have chosen by the advice of the brethren, rules the monastery; and all the priests, deacons, singers and readers and the other ecclesiastical grades, together with the bishop himself, keep the monastic rule in all things.[1]

Although we have no corresponding accounts, it seems probable that the other monasteries in Northumbria where Celtic ways were once observed were similarly organized. During his brief period as bishop, Cuthbert acted after the fashion of his time, travelling freely over the kingdom of Northumbria, preaching, baptizing, confirming and dedicating churches, but having no episcopal seat apart from his monastery, no cathedral church, and returning in the end to the hermit's life in the complete solitariness of Farne. Bede does indeed write of a regular episcopal succession not only in Northumbria but also in Mercia, but at the time when he was writing two generations had passed since the great reorganization of the Church in England which had been set on foot by Theodore, and it may be that he tended, perhaps by deliberate design, to invest the seventh-century church in these areas with the appearance of that more regular diocesan organization which it had in fact acquired by the eighth. From all that is known of the Irish Church and of its influence in England, it seems very unlikely that in the whole vast area of Northumbria and the scarcely less extensive Mercia there would only be a single bishop at any one time in each of the two kingdoms. We might rather have expected to find a number of monks in episcopal orders living in their various monasteries and exercising spiritual functions under their abbots.

The decisions taken at the synod of Whitby marked only the first step towards the ascendancy of the Roman Church in England. In the years which followed, the leading parts in the work of organization and reform which was necessary to give effect to those decisions were played by three men, Wilfrid, Theodore of Tarsus and Benedict Biscop. The knowledge which enabled Wilfrid to act so effectively as spokesman for the Roman party at Whitby had been acquired during the five years which he had

---

[1] Bede's *Life of Cuthbert*, ch. XVI, B. Colgrave's translation, pp. 207–9.

previously spent in Gaul and Italy. At the time of the synod he was ruling a monastic community at Ripon and after the meeting he was appointed bishop in the western parts of Deira with Ripon as his seat. Anxious that the validity of his consecration should be beyond all question, he went to Gaul for the ceremony.

The circumstances which brought Theodore to England were wholly fortuitous. Soon after the synod of Whitby, Deusdedit, the archbishop of Canterbury, died and it is probable that the delay of three years in appointing his successor was largely due to a particularly severe visitation of plague which carried off many of the leading churchmen in England at this time and which led also to a relapse to heathenism in parts of the country. It was not until 667 that Wighard, a priest of Canterbury, was selected for the office and sent to Rome for his consecration. He was on the point of setting forth on his journey home when he too died of plague, and in these circumstances the pope, who was doubtless informed of the serious situation in England, took the appointment into his own hands. His first choice was Hadrian, a monk of African origin who was at that time abbot of a monastery near Naples, but Hadrian thought himself unequal to the task and suggested instead Theodore, a native of Tarsus then living in Rome. Theodore accepted and the two set off for England together, having as their guide on the journey Biscop Baducing, more commonly known as Benedict Biscop, a member of the Northumbrian nobility who had become a monk and was at the time paying his third visit to Rome.

Theodore, Hadrian and Benedict Biscop reached England together in 669 to find a Church which was vigorous enough in its lower orders, but which was almost entirely bereft of leaders, and a people rebuilding their heathen temples in what had once been the diocese ruled by Mellitus from London. In the whole of England only three men are known to have been in bishop's orders at the time, one of them, Wine, had committed the sin of simony by purchasing the see of London from the king of Mercia, the second Ceadda, at York, had been consecrated according to the Celtic rites, and the third was Wilfrid, at Ripon. Theodore removed Ceadda from York because he doubted the validity of his orders and transferred Wilfrid from Ripon to his place. Subsequently he sent Ceadda to Lichfield, impressed by the humility with which he was ready to accept correction. Benedict Biscop became abbot of St Augustine's monastery in Canterbury. Theodore's most urgent task was to increase the number of bishops and he promptly made appointments to Rochester, Dunwich and Winchester. In 672 he summoned a general assembly of the whole English Church.

This synod, which was held at Hertford in September of that year and which was the first of its kind in the history of the English Church, issued a number of canons which were designed mainly to establish the elementary principles of regular administration. Adherence to the Roman method of calculating the date of Easter which had been accepted at Whitby was reaffirmed, bishops were enjoined to confine their activities to their own dioceses, a measure aimed at the peripatetic habits of the Celtic episcopacy, monasteries were given protection against the interference of bishops, and monks and clergy alike were restrained from wandering from place to place without leave of abbot or bishop. It was further agreed that a similar assembly of the whole Church should be held each year on 1 August at a place called *Clofeshoh* whose identity has been lost, and there was a general expression of view that the number of bishoprics should be increased, but on this point no immediate action was taken. Wilfrid himself was not present at the synod, but the attitude which he subsequently adopted suggests that the proctor by whom he was represented may have been instructed to oppose any such move.

During the next few years Theodore took it upon himself to make substantial changes in the midlands and East Anglia (see Map 7, p. 145). He divided the large East Anglian see, retaining one bishopric at Dunwich and establishing a second at North Elmham in Norfolk. He created two new bishoprics in south-western Mercia, one at Worcester and the other at Hereford, and a third in the east to serve the kingdom of Lindsey. There are some indications that he also attempted to create a bishopric, though this did not become permanently established until later, at Leicester in Middle Anglia, and, temporarily, another at

Dorchester on Thames to serve the border district between Wessex and Mercia.

It was, however, in Northumbria that the task of reorganization proved most difficult. Wilfrid, though one of the most staunch supporters of Rome in other respects, vigorously opposed any diminution of his own immense sphere of office as sole bishop in Northumbria. During the period 669–77 he established himself in a position of great strength both in the ecclesiastical and in the secular worlds, seeming, particularly in that love of outward display which found so much favour in the eyes of his biographer and which contrasted so strongly with the more endearing humility of Cuthbert, almost to anticipate the figures of bishops palatine in a later age. He was twice expelled from Northumbria by successive kings, first in 677 by Ecgfrith whose enmity he had incurred by inducing his wife to adopt the religious life, and again in 691 by Aldfrith, the most scholarly of the Northumbrian kings and a man whose devotion to the Celtic Church, particularly its learning, made him wholly unsympathetic to a man of Wilfrid's character. On the occasion of his first expulsion Wilfrid appealed to Rome, where he arrived in 679 after an involuntary visit to Frisia, whither he had been driven by a storm while crossing the sea. Although he received the support of the pope, the Northumbrian council paid no heed to the papal documents which he laid before it. He was at first imprisoned, but later went to Mercia and then to the south where he preached to the South Saxons, the last of the heathen English.

After Ecgfrith's death in 685 he came to an agreement with Theodore and returned to Ripon, but remained dissatisfied with the greatly reduced position which was then allowed to him. On his second expulsion, in 691, he went back to Mercia where he remained for several years, doing much to forward the work of the Church by founding monasteries there. In about 700 he made a second appeal to Rome, this time by proxy, and the pope referred the question to the decision of an English synod. The synod met at Austerfield in 702, but would do no more than allow him to return to Ripon, without the office of bishop. Such a decision could not be acceptable to him and although now a man of over seventy he set off for Rome again. On his return to Northumbria he was finally restored to his monasteries at Ripon and Hexham and he passed the remaining years of his life in peace, dying in 709 in a monastery of his own foundation at Oundle.

The recalcitrance of Wilfrid created a situation of difficulty and embarrassment no less for the Papacy than for Theodore, but his expulsion in 677 gave Theodore the opportunity of introducing into Northumbria the policy which he had already carried out in other parts of the country, though in doing so he yielded something to the Celtic conception of episcopacy by making use of the old system as a bridge towards a more regular diocesan organization. He appointed Bosa, a monk of the community at Whitby which had turned from Celtic to Roman ways at the synod of 663, as bishop of the Deirans with his seat at York. Bosa received his episcopal orders in York from Theodore who also consecrated Eata, abbot of Melrose and, concurrently as it seems, prior of Lindisfarne, as bishop of the Bernicians, allowing him a choice of Lindisfarne or Hexham as his episcopal seat, both of them monasteries, the one largely in the Celtic pattern and the other Benedictine. Soon afterwards Hexham became the seat of a separate bishopric, Eata remaining at first at Lindisfarne, but removing to Hexham during the episcopacy of Cuthbert.

Benedict Biscop's contribution to the final triumph of the Roman Church lay mainly in the opportunities which he provided for others. Some years before the synod of Whitby he had been the friend and companion of Wilfrid on a journey through Gaul and after his return to England with Theodore in 669 he remained in Canterbury for two years as abbot of St Augustine's. He then paid a fourth visit to Rome, collecting there by purchase or gift many books which he brought back with him to England. He at first intended to go to Wessex whose king, Cenwalh, an ardent supporter of the Roman Church, had befriended him on an earlier occasion, but Cenwalh's death caused him to change his plans and he turned instead to his native Northumbria, going to the court of Ecgfrith to whom he expounded what he had learnt of ecclesiastical and monastic usage during his travels and to whom also he showed the books which he had brought back. Ecgfrith gave him a large estate in Durham near the mouth of the Wear, and here, on the site which we know as Monkwearmouth, he established a monastery in the year 674.

With the help of stonemasons and glass-workers brought from Gaul, the buildings were quickly erected, and soon afterwards Benedict Biscop set off to Rome for the fifth time, collecting there more books, as well as relics and paintings and bringing them back to his new foundation, accompanied by John, the archchanter of St Peter's and abbot of St Martin's in Rome. Ecgfrith was so well pleased with the use to which his first gift had been put, that he gave Benedict a second estate in 681 for the establishment of a similar foundation not far away at Jarrow. The original inscription recording the dedication of the church at Jarrow in 685, a few weeks before the death of Ecgfrith at Dunnichen Moss, still survives (see Pl. VI, p. 156). For the sixth and last time Benedict went to Rome to get more equipment for the two monasteries. Soon after his return he was increasingly afflicted with illness and he died in 690. Before his death Benedict had given strict instructions that the library which he had assembled should be diligently kept together and not spoiled by neglect or broken up and dispersed. Among all the monasteries which were so widely scattered over England at this time there can have been few, if any, with so rich a collection of books as Monkwearmouth and Jarrow.

Meanwhile a new generation was coming to the fore. Bede himself was born probably a year or so before the foundation of Monkwearmouth and at the age of seven he was sent there to be under the care of Benedict, but lately returned from Rome. He survived an outbreak of pestilence which removed many of the monks in 685 and either at its foundation or soon afterwards he was moved to Jarrow where he spent the remainder of his life, leaving the monastery only on the rarest occasions. Little of incident has been recorded about his life, beyond what he himself related in the epilogue to his *History*, but it seems probable that he became a deacon at the age of eighteen and it may be presumed that he would not enter the priesthood before the canonical age of thirty. The earliest of his writings which can be precisely dated was completed in 703 and thereafter they flowed from his pen steadily and in great numbers, the last of them being his letter to Egbert, bishop of York, written in 734, the year before his death.

The assembling of libraries and the diffusion through monasteries of some understanding of the power of the written word placed the Roman Church in England in a much stronger position to compete against the scholarship of the Celtic Church. Largely through Bede himself Monkwearmouth and Jarrow became preeminent in this respect during the early decades of the eighth century, but at about the time of Bede's birth Theodore had established a school in Canterbury which attracted many pupils of whom the most distinguished was Aldhelm, a member of the West Saxon royal family and somewhat older than Bede. Aldhelm received his early education from Irish teachers at Malmesbury and after studying under Theodore at Canterbury he returned to Malmesbury as abbot. In 705 he became the first bishop of a newly created West Saxon diocese which served the country west of Selwood and had Sherborne as its seat. Aldhelm died in 709, the same year as Wilfrid.

The work of Theodore, Wilfrid and Benedict Biscop placed the Roman Church in England in a position sufficiently strong to allow it to work actively towards the conformity of the Celtic Churches in more remote areas. Aldhelm himself, while abbot of Malmesbury, wrote a work against the errors of the Britons in their observance of Easter and succeeded in bringing many of those who were subject to the West Saxons into conformity with Rome, and towards the end of the eighth century that part of the northern Irish Church which was not subject to the authority of Iona likewise conformed, as also did others of the Britons, probably those of Strathclyde. Adamnan, the biographer of St Columba and ninth abbot of Iona, himself convinced of the rightness of Roman ways, tried, though without success, to bring the whole community of Iona to his own way of thinking. The ultimate conversion of this community was achieved *c.* 716 by Egbert, a Northumbrian nobleman who became a monk and worked for many years among the northern Irish.

Shortly before 731 an English bishopric was established at Whithorn on a site in the extreme south-west of Scotland which had formerly been occupied by a Celtic monastery and which was almost within view of the Irish coast. The choice as its first bishop of Pecthelm, a man who had been trained by Aldhelm and to whom Boniface, the great West-Saxon missionary, wrote as to an authority on ecclesiastical law, is a sufficient indication that the diocese was intended to serve some purpose of even greater urgency than ministering to the spiritual needs of its immediate neighbourhood. There is much to suggest that that purpose was to secure the predominance of the Roman Church in northern Ireland. It is probable that a similar motive lay behind the establishment some years earlier of another English see, at Abercorn on the southern shore of the Firth of Forth which then marked the boundary between the English and the Picts. In this instance the aim would be to secure the conformity of the Pictish Church. Ecgfrith's defeat by the Picts in 685 was followed by the abandonment of this bishopric and by intermittent warfare between English and Picts for some twenty-five years.

Shortly after 710 Nechtan IV, king of the Picts, sent an embassy to Ceolfrith, abbot of Monkwearmouth and Jarrow, asking for help in his efforts to persuade the Pictish Church to accept the Roman ways which he himself had previously adopted. Ceolfrith sent a letter to Nechtan in which the Easter problem was expounded in all its complexity and which many believe to have been written by Bede himself. The letter achieved its purpose and Nechtan sent instructions throughout all the provinces of his kingdom ordering that the erroneous Easter tables based on the 84-year cycle should be destroyed and that new tables based on the orthodox 19-year cycle should be adopted in their place. With the recognition of Rome's supremacy first by the southern Irish in 633 and then successively by the English at Whitby, by the Britons in south-west England and Strathclyde, by the northern Irish, by the Picts and by the monks of Iona, only in Wales itself did the old Celtic independence of Rome continue and here conformity was not achieved till 768.

5. THE CHURCH IN EARLY ENGLISH SOCIETY

Towards the end of his life Bede went to York to discuss a variety of topics with Egbert, then bishop in York. Illness prevented him from paying a further visit in the following year and instead he wrote Egbert a long letter in which, among other things, he recalled Gregory's instructions to Augustine about the organization of the Church in England. He recommended Egbert to summon an ecclesiastical council and to seek its consent to the establishment of another northern bishopric and from there, Bede thought, he might easily go on to secure the promotion of his own see at York to metropolitan rank. The new bishopric was not in fact created, but Egbert evidently followed Bede's advice and subsequently negotiated with the Papacy, because in 735, the year of Bede's death, Egbert's position as archbishop of York was recognized by the arrival of a pallium from Rome. Henceforward the two archbishoprics continued in existence. There is no evidence from within the Anglo-Saxon period of that system of alternating precedence which Gregory had recommended, but in later times the archbishops of York sought to establish their independence on the basis of Gregory's recommendation. For a short while towards the end of the eighth century a third archbishopric existed with its seat at Lichfield. It came into being partly because of a personal quarrel between Offa, king of Mercia, and Jænberht, archbishop of Canterbury, and partly because of difficulties which Offa encountered in seeking to maintain effective control over Kent, but there was only one holder of the office and the unity of the southern province was re-established early in the ninth century.

Only two of the eight holders of the see of Canterbury between 597 and 690 were of English birth, Deusdedit, a West Saxon who was in office 655–64, and Wighard who died soon after his consecration in Rome. The regular succession of English archbishops began with the consecration of Berhtwald in 693. Previously abbot of Reculver, he was elected archbishop in July 692, consecrated by the metropolitan of Gaul in 693 and enthroned at Canterbury later in the same year. His three successors were respectively abbot of Breedon in Leicestershire, priest in London and bishop in Hereford before their consecration to Canterbury. Information about procedure in the appointment of particular archbishops is scanty, but election, consecration and enthronement are clearly marked as distinct stages. There was in addition a further stage, the gift of a pallium from Rome. Though originally no more than a mark of honour which the pope might confer upon his vicars as he chose, the pallium came to be regarded in the English Church as a necessary token of archiepiscopal rank without which the holder of the office could not properly perform his duties. Before the Danish invasions the pallium was regularly sent to England from Rome and it was not until the tenth century that the custom began to arise of the archbishops themselves going to Rome to receive it. Between the death of Theodore in 690 and the Danish invasion in 865 there were ten archbishops of Canterbury and ten also of York. Although the records are not explicit in every case, there is enough evidence to indicate that it was the regular custom to send a pallium to each successive holder of the two offices. The periodical dispatch of a pallium in this way was one means whereby the pope was able to maintain a considerable measure of control over the Church in England without frequent legatine visitations. After 597 there was no such visitation until 786 when Pope Hadrian sent George, bishop of Ostia, and Theophylact, bishop of Todi, to England as his legates.

In 735 the northern province consisted of four dioceses, York, Hexham, Lindisfarne and Whithorn (see Map 7). The bishops of Hexham and Lindisfarne were also heads of monasteries and it is probable that those of Whithorn were likewise. The southern province contained twelve sees, Canterbury, Rochester, Selsey, Winchester, Sherborne, London, Dunwich, North Elmham, Worcester, Hereford, Lichfield and Lindsey. There was a bishop at Dorchester *c*. 680, but this may have been due to a temporary arrangement. An additional see was established at Leicester in 737. The seat of the Lindsey bishops, called *Syddensis civitas*, has not been identified. The cathedral churches in the southern province seem in the few instances for which there is evidence to have been served by bodies of clergy living a communal life but not as professed monks. Most of the seventh- and eighth-century bishops and archbishops are now represented by little more than their names in the episcopal lists which were kept in various religious houses, but so far as the evidence goes it suggests that the Church was served by many men of considerable intellectual ability. The decline in the political importance of Kent, particularly in the eighth century when the kingdom became a dependency of Mercia, may have tended to lessen the stature of the archbishops of Canterbury, but at York Egbert, brother of one of the most powerful of the Northumbrian kings, was the first of three distinguished men who held office in the eighth century and who created and maintained a famous school of learning, a school which produced Alcuin as its greatest pupil and which possessed a library whose contents were unequalled in the western Europe of its day. Acca, bishop of Hexham, to whom Bede dedicated many of his works, assembled a large library at his own church, and in the southern province Aldhelm, bishop of Sherborne, commanded great, though somewhat abstruse, learning. The English clergy as a whole followed the progress of the Anglo-Saxon missionaries on the Continent in the eighth century with close interest and the surviving correspondence between these missionaries, notably Boniface, and such men as Cuthbert, archbishop of Canterbury, Milred of Worcester, Daniel of Winchester, Torhthelm of Leicester and Pecthelm of Whithorn, testifies to a widespread degree of intellectual attainment among the Anglo-Saxon episcopacy at this time.

Saving only the monastic church at Hexham, there are no substantial architectural remains of any English cathedral church, whether monastic or otherwise, of a date earlier than the tenth century and there is very little even from the later period, a fact which is sometimes overlooked in judgements upon the achievements of the Anglo-Saxons in ecclesiastical architecture. According to Bede, Augustine used as his first cathedral in Canterbury a church which was believed to have been built in the Roman period. It lay upon the site occupied by the present cathedral, but although there is a description of the building which stood there in 1067, this account provides no reliable evidence for the

Map 7. Approximate diocesan boundaries *c*. 750. For Dorchester see p. 143.

appearance of the church before the Scandinavian invasions. Nothing is known of any Christian church at York in the Roman period, though it is likely that one existed. The earliest Anglo-Saxon church there was a small wooden oratory built by Edwin in preparation for his baptism in 627 on a site which lay almost at the centre of the Roman legionary fortress. Edwin began to enclose this oratory within the walls of a larger stone church, but it was not completed until the reign of Oswald, his successor. By 670 the roof of this building was collapsing, there was no glass in its windows and its walls were disfigured by exposure to the weather and by the birds which were using the church as their nesting place. Wilfrid repaired the roof, covering it with lead, glazed the windows and whitewashed the walls. He also endowed the church with altar vessels and other furnishings. The gold altar cross and chalice which Edwin had given to York were taken to Canterbury after his death and were still to be seen there in Bede's time. As at York and Canterbury, so elsewhere the sites of the earliest churches remained in constant use and the oldest buildings became submerged beneath the work of later times.

The establishment of a regular diocesan organization provided the Church in England with a means of orderly government which would allow it to override narrow political boundaries and to act as a unit in a country where political unity did not yet exist, but in the seventh century and much of the eighth the English Church found its greatest inspiration in monasticism. Communal life could do much not only to provide intellectual and spiritual comfort, but also to offer an escape from at least some of the more severe physical hardships of life in a primitive age. During this period religious houses were founded throughout the country in large numbers. North of Tweed there were such houses at Abercorn, Coldingham, Melrose and Whithorn; between Tweed and Humber at Lindisfarne, Coquet Island, Hexham, Tyne-mouth, Monkwearmouth, Jarrow, Hackness, Hartlepool, Gainford, Sockburn, Lastingham, Gilling, Ripon, Whitby and York; and south of Humber at Barrow and Partney in Lincolnshire, Peterborough, Oundle, Bury St Edmunds, Ely, Brixworth, Repton, Breedon in Leicestershire, *Icanho* (an unidentified place in East Anglia), Barking, Woking, Bermondsey, Chertsey, Abingdon, Canterbury, Dover, Folkestone, Lyminge, Minster in Thanet, Reculver, Wimborne, Nursling, Tisbury, Exeter, Malmesbury, Glastonbury, Much Wenlock, Frome and Bradford-on-Avon. This long list of names[1] gives some indication of the important part which was played by monasticism in the early English Church. In addition there are several references in early sources to monasteries which are not named and no doubt many others have perished without leaving trace in the records. The history of Monkwearmouth and Jarrow can be followed in some detail from their foundation until 716, but in most other cases little has been recorded beyond occasional incident.

Eddius claimed that Wilfrid was the first to introduce the rule of St Benedict into Northumbria and under Wilfrid's influence this rule was established at Hexham and Ripon as well as in the houses which he founded in the midlands. The Benedictine rule was also observed at Malmesbury in Aldhelm's time, at Nursling and presumably at St Augustine's whose founder had been trained under it. Cuthbert himself drew up a rule for Lindisfarne, but the Benedictine rule was being observed there as well before the end of the seventh century. According to Bede, Benedict Biscop compiled for his foundations at Monkwearmouth and Jarrow a rule composed of all that he had found best in seventeen monasteries which he had visited during his travels, but it is probable that the Benedictine rule served as its foundation. Elsewhere it is likely that there was wide variation between one house and another. Monkwearmouth and Jarrow were ruled jointly by a single abbot and in other parts of the country there was a tendency for federations to arise between parent houses, such as Peterborough and Malmesbury, and their offshoots.

Women played an important part in the religious life of this age and there were several nunneries as well as double houses in which monks and nuns lived under the rule of an abbess. Coldingham, Hartlepool and Whitby were double houses, as also were Repton, Ely, Barking and Minster in Thanet. There are said to

[1] It is not intended to be complete, but merely to indicate the geographical spread of monasticism at this time.

have been about 600 monks at Monkwearmouth and Jarrow together in 716, but there is no evidence about the numbers at other houses and it is unlikely that many were as big. In some instances Bede records the extent of the estates with which monasteries were endowed in terms of the number of households supported by the estates in question. Monkwearmouth and Jarrow were originally endowed with the lands of 70 and 40 households respectively. Hild, abbess of Hartlepool, bought the land of 10 households for the endowment of Whitby. After his victory over Penda in the battle at the *Winwæd*, Osuiu of Northumbria gave twelve estates of 10 households each for the endowment of monasteries. It is not possible to reckon the size of these endowments in terms of acres, but that they were substantial is apparent from Bede's evidence about Wilfrid's monastery at Selsey. This was endowed with the land of 87 households at a time when the entire kingdom of the South Saxons was reckoned at 7,000 households. If a single monastery received at its foundation so large a share of the landed wealth of the kingdom in which it lay, we can understand why Bede thought that it might be difficult for Egbert of York to find lands for the endowment of another bishopric in Northumbria where monasteries were so numerous.

The O.E. word *mynster*, derived from the Latin *monasterium*, was used somewhat loosely both of a community whose members were monks, a monastery in the modern sense, and of a group of clergy who served a particular church and lived a communal life, but not necessarily as monks. In its material sense a *mynster* was a group of buildings, including one or more churches, inhabited by such a community. At a number of sites there are substantial remains of monastic churches, but little or nothing survives of monastic buildings. The church of St Peter and St Paul at Canterbury, within St Augustine's monastery, was begun in 597. Its superstructure has perished, but its foundations have been traced beneath the nave of the church which was built on the same site by Abbot Scotland late in the eleventh century. It consisted of a nave about 40 feet long, flanked on either side by two chapels and with a narthex across its western end (Fig. 2). The east end

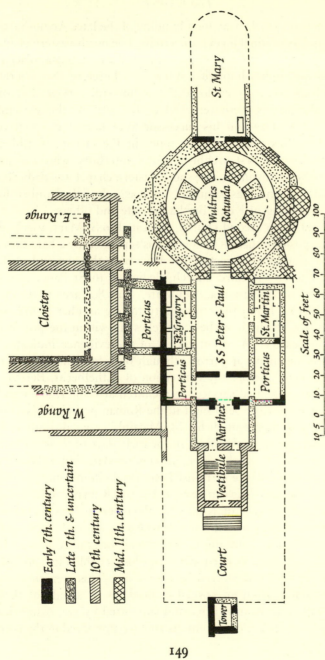

Fig. 2. St Augustine's Abbey, Canterbury: ground plan.

was removed to make way for a building of the later Anglo-Saxon period and its original form is uncertain. The north-eastern chapel was dedicated to St Gregory and was used as the burial place of the first five archbishops of Canterbury. Three of the concrete cases which originally enclosed the coffins still survive, but the coffins themselves were removed at the end of the eleventh century. Theodore and his successor were buried in the nave, since there was then no more room in the chapel. Cuthbert (d. 760) was the first archbishop of Canterbury who was not buried at St Augustine's. The south-eastern chapel was dedicated to St Martin and was similarly used as a burial chamber for Æthelberht, king of Kent, Bertha his wife and others.

In about 620 a second church, dedicated to St Mary, was built in such a position that its west end was separated by a bare dozen yards from what is conjectured to have been the east end of the original church. A third church, dedicated to St Pancras, was built, as its surviving remains indicate, some 80 yards to the east of St Mary's. From their proximity to one another it may be inferred that all three of these churches lay within the precincts of the monastery. A recent review of the evidence indicates a similar arrangement at Jarrow, though only two churches were involved there. Before the conversion of Æthelberht, Bertha is said to have attended services in a church at Canterbury which was believed to have been built in the Roman period. This same church, now represented by St Martin's, was also used by Augustine and his companions in the early days of their mission. Much of it is of seventh- or eighth-century date, but although it contains an abundance of re-used Roman building material, no part of its present fabric can be regarded as of Roman construction.

In 669 king Egbert of Kent gave Reculver to Bassa, a priest, as a site for a *mynster*. The church which he built, though much altered, remained in use until 1805 when it was pulled down. Its destruction, though in itself a grievous loss, enabled its complete ground plan to be recovered by excavation. This consisted of a nave separated from an apsidal chancel by an arcade of three arches turned in Roman brick and supported by two cylindrical columns (Fig. 3 a). These columns are now preserved in the crypt

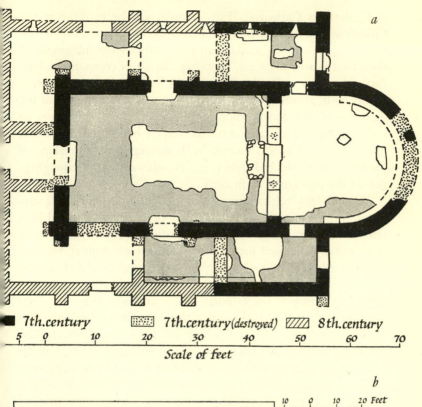

7th. century   7th. century(destroyed)   8th. century

5   0   10   20   30   40   50   60   70

Scale of feet

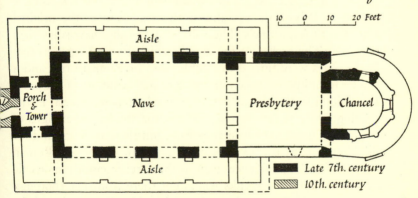

10   0   10   20 Feet

Aisle

Porch & Tower

Nave

Presbytery

Chancel

Aisle

Late 7th. century

10th. century

3. *a* (above), Reculver Church: ground plan; *b* (below), Brixworth Church: ground plan.

of Canterbury Cathedral. Two chapels, similar to those in the Church of St Peter and St Paul, overlapped nave and chancel and other chapels were later added so as to embrace the full circuit of the nave towards the west. Another church of comparable date, that of St Peter at Bradwell-on-Sea in Essex, has a similar plan. It was built, almost entirely from Roman masonry, in one of the gateways of the Saxon shore fort known in Roman times as Othona. Its chancel and external chapels have been destroyed, but its nave still stands though badly damaged by the making of openings, now blocked again, in its sidewalls large enough to permit the passage of farm carts.

The only seventh-century monastic building which has survived in the midlands is the church at Brixworth, described by a scholar who was not given to exaggeration as 'perhaps the most imposing architectural memorial of the seventh century yet surviving north of the Alps'.[1] Its plan was that of an aisled basilica of four bays with a two-storied western porch giving access to adjoining chambers on its north and south sides (Fig. 3*b*). The east end of the nave led through a triple arcade, now removed, to a square presbytery beyond which lay an apsidal chancel. The chancel seems to have been intended to enclose a crypt, but the only remaining trace of this is an external encircling corridor sunk below ground level. With an overall length of about 150 feet the church at Brixworth was almost twice as long as the original church at St Augustine's. The aisles of the basilica have since been removed. The arches of the arcade which formerly gave access to the aisles were turned in double rows of Roman brick and a similar technique was used in the clerestory windows of the nave. In addition to the abundance of re-used Roman material in the existing fabric of the church, the site has yielded other signs of occupation during the Roman period, but there is no ground for thinking that any part of the church as it now stands is of Roman construction. The evidence suggests that it represents the monastic church built by the monks who went there from Peterborough *c*. 670. The austere grandeur of the church at Brixworth and the

[1] A. W. Clapham, *English Romanesque Architecture Before the Conquest* (Oxford, 1930), p. 33.

rich series of eighth-century sculptured stones now embodied in the walls of a much later church at Breedon in Leicestershire testify to the strength of the evangelizing movement which spread into the midlands from Peterborough in the seventh and eighth centuries, leaving scarcely any trace in documentary records.

The earliest recorded church at Lindisfarne was built by Finan, Aidan's successor. It was fashioned *more Scottorum*, that is of oak timbers with a thatched roof. Later in the seventh century the thatch was replaced by a lead roof and the timber walls were also covered with lead. Wilfrid introduced a much more elaborate kind of architecture into Northumbria. His biographer Eddius said of the church at Hexham that he had heard of no other on a grander scale on this side of the Alps. From his account we may learn that it had a colonnaded nave with aisles, chapels, a crypt and spiral stairways leading to its upper levels. This church was still standing in the middle of the eighth century, but it was destroyed during the Danish invasions. Wilfrid's crypts survive at both Hexham and Ripon beneath the existing churches and some other foundations were traced at Hexham when the modern nave was built, though unhappily the opportunity of recovering the complete plan was lost. A stone seat preserved at Hexham probably represents the bishop's or abbot's stool of early times. There is a similar seat at Beverley.

Although remains of monastic churches are fairly numerous, there is only one site in the country at which any substantial traces have been found of the other buildings of an early Anglo-Saxon monastery. This is at Whitby, a double house founded by Hild in 657 and the scene of the debate on the Easter controversy in 663. Early in this century when the ground to the north of the medieval abbey was being cleared, traces were found of a number of buildings which undoubtedly belonged to the early monastery. Their walls, all of stone, rarely survived above the foundations and much disturbance had been caused by the use of the ground as a cemetery from the twelfth century onwards. Nevertheless, it was possible to recover the plans of seven buildings. One of these seems to have been a smithy and four of the others, though not identical, were similar to one another in plan, measuring about 18 ft. by

11 ft. and with structural details suggesting an internal division into two rooms, the one serving as a living-room with a hearth and the other as a sleeping-room with a lavatory in one corner connected to an external drain. It is possible that these buildings represent the cells (*domunculae*) occupied by individual monks or nuns. They suggest a degree of comfort much greater than that indicated by the little that is known about dwelling-places in early Anglo-Saxon villages.

In addition to the architectural remains there were many fragments of sculptured stones, some of them funereal monuments inscribed in Old English with runes or in Latin. There were also fragments of metal from book-covers, some decorated metal tags seeming to be parts of book-markers, some *styli* for writing and a variety of other objects, including spindle whorls and one small piece of woollen textile. The remains were found scattered over an area 300 ft. long and nearly 200 ft. wide and since there were no signs of any boundary wall, save on one side, it is evident that the whole monastery covered a large area. No trace was found of any early church nor were any buildings discovered which could be identified as dormitories, refectories or the like. Early in the nineteenth century workmen building houses at Hartlepool broke into the cemetery of the monastery which was founded there *c*. 640. A number of Christian tombstones were found of a type known from other parts of Northumbria, notably Lindisfarne. Tombstones of this type are shaped as thin slabs, usually less than 1 ft. sq., sometimes with square heads, sometimes rounded. They are plain on the back but on the front they commonly bear a simple cross, either incised or in low relief. Several examples carry the name of the person commemorated, carved in runes or in the Northumbrian form of the Latin alphabet.

The first church at Monkwearmouth, founded in 674, was built by stonemasons brought from Gaul by Benedict Biscop. Gaulish glassmakers were also employed because, according to Bede, the art was not then known to the English. In addition to vestments, relics and altar vessels for the service of the church, Benedict brought from abroad a number of sacred pictures for its adornment. These included paintings of the Virgin Mary, the twelve Apostles, scenes from the Gospels and from the Book of Revelation. These paintings were hung on the walls of the church for the instruction of those who could not read. All Benedict's paintings and other gifts have perished, but it is thought that parts of his church survive. These include the west wall of the nave, narrow and of great height, and a two-storied western porch now serving as the lower stages of a tower erected upon it late in the eleventh century. The ground floor of this porch has a stone barrel vault and on its western side an elaborately constructed outer arch whose plinth is constructed of flat slabs of stone decorated with interlaced animals and supporting a pair of stone balusters on either side. In the gable of the porch was a standing figure carved in relief, but this is now almost entirely weathered away. Among the many fragments of carved stonework now preserved in the church are two which formed parts of the substructure of the abbot's stall and of the bench-end of the presbyter's bench.

The existing church at Jarrow consists basically of a small chancel of early Anglo-Saxon date, a central early Norman tower and a modern nave. The awkward appearance of the Norman tower, seeming to have been pressed into a space too small for it, and the analogy of St Augustine's do much to support the view, recently advanced on the evidence of plans and drawings made before the modern nave was built, that in Bede's time there were two churches on this site built upon the same axis and with only a few feet between the east end of one and the west end of the other. The earliest church at Jarrow was dedicated on 23 April 685, as may be seen from the original dedication inscription which . is now above the western arch of the tower (Pl. VI). This inscription has the additional interest of being the earliest written record of the Anglo-Saxon period in Northumbria which can be dated both confidently and accurately. There are references to common dormitories and refectories at Monkwearmouth and Jarrow but it is probable that some of the monks lived in separate cells of the kind in which Bede himself died, though no trace of these buildings has yet been found.

A code of laws issued in 1014 distinguishes four different kinds

PLATE VI

DEDICATION STONE OF THE CHURCH OF ST PAUL AT JARROW

☧ DEDICATIO BASILICAE / S[AN]C[T]I PAVLI VIIII K[A]L[ENDAS] MAI[AS] / ANNO
XV ECFRIDI REG [IS] / CEOLFRIDI ABB[ATIS] EIUSDEM (Q) / Q[UE] ECCLES[IAE]
D[E]O AVCTORE / CONDITORIS ANNO IIII

'The dedication of the church of St Paul on 23 April in the fifteenth year of king Ecgfrith and the
fourth year of Ceolfrith abbot and, under God's guidance, founder of this same church.'

Bede (*H.E.* IV, 26, v, 24) records that Ecgfrith was killed on 20 May 685 in the fifteenth year of his
reign. In 685 23 April fell on a Sunday and the dedication should be referred to this date. The last
letter of the fourth line, less deeply cut than the remainder of the inscription, seems to be unfinished.
Evidently finding himself with insufficient room, the carver has repeated the letter at the beginning
of the next line. The inscription is now placed inside the church above the western arch of the tower.

Photograph by T. Romans from a cast in the library of the Dean and Chapter, Durham.

156

PLATE VI

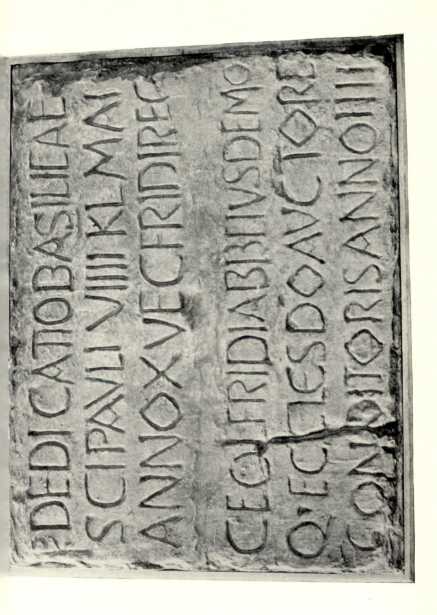

PLATE VII

INTERIOR OF ESCOMB CHURCH, COUNTY DURHAM
Probably seventh or eighth century

of churches, the 'head-minster', the 'ordinary minster', the lesser church with a graveyard and the 'field church', but this classification refers to an organization which had been developing over several centuries. The growth of the lesser churches and of some form of parochial system is obscure, particularly in the early period. No regular parochial system existed in the time of Theodore and there were still areas for which no adequate provision had been made even for preaching and baptism at the time of Bede's death. Several passages in the *Lives of Cuthbert* refer to the dedication of churches and to evangelizing work in the remoter parts of the countryside. On one occasion, as Bede relates, country people jeered at some monks who had been caught by wind and tide and were being carried out to sea on rafts. Let nobody pray for them, they said, because they have robbed men of the old ways of worship and nobody knows how the new worship is to be conducted. In his letter to Egbert Bede urged that more priests should be ordained so that the word of God could be preached in villages. Parish churches, as they may be called, seem normally to have been founded by lay notables who appointed the priests and regarded the churches as property which yielded an income for their founder and which could be bequeathed, sold, moved elsewhere or even dismantled. A Durham document refers to the complete dismantlement of the church at Lindisfarne and its re-erection at Norham.

Only one parish church of the early period has survived virtually complete. It is the church at Escomb in the county of Durham which remained in use till 1860 when a new church was built on another site (Pl. VII). The old church fell into disrepair, but was carefully restored before the end of the century. It is very small in its overall length, but its rectangular nave is of great height in proportion to its length. A tall and narrow arch opens into a chancel no more than 10 ft. sq. Much of the fabric is built of Roman masonry and it is possible that the chancel arch, formed of well-shaped radial voussoirs is a rebuilt Roman arch brought from the nearby fort at Binchester. It has two square-headed doorways, one now blocked but formerly opening into the chancel, and the other into the nave. The jambs of the doorways, as well as of the chancel arch, are built in the long-and-short technique whereby large slabs of stone were laid alternately upright and flat. Original lights remain on either side of the nave, two round-headed and two square-headed. These external apertures are very small, but they are widely splayed inside. There is no documentary evidence about the early history of this church, but there is general agreement, on the basis of its architectural details, that the building belongs to the seventh or eighth century.

A freestanding cross, either of wood or of stone, may have been the forerunner of the parish church in many parts of the country. It was believed in Bede's time that the wooden cross which Oswald put up before the battle in which he defeated Cadwallon in 633 was the first outward emblem of Christianity to be seen in Bernicia. Fragments of sculptured stone crosses which survive in large numbers mainly in Northumbria and Mercia, suggest that such objects were common features of the countryside in the eighth century. Although they were probably most numerous in the north, they were not unknown in the south. William of Malmesbury records that two such monuments were to be seen at Glastonbury in his own day and from his account of the inscriptions which they bore they commemorated a king of Wessex and a West Saxon bishop who lived in the seventh century. William also records that stone crosses were set up every seven miles along the route followed by Aldhelm's funeral procession from Doulting to Malmesbury.

When Leland, the Elizabethan antiquary, visited Reculver he saw a cross with inscriptions and painted images standing in the church between the chancel and the nave. The base for such a cross has been discovered embedded in the original seventh-century floor of the church in such a way as to demonstrate that the base was made before the floor. The cross which Leland saw may be represented by some sculptured fragments now preserved in Canterbury Cathedral, but even though a recent opinion has denied the seventh-century date which others have ascribed to these fragments, the existence of the early base suggests that when Bassa built his church in 669 he may have enclosed an already existing stone cross within its walls. The Glastonbury crosses

PLATE VIII

BEWCASTLE CROSS, WEST AND SOUTH FACES

were evidently memorials to the dead and if we may trust the apparent reading of the main runic inscription which it bears, the famous cross-shaft which stands in the churchyard at Bewcastle in Cumberland was also a funeral monument. A twelfth-century Northumbrian source records that the grave of Acca, bishop of Hexham, who died in 740, was marked by two sculptured crosses and it is commonly held that one of these is represented by a shaft which was formerly preserved at Durham but is now at Hexham.

The Bewcastle cross, whose head is missing, is carved from a single block of stone now just under 15 ft. high (Pl. VIII). On its west face it bears three full-length figures of which the uppermost is that of John the Baptist carrying the Agnus Dei on his left arm. The central panel is occupied by the figure of Christ in glory with his feet resting on two beasts, a scroll in his left hand and his right hand raised. Beneath the figure of Christ is a long runic inscription, seeming to record the dedication of the cross, and in the lowermost panel stands the figure of a falconer. His left arm is bent at the elbow and he wears a heavy gauntlet upon which a falcon rests. Below the bird is a T-shaped perch. It would be difficult to account for the presence of a wholly secular figure in the company of Christ and John the Baptist and it may be that the falconer is to be regarded as representing John the Evangelist and his eagle in a more homely and familiar guise. On the east face a vinescroll runs the full length of the shaft, swinging from side to side in rhythmical curves with tendrils breaking out from the main stem at regular intervals and ending in bunches of grapes at which birds and animals peck. This vinescroll pattern is one of the dominant motifs in the stone sculpture of this age. Although patterns based on the vine are found on Romano-British objects, it is probable that the vinescroll of the Bewcastle type reached Northumbria from the Mediterranean where it was widely used. Imported fabrics seem the most likely medium for the introduction of such a design. By great good fortune the very small quantity of fabric which still survives from the Anglo-Saxon period includes some pieces of Byzantine fabric which bear a vinescroll pattern and were found in St Cuthbert's tomb. These fragments are now preserved at Durham.

Closely resembling the Bewcastle shaft both in its size and in its decoration is the great cross which rises to a height of 18 ft. inside the church at Ruthwell in Dumfriesshire. Whereas the outlines of the Bewcastle shaft have been somewhat blurred by centuries of exposure to the weather, the Ruthwell shaft preserves such sharpness of detail as to suggest that for much of its early history it stood indoors, perhaps enclosed like the Reculver cross within a church. In the seventeenth century it was overthrown and broken into pieces by Scottish Covenanters and it was not until 1887 that it was placed where it now stands in an apse built to contain it. The arms of the cross head, two of which are still preserved, seem to have portrayed the four evangelists with their appropriate attributes. There are five panels of figure sculpture on each of the two broad faces of the shaft, on the one face John the Baptist, Christ in majesty, the hermits Paul and Anthony breaking a loaf of bread in the desert, the flight into Egypt and lowermost a scene which is much defaced but is perhaps of the Nativity, and on the opposite face the Visitation, Mary Magdalene washing the feet of Christ, Christ healing the blind man, the Annunciation and the Crucifixion. The margins separating the sculptured panels bear Latin inscriptions describing the scenes to which they refer. The two narrow faces bear panels of vinescroll ornament with birds and beasts pecking at bunches of grapes. The margins of the lower panels on each of the narrow faces are inscribed in runes with passages from the *Dream of the Rood*, an old English poem of profoundly moving beauty in which the cross is made to tell the story of the Crucifixion.

The year 731 marks the end of Bede's *Ecclesiastical History* and the beginning of a period in which the materials of all kinds of English history are so scanty that it is difficult to reach any firm conclusions about the condition of the English Church during the next hundred years. Several of the men who held episcopal office in 731, such as Acca of Hexham and Pecthelm of Whithorn, were scholars of distinction, and it seemed to Bede that at that time both the civil and ecclesiastical powers were strong enough to overcome any external dangers which might threaten. Nevertheless, there are some indications if not of a falling away at least of some adulteration of the high ideals which had inspired the Church since the days of Theodore. In the long letter which Bede wrote in 734 to Egbert, then bishop of York, he seems to have been concerned rather with drawing attention to ills which needed remedying than with praising what he found to be good. It was common report, he wrote, that some bishops were given to revelling, drunkenness and dissolute living and there were many hamlets which saw no bishops for years together, though they were not exempted from paying their dues to the Church. But more serious than this was the growth of large numbers of spurious monasteries. For a generation past laymen with no pretence of leading a religious life had established themselves together with their wives and families on estates which they acquired by royal charter and which, because they passed under the name of monasteries, were quit of all secular services. In his day, Bede wrote, almost every officer of government had provided for himself in this way. So widespread had this practice become that the sons of noblemen or others who had served with the armies could find no lands on which to settle and in consequence they either spent their days in idleness or passed overseas to seek lands elsewhere. Bede feared that if this practice were allowed to continue unchecked the size of the armies would be so reduced as to make the defences of the kingdom inadequate. The events of 866 suggest that his fears were well-founded.

Bede was here writing of the Church in Northumbria, but some of his charges, particularly those which relate to dissolute living, are repeated in later sources of wider application. For example, canons passed by a synod held at *Clofeshoh* in 747 referred to priests prating in church like secular bards, to monks and nuns dressing themselves in gorgeous apparel, to monasteries becoming retreats for versifiers, harpers and buffoons, and to nunneries becoming secret meeting-places for evil talk, drunkenness and luxury. At about the same time Boniface wrote to the archbishop of Canterbury inveighing strongly against the evils of drunkenness and fine clothing. Not only did bishops themselves get drunk, he had been told, but they forced others to drunkenness as well by offering them overlarge cups. The English Church was also being brought into disrepute abroad by nuns who went on pilgrimage and succumbed to temptation by the way, so that English harlots were to be found in most towns in Gaul and Lombardy. Later in the century Alcuin wrote frequently from abroad exhorting monks to observe their vows, to avoid luxury in dress and to listen in the refectory to holy Scripture rather than to heathen songs. There are some signs too of a weakening of that complete interdependence of Church and State which had been characteristic of early times. In his letter to the archbishop of Canterbury Boniface remarked upon the forced labour of monks upon royal buildings and other works as a thing unheard of save in England. Boniface also joined with a number of other bishops in Germany in sending a stern letter to Æthelbald, king of Mercia, rebuking him for the evil example he was setting by his own life and also for destroying many privileges of churches and robbing some of them of their property. Boniface had also heard that Æthelbald's officers of government were treating monks with greater violence and extortion than any Christian kings had ever done before.

Even though these charges may have been well-founded, they provide a wholly inadequate basis for any general opinion about the condition of the English Church as a whole in the age which followed the death of Bede. The records of the legatine mission which visited England in 787 refer incidentally to heathen practices and other current evils which needed remedying, but taken as a whole they suggest that the legates were satisfied with what they found. The school at York attained its highest degree of intellectual achievement in the second half of the eighth century and the great work of Anglo-Saxon missionaries on the Continent in this century is evidence for the state of the Church from which they came which must be set fairly in the balance.

6. THE ENGLISH MISSION TO THE CONTINENT

The English mission to the Germanic peoples on the mainland of western Europe can fairly be regarded as one of the most remarkable achievements in the whole history of the Church in England. The story which begins with the deposition of Wilfrid in 678 for his opposition to Archbishop Theodore, can here be sketched only in the barest outline, but its consequences for Europe were so profound and its subsequent reactions upon England so important that it cannot be ignored. When Wilfrid set off to Rome to state his case before the pope, the direct route across the Channel was closed to him because of the hostility of those who controlled its southern shore and he accordingly made his way to Frisia. He passed the winter of 678–9 among the Frisians and had considerable success in his efforts to convert the peoples among whom he found himself. The importance of his visit lay not so much in its results in Frisia, for these were ephemeral, as in the inspiration which it provided for others of his countrymen to follow in the path which he himself had been the first to tread.

A fellow Northumbrian, Egbert, who passed most of his long life as an exile in Ireland, was prevented only by divine intervention, as it was said, from fulfilling his own ardent wish to preach in Frisia. Instead he sent one of his English companions who met with little success. Thereupon he assembled a larger band amongst whom was Willibrord, the son of a Northumbrian whose latter years had been spent as a hermit. Willibrord was a young child at the time of the synod of Whitby and he received his education first in Wilfrid's monastery at Ripon and subsequently in Ireland. He and his companions reached Frisia in 690 and soon after they had begun their work Willibrord went to Rome to secure papal blessing for the enterprise, an act of great consequence because it brought the new Frisian Church into direct contact with Rome from the moment of its birth. During Willibrord's absence another of the missionaries returned to England where he was consecrated bishop by Wilfrid. A see was established for him in Frisia, but he left it soon afterwards to preach in Westphalia. His work in Westphalia was undone by hostile invasion and he withdrew to Kaiserswerth on the Rhine where he died in a monastery which he had founded himself. Two others of the company, Black Hewald and White Hewald, ventured into Saxon country, but both were killed. The remainder of the mission found refuge for a while with the Franks and soon afterwards Willibrord, with the support of

Pippin, Frankish mayor of the palace, went a second time to Rome where the pope consecrated him archbishop of Frisia in November 695. On his return to Frisia he received a site for his cathedral at Utrecht and with this for his base he worked for more than forty years at the organization of this new province of the Roman Church. With the support and protection of the Franks and a supply of helpers from England, monasteries were founded, churches built and the Frisians themselves trained for the priesthood. Willibrord died in 739 in his monastery at Echternach.

He and his companions were all Northumbrians, but in the next stage the appeal of missionary work began to widen. Boniface, perhaps the greatest figure in this movement, was a West Saxon said to have been born near Crediton about 675. He was received into the monastery at Exeter while still a child and from there he went to Nursling near Southampton, where he was able to profit both from the new learning which had been brought to Canterbury by Theodore and Hadrian and from the teaching and writing of Aldhelm by whom he was strongly influenced. His first visit to Frisia was in 716, but the times were not propitious and he returned to England in the next year. He set off once more in 718, never again to return to his own country. He visited Rome in 719 to receive a general commission from the pope to preach to the heathen and again in 722 to receive episcopal consecration. He was consecrated in 732 and after working for more than twenty years among Germans and Franks he went back to Frisia and here, at Dokkum near the coast, he and some fifty of his companions were massacred by a band of pagans in June 754. Such in its barest outline was the most remarkable career of this man.

His work, first in creating and organizing a Church in Germany and later in reforming the Frankish Church, forms an important chapter in European history. At home in England it was followed with close interest and attention by clergy and laity alike. Boniface had to meet many difficult problems concerning the faith, and in such matters as baptism, marriage and relations with heretical priests he frequently turned to the English clergy for help and advice. His own surviving letters and those of his successor

Lullus, another Englishman, testify to the frequency of inter-course between England and the Continent at this time. In this way close personal contact was maintained and many helpers, in-cluding a number of women, were encouraged to go out to his assistance. In particular, English monasteries were in a position to meet the urgent need of books for the newly founded Con-tinental monasteries. Writing with great affection, Boniface offers sympathy and encouragement to Daniel of Winchester, his old bishop, news of whose blindness had lately reached him. As a token of his love he sends a towel of silk mixed with rough goat's hair and as a solace in his own difficulties he asks the bishop if he will send him the book of the six Prophets which had belonged to his former teacher and which he remembered to have been in a single volume in clear letters. 'I cannot procure in this country such a book of the Prophets as I need, and with my fading sight I cannot read well writing which is small and filled with abbrevia-tions.'[1] News had reached him of the writings of Bede and more than once he wrote to Bede's pupil Egbert, then archbishop of York, and to the abbot of Monkwearmouth asking that copies of some of Bede's Biblical commentaries might be sent to him. On one occasion he sent Egbert a cloak and a towel and on another two small casks of wine 'for a merry day with the brethren'.[2]

Two other figures played an important part later in the eighth century when this period of English activity on the Continent reached its consummation. Both were Northumbrians. The first, Willehad, went to Frisia in about 770 and worked in the district where Boniface had been martyred. In 780 he was sent by Charle-magne to the Saxons between the Elbe and the Weser. Saxon insurrections against the Franks created difficulties for him and he was compelled to withdraw to Echternach. He later returned to Saxon territory and in 787 he was consecrated bishop of Bremen. He died in 789 and was buried in the cathedral which he had consecrated only a week before.

The second was Alcuin, the most distinguished pupil of the school which had been founded at York by Archbishop Egbert

---

[1] E. Emerton, *The Letters of St Boniface* (Columbia, 1940), p. 116.
[2] *Ibid.* p. 169.

and which, inheriting through its founder much of the teaching of Bede, came to be the greatest centre of English learning in the later eighth century. In 767 Alcuin became master of the York school and in the course of the next fifteen years he established for himself a reputation as a scholar of distinction. In 782, in consequence of an earlier meeting with Charlemagne while returning from a visit to Rome, he accepted an invitation to settle himself permanently at the Frankish court where he became head of the palace school. He served as Charlemagne's principal collaborator in educational work and played an important part in the revival of theological and philosophical studies among the Franks.

7. THE CHURCH AND THE VIKINGS

Even when due allowance is made for the natural prejudices of monastic writers, there can be no doubt that the Church in England suffered severe losses at the hands of the Vikings, particularly in the twenty years following the landing of the great Danish army in 865. These losses seem all the more serious in contrast with the long period of comparative peace which England enjoyed between the arrival of Theodore in 669 and the sack of Lindisfarne in 793. Yet it is well to remember that this phase was an isolated phenomenon peculiar to England amid centuries both earlier and later in which intermittent warfare was a normal feature of life in Europe as a whole. The devotion of the Vikings to their own gods was not so great as to inspire them with active hostility to Christianity itself and in consequence they presented a far less serious challenge to the continued existence of the Christian Church in Britain than had the English themselves in the fifth and sixth centuries. They were capable of inflicting heavy material losses and of creating conditions unfavourable to the continued prosperity of intellectual and spiritual life, but no part of England became so completely paganized as to require prolonged missionary activity for the restoration of Christianity. Guthrum, the Danish leader who became king of East Anglia, was baptized in 878 in fulfilment of the terms of peace made with Alfred, and within less than a generation Edmund who had been killed by the Danes in 869 was being venerated there as a saint.

There are no detailed records of the progress of Christianity among the Danish settlers east of Watling Street, but despite the widespread destruction of the numerous monasteries in East Anglia and the fens it is unlikely that the Danish settlements were anywhere so dense as to obliterate Christianity among the native English.[1] The territory of the Five Boroughs, between Welland and Humber, was regarded as a Christian area in 942. By this date, however, in addition to the original Danish settlements in Yorkshire, Northumbria had received an influx of Norsemen from the west and the resulting tangle of racial and political confusion seems to have led to a more varied mixture of religious practices than is to be found in the more southerly parts of the country. There had been a Christian Danish king in Northumbria before the end of the ninth century, but for about a generation, ending with the expulsion of Eric Bloodaxe in 954, York itself was at once the seat of an archbishopric and the capital of a line of semi-pagan kings.

Heathen cults associated with Thor and Othin have left traces here and there in place-names, notably in the name 'Othin's Hill' (*Othenesberg*), now Roseberry Topping in the North Riding of Yorkshire, which is the Scandinavian equivalent of the Old English 'Woden's Hill' (*Wodenesbeorg*, Wednesbury in Stafford-shire). At several places in north-western England sculptured stone crosses, such as those at Halton in Lancashire and Gosforth in Cumberland, portray scenes from Scandinavian mythology. Though testifying to the currency of stories about heathen gods, the form of the monuments themselves is likewise testimony that those who set them up were in their own eyes Christians. It is probable that many of the mixed Irish-Norse settlers in north-western England came there as Christians and several church dedications to St Patrick in this area may be due to their influence.

The effect of the Scandinavian settlements upon the diocesan organization of the Church in England was most strongly marked in the northern and eastern parts of the country where the resulting

---

[1] D. Whitelock, *E.H.R.* LVI (1941), pp. 1–21, finds ground for thinking that the East Anglian Danes may not have come so quickly under the influence of the Church as had been previously thought. See also *ibid.* LXX (1955), pp. 72–85.

changes were very considerable (see Map 8). Of the four dioceses
which comprised the northern province in 735 only two survived,
both of them in greatly altered circumstances. Hexham and
Whithorn perished, though the date and circumstances of their
destruction as dioceses cannot be determined owing to a failure
in the records of episcopal succession soon after 800. York was
occupied by the Danes in 866 and the archbishop was compelled
to seek refuge farther west. For the next fifty years the history
of the archbishopric is obscure. There was no break in the succession, but the see was greatly impoverished by the loss of its
estates and long remained so. Soon after the middle of the tenth
century it began to receive additional endowments, notably from
a large estate at Southwell in Nottinghamshire, and at about the
same time the practice began of appointing men of southern upbringing to York, an innovation which prepared the way for a
more revolutionary change whereby York came to be held in
plurality with the see of Worcester. This arrangement, which
lasted from 972 till 1016 and was revived again in 1040 for a short
while, had material advantages for the holder of the two sees as
well as political advantages for the kings of England, who may
thus have thought to secure greater control over those parts of
their realm in which the dangers of separatist movements were
likely to be greatest.

The relations between York and Canterbury did not become a
matter of urgency until the time of William the Conqueror and
Lanfranc. Lindisfarne, which had been the seat of bishops since
635, was abandoned by the monks in 875. They took with them
the body of St Cuthbert and other treasures, including the famous
Lindisfarne Gospels, and after wandering from place to place for
several years, even contemplating a flight to Ireland as tradition
relates, they settled at Chester-le-Street in 883. Here the see
began to benefit greatly from the veneration attaching to the saint
himself, and fresh endowments, added to what remained of the
material legacy from earlier times, laid the foundations upon
which rested the ecclesiastical and political power of the Norman
bishops of Durham. The final move from Chester-le-Street to
Durham was made in 995.

There were probably twelve dioceses in the southern province in 735 and another had been added two years later with its seat at Leicester. The six which lay on the eastern side of the country—Lindsey, Leicester, Dorchester(?), Elmham, Dunwich and London—were all affected in greater or lesser degree by the Danish settlements. Dunwich, one of the two East Anglian sees, was destroyed and never again revived. Elmham was likewise destroyed, though not permanently. The break in the succession of East Anglian bishops seems to have lasted from 870 until 956, though it is probable that Norfolk and Suffolk, as well as Essex, came under the control of the bishops of London as the English frontier was pushed northwards during the reign of Edward the Elder. Later in the tenth century Norfolk and Suffolk were re-formed as a separate diocese, with the bishop's seat at North Elmham, Essex remaining as it had been from the first within the diocese of London. The succession of bishops at Elmham continued without any further break until after the Norman Conquest when moves were made first to Thetford in about 1072 and finally a few years later to Norwich.

In the eastern midlands the diocese of Lindsey which marched with Lichfield on the west, was destroyed and not again revived as a permanent unit. Leicester became untenable and the bishop's headquarters were withdrawn as far south as Dorchester-on-Thames. At the end of the Anglo-Saxon period the bishop of Dorchester controlled the whole of the east midlands from the middle Thames in the south to the Humber estuary in the north. After the Norman Conquest the bishop's seat was moved from Dorchester to Lincoln. Lichfield, Hereford, and Worcester all suffered from periodical incursions by raiding Danish armies, but, except in parts of the large see of Lichfield, there were no permanent Scandinavian settlements here and the continuity of episcopal organization was not interrupted, unless perhaps for a short time at Lichfield. Similarly there were no major changes in the three south-eastern dioceses, Canterbury, Rochester and Selsey, though here again, and particularly in Kent, it may be supposed that the Church suffered much loss.

In the south-west Winchester and Sherborne, the two ancient

West Saxon dioceses, were subdivided and three additional sees created during the reign of Edward the Elder. These changes seem to have been prompted not so much by the consequences of the Danish incursions as by the evident fact that Winchester and Sherborne were too large for the effective control of a single bishop. Winchester was reduced to Hampshire and Surrey by the transfer of Berkshire and Wiltshire to a newly established see at Ramsbury. Sherborne was left with Dorset and two new sees were created, the one for Somerset with its cathedral church at Wells, and the other for Devon and Cornwall with its headquarters at Crediton. In Æthelstan's reign an independent see of St Germans was created for Cornwall. These six West Saxon sees—Winchester, Sherborne, Ramsbury, Wells, Crediton and St Germans—continued in being throughout the remainder of the tenth century and for much of the eleventh, but subdivision had gone too far and the resources of a single shire proved inadequate for the support of a bishop and his household. In 1027 Lyfing, who had been abbot of Tavistock and had lately accompanied Cnut to Rome, was appointed bishop of both Crediton and St Germans. The two sees remained united in the hands of his successor Leofric who transferred his seat from Crediton to Exeter in 1050. The see of Ramsbury was similarly absorbed into that of Sherborne in 1058 when Hereman, who had previously held Ramsbury alone, became bishop of Sherborne and Ramsbury together. In 1070 the episcopal seat was moved to Old Sarum. The situation of Wells remained unchanged and there was a regular succession of bishops there during the remainder of the Anglo-Saxon period.

There is very little evidence about the way in which the cathedral churches were served by clergy in the tenth century and of the buildings themselves there is only one, the cathedral at North Elmham in Norfolk, of which any substantial remains have survived. This building, whose architectural features suggest a date late in the tenth or early in the eleventh century, was scarcely more than 120 ft. long, greatly less than a quarter of the overall length of the existing cathedral at Ely. It consisted of a narrow nave with a transept at its eastern end from which projected a small apse. Two small towers stood one on either side in the angles

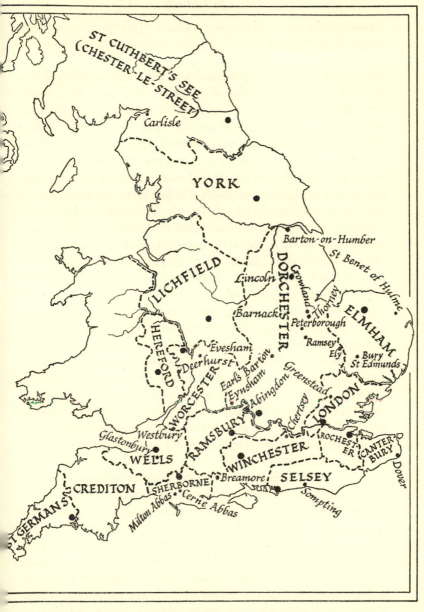

ST CUTHBERT'S SEE
(CHESTER-LE-STREET)

Carlisle

YORK

Barton-on-Humber

LICHFIELD

DORCHESTER

Lincoln

St Benet of Hulme

ELMHAM

Crowland

Thorney

Barnack

Peterborough

Ramsey

Ely

Bury
St Edmunds

HEREFORD

Evesham

Deerhurst

WORCESTER

Earls Barton

Eynsham

Abingdon

Greenstead

Chertsey

LONDON

ROCHEST-
ER

CANTER-
BURY

Dover

Glastonbury

Westbury

RAMSBURY

WELLS

WINCHESTER

SELSEY

CREDITON

SHERBORNE

Breamore

Sompting

S GERMANS

Milton Abbas

Cerne Abbas

Map 8. The dioceses of the later Anglo-Saxon period, showing approximate
boundaries in the tenth century.

formed by the nave and transept walls. A larger tower stood at the west end of the nave.

It was perhaps in the destruction of monasteries that the English Church suffered its most grievous losses at the hands of the Vikings. Bede gives more than a hint of conditions in his own time, which were likely, if left unchecked, to bring monastic life into disrepute and it may well be that the absorption of many of its most ardent followers into missionary work on the Continent deprived those who remained at home of the men and women who might otherwise have been their spiritual and intellectual leaders. We have not enough evidence to establish whether there had been marked and widespread deterioration before the Viking attacks began, but it seems clear that these attacks and the permanent settlements which followed them led to the complete destruction of all forms of monastic life throughout eastern England from the Thames in the south to Coldingham in the north. The guardians of St Cuthbert's relics formed the only monastic community which could claim some continuity of life with the past. Posterity may perhaps regard the destruction of the monastic libraries, whose contents no amount of subsequent endeavour could restore, as the most disastrous aspect of this loss. It is for this reason that the history of East Anglia and the eastern midlands is almost wholly unknown for much of the Anglo-Saxon period, and for this reason too that the history of Northumbria is known so largely from the writings of a single man whose reputation was great enough to ensure that his writings were copied frequently and widely distributed abroad as well as at home.

Evidence deriving both from contemporary witnesses, such as Alfred and Asser, and from later authorities indicates that regular monastic life had disappeared from western Mercia and southern England, as well as from the east and north, by the year 900. The bulk of this evidence is not large, but its weight seems heavy enough to establish the fact of disappearance, even though we cannot discern how much was due to the destruction caused by warfare and how much to earlier decay in the monasteries themselves. No doubt there were many religious houses in the south and in the western midlands which suffered from attack by raiding

Danish armies, but by Alfred's own account the state of learning in England when he came to the throne was such that there can then have been very few of the clergy capable of corresponding with one another in Latin as had their predecessors in the eighth century with the English missionaries abroad. It may be that in his enthusiasm for better things Alfred somewhat exaggerated the decay of English scholarship, but at the time of which he wrote the full force of the Danish attack was yet to be felt. Evidence from many individual houses shows that when the reform movement began to gather weight towards the middle of the tenth century monks had been displaced by communities of clerks who did not observe the regular life. Such was undoubtedly the case at Winchester, Milton, Chertsey, Cerne and Christ Church, Canterbury. Monastic life had ceased at Abingdon and Bath and the buildings of both had fallen into ruins. Glastonbury and Evesham seem similarly to have been served by clerks. To whatever part of the country we turn there is no ground for dissenting from the view 'that we are justified in regarding England in the reign of Athelstan as being wholly without any organized monastic life'.[1]

8. THE MONASTIC REVIVAL

Shortly before the middle of the tenth century three men of outstanding ability inspired and directed a remarkable monastic revival which gave fresh life to a Church brought almost to the point of exhaustion by its long period of suffering. They were Dunstan who was born in *c.* 909 of a Somerset family some of whose members are found in attendance at the court of Athelstan, his friend and close contemporary Æthelwold, a native of Winchester, and Oswald, a man of Danish family who numbered two archbishops, one of Canterbury and one of York, among his near relations. Biographies of each of these three men were written shortly before or after the year 1000, a circumstance which may have tended to obscure the parts played by some of their contemporaries, notably by Oda, archbishop of Canterbury (942–58), who found no biographer until more than a century and a half after his death. From Oda's surviving ecclesiastical legislation

[1] Dom D. Knowles, *The Monastic Order in England* (Cambridge, 1949), p. 36.

and from the part which he played with his fellow-archbishop of York in arranging a treaty between Edmund and Olaf Guthfrithson after the latter's invasion of England in 939, it may be judged that he worked strenuously to create the conditions in which ecclesiastical reform might prosper. It should be remembered that Oda was the uncle of Oswald and that Ælfheah, a monk who became bishop of Winchester in 934, was the uncle of Dunstan, and that he not only persuaded Dunstan to become a monk, but also himself ordained both Dunstan and Æthelwold.

Dunstan passed the early years of his life at Glastonbury where the memory of its past history, the old books which its library still contained and its yet living connexions with Irish scholarship offered him great opportunities. As a young man, and perhaps because he was cleverer with brain and hand than other young men, he was apt to provoke the envy of his fellows. It is of interest to note that one of the grounds advanced by his earliest biographer for the hostility of his comrades and kinsfolk was that he showed more interest in studying the poetry of heathen times than in the books which might have brought greater profit to his soul. It is likely enough that Ovid was among the heathen poets whom Dunstan studied, since there was a copy of his work in the Glastonbury library. Now in the Bodleian, it contains a fine drawing, judged to have been executed *c.* 960, showing Dunstan as a monk prostrate at the feet of Christ (Pl. IX). A note added by a later hand ascribes the drawing to Dunstan himself. It is known that he was an active patron of the arts and that he was skilled both as a musician and as a metal-worker. As a young man he had thoughts of marriage and it was only after the trial of a severe illness and through the persuasion of his uncle, Ælfheah, that he finally determined to devote himself to the monastic life. He was ordained priest at Winchester on the same day as Æthelwold and after the death of king Athelstan we find him in attendance at the court of his successor Edmund. Here he became the victim of intrigue and he was on the point of banishment from the country when the king experienced a providential escape from death while hunting a stag in Cheddar Gorge. Dunstan's biographer relates that in gratitude for his good fortune Edmund reversed his earlier

PLATE IX

CHRIST WITH ST DUNSTAN PROSTRATE BEFORE HIM

decision and rode forthwith to Glastonbury where he installed Dunstan as abbot. This event took place in 943 or 944 and it may be taken to mark the beginning of a movement which spread rapidly over southern England, the midlands and East Anglia. For the next fifteen years Dunstan remained at Glastonbury where he rebuilt the old monastery and established within its walls a community whose life was based upon the rule of St Benedict.

The disappearance of monastic life in the second half of the ninth century was by no means confined to England. The same process is to be observed throughout western Europe. In 910, a full generation before Dunstan's installation as abbot at Glastonbury, the beginning of Continental reform was marked by the foundation of a monastery at Cluny in Burgundy. Under its first two abbots the movement spread to other houses, among them being the house of Fleury on the Loire which came under the influence of Cluny *c*. 930. Similar movements began simultaneously in Lorraine and spread rapidly to Flanders where the houses of Ghent and St Omer were among those affected. Although there is little evidence of direct contact between the reformed centres of England and the Continent before the arrival of Dunstan at Ghent as an exile in 956, it is difficult to believe that in its earliest years the English movement was wholly indigenous and without some influence from abroad. Contemporary records of English history in the first half of the tenth century are very slight and the biographers from whose works the history of the English revival is so largely derived were writing close on a century after the foundation of Cluny. The brief entry made by the West-Saxon annalist under the year 889—'in this year there was no embassy to Rome, but king Alfred sent two couriers with letters'—is a warning against any assumption that the effects of warfare upon foreign travel in the Anglo-Saxon period were similar to its effects in recent times. Indeed, the frequency of Anglo-Saxon intercourse with countries overseas strikes the modern eye as one of the more surprising features of the period.

Among those who joined Dunstan's community at Glastonbury was Æthelwold, but after some time, perhaps because he found his vigorous and austere temperament curbed by his presence in the same house with Dunstan, he became anxious to go overseas. Dissuaded by King Eadred from leaving the country, he accepted the task of restoring the monastery at Abingdon. Two years later, in 956, Dunstan was exiled from England as the result of a personal quarrel with King Eadwig. He went to Flanders where he found refuge at the newly reformed monastery at Ghent. Oda, archbishop of Canterbury, is known to have visited Fleury some years before his death in 958 and it is probable that his visit had already taken place some little time before Dunstan reached Ghent. After his return to England Oda sent his nephew Oswald to study the practices of Fleury and at some uncertain date after 956 Æthelwold, perhaps having wished to go to Fleury himself, sent instead one of his monks from Abingdon for the same purpose. By these means the three leaders of the reform movement in England established contact with the two principal centres of reform on the Continent. So long as Eadwig remained king, there was little prospect of further advance, but in 957 his brother Edgar was set up as king in Mercia. He immediately recalled Dunstan and gave him the sees of Worcester and London. Two years later, on the death of Eadwig, Edgar became king south of Thames as well and he moved Dunstan to Canterbury as successor to Oda who had died the previous year. Oswald went as bishop to Worcester and in 963 Æthelwold became bishop of Winchester. With three monastic bishops thus possessed of well-endowed sees and the throne occupied by a young man who was ardently devoted to Christianity the way ahead was clear.

The reign of Edgar, who in no way lagged behind the most ardent of the reformers, lasted till 975 and of the three bishops Æthelwold lived till 984, Dunstan till 988 and Oswald till 992. Time was thus given within the lives of these three for the reform of the old foundations, the creation of new, the establishment of some form of observance common to all English monks and, not least in importance, the training of a second generation in centres so widely scattered that much was able to survive the second Scandinavian onslaught. Dunstan, who had led the way at Glastonbury, seems to have been less active as a reformer after his move to Canterbury, preferring rather to give his attention to the many-sided business of his office as archbishop. We cannot even be certain that the community at Christ Church became wholly monastic, though we may think it likely that clerks would be gradually displaced by monks as opportunity arose. This was certainly the method which was followed by Oswald at Worcester, in contrast with the dramatic incident which transformed the situation at Winchester at one stroke by the sudden, and perhaps even violent, ejection of the clerks from both the Old and the New Minsters in 964. A similar course was taken in the same year at Chertsey in Surrey and Milton Abbas in Dorset. A contemporary chronicler, probably writing in Winchester itself, ascribed these actions to Edgar the king, but Ælfric, a former pupil of Æthelwold's, writing shortly before or after the year 1000, claimed the major part in the deed for his master, to the great hurt of his master's reputation in recent times.

It is not necessary to follow the further progress of the revival in southern England, but some attention must be given to a number of important foundations in two other areas, the west midlands and East Anglia. In about 962 Oswald established a small offshoot from Worcester at Westbury-on-Trym near Bristol, but not wholly satisfied with its situation he sought opportunities elsewhere. He finally acquired from Æthelwine, ealdorman of East Anglia, a site at Ramsey near the western edge of the fens and to this distant place in an area which had been strongly affected by the Danish settlements he moved the greater part of the community at Westbury. He ensured the success of this bold venture by enlisting aid from Fleury whence came Abbo, one of the most learned of its monks, to teach at the new foundation. He remained there for two years and the community at Ramsey prospered so greatly that it was able to repay its debt to the west midlands by sending monks not only to Worcester itself, but also to Winchcombe and soon afterwards to Pershore and Evesham. It was from these areas and particularly from Evesham that late in the eleventh century monasticism was carried to the north of England and even farther afield to Denmark, but this was not until some years after the Norman Conquest. Meanwhile Æthelwold perceived the opportunities which the islands in the fens of

East Anglia offered for the pursuit of monastic life free from external interference. Several of them had supported monasteries in the seventh century and Æthelwold set himself with great energy not only to acquire the derelict sites but to ensure that they were richly endowed with lands. In this way monasticism was restored to Peterborough (966), Ely (970) and Thorney (972). From Ely, during the reign of Cnut, colonists went to two other East Anglian sites which bred famous houses, Bury St Edmunds and St Benet of Hulme.

During the eighth century, though some houses observed the rule of St Benedict, there was great diversity of practice among the many religious houses which then existed in England. The risk of a similar situation arising in the latter part of the tenth century was considerable. To meet this risk a synodal council was summoned at Winchester in about the year 970 to construct a common rule of life to be observed by all monasteries. The task of compiling this rule was entrusted to Æthelwold who was helped in his work by monks from Fleury and Ghent. The *Regularis Concordia*, the name by which Æthelwold's compilation came to be known, was derived from a variety of customaries in use in western Europe and it contained very little that was peculiar to England. If it yields but slight signs of innovation on the one hand, it contains no suggestion at all of any desire to revive the practices of early Celtic monasticism on the other. As a result perhaps of the active help which Dunstan and his companions had received from Edgar it was enjoined that prayers should be said for the king and his family who were to be regarded as the particular defenders of the monastic order in England. The *Regularis Concordia* differed from Continental practices in one other important respect, namely in the adoption of a procedure for the election of bishops which led in practice to a predominantly monastic episcopacy.

9. THE LAST CENTURY OF THE ANGLO-SAXON CHURCH

Historians of a previous generation, paying over-much attention to the ill-informed comments of Norman writers and perhaps influenced as well by the atmosphere of romance which can too easily be associated with the splendours of English ecclesiastical architecture in Norman and later times, have done less than justice to the good qualities of the later Anglo-Saxon Church. Some reparation has been achieved through the researches of more recent writers, but there is much work yet remaining to be done. It is already clear that the tenth-century reformers were as much interested in the well-being of the Church as a whole as in the revival of monasticism itself, and furthermore that the influence of their invigorating work had not greatly lessened even by the time of the Norman Conquest. After Edgar's death in 975 some of the Mercian monasteries were despoiled, but this may have been due less to reaction against monasticism as such than to circumstances arising ultimately from the disputed succession to the throne.[1] Even before this date an end had come to the short period of immunity from Viking attack which had allowed the reform movement to make such rapid progress. But although the further establishment of new monasteries almost ceased, thereby leaving substantial areas in the midlands and the whole of the north beyond the direct influence of the movement, renewed Viking attack, even culminating in the accession of a foreign conqueror to the English throne, was not able to overthrow what had been achieved. The hope to which the *Regularis Concordia* gave expression, that the king would serve as the special protector of the monastic order, proved in the event to be no vain one. Of the ninety-odd years between the death of Edgar and the battle of Hastings, more than eighty were covered by the reigns of Æthelred, Cnut and Edward the Confessor, and all three of them gave active help to the Church, especially, as perhaps need hardly be said, the last. No doubt some monasteries and churches suffered during the wars of Æthelred and many of them must have had to find large sums as their contribution to the tribute paid to the attackers. The barbarous murder of Archbishop Ælfheah at Greenwich in 1012 by a mob of drunken Vikings was an isolated episode carried through in the face of an attempt by one of their leaders to save the archbishop's life.

For the future prosperity of the Church much, if not all,

[1] So D. J. V. Fisher, *Cambridge Hist. Journ.* x, no. 3 (1952), pp. 254–70.

depended upon the attitude of Cnut and it was a stroke of good fortune that in their conqueror the English found a man who from the beginning of his reign devoted himself to the interests of the Church with an enthusiasm which was not the less sincere because it was also politic. In a proclamation which he issued in 1020 on his return from the first of his expeditions to Scandinavia, he referred to the messages which Archbishop Lyfing had brought him from the pope and he repeatedly emphasized the duty which both he and his subjects owed to God. In the same year he went with a large company of bishops, abbots and monks to Ashingdon in Essex to attend the consecration of a new church built at the place where he had defeated Edmund in 1016. Among those who were present was Wulfstan, archbishop of York, an ecclesiastical statesman of high distinction, whose guiding influence upon Cnut is becoming increasingly clear.

A second proclamation issued in 1027 contains still more striking evidence of his service to the Church. At the time of its issue Cnut was on his homeward journey from a visit to Rome where he had had profitable intercourse with the pope himself, with the Emperor Conrad whose coronation had taken place during his visit, and with many other ruling princes. Opportunities awaited one who went to Rome both as a pilgrim and as a powerful ruler whose ships and armies represented the most efficient fighting forces seen in Europe since Roman times. With obvious pride in his achievements, Cnut tells of the privileges which he has secured in the relaxation of tolls and of other hindrances to the free progress of pilgrims and merchants travelling to Rome. In particular he had expressed his great displeasure at the exaction of large sums from his two archbishops as the price of the pallium for which they travelled all the way to Rome. No doubt the results of this meeting were not solely to the advantage of Cnut and something of the other side emerges towards the end of his proclamation in injunctions that full payments should be made of all that was due to God—plough-alms, tithe of animals, Peter's Pence, tithe of fruits in the middle of August, and the first-fruits of the crops at the feast of St Martin; every man must pay his dues to the church of the parish in which he lived.

The close connexions with Rome which had been characteristic of the English Church from its earliest days and which had been strengthened by the interest with which the Papacy had followed the progress of English missionary work on the Continent were never completely broken during the Danish invasion. Alms were sent to Rome by Alfred in most years when circumstances allowed and it is probable that these alms whose payment was enforced in the legislation of Edmund and Edgar, represent the dues called Peter's Pence in Cnut's proclamation of 1027. Throughout the eighth century it had been the regular practice of the Papacy to send pallia to England for the two archbishops, but in later times even closer contact was established with the growth of the custom which required the archbishops to receive the pallium in Rome itself. The expenditure, as well as the dangers, involved in making the long journey, inflicted considerable hardship on the recipients of this distinction. Ælfsige, archbishop-elect of Canterbury, met his death while crossing the Alps in 959, and most of those who held the office between 925 and 1066 are known to have made the journey. In a letter which was formerly ascribed to the year 805 but which is now held to belong to the early years of the eleventh century, the English bishops made a strong protest not only against the imposition of such a journey but also against the sin of simony which they believed to be involved in the payments demanded. This was one of the matters discussed with the pope by Cnut who referred in his proclamation of 1027 to some allevia- tion which he had been able to achieve in papal demands, though not to the extent of a reversion to eighth-century practice. During the eleventh century the influence of the Papacy became steadily greater, amounting on one occasion to an instruction to the arch- bishop of Canterbury to refuse consecration to Edward the Con- fessor's nominee to the see of London.

Detailed analysis has shown that of 116 occupants of eighteen English sees between 960 and 1066 no fewer than sixty-seven are known to have been monks.[1] Of the fourteen or so known to have been secular clerks, the great majority belong to the reign of Edward the Confessor. With allowances made for the lack of

Dom D. Knowles, *op. cit.* pp. 697–701.

information about the East Anglian and Mercian sees, it has been estimated that in this whole period about three-quarters of the whole number of bishops in England were monks, and that for the shorter period from 960 till the accession of Edward the Confessor in 1042 the proportion would be nearer nine-tenths. A great many of these monastic bishops were recruited from houses founded or reformed by Dunstan and Æthelwold. From the time of Cnut onwards a few bishops are found achieving their office as reward for service done in the king's writing office. A few foreign bishops are found, but no more than might be expected as the natural consequence of the close Continental contacts in the eleventh century.

The predominance of a monastic episcopate did not, however, lead to the exaggeration of exclusively monastic interests at the expense of other aspects of the Church. The administration of the Church proceeded through the machinery of ecclesiastical council and diocesan synod and there is much evidence of successful effort to secure the building and endowment of parish churches and the proper instruction of their clergy. Æthelred's legislation, subsequently embodied by Cnut in his own legal codes, gave close attention to the status, privileges and responsibilities of the priesthood, amongst whom it recognized two main groups, those who lived according to rule, the monastic priests, and those who did not, the secular clergy. Many of the parochial clergy were married, though clerical marriage was forbidden in the laws of Edmund, Æthelred and Cnut. The income of individual churches was derived in part from endowments in land, but to a greater extent from the various dues whose payment was enforced by law: plough-alms, tithe, church-scot (a due mentioned as early as the seventh century in a West Saxon code), burial fees and the like. The number of churches in private ownership at the end of the eleventh century was considerable and where their endowment was substantial they might on occasion be treated like any other profitable business.

The spiritual and intellectual force of the ecclesiastical revival can be perceived more easily in its written memorials than in its architecture. There still exist in England some 200 churches whose fabric is in varying degree of tenth- or eleventh-century workmanship, although from this later, as from the earlier, Anglo-Saxon period there are very few complete or even nearly complete examples. Apart from the varied hazards of war, fire, faulty workmanship, neglect and the mere passage of time, two other factors have had some effect upon the distribution and numbers of the survivors—the ease with which good building stone could be won and the relative fame or obscurity of the site in later times. Most of the later Anglo-Saxon churches are to be found either on the limestone belt which runs southwards from the Yorkshire coast through Lincolnshire and past the western edge of the Fens, then turning south-westwards by way of the Cotswolds to the Dorset coast, or on the chalklands which run almost parallel to it from the north coast of Norfolk to Salisbury Plain with a long finger running back through Sussex to Beachy Head.

So far as we know, Anglo-Saxon builders used stone for their churches only, generally keeping to the traditional wood for other forms of building, and there can be little doubt that wooden churches were built in places where stone could not easily be had. The church at Greenstead in Essex is the only surviving example of a kind which we may suppose to have been numerous. The chances of a wooden church surviving for more than a century or two must have been extremely slight and it is to be admitted that there is no proof of the timbers even at Greenstead being as old as the eleventh century. Greenstead lies, significantly, in the forest-lands of Essex and we need not hesitate to think that wooden churches were common in other forest areas. There are literary references to wooden churches at, for example, Wilton, Lewes and Chester-le-Street. In some instances, notably at Earl's Barton, the external decoration in stone is strongly reminiscent of half-timbered or framework construction, though it is impossible to say whether this decoration was copied from wooden prototypes in England or whether the change from wood to stone was made on the Continent and the resulting style carried thence to England.

Old buildings may perish by accidental loss or by mere decay, but they may also perish by deliberate destruction intended to clear the ground for the erection of new buildings designed to meet changing needs. Deliberate destruction was most likely to occur at the more prominent ecclesiastical centres and the prospects of surviving this hazard were considerably greater for the smaller monastic or parish churches than for the more important establishments. It is important that the operation of this factor should be recognized, lest the qualities and defects of Anglo-Saxon ecclesiastical architecture should be judged solely from the remains of its minor buildings. There are written accounts of the cathedral church built at Canterbury by Archbishop Oda and of other important buildings constructed in the tenth century at Winchester, Worcester, Ely, Ramsey, Thorney, Peterborough, Durham and elsewhere.

It is evident that large buildings of elaborate construction were by no means beyond the competence of the age, but the mind cannot visualize the appearance of the Anglo-Saxon cathedrals or their great monastic churches when their image must be reconstructed from written accounts. Nor should the only surviving ground plan of a tenth-century cathedral church in England, that of North Elmham (Fig. 4a), be regarded as typical of its age, for Elmham lay in an area which had been greatly affected by the Danish invasions and its modest scale may well be a reflexion of the small resources available in this area. Remains of the monastic buildings erected by Dunstan at Glastonbury in the middle of the tenth century have lately been identified by excavation.[1] Little but foundations survive and even these were found to be much mutilated by later work, but their extent suggests that Dunstan's monastery was on a scale comparable with the largest contemporary houses on the Continent. Some slight remains of the church built at Abingdon by Æthelwold have also been discovered, but not enough to indicate the peculiarities of its plan which is described as consisting of a circular chancel, a circular nave with twice the diameter of the chancel and a circular tower. About the middle of the eleventh century Wulfric, abbot of St Augustine's, began to build a church which seems to have been intended to

---

[1] C. A. Ralegh Radford, *Antiquity*, XXIX (1955), pp. 33–4, and *Trans. Somersets. Arch. and Nat. Hist. Soc.* XCVII (1953), p. 21.

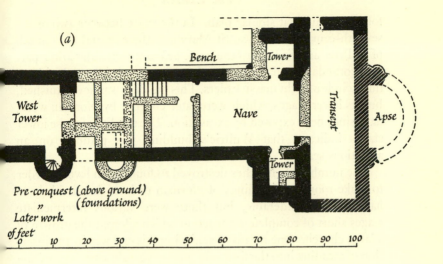

(a)

West Tower

Bench

Tower

Nave

Transept

Apse

Tower

Pre-conquest (above ground)
      "   (foundations)
Later work
of feet
0   10   20   30   40   50   60   70   80   90   100

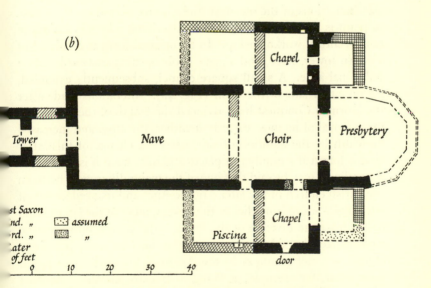

(b)

Chapel

Tower

Nave

Choir

Presbytery

Chapel

Piscina

door

st Saxon
nd. "   assumed
rd. "   "
ater
of feet
0   10   20   30   40

Fig. 4. *a*, North Elmham: ground plan of Saxon Cathedral;
b, Deerhurst Church: ground plan.

185

follow a somewhat similar plan. In the space between two of the seventh-century churches, St Mary's to the east and the church of St Peter and St Paul to the west, he constructed the lower part of a rotunda, circular inside and octagonal outside, and with an inner circle of eight massive piers. This building was never finished, but its lower stages, which were later covered by Norman work, have since been exposed by excavation. The solidity of these lower stages indicates that Wulfric's building was planned on an ambitious scale.

The number of churches destroyed to foundation level in order to make room for buildings of Norman or later date is likely to have been considerable, but there were various intermediate stages short of complete destruction which allowed the growth of a large church. One means of achieving this end was by the insertion of arcading into the formerly solid nave walls and the addition of side aisles, a method of reconstruction which tended to preserve the dimensions of the old nave and also its western wall. A case in point is the monastic church at Deerhurst which is mainly of tenth-century workmanship. In its original form it consisted of western tower, nave, and square choir opening eastwards into a polygonal apse. A small square chapel, subsequently extended, lay on either side of the choir (Fig. 4*b*). Alterations made after the Norman Conquest have reduced the length of the church by the removal of its most easterly member, the apse, and increased its width by the addition of side aisles. A change of this latter kind is found at a number of places and in so far as it is possible to generalize it may be said that one of the major differences between the parish church of the later Middle Ages and its predecessor of late Anglo-Saxon times lies in the development in the later period of the tripartite division of the body of the church into a central nave flanked by side aisles. So far as may be seen, the aisled church was not common in the Anglo-Saxon period, though it does occur, for example, at Wing in Buckinghamshire. Another difference lies in the growth of transepts and the resulting cruciform plan. Throughout almost the whole of the Anglo-Saxon period the external adjunct to the nave which has been variously called porch, porticus and chapel, remained in favour. Such

PLATE X

ANGLO-SAXON INSCRIPTION AT BREAMORE,
HAMPSHIRE

The inscription is cut on the head of the arch which opens below
the south wall of the central tower and leads into the south porticus.

Reading

HER SWVTELAÐ SEO GECWYDRÆDNES ÐE

Translation

'In this place the Word is revealed unto thee'

adjuncts are a regular feature of the seventh-century churches in Kent and they remain a prominent feature in the plan of Deerhurst. At this church they remain chapels entered by means of a doorway from the choir, but at various churches considerably wider openings are found with a correspondingly nearer approach to a transeptal plan. These modifications may be seen at Breamore in Hampshire where the openings remain little more than doorways (Pl. X), at Worth in Sussex, at Hadstock in Essex where a transeptal plan may be said to exist though the openings into the transepts are still a little less than the full width of the choir, and also at St Mary-in-Castro, Dover.

Owing to the incorporation of almost the whole of the tenth-century church in the later fabric, the amount of Anglo-Saxon workmanship still surviving at Deerhurst is exceptionally large. In times of reconstruction, where anything less than complete clearance occurred, it was more usual to demolish almost everything save the tower. It is unlikely that the earliest Anglo-Saxon churches, either in the south-east or in Northumbria, possessed towers, but in the later period towers are a common, if not almost universal, feature in all save the smallest buildings. Most of those which survive, and their number is considerable, are western towers, but central towers were built, as also were lesser towers to contain stairways. It is more than probable that many of the major towers, and particularly those which were centrally placed were built of timber. Such was probably the case at Deerhurst and at Breamore where the supporting walls are too slight to have supported a tower wholly of stone. The existing stone tower at the west end of Deerhurst is of tenth-century date, save for some window and belfry openings of later date. The main function of the western tower was to house the church bells and we may associate the development of a widespread and characteristic type of belfry opening with that delight in the ringing of church bells which is apparent from several passages in the *Regularis Concordia*. To this custom too may be attributed the strength and solidity of workmanship which has enabled so many Anglo-Saxon towers to survive till the present time. The characteristic belfry openings are not to be seen at Deerhurst whose tower is indeed somewhat unusually severe and plain, though it is not wholly unparalleled in this respect. More commonly the later Anglo-Saxon church tower rose in three or four receding stages, each being marked by a horizontal string-course, and the uppermost containing the belfry openings. This arrangement, with the characteristic belfry openings, can be seen at St Bene't's, Cambridge (see Pl. XI), Barnack and Barton-on-Humber and farther north, where the fashion continued in use after the Norman Conquest, at Monk-wearmouth and Billingham in Durham, at Bywell and Ovingham on the Tyne and at Appleton-le-Street in Yorkshire.

The tower of St Bene't's, Cambridge, provides a good example of the method of constructing quoins in the 'long and short' technique whereby massive stones are set alternately flat and upright. The towers of Barnack and Barton-on-Humber show the use of a device known as the pilaster-strip which is perhaps the most characteristic decorative feature of later Anglo-Saxon architecture and which is now to be seen at its greatest development in the tower at Earl's Barton. The pilaster-strip takes the form of narrow bands of stonework which project an inch or two beyond the surface of the walls which they adorn. In appearance they create an effect similar to the half-timbered framework characteristic of some types of later domestic architecture, a method of construction which is likely to have been used in the Anglo-Saxon period, but the function of the pilaster-strip was nearer to that of the modern adulterated copies of Tudor half-timbered work in that it was mainly decorative and superficial, though it may have served some minor structural purpose in helping to hold the intermediate masonry together. Pilaster-strips, which are commonly found running vertically up the full height of tower or other walls, were sometimes adapted to form an arcading with semicircular heads or a triangular trellis-like pattern. Plain vertical strips may be seen at Barnack and Wing, while more elaborate forms employing both semicircular and triangular arcading are found at Barton-on-Humber and Earl's Barton. There is some evidence that the intermediate spaces were covered with plaster or stucco, thus presenting to the view a flush surface. The belfry openings at Earl's Barton reached a high degree of

PLATE XI

TOWER OF ST BENE'T'S CHURCH, CAMBRIDGE

elaboration, consisting of five openings separated from one another by baluster shafts in each of the four faces of the tower, as if particular pains had been taken to make the most of the commanding site on which this church was built. A common and somewhat puzzling feature of several towers of this period is the occurrence in the upper stages of external doorways to which the approach must have been by way of a ladder. The topmost stages of all save one of the surviving Anglo-Saxon towers have been substantially modified by the additions of later times. The exception is the tower at Sompting whose roof, though not original in itself, retains the original structural form. This form consists of a tiled pyramidal shape resting upon the four walls each of which is carried up to a pointed gable. Certain structural details suggest that the original roof of St Bene't's, Cambridge, was of a similar form, and roofs of this kind may have been common.

The east wall of the tower at Deerhurst contains a round-headed doorway which seems to have given access to a gallery across the west end of the nave and in the stage above it are two triangular-headed openings which likewise give on to the nave. The triangular head was not uncommonly used for both door-ways and windows in the churches of this period, though the round head may be regarded as the normal for both features. In general, surviving windows are small and placed at a great height above the ground. One of the most distinctive features of later Anglo-Saxon architecture is the window which has an equal splay both inside and outside. Wherever this double-splay window, as it is called, occurs in English churches, it is held to be conclusive evidence of tenth- or eleventh-century Anglo-Saxon workmanship. We have noted that Benedict Biscop employed Gaulish glass-makers for his churches at Monkwearmouth and Jarrow, and also that Wilfrid caused the windows of the church at York to be glazed. It is uncertain to what extent window glass was used later in the Anglo-Saxon period, but it is known that in some instances window openings were closed by the insertion of wooden boards, presumably pierced by small openings. The remains of such a device are to be seen at Birstall in Leicestershire, and at Barnack there are in three of the tower openings stone slabs pierced so as to form an openwork interlace design.

To judge from the surviving remains the nave was the dominant feature of most Anglo-Saxon churches, whether early or late. Although the overall size of most of these churches was not great, the nave was often long and of great height in proportion to its width. This feature, combined with the smallness of the chancel, the absence of side aisles and the small windows placed at considerable height, must have presented a large expanse of wall surface to the eye of worshippers. It would be natural to suppose that these surfaces, as in later medieval times, were either hung with pictures after the fashion described by Bede at Jarrow or themselves painted. No such paintings survive, but here and there are found fragments of sculptured panels evidently intended to give some relief to the flat surfaces. Some of these fragments are of high artistic quality, notably the pair of winged angels which adorn the church of St Lawrence at Bradford-on-Avon. This church, a miniature in its dimensions, is largely, if not wholly, tenth-century work, but its builders made great efforts to enrich its decorative effect by the use of pilaster-strips, fluted columns and blank arcading on its external surface. Similar figures of angels are to be seen at Winterborne Steepleton in Dorset and at Deerhurst.

It may be surmised that such figures once formed part of a rood, such as is found at Breamore, at Romsey and at Headbourne Worthy, all in Hampshire. The crucifixion scene, occurring already on the Ruthwell cross, became common later in the Anglo-Saxon period and among examples which may be noted are those on a second slab at Romsey, at Langford in Oxfordshire, at Daglingworth in Gloucestershire and at St Dunstan's Stepney. Two northern examples, both on cross shafts, may be noted, one at Aycliffe in Durham and another in Alnwick museum, coming from the site of the old church at Alnmouth. On some of these examples the figure of Christ crucified is accompanied by those of the Virgin and St John and of Longinus and Stephaton, carrying respectively a lance and a reed. The high quality of workmanship found in some of these pieces and in others such as

the seated figure of Christ at Barnack and the cross shaft at Cod-
ford St Peter in Wiltshire, suggests that the later Anglo-Saxon
churches housed a considerable quantity of sculptured monuments.
The chances of survival through centuries of change both in taste
and in religious belief were not great. With the outstanding exception of the York Virgin, whose eleventh-century date is not wholly
undisputed, northern English sculpture of this later period is
more notable for its bulk than for its artistry.

There need be no hesitation in believing that the revived
English Church came to be richly endowed with great and
splendid treasures of plate, vestments and the lesser accompaniments of its services. Although virtually all endowments of
this kind have perished, there is no lack of written evidence testifying to its former existence. Among the treasures given to the
restored house at Peterborough by Bishop Æthelwold are said to
have been three crosses adorned with silver, two silver candle-
sticks and two covered with gold, one silver censer and one of
brass, one silver water vessel, two silver bells, four silver chalices
and four patens. There were also ten hanging bells and seven
handbells. A very substantial wardrobe of ecclesiastical garments
included six Mass vestments, four copes, eight stoles, eleven
subuculas and nineteen albs, as well as curtains, seat-covers and
two gilded altar cloths. The treasury at Bury St Edmunds in the
eleventh century contained an even richer collection of vestments.
Peterborough and Bury were of course among the wealthier
houses, but Ramsey, Ely, Thorney, Winchester, Abingdon,
Glastonbury, and Worcester are not likely to have been any less
wealthy in this respect, as we may see in some instances from
surviving inventories. In the north it is recorded that Aldred,
bishop of Worcester 1044–62 and archbishop of York 1062–9,
had a screen made of bronze, gold and silver to enclose the choir
at Beverley. An inscribed sundial at Kirkdale in the North
Riding of Yorkshire records the rebuilding of a church there in
the last decade of the Anglo-Saxon period (Pl. XII).

Although such wealth should not be attributed to the lesser
churches, it is likely that they had their due share. The English
acquired a high reputation abroad as metalworkers and their

PLATE XII

THE KIRKDALE INSCRIPTION

(Now placed above the south porch of the church at Kirkdale in the North Riding of Yorkshire, this is the best surviving example of an inscribed Anglo-Saxon sundial.)

Dexter panel

✠ ORM GAMAL/SVNA BOHTE S(AN)C(TV)S / GREGORIVS MIN/STER ÐONNE HI/T WES ÆL TOBRO/

Sinister panel

CAN 7 TOFALAN 7 HE / HIT LET MACAN NEWAN FROM / GRUNDE XPE 7 S(AN)C(TV)S GREGORI/VS IN EADWARD DAGVM C(I)NG/ 7 (I)N TOSTI DAGVM EORL ✠

Centre panel

✠ ÞIS IS DÆGES SOLMERCA ✠ / ÆT ILCVM TIDE / ✠ 7 HAWARÐ ME WROHTE 7 BRAND PR̄S /

'Orm, son of Gamal, bought St Gregory's church when it was all ruined and tumbled down and he caused it to be built afresh from the foundation (in honour of) Christ and St Gregory in the days of king Edward and in the days of earl Tosti.

This is the day's sun-marking at every hour. And Hawarð made me, and Brand, priest (?).'

The dial shows the octaval system of time reckoning whereby the 24 hours were divided into 8 equal periods. Each 3-hour period was called a *tid*. The lines marked with a single cross-bar correspond with 6 a.m., 9 a.m., noon, 3 p.m., and 6 p.m. Intermediate lines divide each *tid* into periods of 1½ hours. One of these intermediate lines, marked with a cross, denotes *dægmæl*, corresponding with 7.30 a.m. This word usually means 'dial', but here it denotes 'day-time'.

Tosti (Tostig), brother of Harold Godwineson, became earl of Northumbria in 1055. He was expelled in 1065 and killed in September 1066. The dial should accordingly be ascribed to the decade 1055–65.

The inscription shows the neglect of inflections in the oblique cases which is characteristic of the late Northumbrian dialect of O.E. *Solmerca* is a Scandinavian loanword from O.N. *sólmerki*. The personal names *Orm*,

192

PLATE XII

PLATE XIII

PART OF ÆLFFLÆD'S STOLE FROM CUTHBERT'S TOMB

decorated textiles were of such excellence that they gained the reputation of being pre-eminent in this art. The whole of this treasure of metalwork and vestments has perished save for one or two fragments of which the most notable are parts of a stole and of a maniple which were among a number of gifts made by Athelstan to the shrine of Cuthbert in 934 (see Pl. XIII). From inscriptions which they bear it may be learnt that these vestments were worked at the behest of Ælfflæd, the second wife of Edward the Elder, between 909 and 916. On all the surviving fragments (the largest being 2⅜ in. wide by about 6 ft. long) figures of saints and prophets with decorative acanthus scrolls and pairs of animals are thickly, but delicately, embroidered in silk threads. If work of this quality in textiles and of the quality of the Alfred jewel in metalwork was being produced in southern England between 870 and 920, it may be confidently supposed that much of the work which adorned the new churches later in the century was of outstanding excellence. The same high quality is to be found in the small number of ivories which survive from this period. Indeed, to whichever of the arts we turn, carving in stone or ivory, metalwork, embroidery, the paintings in Æthelwold's *Benedictional* or the line drawings in the Canterbury copy of the *Utrecht Psalter*, we find evidence, sometimes small in quantity, but always convincing in quality, that the artistic expression of the ecclesiastical revival in no way lagged behind its spiritual and intellectual achievements. In later centuries the buildings themselves became more and more enriched, but there cannot have been many ages when the objects which they housed were of greater beauty than in the last century of the Anglo-Saxon Church.

CHAPTER IV

GOVERNMENT

I. THE RULE OF KINGS

THE misuse of Anglo-Saxon records by lawyers and antiquaries of the seventeenth century as a storehouse of information which could be made to yield arguments against the prevalent theories of monarchical government was largely responsible for the birth of long-lived misconceptions about the democracy of the early Anglo-Saxon state. Under the influence of movements for parliamentary reform and of the development of joint-stock principles in commerce such misconceptions prevailed into the Victorian era.[1] The publication in 1907 of H. M. Chadwick's book *The Origin of the English Nation* finally exposed the false bases upon which such beliefs rested and none would now be found to dispute the view that from the first the Anglo-Saxon invasions of Britain took place under the leadership of kings and princes and that the effective government of the country remained in the hands of such men supported by a strong aristocracy. In no part of Anglo-Saxon England and at no time in its history is any trace to be found of a system of government knowing nothing of the rule of kings.

There seems yet to be no ground for challenging Chadwick's views on these matters, but it may be that his demonstration of the strongly aristocratic nature of society among the peoples whence came the invaders of Britain, combined with the detailed attention latterly given to Anglo-Saxon poetry which again reflects a strongly aristocratic background, has led to some depreciation of the part played by the lesser orders at least in the lesser parts of

[1] Thus J. M. Kemble, *The Saxons in England* (London, 1849), II, p. 182, writes of the Anglo-Saxon invasions: 'If we carefully examine the nature of these adventures, we shall I think come to the conclusion that they were carried on upon what may be familiarly termed the joint-stock principle.'

194

government. It is well to remark that most of the administrative boundaries of early nineteenth-century England were created between the departure of the Romans and the arrival of the Normans. Hundred and parish boundaries were not defined for nothing, but as units they are often so small and so numerous that we can hardly avoid supposing that their control was frequently in the hands of those who were not noble born. Perhaps the primitive folk-moot did have some substance, not indeed after the Victorian notion of a body of free men delegating authority to one of their number in a central parliament, but as a body of men small enough to have intimate knowledge of a small area and thus to be able both to attend to its affairs and to place ultimately upon the back of an individual his own share of the burdens and duties imposed by a king.

The modern title 'king' derives from O.E. *cyning*. It is probable that the frequent use of this word as a title following a proper name, e.g. *Æþelbald cyning*, where it would not be heavily stressed, led to the adoption of a syncopated form *cyng* at an earlier date than might otherwise have been expected. The shortened form is found as early as the late ninth century in the *Anglo-Saxon Chronicle* (text A) and had become regular by the time of Ælfric. The second element of the unsyncopated form *cyning* appears to be the regular Old English patronymic meaning 'son of' and it has been suggested, though it is not certain, that the word *cyning* originally meant 'son of the *cyn*' or 'member of the family' with particular application to a royal family. The distribution of the word which is found in Old German *cuning* and in Old Norse *konungr* makes it very probable that it was in use over much of north-western Europe before the Anglo-Saxons invaded Britain. The authority which a *cyning* exercised or the territory in which he exercised it might be called *cynedom*, from which the modern English 'kingdom' derives, but in Old English texts and throughout the Anglo-Saxon period it was far more commonly called *rice*, a word cognate with the Gothic *reiks* which is held to represent an early Teutonic adoption of Celtic **rix*, cf. Latin *rex*. This word *rice*, seemingly much older than *cyning*, retains its political significance in, for example, German *Reich* and in the second element of *Sverige*, formerly *Svéaríki*, the native name of the country known to English speakers as Sweden.

Scandinavian traditions which relate to times as early as the latter half of the fourth century indicate that government by kings was then universal in the north. The *Germania* of Tacitus, which refers to much earlier times, may give the impression that Tacitus regarded the kind of state which was ruled by a king as being the exception rather than the rule, yet by his own evidence some of the Germanic states were governed by kings in the first century A.D. and a general survey of his evidence suggests that the power of the king tended to become more absolute as the peoples concerned were more geographically remote from the frontiers of the Roman Empire. With one possible exception, the rule of kings was universal among the peoples of north-western Europe in the seventh century. Some other form of government may have been customary among the Saxons. Writing of the Old Saxons, as they came to be called in distinction from the Anglo-Saxons, Bede said that they had no kings, but a number of officials (*satrapae*) from amongst whom one was chosen by lot as leader in time of war, but this remark applied to the late seventh century and we do not know what the situation was in the fifth. There can be no doubt, whatever the basic meaning of the word *cyning*, that the all-important qualification, without which no claim to the title of king could be upheld, was that the claimant should be born to his office.

Documents relating to the Anglo-Saxon period, and particularly to its earlier part, devote much space to royal genealogies, and it may indeed be said that a king's genealogy came to be regarded as one of the most important of his possessions.[1] It may be observed that Bede seldom fails to recite the forbears for three or four generations of the kings to whom he refers and that the A text of the *Anglo-Saxon Chronicle* begins with a long genealogy setting out the ancestry of the house of Wessex. Parts of this and of other genealogies constantly recur in the annals of the *Chronicle* and there can be little doubt that documents containing the genealogies

---

[1] See K. Sisam, 'Anglo-Saxon Royal Genealogies', *Proc. Brit. Acad.* XXXIX (1953), 287–348.

of the royal families were widely distributed in places where records were kept by the eighth century. It is of interest to note the phrase *ungecynde cyning*[1] used by an annalist of a man not of royal race who had been chosen by the Northumbrians in preference to their lawful king shortly before the Danish attack on York in 866. The enduring strength of the hereditary aspect of kingships may be seen in both English and Scandinavian lands in later times. Æthelred, the powerful earl of Mercia, was always known by the title *ealdorman*. The high-reeves of Bamburgh who ruled there after the extinction of the old Bernician royal line were never themselves known as kings. The earls of Hlaðir in Norway, who achieved and long maintained a position of eminence which far surpassed that of many kings, were always known as earls, as also were the even more eminent Norse rulers of Orkney who ruled the islands for many generations.

The ancestry of the Anglo-Saxon dynasties is invariably traced back to the gods, to Woden in seven of the eight surviving genealogies and to Seaxnot in the remaining one, the East Saxon dynasty. In later times antiquarian ingenuity enabled some genealogies to be carried back to Noah and even to Adam. Such spurious additions can easily be recognized for what they are, but it is more difficult to discern how far the Germanic elements are fictitious and how far they are historical. Assertions of divine origin need not necessarily discredit the genealogies in which they are found, because there is evidence for the deification not only of dead but also of living kings among some of the northern peoples in early times. So far it has proved possible only in one case to establish a connexion between kings who ruled in England and ancestors who ruled on the other side of the North Sea before the invasions. This was the house of Mercia whose most distinguished member, Offa, was descended from kings who ruled near Slesvig late in the fourth and early in the fifth centuries. Although only eight royal genealogies are preserved, it is certain that the number of royal families in seventh-century England was greater than this. In some instances they were known by dynastic names, as with the *Iclingas* of Mercia, the *Wuffingas* of East Anglia and the

[1] *A.S.C.* 867 A.

197

Oiscingas of Kent. It is not improbable that the dynasties were named from the first member of the line to rule in England.

2. THE GROWTH OF MONARCHY

Although it is proper to emphasize the hereditary aspect of the rule of kings in Anglo-Saxon England, it should be stated with equal emphasis that the principle of primogeniture played no part in the succession. At no time within the period did it become the practice for the dead king's eldest son to succeed automatically to his father's position, nor was it necessary even that a son should succeed a father. Indeed, of the eight kings who reigned in the tenth century only three were sons who immediately succeeded their fathers, Edward the Elder, his son Athelstan, and Edward the Martyr, son of Edgar. Edmund, Eadred, Eadgar and Æthelred all succeeded brothers, Eadwig an uncle. There are a number of passages in Bede's *History* which suggest that the reigning king himself designated his successor during his own lifetime. In the *Anglo-Saxon Chronicle* we commonly find the expression *feng to rice*, an indefinite phrase which simply records the fact that so-and-so 'acquired the kingdom' and tells nothing of the way in which the decision was reached. On the other hand the lack of any established rule of automatic succession left room for the elective principle to play its part within certain limits. In addition to *feng to rice* we meet the phrase *ceosan to cyninge*, 'choose as king', an expression which implies some freedom of choice, though the phrase should not be further interpreted as implying the existence of a clearly defined body of electors. The parallel phrase *ceosan to hlaforde* meant the giving of allegiance to some higher authority, an act involving the relationship of lord and man. The death of a king meant that his nobles were deprived of the offices which they had previously held and consequently of the profits arising therefrom. The appointment of his successor was not automatic on the one hand nor was it an act of election on the other, but something between the two, consisting in the choice or selection of the most suitable man from among those who were otherwise qualified, the most important qualification being that of royal birth. Although within the historical period there was not usually more than one man holding the title and office of king in each kingdom, traces are to be found in Sussex and Essex of a different system which recognized the contemporary existence of three or four kings within the same kingdom.

Not less than twelve kingdoms existed in England about the year 600. There is no reason to think that they were in any way tribal or national in origin. There does not seem to be any significant relationship between the distribution of the Anglo-Saxon kingdoms and the Romano-British *civitates* which had preceded them, save in the case of Kent and possibly Sussex, but in both these instances physical geography may well have been the deciding factor, and in general it may be thought that most of the Anglo-Saxon kingdoms came into being through military conquest and the disintegration of any centralizing authority which may have existed at the time of the invasion. Between 600 and 865 there was a substantial advance towards political unity as authority came to lie with the three or four more powerful kingdoms whose rulers were able to reduce the status of their weaker neighbours to that of dependent provinces. In this way Kent, Sussex, Essex, Lindsey and Wight, as well as the *Hwicce* and the *Magonsætan*, all of which were once independent states ruled by their own kings, gradually ceased to possess any political importance save as elements within a larger state. The Scandinavian invasions, by virtually destroying all save one of those larger units, played a decisive part in the creation of the English monarchy.

Although it was long before the power of an English king became so great that the country could not contain more than one at any time, the pre-eminence of certain kings above their fellow kings was recognized from very early times. In a chapter which is primarily concerned with an account of the pagan reaction in south-eastern England after the death of Æthelberht, Bede describes Æthelberht as the third king who governed all the southern provinces of the English race, and the word he uses is *imperavit* which in this context is undoubtedly intended to signify something more than *regnavit*.

At this point Bede interrupts the flow of his narrative in order to amplify his remark about the peculiar distinction of Æthelberht and the interruption takes the form of a list containing altogether seven names, two earlier and four later than Æthelberht, of other kings who had been similarly distinguished. The first name is that of Ælle whose arrival in England is placed under the year 477 in the *Chronicle* and who came to be regarded as the founder of the South Saxon kingdom. The second name in the list is that of Ceawlin, a king of the West Saxons, who flourished about a century later than the times with which Ælle is associated. Enough is known of the activities of Ceawlin to show that he was prominent in his day and that it was he who was responsible for the conquest of much of southern England from the British. The third was Æthelberht of Kent. It may be noted that his reign coincided almost exactly with that of Æthelfrith of Northumbria of whom Bede says that he conquered more British territory than any other English king, but despite his conquests Bede does not describe him as holding *imperium*. Fourth in the list is Rædwald of East Anglia, of whom Bede says that he was gaining the leadership—*ducatus*—for his own kingdom while Æthelberht was still ruling Kent. This phrase seems to suggest that the *ducatus* or *imperium* was a condition which was capable of at least some kind of definition and which conferred substantial benefits upon its holder. It will be observed that the first four in this list were all rulers of one or other of the kingdoms south of Humber. The next three, Edwin, Oswald and Osuiu, were all kings of Northumbria, but in addition to their extensive northern territories, they all held dominion over the southern provinces. The reality of this control seems to be underlined by Bede's words about Edwin of whom he said that he had authority over all the people of Britain, English and British alike, save only the people of Kent.

After referring to Osuiu, Bede seems to have thought that he had digressed far enough from his purpose in this chapter, which was to trace the events following the death of Æthelberht of Kent, and with the words *sed haec postmodum* he returns from his digression. Bede's list supplies the names of six kings who ruled variously in Wessex, Kent, East Anglia and Northumbria and in general succession. Their joint reigns covered approximately a hundred years from *c.* 570 to 671. Ælle, the first in the list, stands apart as one who died long before Ceawlin's reign began (see above, p. 49). Bede evidently intended to return to this topic at a later stage and perhaps to add further names to the list for the period between 671 and 731, but unfortunately he never did so. Nevertheless it ought not to be assumed from Bede's seeming oversight that there were no kings during this later period holding a position of similar eminence above their fellow rulers. It has been demonstrated from other sources that Æthelbald and Offa, the two great Mercian kings whose reigns spanned the greater part of the eighth century, held a position similar to that which Bede ascribed to the seven named in his list.

Under the year 827 the scribe of the A text of the *Chronicle* records that Egbert, king of the West Saxons, overran Mercia and all that lay south of Humber. He adds that Egbert was the eighth king who was *Bretwalda* and he then recites the names of the previous seven kings who had enjoyed the same distinction. These seven names are those given by Bede from whom they were evidently derived, but the last name in Bede's list is that of Osuiu who died in 670, whereas Egbert belongs to the earlier part of the ninth century. It seems certain that the annalist is in error here by omitting, perhaps deliberately, the names of the two Mercians, Æthelbald and Offa. If these two names are inserted, it is apparent that for rather more than two and a half centuries from late in the sixth to the beginning of the ninth, the English kingdoms were normally subject to a common overlord and that at least by the ninth century the position held by that overlord was so far recognizable that it could be known by a particular title. More often than not the overlord was the ruler of one of the southern English kingdoms, but three successive kings of Northumbria held the position in the seventh century.

The title *Bretwalda* means literally 'Britain-ruler', but its interpretation raises many difficulties. It has been suggested that the expression itself belongs to the sphere of Germanic encomiastic poetry and that it is parallel with such terms as 'bracelet-giver', 'deed-doer' and other comparable expressions in Germanic heroic poetry. Others have interpreted it as a more formal title and have been ready to think that it reflects the acquisition by English rulers of a position of authority established in Britain by the native British as the Roman occupation came to its end. The traditional connexion of Magnus Maximus with Vortigern, the fact that this latter name is apparently a title meaning 'chief lord', the coincidence, if it is nothing more, that the first of the Anglo-Saxon *Bretwaldas* belonged to that part of the country in which Vortigern had sought to establish his authority, the direct claim to rule, not England or the Anglo-Saxons, but Britain which the title itself conveys—these are grounds at least for hesitation before rejecting outright any idea that the growth of political unity among the Anglo-Saxons may have been furthered by a memory inherited from earlier times that Britain was one country to be governed by one ruler. Whatever may be thought of this difficult problem, it is clear that the recognition over a long period of successive kings as holding a pre-eminent position was an important influence in the growth of a strictly monarchical government having authority over the whole country. By the end of Offa's long reign (796), of the dozen or more kingdoms which had existed *c.* 600, there remained only four whose size and resources were great enough to allow a succession of forceful rulers to establish the supremacy of any one of them—Northumbria, Mercia, East Anglia and Wessex.

Mercian supremacy, which had already begun to fade, was finally eclipsed by the victories of Egbert in 825 and 829. Egbert is in fact the only king specifically called *Bretwalda* by a contemporary (the other seven in the *Chronicle* list are all borrowed from Bede who does not himself use the title) and it is of interest to note the phrases used in the *Chronicle* of his rise to that position. First the people of Kent, Surrey, Sussex and Essex 'submitted to him' (*him to cirdon*), and in the same year the king of the East Angles, and his people, 'sought the peace and protection of king Egbert' for fear of the Mercians (*gesohte Ecgbryht cyning him to friþe 7 to mundboran, s.a.* 823 A). And four years later, after overrunning Mercia, Egbert led his army to Dore, on the Northumbrian border and the Northumbrians 'there offered him submission and peace' (*hie him þær eaþmedo budon 7 geþuærnesse, s.a.* 827 A). And again a year later, Egbert led an army against the Welsh 'and he reduced them to humble submission' (7 *he hie to eaþmodre hersumnesse gedyde, s.a.* 828 A). These various expressions show that the basis of Egbert's authority as *Bretwalda* was armed force which might be used to defeat an enemy and impose terms upon him, as happened with Mercia, or which might prompt a weaker state to seek the protection of its wielder against a threatening neighbour, as was the case with East Anglia. It is not to be doubted that such occasions, when terms were imposed or protection granted, were marked by formal gatherings which brought substantial benefits and corresponding obligations to the parties concerned. So long as the succession of other dynasties endured, there could be no single king of England, but we may be sure that both Egbert and his predecessors in the position of *Bretwalda* felt themselves entitled and able to interfere directly in the affairs of states which lay beyond the boundaries of their own kingdoms.

Further movement towards political unity, at first interrupted by the Viking attacks which had already begun before the end of the eighth century, was in the end hastened by those same attacks which destroyed the dynasties of Northumbria, East Anglia and Mercia and left the house of Wessex as the sole survivor. The supremacy of Wessex under Egbert was short-lived and almost a century passed before another member of the house, Edward the Elder, found himself established in a position of authority similar to that which had been momentarily achieved by his great-grandfather, but the basis of Edward's authority was very much wider than his great-grandfather's had been. In 918 he was recognized by all the people of Mercia, English and Danes alike, as well as by a number of Welsh princes and their subjects who 'sought him as their lord' (*hine sohton him to hlaforde, s.a.* 922 A) and his power was further extended in 920 when the king of Scots and all the Scottish people 'chose him as father and lord' (*hine geces þa to fæder 7 to hlaforde, s.a.* 924 A). All the people of Northumbria and the king of the Strathclyde Welsh likewise submitted to him.

With these events it may be said that a kingdom of England ruled by a monarch had come into being, but its continued existence depended almost wholly upon a succession of kings who could fight and win battles. Such kings were found both in Athelstan whose victory at *Brunanburh* in 937 confirmed him in the position which he had already established for himself at the great gathering at the Eamont ten years previously, and in his successor and brother Edmund whose military strength was great enough to enable him to repair the losses sustained in a Scandinavian assault delivered immediately after Athelstan's death. The expulsion of Eric Bloodaxe in 954 and the consequent extinction of the Norse line of rulers in York marked another important advance. Soon afterwards there was a temporary split in the realm when the Mercians and Northumbrians rejected the rule of Eadwig of Wessex in favour of his brother, Edgar, but on the death of Eadwig in 959, Edgar succeeded peacefully to the whole kingdom. Edgar's reign, and particularly the ceremonial attending his coronation, marks the consummation of this long and slow movement towards political unity. The recognition of Edgar's position as king of England is embodied in the tradition, seemingly well-founded, which tells how the other kings in Britain came to do him homage at Chester and rowed him in a boat on the Dee.

3. KING AND COURT

(a) Ceremonial

Nothing is known of the rites which attended the making of a king in pagan Saxon times and very little even in the early Christian period. Two of the objects found at Sutton Hoo can most readily be interpreted as emblems of sovereignty. One of these is a massive stone object fashioned in the manner of a whetstone but clearly never intended to be used as such. Its tapering ends terminate each in a lobed knob originally painted red and encased within a bronze framework. A human mask is cut on each of the four stone faces at either end. There are no known parallels to this remarkable object, and even though its meaning is never likely to be wholly understood, we can hardly doubt that it was an emblem of authority, pagan rather than Christian, and that it was used on ceremonial occasions. The other object is an iron

standard, something over 6 ft. high, bearing at its upper end a
bronze stag with spreading antlers and so fashioned at its lower
end that it could be stood upright in the ground. Bede records of
Edwin, king of Northumbria, that standards (*vexilla*) were carried
before him in time of battle and that when he rode through his
kingdom in peace-time he was preceded by a standard-bearer
(*signifer*). In addition, he had a particular kind of standard which,
according to Bede, the Romans called *tufa* and the English *thuuf*.
In addition to the *tufa*, Vegetius mentions several other kinds of
standard used by the Romans. Some of these were decorated
with animals. There are several references to gilded banners in
Beowulf and in one instance to a banner bearing the emblem of
a boar's head, an emblem which was also used to decorate helmets.

The expression *feng to rice* commonly used by the *Chronicle*
to record the accession of a king in itself yields no indication of
the accompanying ceremonies. On a few occasions the expression
to cyninge gehalgod is used. *Gehalgian* is the word which is normally used of the consecration of bishops and churches in Anglo-
Saxon texts, and it is a clear indication of ecclesiastical influence
in the development of a ritual for the making of kings. An
O.E. *gecoronian* is recorded, but it is an unfamiliar word and
there is no doubt that consecration, presumably by anointing, was
a much more important part of the ritual than the placing of a
crown upon the king's head. The first Anglo-Saxon king of whom
Christian consecration is recorded was Ecgferth, son of Offa, who
was consecrated (*to cyninge gehalgod*) in 787 while his father was
still alive. At this time Alcuin was at the court of Charlemagne
and six years previously Charlemagne's two sons had been
anointed by the Pope. In 796 Eadwulf was consecrated king of
Northumbria in the church of St Peter at York. The Northumbrian annals which tell of this event also record that Coenwulf
received the diadem of the kingdom of Mercia in the same year
(*diadema regni Merciorum suscepit*)[1] and that in 802 Egbert of
Wessex placed the diadem of the whole kingdom upon his head
(*diadema totius regni capiti imposuit*).[2] It is not certain, however,

[1] Symeon of Durham, *Historia Regum*, s.a. 796.
[2] *Ibid.* s.a. 802.

whether these words refer to a tangible emblem of sovereignty or whether they are merely figurative expressions.

A detailed account of the coronation of Charlemagne in Rome on Christmas Day of 800 reached Northumbria soon after the event.[1] The ceremonial included the robing of Charlemagne in royal purple and the placing of a gold crown upon his head and a sceptre in his hand. In 853 Alfred, then a child of only four years, visited Rome, where the pope invested him with consular insignia. This ceremony which may indeed have included the act of placing a crown upon his head, was misinterpreted, perhaps by Alfred himself, as marking his coronation as king. In much later times the monks of Westminster, seeking to establish their claim that the English kings had always been crowned in the abbey, went as far as they could with Alfred by asserting that the crown with which he was crowned in Rome was brought back to England and still preserved among the regalia in the Abbey. The 'crown of king Alfred', which is alleged to have been melted down at the time of the Commonwealth, seems not in fact to have been ascribed to him before the fourteenth century. If this was an ancient crown, it may have been Edward the Confessor's, but it is very unlikely to have been Alfred's.[2]

Dunstan's earliest biographer tells how those who went to recall the young Eadwig from his amusements to his proper place at the coronation feast found the royal crown, wrought of gold, silver and precious stones, lying neglected upon the floor, but perhaps this is no more than fictitious colouring in a story which was intended to discredit Eadwig. The *ordo* which was compiled for Edgar's coronation in 973, provided for the covering of the head with a crown. In the Bayeux tapestry Edward the Confessor is shown wearing what may be loosely called a crown, but which is really no more than a narrow fillet of metal, presumably gold, which encircles his head and from which, towards the front, rise three gold fleurs-de-lys. He carries a sceptre in his left hand.

[1] Symeon of Durham, *Historia Regum, s.a.* 800.
[2] See the comments by W. H. Stevenson, *Asser's Life of King Alfred* (Oxford, 1904), pp. 180–3. Stevenson effectively discredited the legend of Alfred's crown, but it is repeated by O. Warner, *The Crown Jewels* (King Penguin Books; London, 1951), p. 9.

Harold is shown with a similar coronet or diadem and carrying an orb in his left hand and a sceptre in his right.

The scene of royal consecrations varied. Athelstan was consecrated at Kingston-on-Thames on 4 September 925 and so also was Æthelred the Unready in 978. There were ceremonies in Cnut's reign both in Oxford and London, and Edward the Confessor was crowned at Winchester. The coronation of Edgar took place at Bath in 973 after he had been reigning for fourteen years and only two years before his death. The delay may well have been deliberate, for in 973 Edgar reached the age of thirty, the minimum canonical age for ordination to the priesthood.

The order of service which was compiled specially for the occasion laid great emphasis upon the religious nature of the ceremony, thereby exalting the part played by the Church. An eyewitness has left a vivid description of this great occasion. The king, robed and already wearing his crown, was led in procession to the church by two bishops, each of whom held him by the hand. When they had entered the church, the king removed the crown from his head and prostrated himself before the altar while Dunstan led the singing of the *Te Deum*. When this hymn of praise was finished, the bishops raised the prostrate king who then took a coronation oath in the form of answers to questions put to him by the archbishop. He undertook that true peace should be observed throughout his kingdom, that robberies and all other evils should be forbidden and that equity and mercy should temper all judgements. When these promises had been given, Dunstan offered prayers for the king who was then solemnly anointed to the acclamation of *Vivat rex in aeternum*. The archbishop then placed a ring upon the king's finger, girded him with a sword, put the crown upon his head and pronounced a blessing. Mass was celebrated and finally the king was enthroned in company with Dunstan and Oswald. These ceremonies were followed by a coronation banquet.

It is apparent both from this account and from the order of service that the main emphasis of the ceremony lay in the solemn act whereby the king, like priest or bishop, was consecrated to the service of God. Constitutionally the most important innovation was the taking of the coronation oath. Edmund (939–6) had required an oath of allegiance from his subjects and with Edgar's coronation we get the counterpart to this in the *promissio* or oath taken by the king towards his subjects, thus recognizing the principle that the king is under obligations towards his subjects. A similar oath was taken by Æthelred the Unready. The elaborate ceremonial surrounding the coronation of Edgar and the prominent part played in it by the Church did much to enhance the dignity of the office of king apart from the personal failings of individual holders and to create an attitude towards it which enabled an eleventh-century writer to say that a Christian king is Christ's deputy among Christian people.

(b) *Household*

It need hardly be said that the king's household is as old as the rule of kings, and there can never have been a time when attendance upon a ruler did not bring with it opportunities both for personal advancement and for exercising influence upon decisions of all kinds. No remains have yet been discovered of any Anglo-Saxon royal dwelling place, or even of a nobleman's house. A palace existed at Westminster between the abbey and the river before the Norman Conquest. Edward the Confessor may be seen depicted in the Bayeux tapestry seated on a throne in a lofty hall whose outer walls seem to be represented as stone and in the death-bed scene the king is shown in an upper story, but it remains uncertain whether the tapestry was worked in Normandy or England and therefore whether the buildings represented by it in England are of Anglo-Saxon or Norman style. Any substantial building made of wood, the customary building material of the Anglo-Saxons, tends to take the form of an oblong hall. The hall called *Heorot*, described in *Beowulf*, was of this shape with wooden walls clamped together with iron. Benches were ranged along its sides wide enough to allow men to sleep on them, its floor was paved and variegated and its doors wide enough to admit horses. On festive occasions its walls were hung with tapestry. But *Heorot* is set in Denmark late in the fifth or early in the sixth century and even though the discoveries at Sutton Hoo have confirmed the reality behind what may have seemed fanciful imaginings in *Beowulf*, it would be wiser to wait upon the hope of archaeological discovery before supposing that Anglo-Saxon kings lived in halls such as Hrothgar built. The hope is not entirely a vain one, since the sites of several seventh-century royal estates are known at least by name. One such lay at Rendlesham in East Anglia and near to Sutton Hoo whose several mounds in all probability represent the royal burial ground. Others lay at Yeavering in the north-eastern foothills of Cheviot—this was abandoned in favour of another estate at an unidentified place called *Maelmin*—and at Catterick which was the scene of a royal marriage in the eighth century, and near the Yorkshire Derwent.[1]

An Anglo-Saxon royal household of the seventh century seems not to have been greatly different either in its membership or in its ideals from the household of a Germanic chieftain in the first century A.D. In his *Germania* Tacitus noted the virtues and characteristics which distinguished the members of a chieftain's following or *comitatus*, as well as the chieftain himself. For the chief it was a disgrace to be surpassed in valour by his companions and for the companions it was lifelong infamy to leave the battle-field alive after their chief had fallen. Their whole duty lay in defending and protecting their chief who in return was expected to reward their self-sacrifice with the spoils of war as well as their daily sustenance. These are the ideals of the Teutonic Heroic Age which find expression in heroic poetry where the companions of heroes are constantly faced with situations in which they experience the rewards of loyalty and the penalties of failure to sacrifice themselves to the utmost in defence of their chief. Outside heroic poetry it is sometimes necessary to look a little way below the surface, but the same ideals are reflected in the court of seventh-century Northumbria beneath the Christian colouring of Bede's *History*. The story of Osuine may serve to illustrate the point.

---

[1] References will be found to all these sites in Bede's *History*. On Rendlesham see R.L.S. Bruce-Mitford, *Proc. Suffolk Inst. Arch. and Nat. Hist.* XXIV (1948), pp. 228–51. An aerial photograph showing ground markings at Old Yeavering and at Milfield nearby is reproduced in D. Knowles and J. K. St Joseph, *Monastic Sites from the Air* (Cambridge, 1952), pls. 125, 126. Excavations were begun at Old Yeavering in 1953 and have been proceeding since. They have revealed extensive signs of habitation, but no results have yet been published.

Osuine belonged to the house of Deira where he ruled for some years in great prosperity, while Osuiu reigned in Bernicia. Later the two disagreed and went to war. Their armies assembled near Catterick and Osuine, perceiving the enemy to be in much greater strength, dismissed his own army. One faithful companion, Tondheri, remained with him, and the two concealed themselves in the house of one whom Osuine regarded as the most trust-worthy of his followers, but he betrayed the trust and Osuine was killed. Even Bede was moved to stern language by the heinous-ness of this crime brought about by the treachery of a trusted warrior. Bede is full of praise for the murdered Osuine and it is of interest to note the qualities for which he praises him—his tall stature and graceful appearance, his friendly courtesy and his generosity, qualities which inspired men of the highest rank to come from neighbouring provinces to seek service with him. Other stories, such as that of Lilla who leapt forward to take him-self the dagger blow a would-be assassin aimed at King Edwin, and that of the vain attempts to persuade Rædwald of East Anglia to murder Edwin who was then seeking refuge as an exile at Rædwald's court, these demonstrate the same standards of values which were far from being the mere conventions of literary artists.

An incident of later times which is recorded in great detail in the *Chronicle* provides a perfect example of the same ideals in practice. It occurred in 786[1] when Cynewulf, king of Wessex, was killed in a surprise attack made by night. Although the dead king's thegns found themselves in a hopeless position, they refused to surrender, preferring to fight 'until they all lay dead, except for one Welsh hostage, and he was severely wounded'. Yet again a century later, to die for one's lord, in battle, even though he himself had fallen already, and to fly in disgrace from the battlefield, are represented in the poem on the battle of Maldon (991) as the two extremes of noble and evil conduct. Kings and heroes, loyalty and treachery, self-sacrifice and rewards, these are the themes which constantly occur in the works of those who wrote about court life in early days. Till at least the eighth century, the Anglo-Saxon royal household wears an almost wholly

---

[1] The story is related under the year 755 in the *Chronicle*.

military aspect and there is little room for much beyond. The personality of the king himself created, or failed to create, a household to which fighting men were attracted. The main duties of such men were courage and loyalty, their rewards the simple ones of land, treasure, food and drink.

The influence of the Church was the most important factor tending to direct the royal household away from the ideals governing the *comitatus* and towards more sophisticated ways. Augustine's mission was directed at the rulers of kingdoms from the first and throughout the seventh century missionary progress was dependent on close and lasting contact with the royal households. The wife of Æthelberht of Kent had a priest in attendance and in the middle of the seventh century there was a priest called Utta who was held in high honour at the Northumbrian court. A few years later another priest, one of four brothers of whom two became bishops, attended Æthelwald in Deira. Aldfrith of Northumbria (685–704) anticipated Alfred in his cultivation of letters and learning. His interest in such matters is strikingly illustrated by his gift of an estate to Monkwearmouth in exchange for a work on cosmography which Benedict Biscop had brought from Rome. Bede dedicated his *Ecclesiastical History* to Ceolwulf (729–37) and both he and his successor, Eadberht (737–58), gave up the throne to enter the religious life as monks. It is unfortunate that there is no contemporary account of the Mercian court during the reigns of Æthelbald and Offa, but the establishment of the archbishopric at Lichfield and the reform of the coinage are two incidents of Offa's reign which illustrate the growing complexity of the affairs of government.

There is a fuller picture of the royal household in Alfred's reign to be gained from Asser, his biographer.[1] Alfred is said to have built new halls and royal chambers in both stone and wood and to have reconstructed older stone buildings in more suitable places. Both from England and from abroad he gathered about him men of learning to assist him in his educational work. Many

[1] A note of scepticism about the authenticity of at least parts of Asser's *Life of Alfred* is sounded by V. H. Galbraith in *Historical Research in Medieval England* (Creighton Lecture in History, 1949; Athlone Press, 1951), but most scholars accept the work as genuine.

visitors came to the court, among them two sea-captains, Wulfstan and Ohthere, who told him what they had seen on their
travels. The sons of noblemen came to the court to receive their
education. Alfred's reign seems to mark a stage in the process
whereby the king's companions gradually ceased to be in direct
personal attendance upon the king and became instead landed
proprietors whose duties at the court were more limited. We are
told by Asser that Alfred divided his companions into three groups,
each to live at the court for one month and to return to their own
estates for the next two.

The court was also attended by priests (*mæsse-preostas*) who
are called chaplains (*cappellani*) by Asser, but this latter name is
a Frankish term which seems not to have come into regular use
in England until after the Norman Conquest. In addition to their
religious duties such men are likely to have been concerned from
early times with the keeping of records and with the composition
of written instruments of government. It is probable that something closely resembling the king's writ of later times was in use
during Alfred's reign, and for the composition of such writs, as
well as of royal charters, proclamations, legal codes and other
documents concerning the business of government, we may
suppose the existence of a royal secretariat which had passed
beyond the elementary stages of its development before the
Norman Conquest, though perhaps it had not developed so far
that it can properly be called a Chancery. It has not yet been
shown beyond all doubt that the term *cancellarius* was used in
England before the Norman Conquest, but the evidence relating
to Regenbald, a priest first of Edward the Confessor and later of
William I, comes very near to indicating that he was the first
Chancellor of England both in fact and in name.[1]

Alfred reorganized the finances of his household and Asser's
account of this is the earliest evidence for the manner in which
the king's revenue was employed. The whole was divided into two
parts, of which one was given to the Church. The other part was
itself divided into three shares, one for the nobles in attendance
at his court, another for his workmen and a third for those who

[1] F. E. Harmer, *Anglo-Saxon Writs* (Manchester, 1952), pp. 57–61, 211–14.

visited the court. The sources of the royal income in the Anglo-Saxon period were many and various. An important item was the food-rent, known in Old English as *feorm* and in Latin as *firma*, which was due from all lands in the kingdom save those which were specially exempted from it. In origin it consisted of an amount of provision sufficient to maintain the king and his household for a day and a night. It was imposed upon groups of villages and was generally paid in the form of ale, corn, livestock, honey, cheese and the like, though occasionally it was commuted for a money payment. In addition the king received tribute from subject kings, as well as income from the royal estates, from the proceeds of justice, from tolls on trade, from the sale of privileges and from a great variety of customary dues. For most of the Anglo-Saxon period kings moved about the country without any permanent capital, living upon royal estates or upon their subjects. There is some evidence that by the beginning of the eleventh century Winchester had come to be regarded as the permanent resting-place of the king's treasure chests. It is unlikely that any substantial part of an Anglo-Saxon king's revenue was in the form of bullion and it is certain that there was no distinction between the king's own income and the national income. Although there is little evidence for the existence of a specialized office of Treasurer during the Anglo-Saxon period, it seems probable that the raising of taxes to pay the men who fought against the Danes and to pay also the very large sums of tribute which were exacted by the Danes during the reign of Æthelred the Unready would demand a considerable degree of organization.

The growth of lay offices in the royal household with specialized duties did not proceed very far in the Anglo-Saxon period, though some positions originating in intimate household duties had begun to be of importance by the tenth century. Alfred's will seems to hint at some kind of differentiation of rank among court officials and to suggest that there were groups possessing a recognized precedence over others, but there is no reference to individual household officials by title. Eadred's will, which dates from 955 or a little earlier, is more detailed. After making bequests to the archbishop, the bishops and the ealdormen, Eadred leaves sums of money to each duly appointed seneschal, chamberlain and butler, to the priests whom he had placed in charge of his relics, to his other priests, to each duly appointed steward and to other members of his household.

The term translated 'seneschal' is O.E. *discðegn*, a word which suggests that the person so called was originally concerned with the king's plate and service at the royal table.[1] It is equated in vocabularies with Latin *discifer* or *dapifer*. Charters of Eadwig and Edgar are witnessed by *disciferi* and the first genuine appearance of this title among the witnesses of charters seems to belong to the reign of Athelstan. The office of seneschal was not exclusive to the king. In the record of a lawsuit dating *c.* 990, there is a reference to Æfic, the seneschal of the æthelings (i.e. of the princes), and one Leofwine, the æthelings' seneschal, was among those who witnessed a lease of land by the community at Sherborne *c.* 1030.

The term translated chamberlain is *hræglðegn* whose first element means 'robe', 'clothing'. The holder of this office was evidently concerned with the royal apartments and in particular with the king's wardrobe. He is perhaps to be equated with an official who is sometimes found witnessing charters with the title *burðegn*. The office of butler, translated from O.E. *byrele* and equivalent to the Latin *pincerna*, is likely to have developed at an early stage in a society much given to feasting and drinking. The word itself occurs in the laws of Æthelberht of Kent, though it is there used in the sense of serving-maid. Cup-bearers (*byrelas*) are mentioned in *Beowulf*.

4. THE KING'S COUNCIL

The history of the Anglo-Saxon king's council can be, and perhaps ought to be, approached from two different points of view—by the study of what seem to be the established facts within the period and by considering the interpretation put upon those facts by successive generations of modern historians. Where so much

---

[1] Professor B. Dickins draws my attention to the occurrence of the word *distein*, evidently from O.E. *discðegn*, in the laws of Howel the Good (Hywel Dda) who is known to have visited frequently at the court of Athelstan; A. W. Wade-Evans, *Welsh Medieval Law* (Oxford, 1909), index under *distein* and *distein brenhines*.

of English constitutional history turns upon the relations between king and parliament, it is all but impossible to escape comparisons between the composition and functions of the medieval and modern parliament and those of what has been taken for its Anglo-Saxon counterpart. Kemble, writing in 1849, regarded the *witan* as a representative body in a real sense. Just as the conquest of Britain was achieved in a series of undertakings carried out by the counsel, leave and consent of their various members, so in their various assemblies the Anglo-Saxons met as free men on terms of equality. Realizing the difficulties entailed in attending such assemblies and the burdens which attendance laid upon their members, Kemble argued to a representative system whereby the mass of the people were relieved from this duty. He maintained that the signatures of the nobility who witnessed the transactions of the *witan* were unquestionably looked upon as representing the whole body of the people. He admitted that in Anglo-Saxon times the members were not chosen from a defined body of electors, but he implied that such had once been the case and he thought that there might have been separate bodies for the clergy and the laity. In other words, Kemble was representing the contemporary reform movement not as seeking to introduce innovations, but as a return to the Anglo-Saxon commonwealth system.

Liebermann, writing in 1913 in a book which he called *The National Assembly*, held a curiously high opinion of the views of Kemble who, he maintained, had drawn a firm and clear picture which had left little for Stubbs to improve upon, but in fact Stubbs[1] differed from Kemble on a number of important points. For example he held, rightly as we should still think, that the *witan* was not representative in any modern sense. Its members were the mere retainers of the king who could only be regarded as representing the people by an uneasy fiction. He made two points which still seem to be important, first that each kingdom had its own assembly and that it was only the ecclesiastical councils which met frequently from the time of Theodore onwards that could be regarded as overriding provincial boundaries and therefore in a sense national, and secondly that the larger the council

[1] W. Stubbs, *Constitutional History of England*, I, ch. vi (Oxford, 1897).

and the larger the number of signatories witnessing its acts, the greater the efficacy of the acts so witnessed. Effectiveness and security were achieved by greater publicity rather than by the observance of legal or constitutional routine. In arguing thus Stubbs had moved a long way from Kemble, but both he and Liebermann maintained that, even if the *witan* took on the appearance of a king's council in the seventh century, this was only because of a movement away from an earlier republican age. Chadwick, writing in 1905,[1] a few years before Liebermann, had indeed effectively demonstrated that no trace of an elective principle being applied to the Anglo-Saxon *witan* was anywhere to be found in the records. Though he wrote of the assembly as the National Council, he was in no doubt that it was from the first an aristocratic body and that its lay members were the king's nominees. However far back the records carried, there was no trace of the lost republican age which the nineteenth century wished to find. To Sir Frank Stenton, the *witan* is no longer the National Assembly but the King's Council.

The full title *witenagemot* is not found in common use in written records until the eleventh century. *Witena* is the genitive plural of a weak masculine noun *wita* which in its primary sense means 'one who knows'. Even though Latin writers commonly translated *witan* by *sapientes*, it would be foolish to lay too much stress on this primary meaning. The men called *witan* were not necessarily any more distinguished for their wisdom than were the *ealdormenn* for their age. *Witan* in fact means 'the king's councillors' and *witenagemot* is the meeting of the king's councillors, not the meeting of the wise men. Another and significant name used by Latin writers is *synodus* which became O.E. *seonoð* and which did not necessarily mean an ecclesiastical assembly though it is indicative of ecclesiastical influence on the growth of the king's council. *Seonoð* (*synodus*) and *gemot* may be different names for the same thing.

Even though it may not be possible to demonstrate the fact in every instance, there can be little doubt that something resembling a primitive king's council functioned in each of the seventh-

---

[1] H. M. Chadwick, *Studies on Anglo-Saxon Institutions*, ch. ix.

century kingdoms. Such bodies may in fact have been no more than the king's household itself attending to matters of state as they arose. Bede says that Æthelberht of Kent issued his code of laws with the advice of his councillors (*cum consilio sapientium*). The code of king Wihtred of Kent, dating 695, begins with a prologue which shows the royal council performing what long remained one of its chief functions, assisting the king in the promulgation of laws. It refers to the summoning of a deliberative assembly of laity and clergy which proceeded to draw up the decrees which we now know as the Laws of Wihtred and to add them to the legal usages of Kent. The only individuals referred to by name or title are the king himself, the archbishop of Canterbury and the bishop of Rochester. At about the same time Ine, king of Wessex, issued a code of laws in whose compilation he had been assisted by his father, by two bishops and by all his ealdormen and the chief councillors of his people.

The gathering of a large assembly of this kind should by no means be interpreted as meaning that the persons assembled had the right to be consulted, but rather as indicating a desire to secure that the laws should be the better observed by the mere fact of their being made known to and approved by those who mattered most in the affairs of the kingdom. The close concern of the king's council with the promulgation of laws can be observed throughout the Anglo-Saxon period. In the days of Wihtred and Ine in the seventh century such laws were of limited application geographically, but by the time of Æthelred the Unready their scope had become national. Three of Æthelred's codes were drawn up at meetings of his council held respectively at Woodstock, Wantage and Bath, and a code of Cnut's was compiled in a similar way at Winchester. For some five centuries the laws of kings were in fact normally approved and sanctioned by the king's councillors and such long-continuing practice cannot have failed to enhance the authority of the king's council.

A famous passage in Bede's *History* illustrates a meeting of the king's council in seventh-century Northumbria. Edwin, as yet heathen, had been called upon by Paulinus to redeem a pledge, given in exile, that he would become Christian when the appointed time came. He replied that he must first confer with his friends and councillors among the nobility (*cum amicis principibus et consiliariis suis*). A meeting was accordingly summoned (*habito enim cum sapientibus consilio*)—it may be suspected that Bede wrote *sapientibus* for the vernacular *witum*—and each in turn was asked what he thought. Coifi, the heathen priest, was the first to speak. It was to one of the nobles (*alius optimatum regis*) that Bede attributed the famous comparison of the life of man with the flight of a sparrow through the hall while the storms of winter raged outside and the king sat at meat with his thegns and ealdormen (*cum ministris et ducibus*). Here Bede has left us a picture within a picture, the Northumbrian *witan* performing one of its main functions, that of deliberative discussion, and the royal household itself used as illustration of an argument. The two are surely the same and both scarcely distinguishable from the *comitatus* of Tacitus.

The change from this kind of gathering to the more formal assemblies of the tenth and eleventh centuries necessarily kept pace with the growth of the monarchy and the increasing complexity of the business of government. From the first the Church was closely concerned. The synod of Whitby is a notable instance of a predominantly Northumbrian assembly whose business was wholly ecclesiastical, but whose decisions affected the laity as well as the clergy. The reorganization of the Church which followed during the primacy of Theodore led to the summoning of a general council of the whole English Church at Hertford in 672. One of its decisions was that a synod of the Church should be held each year at *Clofeshoh*. At one such synod held in 747, there were present not only the archbishop and all the bishops of the southern province, but also Æthelbald, king of Mercia, together with his governors and ealdormen (*cum suis principibus ac ducibus*).

From the second half of the eighth century when Offa held a dominating position in England south of Humber there are a number of documents which indicate the frequent holding of assemblies. There is no complete record of all the proceedings of any one of these assemblies, but from surviving charters which form part of the record of what was done, it appears that their business was frequently concerned with problems arising from the transfer or ownership of land. A charter recording part of the proceedings of an assembly held at Brentford in 781 may serve to illustrate this aspect of the work of an eighth-century assembly. Much of the document is written in the first person, though it is not the same person throughout. The first speaker is the bishop of the *Hwicce* whose seat was at Worcester. He records that a dispute had arisen between Offa and the church of Worcester about certain small pieces of land at Bath and elsewhere. Offa had alleged that the community at Worcester was holding un-lawful possession of property to which they had no hereditary right and which had belonged to his predecessor Æthelbald. After the bishop had made careful inquiry, the dispute was brought before a synodal council (*in sinodali conciliabulo*) at Brentford. It was agreed on the one side that Worcester should hand over the property at Bath to Offa and on the other that Offa should confirm Worcester in possession of the other properties in dispute. Towards the end of the document Offa, represented as speaking in the first person, confirms this decision. The document ends with the names of those who witnessed these decisions. They consist of Offa's own name, those of the archbishop of Canter-bury, of twelve bishops representing between them all the sees of the southern province and of six men with the title *princeps*, a title implying that the men who hold it were members of the lay nobility.

The synods which were held a few years later in connexion with the visit of the two papal legates were on a much larger scale. After going first to Canterbury, the two legates met Offa of Mercia and Cynewulf of Wessex. They then separated, one going to Northumbria and the other to Mercia. An assembly held in Northumbria was attended by the archbishop of York, by the bishops of the other northern sees and by members of the nobility (called *judices, optimates et nobiles*). A similar assembly in Mercia was attended by the archbishop of Canterbury, the southern bishops, several abbots and a number of laymen variously styled *dux* or *comes*. These two assemblies were clearly important formal gatherings whose membership transcended narrow provincial boundaries. Their business was primarily ecclesiastical and we should naturally call them synods, but in so doing we should be implying a distinction between Church and State such as contemporaries would not have recognized. That most surviving records of the assemblies of these times relate to ecclesiastical affairs is simply a reflection of the fact that the clergy knew how to write and appreciated the importance of the written record of what had been agreed.

The Legatine mission took place only a few years before the first of the Viking attacks. There is a fairly long period, ending with the reign of Edward the Elder, for which there is little or no evidence about the composition of the king's council, but with the reign of Athelstan there is again a series of charters recording and witnessing some of its decisions and revealing the existence of a body very different in its composition from the eighth-century Mercian assemblies and with the lay nobility now present on a large scale. Meetings of this greatly enlarged council took place frequently during Athelstan's reign, though so far as can be seen neither the time nor the place was subject to particular rules, although councils were commonly held at Christmas, Easter and Pentecost. There is no document dealing with it in general terms, and for information about its membership and its business we are dependent still upon the charters which it issued, remembering that such documents are not full records of its proceedings but testimony only of a particular piece of business transacted. A document issued after a meeting of the king's council at the royal manor of Frome on 18 December 934 may serve as a particular instance. The document records the gift by Athelstan of thirty hides of land to the community at the Old Minster in Winchester. This transaction, small in itself, is witnessed by no fewer than forty-five persons. Athelstan himself headed the list of witnesses and he was followed by Howel, called Underking. This was Howel the Good, king of Dyfed, who attests a number of Athelstan's charters. Next came the archbishops of Canterbury and York, fifteen bishops, one ealdorman and then the names of no fewer than twenty-five men who bear the title *minister*, a word which may be broadly interpreted in this context as thegn.

It is in the largely increased lay element, the *ministri*, that the contrast with the eighth-century synodal councils is most marked. On Kemble's view of the *witan*, these men represented the lower orders in different parts of Athelstan's kingdom. We cannot now admit that the lower orders had any say at all in the affairs of the king's council, but would rather interpret the enlargement of the council to the mere physical enlargement of Athelstan's kingdom, to the resulting difficulty of being in close touch with all parts of it and to the desire of securing greater effectiveness for the decisions reached by widening the limits of those whose agreement was given. It would be folly to suppose that this very large gathering of distinguished people assembled at Frome for the purpose of giving a mere thirty hides of land to the community at Winchester, but their attestation of the gift would undoubtedly give the community much greater security of possession than any less public act would have done. Yet the meeting of the king's council at Frome was by no means the largest of Athelstan's reign. At a council held at Colchester in 931 as many as fifty members of the lay nobility were present.

Surviving records show that the king's council met on at least seventy occasions during the tenth and eleventh centuries and no doubt there were many other meetings of which no record remains. Those of Athelstan's reign seem normally to have been attended by about sixty or seventy men of distinction from among the clergy and the laity. Even though there is no reason to suppose that the king was bound to take the advice of his council, the mere fact of consultation over a long period with the most influential men in the kingdom marked some degree of enfranchisement and prepared the way for occasions when consent might be withheld. It is not possible to define the membership of the council with any precision nor can its functions be exactly described. In practice it was concerned with the drawing up of laws, with the transfer of estates, with foreign affairs and the raising of taxes, and there were brief occasions when virtually the whole government of the country must have rested in its hands. It can hardly be doubted that a body of this kind played an important part in the work of government, particularly in the tenth and eleventh centuries, even though it never established its position so firmly by right that effective government could not continue without it.

5. LOCAL GOVERNMENT

During the tenth century political unity advanced to the point at which the country became a monarchy in the literal sense, a country in which a single king ruled, but apparent unity of this kind could by no means override fundamental divisions which were the legacy of two periods of invasion and settlement, the English in the fifth and sixth centuries and the Scandinavian in the ninth and tenth. Both peoples soon reached a condition in which they could regard themselves as subjects of the same king, whether it was the English Edgar or the Danish Cnut, but the country as a whole remained far removed from uniformity in race, language and custom. Eleventh-century laws recognize a three-fold division into Wessex, Mercia and the Danelaw. Later documents which give a more detailed definition of these divisions indicate that Wessex comprised all the counties adjacent to the sea from Kent to Cornwall and in addition the counties of Surrey, Berkshire, Wiltshire and Somerset. Mercia consisted of the western midlands.

The earliest definition of the boundary between Mercia and what came to be called the Danelaw is to be found in the treaty made between Alfred and Guthrum shortly before 890. It was here agreed that the boundary should be marked by the Thames estuary as far upstream as the Lea. It was then to turn northwards, leaving London itself in Alfred's hands, and to follow the Lea to its source. This course took it along what is still the western boundary of Essex from the Thames northwards to Broxbourne, but at the latter point the Lea swings westwards across Hertfordshire and into Bedfordshire, taking its rise near Dunstable. From the source of the Lea the boundary was to run in a straight line to Bedford and thence it was to follow the Ouse upstream to the point at which it was crossed by Watling Street, that is at Fenny Stratford. It is interesting to note that the boundary thus defined, while following part of the existing boundary of Essex, a county which had once formed an independent kingdom, nowhere coincides with the boundaries of Hertfordshire, Bedfordshire or Buckinghamshire. This last shire, though mainly on the English side of the border, was later reckoned to be part of the Danelaw. Later evidence assigns eight shires to Mercia, those of Oxford, Warwick, Gloucester, Worcester, Hereford, Stafford, Salop and Chester.

The remainder of the country as far north as Tees comprised the Danelaw, a term which originally referred to Danish law or custom, in contrast with Mercian, West-Saxon or other custom, and which came to be used territorially of the area in which such Danish law prevailed. The Danelaw was far from being uniform within itself. East Anglia became a Danish kingdom for a short while, but kings soon gave place to earls. The south-eastern midlands show certain peculiarities which distinguish them both from East Anglia and from the counties between Welland and Humber. In this latter area lay a Danish confederation known as the Five Boroughs, the boroughs in question being Stamford, Leicester, Derby, Nottingham and Lincoln. And beyond the Five Boroughs lay the kingdom of York, the seat of a line of Scandinavian kings until the expulsion of Eric Bloodaxe in 954. After Eric's death Northumbria was ruled by earls. Their territories were not reckoned to be part of the Danelaw and they were indeed beyond the effective control of the central government.

(a) The Shires

Saving only the four most northerly counties, together with Lancashire and Rutland, all the English counties were in existence and serving as the basis of local administration at the time of the Norman Conquest. Their boundaries were substantially the same then as they are now. Eadred's will, dating *c*. 955, provides evidence which demonstrates the existence of the shires south of Thames a hundred years and more before this date. Eadred bequeathed 1,600 pounds for the relief of his people from need and from the ravages of Viking armies. This sum was to be divided into four lots of which one, of 400 pounds, was to be entrusted to the archbishop of Canterbury to help the people of Kent, Surrey, Sussex and Berkshire, and another, also of 400 pounds, to the bishop of Winchester for the people of Hampshire, Wiltshire and Dorset. The sum of 200 pounds was given to Dunstan for the people of Somerset and Devon and another 200 was to be kept at Winchester for whichever shire might need it most. The remaining 400 pounds was entrusted to the bishop of Dorchester for the use of the Mercians. It will be seen that this document refers to all save one of the existing shires south of Thames, the exception being Cornwall, but that there is no reference to the individual shires of Mercia. Two of the southern shires, Kent and Sussex, were originally independent kingdoms which were absorbed in the kingdom of Wessex. Cornwall similarly represents the remnant of a former Welsh kingdom. Most of the other southern shires can be traced back for at least another hundred years before the time of Eadred.

Under the year 837 in the *Chronicle* there is a reference to an engagement between the Danes and the ealdorman Æthelhelm leading the men of Dorset—*mid Dornsætum*. The first element of this name is related to the first element of the name 'Dorchester' and the second element means 'inhabitants', 'dwellers'. This second element in the nominative plural forms *sæte* or *sætan* is commonly found as part of a compound name referring originally to the people inhabiting a particular area and being subsequently transferred to the area inhabited by them. It is found in the midlands also in the Old English names *Tomsætan*, *Wreocensætan* and *Pecsætan* referring respectively to those who dwelt by the Tame, the Wrekin and the Peak, but it now survives only in the two southern English names Dorset and Somerset. The first element of Somerset is to be associated with the first element of Somerton and there is a reference to the *Sumursæte* and their ealdorman under the year 845 in the *Chronicle*. The element 'shire', from O.E. *scir*, is first recorded in association with Dorset in the tenth century. In the case of Somerset it is not recorded before the twelfth century, but the term is used of Wiltshire at a much earlier date. The death of one Æðelm, called ealdorman of Wiltshire, is recorded under 898 in the *Chronicle*—*Æðelm Wiltunscire ealdormon*, but here too the territorial name has displaced an earlier name which referred to the people who lived there rather than to the area in which they lived. As early as 800 the *Chronicle* refers to an engagement in which an ealdorman of the *Hwicce* was defeated by an ealdorman leading the *Wilsætan*, a name which derives its first element from the river-name Wylye. There is a reference to Hampshire, in the form *Hamtunscire*, under the year 755 in the *Chronicle*, but this particular passage cannot safely be used as evidence for the currency of the term 'shire' in the territorial sense at this date.

Evidence of this kind, and similar evidence relating to Berkshire and Surrey, indicates that in the first half of the ninth century there were in Wessex recognizable groups of people who were called by names corresponding with those of the modern counties and who were led in time of war by an official called an ealdorman. By this date the Viking attacks had begun, but they had not yet become so grave a menace as to have had any great effect upon the existing methods of defence and administration. We may therefore regard it as probable that by about the year 800 the kingdom of Wessex was already divided into what we may loosely call shires, even though there may be some anachronism in applying the term to that date, and that such shires were administered by an ealdorman, one of whose functions was to lead his men in battle. A passage in the laws issued *c.* 690 by Ine, king of Wessex, states that as penalty for certain offences an *ealdorman* is to lose his *scir*. This passage might be used as evidence that the West Saxon shires are as old as the seventh century, but the term *scir* in Old English is also used in the abstract sense of 'office'. For example the office of bishop, abbot or bailiff could be called *scir* and it would be unwise to assume that the word *scir* in Ine's code necessarily has the meaning 'shire' which it bore in later times. It is of course impossible to define precisely the areas occupied by the *Wilsætan* or the *Sumursætan* in the ninth century, but it is reasonable to suppose that the requirements of defence, amongst other things, had led to a fairly exact definition of boundaries before the end of Alfred's reign.

The West Saxon shires seem largely to have grown by some unrecorded process from the areas first settled by the English

invaders. They bear a primitive and natural aspect generally con-
forming with geographical boundaries, but this is by no means
the case with the midland shires which are altogether more
regular and artificial and have almost wholly obscured the
boundaries of early times. This artificiality is apparent on both
sides of the boundary between English Mercia and the Danelaw.
The shires of Gloucester, Worcester and Warwick correspond in
extent with the diocese of Worcester and seem to represent the
territory embraced by the old kingdom of the *Hwicce*. There is no
evidence to show how old these shires are, but there is some
ground for thinking that there were substantial alterations in their
boundaries in the eleventh century. The hidage assigned to
Gloucestershire in Domesday Book is almost double that of the
other two and it is possible that Gloucestershire had by then
swallowed an older territorial unit based on Winchcombe. The
extreme irregularity of the northern boundary of Gloucestershire
seems to have resulted from the actions of Eadric Streona early
in the eleventh century. In the west midlands generally such
groups of peoples as the *Magonsætan*, the *Tomsætan*, the *Wreocensætan* and the *Pecsætan*, unlike their counterparts in Wessex,
have left no trace in the nomenclature of the shires.

In most instances in both the west and the east midlands the
shires take their names from the county towns which are usually
placed centrally amid the surrounding shire. It is possible that
this marked degree of regularity arose in English Mercia from the
adoption of the burghal system whereby the burden of fortifying
and defending a chosen centre against Danish attacks was laid
upon the inhabitants of its surrounding territory. Such may have
been the case with Shropshire, whose territory, based upon
Shrewsbury, had once belonged in part to the *Magonsætan* and in
part to the *Wreocensætan*, and perhaps also with the shires of
Oxford, Stafford and Hertford. Hertfordshire has no geographical
unity. Its territory had previously belonged to two, if not three,
earlier units, the east to the kingdom of Essex, the north to
Middle Anglia and the south perhaps to the Middle Saxons, now
represented by Middlesex. The shire is not mentioned as such
until the eleventh century, but it is possible that its origin is to be

seen in an entry in the *Chronicle* under the year 912 in which it is recorded that Edward the Elder caused two fortifications to be built at Hertford, one on each side of the Lea. The maintenance of these fortifications may be supposed to have been laid upon those who lived in their neighbourhood.

It has already been remarked that the boundary agreed upon by Alfred and Guthrum cuts across the middle of Hertfordshire, as though suggesting that the shire itself did not then exist. The east midland shires seem to be wholly of Danish origin, representing the division of the conquered parts of Mercia between the various units of the Danish armies which settled there. The shire of Cambridge is first mentioned as such in 1010, but under the year 921 in the *Chronicle* there is a reference to the submission of the Danish army at Cambridge to Edward the Elder. There are similar references to the submission of Danish armies to Edward at Bedford, Huntingdon and Northampton. Rutland formed part of Northamptonshire in the time of Edward the Confessor. It became customary to bestow its land as part of the dowry of the English queen and in this way it eventually achieved separate existence as a shire in itself.

The shires of Leicester, Derby, Nottingham and Lincoln represent the territories of four of the Five Boroughs, a Danish confederacy which grew out of the settlement of the Danish armies in these areas in the time of Alfred. The fifth of the Boroughs was Stamford, the only one of the five which has not become a county town. It now holds an anomalous position nearby the junction of the boundaries of Rutland, the Soke of Peterborough and the Parts of Holland. The Humber estuary and parts of the northern boundary of Derbyshire mark the ancient line of division between the northern and the southern English. Beyond this line to the north the existing counties are of more recent origin, with the exception probably of Yorkshire whose extent may be taken to correspond with the lands settled by Halfdan's army in 876. Lancashire first becomes recognizable in the thirteenth century. There is a reference to *Westmoringa land* under the year 966 in the *Chronicle*, but there is no certainty that its extent corresponded with that of Westmorland as we now know it. Durham was very largely ecclesiastical in origin and the remaining two counties, Cumberland and Northumberland, represent by their names two ancient kingdoms, Welsh Strathclyde and English Northumbria, the former now remote from Clyde and the latter no less remote from Humber.

The shire may perhaps be regarded as the most important unit of government in the later Anglo-Saxon period, because it was through this unit and its presiding officers that the king was able to exercise a considerable degree of control over local affairs. The shire court was both the recipient of the royal writ containing the king's commands addressed directly to it and at the same time a body competent to transact much important local business of less immediate concern to the king. Such a court was at work in the shires of Wessex during the reign of Alfred, although we find the first specific reference to the *scirgemot* by that name in an ordinance of Edgar which directs that it shall meet twice a year and that the bishop of the diocese and the ealdorman shall supervise the proper observance of ecclesiastical and secular law.

The ealdormen were royal officials,[1] sometimes related to the royal family, but more often drawn from the nobility. Their office was not hereditary in its nature, though it tended to become so. Its holder had great privileges, in return for which it was his duty to lead the shire forces in time of war, to preside over the business of the shire court and to see that the king's commands conveyed to him by royal writ were properly carried out. In the days of Alfred the scope of an ealdorman's office south of Thames seems normally to have been limited to a single shire, but during the tenth century there was a steady increase in the scope of an ealdorman's authority and a corresponding diminution in his numbers. At the same time the title *ealdorman* began to yield to that of *eorl*, with the result that by the eleventh century the *ealdorman/eorl* is no longer the royal nominee to an office of local administration but a powerful magnate whose territories embraced many shires and whose strength might rival that of the king himself, though very few became as powerful as the houses of Godwine in Wessex and Leofric in Mercia.

[1] The point is emphasized by H. R. Loyn, *E.H.R.* LXVIII (1953), pp. 513–25.

The place which had been occupied by the ealdorman of Alfred's time came to be filled by one of the king's reeves, 'the shire-reeve' (*scirgerefa*) or sheriff. This official is plainly recognizable in the reign of Æthelred the Unready as the effective president of the shire-court, although the title itself is not recorded before the time of Cnut. In his second code of laws Cnut repeated Edgar's injunction that the court was to meet twice a year, adding that it could meet more often if need arose. The business of the court was concerned with every aspect of local government within the shire, ecclesiastical as well as secular. Its principal suitors were the thegns of the shire. There are occasional references to meetings attended by the magnates of several neighbouring shires, in one instance as many as nine. Much of the shire-court's business was concerned with the settlement of disputed claims to the possession of land. Two cases will serve to illustrate what happened when such claims were brought before the court.

The first case was concerned with the settling of rival claims to estates at Hagbourne and Bradfield in Berkshire in about the year 990.[1] The disputants were Wynflæd, a woman, and Leofwine. Wynflæd claimed that the estates had been given to her by Leofwine's father. She was evidently a woman of great influence and she first established her claim on the testimony of the archbishop of Canterbury, the bishop of Rochester, the ealdorman of Hampshire and the king's mother, all of whom bore witness on her behalf before king Æthelred at Woolmer. The king sent word of this to Leofwine through the archbishop, but Leofwine insisted that the matter should be referred to a meeting of the shire-court. Thereupon the king sent his writ to the shire-court at Cuckamsley in Berkshire ordering the case to be heard before the whole shire who were to settle the dispute as best they could. The archbishop of Canterbury and the bishop of Rochester who had testified on Wynflæd's behalf before King Æthelred sent declarations to the court. It was considered that through the testimony of these and the other witnesses given at Woolmer Wynflæd had successfully invalidated Leofwine's claim to the estates and she was told by the shire-court that she could now substantiate her own claim by

[1] A. J. Robertson, *Anglo-Saxon Charters* (Cambridge, 1939), pp. 136–9.

producing a sufficient number of witnesses who would support her by oath.

This was the normal procedure in an Anglo-Saxon lawsuit. The defendant was not required to produce evidence about the facts of the dispute, but to bring before the court compurgators or oath-helpers who would swear that the oath taken by the defendant was pure and not false as the plaintiff maintained. The number of oath-helpers required varied according to the nature of the accusation involved and the value of each oath similarly varied according to the standing of the individual who made it. If the requisite number of oath-helpers was produced before the court and the oath taken in full, the case was at an end. In the particular case in which Wynflæd was involved, twenty-four people are named as coming forward on her behalf, but there were others who were not enumerated by name. Eleven of the named oath-helpers were men and thirteen were women. When these oath-helpers had been produced, the court was evidently satisfied that Wynflæd had made her case and it accordingly decided that the oath itself should not be taken, because, if it were, friendship between the two sides concerned would thereafter be at an end. Leofwine accepted this decision and without further dispute handed over the estates which he had wrongfully seized to the safe-keeping of the bishop of Sherborne. Although Leofwine had lost his case, Wynflæd was required to hand over to him gold and silver which she had previously had from his father.

The second case[1] concerns a suit which was heard before the shire-court of Hereford meeting at Aylton, near Ledbury, during the reign of Cnut. Although the text of the document recording the suit is late and imperfect, the account itself gives a lively picture of the meeting and illustrates several interesting points of procedure. The case arose from a dispute between a mother and her son over the possession of certain estates. The meeting of the court was attended by the bishop of Hereford, the ealdorman, the sheriff, several noblemen and all the thegns of Herefordshire. Edwin, the son, stated his case to the meeting and the bishop of Hereford then asked whose business it was to answer for his

[1] *Ibid.* pp. 150–3.

mother who was not herself present at the meeting. Thurkil the
White answered that it was his business to do so, but, since he was
not fully informed on the matter, three of the thegns of the shire
were sent to inquire of the mother who was then at Fawley, about
nine miles away from Aylton where the court was meeting. The
mother was angered by her son's conduct and after summoning
her kinswoman Leofflæd, she said to the three thegns of the shire
'"Here sits Leofflæd, my kinswoman, to whom, after my death,
I grant my land and my gold, my clothing and my raiment and all
that I possess." And then she said to the thegns: "Act like thegns,
and duly announce my message to the meeting before all the
worthy men, and tell them to whom I have granted my land,
and not a thing to my own son, and ask them to be witness
of this."'

It will be observed that the mother's defence takes the form of
a simple denial of her son's claim and that she then proceeds to
dispose of her land and all her other possessions by a formal statement made in the presence of witnesses. When this had been done
the thegns rode back to the meeting and delivered their message.
At this point Thurkil the White, Leofflæd's husband, spoke to
the meeting and asked all the thegns to give his wife the lands
which her kinswoman had thus granted to her. This was done and
then with the consent and cognisance of the whole meeting,
Thurkil rode to the cathedral church of Hereford and had an
account of the whole transaction recorded in a gospel book. Among
the several interesting points in this case are the composition of
the court itself with the bishop of the diocese and the ealdorman
present, as was enjoined by the legislation of Edgar and Cnut, the
reference to the sheriff under that title (*scirgerefa*), to the thegns
of the shire and to the important part played by three of their
number, to the oral will made by formal declaration before witnesses, to its endorsement by the whole assembly and finally to
the insertion of a written account of what had been agreed in a
copy of the Gospels in the cathedral at Hereford.

(b) Hundred and Wapentake

At the beginning of the eleventh century the shires of England south of Tees are found to be subdivided into a number of smaller units called hundreds or wapentakes. Hundreds predominate in most of the country, wapentakes being confined to those parts of it in which Scandinavian influence was strongest, notably in the territories of the Five Boroughs and in the North and West Ridings of Yorkshire. These two units served the same ends and whether the one name or the other survives has depended upon the relative strength of the English and Scandinavian languages in the areas concerned. The same unit could on occasion be called by either of the two names. The term 'wapentake' is derived from O.E. *wæpentæc* which in its turn is a loan-word from O.N. *vápnatak*. This latter is a term of legal phraseology and in wholly Scandinavian lands it referred to the act of seizing and brandishing weapons by those assembled at a meeting as a way of signifying approval of a measure. It is only in England that the term is used of an administrative unit.

The hundred first becomes clearly recognizable as a unit of local government in the tenth century. Its working is described in an anonymous royal ordinance which was compiled between 945 and 961 and which is commonly attributed to Edgar, although there is no direct evidence of his connexion with it. This ordinance enjoined that a meeting of the hundred was to be held every four weeks and that at this meeting every man was to do justice to his fellow men. From what follows it is made clear that the meetings of the hundred were largely concerned with bringing thieves to justice and with rounding up stray cattle. One of its members, called 'the hundred man' (*hundredesmann*) was recognized as its chief official and when a theft occurred he was to be informed of it and was to pass on the information to the men of the 'tithings' who were all to go in pursuit of the thief. It is not altogether clear whether 'tithing' in this context refers to groups of ten men organized for police purposes within the hundred or to territorial subdivisions of the hundred. Anyone neglecting his duty to the hundred on this head was to pay a fine to the hundred and to his lord for his first offence, a double fine for his second offence and to suffer outlawry, unless pardoned by the king, for his third. With regard to cattle it was enjoined that no man was to keep any stray beasts without declaring the fact to the men of the hundred or to the chief official of the tithing. If it became necessary to follow the track of man or beast from one hundred into another, the chief official of the latter was to be informed and then to take up the pursuit. All cases which came before the hundred court were to be settled in accordance with customary law and any man who failed to answer the court at the appointed time was to pay a fine, unless he had been prevented from appearing by his lord.

There is no ordinance concerned solely with the organization of the wapentake, but a code which was issued at Wantage by Æthelred the Unready contains some points of interest about it. This code relates mainly to the territories of the Five Boroughs in which it recognizes the existence of a hierarchy of courts, first the court of the Five Boroughs itself over which ealdorman or king's reeve presided, second the court of a single borough, and third the wapentake court. In each wapentake there was to be a body consisting of the twelve leading thegns who, after swearing upon relics which they held in their hands, that they would not accuse the innocent or shield the guilty, were to go out and arrest men of ill repute against whom the reeve was taking proceedings. There is abundant evidence to justify the view that this sworn jury of presentment, an aristocratic body, is in origin a Scandinavian and not an Anglo-Saxon institution. Bodies of twelve 'doomsmen' are familiar in Scandinavian history and literature and their antiquity is stressed by the belief expressed in Norse mythology that the gods themselves were twelve in number. The exact functions of such doomsmen are difficult to discern. The innocence or guilt of an accused man brought before the hundred or wapentake court, and indeed before any higher court, was normally decided either by his ability to produce the required oath in company with his oath-helpers or by the ordeal. Yet some element of judgement rested with this sworn jury, as may be inferred from a later passage in Æthelred's Wantage code which states that a verdict (*dom*) in which the thegns are unanimous shall be held valid, but if they disagree, the verdict of eight of them shall be held valid and those who are outvoted shall pay a fine. This is the earliest recorded occurrence in England of the principle that the view of a majority should prevail, and it may be observed that though the code containing it is written in Old English, the custom which it defines is wholly Scandinavian.

References to similar bodies of twelve are to be found in other contexts, and such a body undoubtedly played its part in the organization of the hundred. A code of Edgar's, dating *c.* 962, declares that a body of twelve standing witnesses shall be chosen for every hundred. Each such witness was to take an oath that neither for money, favour or fear would he deny what he himself had witnessed or declare in testimony what he had not seen or heard. Two or three of the men thus sworn were to be present as witnesses of transactions within the hundred. For example, a man setting off on a journey was to tell his neighbours why he was going and on his return he was to declare who were present as witnesses at the buying of the goods with which he had returned. If a man set off unexpectedly without giving information, he was to do so as soon as he got back, and if he brought cattle with him, they were to be put on the common pasture of the village to which he belonged. If he failed to do so within five days, the villagers were to tell the head man of the hundred and the culprit was to lose his cattle. Even if he were able to demonstrate that he had bought the cattle with the cognisance of men duly appointed as hundred witnesses, he would still lose his cattle for failing to inform his neighbours or the head man of his hundred. To be convicted of false testimony in such a matter was to lose not only cattle and all other possessions, but life as well.

Thus the twelve standing witnesses of the hundred did not serve the same functions as the sworn jury of the wapentake, not at least as these functions are described in the codes of Edgar and Æthelred. The former were a body of men of whom two or three were to be at hand to take account of the business transacted within the hundred and to bear witness in a court of what they had seen and heard. The prime duty of the latter was to arrest wrongdoers and to bring them to the court, though it appears that they possessed some power of giving judgement. In this latter respect they may be compared with bodies of men, usually twelve in number, called *judices* or *lagemanni*, that is 'lawmen'. Traces of such are to be found in Cambridge, Stamford, Lincoln, York and Chester, all places at which Scandinavian influence was strong. On the occasion of an attempt to interfere with the privileges of York in 1106, a commission of twelve men was appointed to find a verdict on the customs of the Church and one of the twelve appointed is described as hereditary lawman of the city.[1] The lawmen played a sufficiently important part in Scandinavian government to leave traces of their existence in most areas of the British Isles where Scandinavian settlement was on a large scale, notably in the Isle of Man, the Western Isles and Orkney. A term corresponding with 'lawman' occurs frequently in Irish records where it is used sometimes as a personal name and sometimes apparently as a kind of tribal name referring in general to Viking settlers.

Cnut's secular code enjoined that every free man over the age of twelve should belong both to a tithing and to a hundred if he wished to have the right of defending himself against a charge of wrongdoing and of being atoned by the payment of his wergild if he was slain. According to the same code no steps were to be taken for the recovery of property unless appeal had been made three times to the hundred court. If justice were not obtained, the case might then be taken to the shire court. The anonymous ordinance about the administration of the hundred which is commonly attributed to Edgar has sometimes been interpreted as though it marked a major administrative innovation, but this is to mistake the nature of Anglo-Saxon legal codes which were not so much concerned with the promulgation of new law as with the codification of established custom. There is little doubt that the hundred was functioning as a unit of local government in the reign of Edmund and also in the reign of Edward the Elder. The frequency of its meetings, the nature of the business with which

[1] *Visitations and Memorials of Southwell Minster*, ed. A. F. Leach (Camden Society, 1891), p. 192—*Ulvet filium Fornonis, hereditario jure lagamen civitatis* (*quod latine potest dici legis lator vel judex*).

it was concerned and the kind of place in which its meetings were held, all suggest that it was an institution with a long history behind it in the tenth century.

The geographical variation in size between hundreds in different parts of the country is very great and their boundaries have tended to be less stable than those of the shires in which they are contained. There were never more than five hundreds in Staffordshire whereas Sussex, much the same in its physical area, came to contain more than sixty. In Cambridgeshire proper there were fourteen, with another four in the Isle of Ely. It is important to distinguish between the hundred as an area of land and the hundred as a unit of assessment for purposes of taxation. A hundred might be assessed for fiscal purposes at 100 hides of land, but this meant only that it was to be made responsible for producing the amount of service in tax or other forms reckoned to be due from 100 hides of land, not that it did in fact contain 100 hides. A West Saxon hundred may be rated as low as 20 hides or as high as 150, but in much of the midlands the fairly frequent assessment of the hundreds at a round 100 hides reveals a degree of symmetry which conforms with the artificial appearance of the midland shires, and suggests that the hundredal organization here may have been deliberately imposed as part of the administrative reorganization which involved the creation of the shires in the first half of the tenth century.

The sites at which the courts of shire, hundred and wapentake were held are commemorated in numerous place-names.[1] Names containing the word *gemot*, as in Mudbury in Dorset or Mutford in Suffolk, are widely distributed over the country. Skirmett in Buckinghamshire derives from *scirgemot* 'shire-moot', and Skyrack in the West Riding of Yorkshire refers to the oak at which a shire-court met. The word *þing* which is common to both Old English and Old Norse in the sense of 'meeting', is found in Thingley in Wiltshire, Thinghill in Herefordshire, Fingest in Buckinghamshire and many other names. Thingoe in Suffolk

---

[1] The comments which follow are based on O. S. Anderson, 'The English Hundred-Names', *Lunds Universitets Årsskrift*, N.F. Avd. 1, Bd. 30, 35, 37 (Lund, 1934 and 1939).

derives from O.N. *þinghaugr* 'moot-hill'. Thingwall in Cheshire and Lancashire as well as Tynwald Mount in the Isle of Man correspond with *Þingvellir* in Iceland, the site at which the *Alþingi*, the Icelandic Parliament, held its meetings. In England, as in Scandinavia, the burial mounds of chieftains were commonly used as meeting-places for assemblies. O.E. *beorg* and *hlaw* and O.N. *haugr* are frequently found in hundred-names, in this sense, although it is not always possible to tell whether such terms refer to artificial burial-mounds or to natural eminences. Cuckamsley in Berkshire, the place at which the shire court met to decide the suit between Wynflæd and Leofwine, derives from O.E. *Cwicelmeshlæw*, a name signifying the burial mound of a man called Cwichelm. Whether, as some have suggested, the man in question was the seventh-century West Saxon king of that name cannot be determined, but there can be no doubting the existence of a barrow called by a more corrupt form of the same name, Scutchamfly Knob. Where a hundred name contains the element *beorg*, *hlaw* or *haugr* combined with a personal name, it is probable that the reference is to a burial-mound rather than to a natural eminence.

The choice of a burial-mound, as of a natural hill, for a hundred meeting-place should be ascribed to no deeper motive than the desire for a site which would be prominent to all concerned. Such was the case with Mutlow Hill in Cambridgeshire which, like its namesake in Essex, derives from *gemot* and *hlaw*, 'assembly hill'. The Cambridgeshire Mutlow Hill is of particular interest in that it consists of a tumulus which itself stands upon the Fleam Dyke, one of the series of massive dykes which cut across the course of the Icknield Way in this neighbourhood. Freed from the trees which now encumber it, the site would command a very wide prospect. The meeting-places of hundreds commonly stand near the centre of the hundreds to which they belong, but the Cambridgeshire Mutlow Hill marks the point at which the boundaries of three adjacent hundreds meet, as though to suggest that there was a common assembly for all three. Such may have been the case in other places, since there are many references to groups of two, three, and even as many as seven and eight hundreds acting together as a unit. A further point of interest in some of the

Cambridgeshire hundreds is to be found in references to names which are now lost but which once contained the Old English word *sceamol*, 'bench'. This element is also found in hundred-names in Kent and Essex and evidently refers to the benches on which members of the hundred court were seated. A reference to some form of wooden platform or flooring is to be found in Dill, the name of one of the Sussex hundreds, which derives from O.E. *þille*, 'boarding', 'flooring', though it may be supposed that in general the hundred court met in the open air.

Beside the few names which refer to structures, the overwhelming majority suggest that some natural feature, such as a ford, a hill, a tree or a stone, marked the site of the meeting-place. The interpretation of hundred-names as evidence for the antiquity of the hundred as an institution presents difficult problems. Several hundred-names in East Anglia are of the *-ingas* type. Such are Loddon in Norfolk and Blything in Suffolk, deriving respectively from *Lodningas* and *Bliþingas*, that is groups of people living by the Rivers Loddon and Blythe. Such also is Happing in Norfolk, deriving from *Hæppingas* whose first element is a personal name *Hæp*. This person also gave his name to the stronghold of the district, now called Happisburgh. Happing is the name of a district rather than of any precise locality and it denotes the area settled by a community who regarded themselves as the followers of *Hæp*. In this particular case it is difficult to avoid the conclusion that the hundred of Happing grew from a community which established itself there at the time of the invasions. But this is not to say that the hundred as such is as old as the sixth century. In many instances hundred boundaries are formed by natural features, and it may frequently have been the case that some kind of community developed within those boundaries many generations before any hundredal organization became necessary.

There are also several hundred-names which refer to heathen gods. Thurstable hundred in Essex derives from O.E. *Þunres-stapol*, 'pillar of Þunor'. There was formerly a hundred in Bedfordshire called *Wodneslawe* and another in Essex called *Thunreslaw*, meaning a hill dedicated to *Woden* and *Þunor* respectively.

These names are undoubtedly interesting evidence of places at which heathen gods had been worshipped, but it does not necessarily follow that meetings of the hundred court were being held on these sites when the heathen gods were still being worshipped. A local eminence which by its prominence was a suitable centre for the worship of a heathen god was for that same reason suitable as the meeting-place of a hundred court. There is indeed evidence both of popular assemblies and of territorial units resembling hundreds in several parts of the country as early as the seventh century, but neither the *-ingas* hundred-names nor those containing the names of heathen gods are evidence for the antiquity of the hundred itself as an institution.[1]

(c) Ward

The hundred and wapentake are not found in the four northern English counties, excepting only the wapentake of Sadbergh in County Durham. In their place the divisions intermediate between the civil county and the ecclesiastical parish are called wards, in Latin *balli(v)ae*. *Ward* derives from O.E. *w(e)ard*, but evidence for the existence of wards as administrative units is not found earlier than the thirteenth century.[2]

(d) Riding and Rape

There are in some parts of England territorial units intermediate between the shire and the hundred or wapentake. The most familiar of these is the riding, represented by the three Ridings of Yorkshire, and the three Ridings of Lindsey which together with the Parts of Kesteven and the Parts of Holland makes up the shire of Lincoln. The modern English 'riding' is derived from the Old Norse *þriðjungr*, 'a third part'. The Ridings of Yorkshire and Lindsey may be thought to have come into being late in the ninth century when their lands were being divided among the disbanded Danish armies. A passage in the Lincolnshire Domesday shows that at one time Kesteven was also known

---

[1] The views of O. S. Anderson on this problem, *op. cit.* pt. III, pp. 213–14, are difficult to accept.

[2] See E.P.N.S. XXII, pp. xiv–xv.

as a riding and if this term is to be strictly interpreted as implying that an area so called was the third part of some larger whole, there ought to have been two other ridings which together with Kesteven would make up the unit. It is possible that those two others consisted of the Parts of Holland and the territory once dependent on Stamford, but there is no evidence of the fact and it is possible that the term 'riding' should not always be interpreted in the literal meaning of 'a third part'. There is indeed some evidence that groups of hundreds working together as a unit for purposes of local government were sometimes called ridings. There is known to have been a riding court and an official known as the riding reeve, but the references to both are found for the most part in documents later than the Norman Conquest.

The system of a unit and its subdivisions, represented only by the riding in England, is found almost universally in countries occupied by Scandinavian peoples during the Viking Age. The riding or third part is found in Orkney, as well as in parts of Norway and Sweden. In the Norwegian Trondelag are to be found not only the third (*þriðjungr*), but also the quarter (*fjórðungr*),[1] the sixth (*séttungr*) and the eighth (*áttungr*). Each of these units had its own assembly and there were intermediate assemblies comprising two or three of the smallest units joined together, as well as an overriding assembly of the whole community, the *Trondelagsþing*. Island communities were particularly well suited to this kind of subdivision and devolution of authority. Something has been said above of the Isle of Man. In the island of Gotland in the Baltic, the *Gutnalþing* formed the highest assembly in the island which was divided overall into thirds, or ridings as it might be, and each third was again subdivided into sixths of the whole.

The Icelandic constitution offers the best example of this system of government. The comparatively small size of the island's total population and the absence of complications arising from relics of earlier methods of administration left the Norse settlers

---

[1] The term *ferding*, O.E. *feorþling*, occurs in East Anglia with reference to the fourth part of a hundred, O. S. Anderson, *op. cit.* pt. I, pp. xviii–xix. Cf. also the *ferlingi* of the borough of Huntingdon, E.P.N.S. xxii, p. xv.

free to devise their own constitution entirely according to their own wishes. The *Alþingi*, the assembly for the whole island, consisted of two bodies, the *Alþingisdómr* to which all lawsuits were referred and the *Lǫgrétta* which had the power of making new laws which were announced by a lawspeaker whose duty it was to memorize the whole law, to recite it to the assembled people and to pronounce decisions on disputed points. By a re-organization carried out in 965 the island was divided into four quarters. Three of these quarters were further subdivided each into three judicial districts and the fourth into four. Each quarter had its own assembly as also did each of its subdivisions. These numerous assemblies, as also the meetings of the *Alþingi* itself, were governed by elaborate rules of procedure. It is unlikely that similarly elaborate forms of government or of legal processes developed in the Danelaw or in the north-western counties of England, if only because the settlers in these areas came to lands which had previously been occupied for some centuries by the English who had developed their own forms of government. Nevertheless the Scandinavian contribution to the local govern-ment of England was very considerable.

The county of Sussex also possessed a division intermediate between shire and hundreds. These are known as 'rapes', a name which is held to be derived from O.E. *rap*, 'rope', and which has been associated with a Germanic practice whereby the area within which the 'peace' attaching to an open-air court was defined by an enclosure marked out by stakes and ropes. There were six rapes in Sussex and owing to the lack of evidence for their existence before the Norman Conquest it has sometimes been maintained that they were Norman innovations. The derivation of the term itself from an Old English word is a strong, if not decisive, argu-ment in favour of their Anglo-Saxon origin.

(e) Primitive Divisions

The machinery of local government in medieval and indeed to a large extent in modern England was an Anglo-Saxon and Scandinavian creation. It owed nothing to the Romans and very little, save in its more efficient use, to the Normans. Most of its various parts can be seen at work in the tenth century and with increasing clarity in the eleventh. Though it is right to recognize this creation as one of the great achievements of the period, care should be taken not to imagine English, Danes and Norse as men greatly preoccupied with their own government. Shire, hundred, and wapentake did not grow upwards from the bottom, but were created in response to the stimulus provided by the demands of the monarchy. A king required men to fight for him and payments, whether in money or in kind, to support him and his household. It is probable that the primitive right of exacting tribute from subjects was a far more potent stimulus towards the growth of local units which might share the burdens imposed upon them from above than any popular desire towards sharing in local government. Throughout the Anglo-Saxon period attendance at local assemblies, though denied to some and therefore in a sense a privilege to others, remained a duty whose neglect was punishable by fines. Looking back to times earlier than the tenth century, many traces of local units are to be found, but the evidence is piecemeal and not such as to present a clear picture for any part of the country, let alone the country as a whole.

The vast area of Northumbria was never divided into shires of the kind found in the midlands and south. The primitive division between Bernicia and Deira continued to be observed after the amalgamation of these two kingdoms, but each of the two covered a large area and we could not avoid inferring the existence of lesser divisions even if there were no evidence of the fact. The writings of Bede and his contemporaries in Northumbria refer to areas which they describe by the word *regio*, but unfortunately it is not possible to determine the word which these writers would have used in the vernacular. One such *regio*, called *Ahse*, lay between Corbridge and Carlisle. Another was called *Kintis* but its whereabouts are unknown, save that it was in the diocese of Lindisfarne. The term *regio* is also applied to Hexham by Eddius, a point of particular interest, because the town of Hexham lies near the centre of a small area which formed a medieval liberty and which is still known as Hexhamshire. According to twelfth-century Hexham tradition, the district of Hexham was given to Æthelthryth as part of her dowry when she married Ecgfrith, king of Northumbria, in the seventh century. It is possible, though there are long gaps in the evidence, that the liberty of Hexham represents one of the ancient divisions of Northumbria. Districts of similar size in the neighbourhood of Coldingham, Bamborough, Norham, Bedlington, Richmond and elsewhere were known as shires in times later than the Norman Conquest, but owing to the meagreness of Northumbrian records in the tenth and eleventh centuries it is impossible to determine whether they are relics of an older system.

Bede also uses the term *regio* or *provincia* of districts in other parts of England. For example, he writes that Wilfrid died *in provincia quae vocatur in Undalum*. It is possible that there may be some connexion between this *provincia* and the later Soke of Peterborough. The name is now preserved as Oundle. It is clearly a district name, but no satisfactory etymology has been suggested. Similarly Bede refers to Ely as a *regio in provincia Orientalium Anglorum*, stating further that it contained 600 households, information which indicates that the *regio* in this case was a district capable of definition. The name 'Ely' derives from O.E. *æl* and *ge*, meaning 'eel-district'. The second element *ge* is a somewhat rare word which is cognate with German *gau*. It is found in a few other place- or district-names and its correlation with *regio* in this instance is not without interest. In the eighth-century life of Guthlac, country neighbouring the Norfolk River Wissey is called *provincia Uissa*. A charter of Æthelbald, king of Mercia, dated 736, refers to a *provincia* called *Husmeræ* near the Worcestershire Stour. The name survives as Ismere House, near Kidderminster. Another of Æthelbald's charters refers to a *regio* called *Geddinges*. This, now preserved as Yeading in Middlesex, is a name of the *-ingas* type. Alongside these *regiones* and *provinciae*, and as parallels with Ely, note may be taken of Vange in Essex, which contains the archaic *ge*, of *Ginge*, now represented in Margaretting and Ingatestone, but formerly referring to a considerable area south-west of Chelmsford, and also of the name Surrey which means 'southern district'. Bede refers to a monastery at Chertsey as being *in regione Sudergeona*, where the second element of *Sudergeona* is the genitive plural of a derivative of *ge* meaning 'inhabitants of a district'. Surrey, 'the southern district', is paralleled in its formation by Eastry, 'the eastern district'. This latter is the name of one of the lathes into which Kent was divided, and it is of significance that two of the other Kentish lathes, Lyminge and Sturry, contain the same element *ge*, 'district'. Kent is peculiar in that it possesses a dual internal division into lathes as well as into hundreds. The hundreds appear to be considerably the later of the two and there is much evidence to suggest that the lathes preserve the outline of a distribution of land which goes back to very early times.

CHAPTER V

ECONOMY

I. THE COUNTRY

THE face of Britain has changed much since the end of the Roman period, but the changes have been due more to the works of man than to the processes of nature. Climatic conditions remain much the same now as they were then and the outline of the coast has altered only a little through causes other than the slow but continuous processes of erosion and deposition. Coastal changes from whatever cause have been mainly confined to the eastern and southern shores from the Wash to Selsey Bill, although there has been some erosion farther to the north, particularly along the coast of Yorkshire and Durham. Evidence of Romano-British dwelling sites at several points along the Thames estuary which now lie some 15 ft. below high-water mark, points to some degree of land subsidence in this area. Since Roman times the tidal limits of the Thames have advanced progressively westwards, in part because of a rate of submergence which has been estimated at 9 in. every hundred years and in part because of modern dredging of the river bed.

Along much of the north coast of Norfolk continuous deposition has created a wide belt of salt marsh between the sea and the coastline of Roman times. One result of this change may be seen at Brancaster where the site of the Roman fort now lies over a mile from the edge of open water, though the tidal surge of 31 January 1953 brought the water temporarily back again to the old line. Along the eastward bulge the sandy cliffs have retreated considerably before the oblique wave action of the North Sea and this process continues. The cumulative erosion in 1,500 years has been considerable. The most striking loss has been the almost complete destruction of Dunwich, the site of the first East Anglian bishopric and still a prosperous market town in Elizabethan times. The graveyard of its only surviving medieval church is now exposed in the cliff face. North of Dunwich the shape of the Yare estuary, now called Breydon Water, has greatly altered, and to the south, Walton Castle, another of the Roman forts of the Saxon shore, has been lost beneath the sea off Felixstowe. Parts of the fort at Bradwell-on-Sea in Essex have been similarly lost.

Across the Thames estuary the shores of Kent have changed considerably (see Map 9). In Roman times the Isle of Thanet was separated from the Kentish mainland by a tidal channel, the Wantsum strait, into which the waters of the greater and the lesser Stour debouched. The Roman forts at Reculver and Richborough guarded the two ends of this strait from its mainland side. Thanet was still an island when Augustine landed there in 597. Bede estimated the width of this strait as 3 furlongs (*stadia*) and said that it could only be forded at two places. It is probable that Thanet remained an island throughout the Anglo-Saxon period. It and the nearby Isle of Sheppey were the first places at which Viking fleets ventured to pass the winter in England, at about the middle of the ninth century, and early in the eleventh the port of Sandwich was for several years the main base for English naval concentrations against the invasion then threatened from Norway. At the southern end of the Wantsum channel silting has now proceeded so far as to remove the coastline 2½ miles from the old Roman harbour at Richborough.

Further west, along the coast of Sussex, changes in the coastal outline have been even more marked than in Kent. The sweeping curve of Dungeness, with Romney and Walland marshes lying behind, has replaced the deeply indented bay which lay here in Roman times, with tidal inlets then reaching as much as 5 miles inland from the present shore. The former harbours at Rye and Winchelsea have been blocked by silt and westwards again Pevensey Levels have grown from the silting of another deep bay, but at the extreme western end of the Sussex coast silting gives place to erosion. The place at which Ælle is said to have landed in 477, *Cymenes-ora*, has been lost beneath the sea off Selsey Bill and traces of Anglo-Saxon dwellings have been exposed in the cliffs nearby. Bede glosses the Old English name of Selsey with the words *insula uituli marini*, 'the island of the sea-calf', though he regarded it as a peninsula rather than as the island which in fact it was until the nineteenth century.

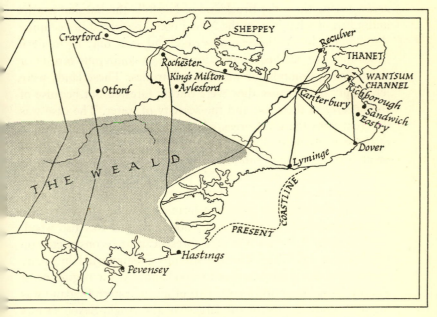

Map 9. The coastline of south-eastern Britain in Anglo-Saxon times. Based on E. W. Gilbert in *Historical Geography of England before 1800*, ed. H. C. Darby, p. 39, fig. 9.

Apart from the consequences of the industrial revolution of modern times, perhaps the most striking changes in the country-side since the end of the Roman period have been in the creation of arable and pasture out of forest and scrub land and in the drainage of fenland. The varying nature of the vegetation produced by underlying geological structure and superficial soil formations was among the decisive factors controlling the distribution and density of settlement at a time when the total population was small. Vegetation affected society at every level, whether locally in the economy of an individual farm or nationally in the configuration of a kingdom. Early settlers were no less strongly attracted by the open country lying above loamy soils and low-lying gravels than they were repelled by the heavy forest-bearing clays or by the sandy areas where the soil was poor and the water table lay deep beneath the surface. Some of the less attractive areas, among them the Breckland of Norfolk, the Bagshot heaths and much of what is now the New Forest, remained unoccupied throughout the Anglo-Saxon period, and it is only in modern times that use has been found for them as coniferous forests or manœuvring grounds for mechanized armies. These lands were left empty not because they were thickly forested but because of the poverty of their soil and the scarcity of water. The case was different with the great areas whose soil encouraged the growth of forest in its natural state. These were left unoccupied at first, or at best only thinly inhabited, because they were less easy of access and offered less favourable dwelling-places than the open gravel terraces to be found along many river banks. The forest, however, had much to give to a farming people whose primary building material was wood and whose only fuel was also wood.

The extent of Britain's natural forests can be reconstructed on the basis of soil maps whose testimony is supported by many place-name elements referring to woodland. At the beginning of the Anglo-Saxon period a large part of south-eastern England was heavily wooded. One of the largest of the Anglo-Saxon forests was sometimes known simply as 'the Forest' (O.E. *weald*) and as the Weald of Kent and Sussex its old name still survives, though it was also known as the forest of *Andred* (*Andredesweald*, *Andredesleah*), a name which is certainly to be connected with that of the Roman fort at Pevensey. Late in the ninth century it was described as being 120 miles long and 30 miles wide, with Lympne marking its eastern end. This description suggests that it was regarded as covering both the Wealden clays and the New Forest sands, but perhaps the chronicler's figures were intended only to convey an impression of great size. More than once the Weald is named as a place of refuge for hunted men. There can be no doubt that it tended to separate the kingdom of Sussex more sharply from its neighbouring kingdoms, than for example Wessex was separated from Mercia. It was not by accident that Sussex was the last of the Anglo-Saxon kingdoms to abandon heathenism.

Yet it would be a mistake to suppose that the Weald formed an impenetrable barrier between those who lived on either side of it or that it was wholly uninhabited. The Romans built three main roads across it southwards from London, to Chichester, to the coast near Hove and to Lewes. Even before the Roman conquest, deposits of iron ore were being worked in the Weald and they continued to be worked throughout the Roman period. Although the Roman roads were not everywhere so solidly built as at Holtye, near East Grinstead, where slag metalling sixteen inches thick has been found, their condition in many stretches today is proof enough that the Weald could be crossed without difficulty in Anglo-Saxon times. It did not attract settlers in large numbers, but its fringes served as valuable swine-pasture for communities living on more open land sometimes far removed from the Weald itself. The Kentish name Tenterden means 'the swine-pasture of the men of Thanet'. Other place-names testify to the existence of scattered groups of herdsmen deep in the forest itself.

Comparable in extent with the Weald, and perhaps even greater, was the wide belt of forest which ran along the northern side of Thames from near the Essex coast as far west as Chiltern. Remnants of its eastern parts survive as the forests of Epping and Hainault and much of Hertfordshire is still heavily wooded. At its widest point this belt was some 40 miles across from north to south. Very few cemeteries indicating early settlement have been found within it, yet its place-names, especially in its eastern-most parts, indicate that it carried a larger population than might have been expected. Place-names in -*ingas* and -*ingaham* are as numerous in Essex as anywhere else in the country, but they are very rare in Hertfordshire. Both counties contain many names with elements such as *leah*, *feld*, *hyrst* and *hryding* which refer to woodland and its clearing. Most of the -*ingas* and -*ingaham* names of Essex lie near the sea or along river valleys and there is little overlapping with the woodland names. It is possible that light rainfall and locally prevalent onshore winds did something to lessen the natural growth of forest in the eastern parts of Essex, but the abundance of early place-names and the lack of early cemeteries remain something of a puzzle.

The ecclesiastical history of Essex in the seventh century yields a further hint of connexion between the tenacity of heathenism and the distribution of forest. The northern edge of the Essex and Chiltern forest belt sloped away from near the Suffolk border towards the Thames at Wallingford. Beyond this edge and traversed by the Icknield Way, lay a narrow strip of open country which was bounded on its far side by *Bruneswald*. This forest has now vanished save for its reflection in the place-names Newton Bromswold and Leighton Bromswold, but it formerly covered much of the shires of Huntingdon and Northampton.

The extent of these three great forest areas, the Weald, the Essex-Chiltern belt and *Bruneswald*, was such that at the beginning of the Anglo-Saxon period about half of the south-eastern quarter of Britain seems likely to have been heavily wooded. Further north there were many other areas of forest—Rockingham, Sherwood and Galtres survive if only in name—but they were mostly of limited extent. In the western midlands Cannock Chase, Morfe, Kinver, Arden and Feckenham combined to form a broad belt of forest covering the divide between the upper waters of Trent and Severn. The kingdom of Wessex was for the most part open country, save for Selwood which formed the boundary between the sees of Winchester and Sherborne and which protected Alfred at the most critical time of his reign.

A passage in a seventh-century West Saxon code of law states that a stranger who travels through a forest off the highway and does not shout or blow a horn shall be assumed to be a thief and as such may be either slain or put to ransom. The same code lays down penalties for setting fire to a tree in a forest, for felling a large number of trees or for felling a tree that can shelter thirty swine. Apart from these, and apart also from occasional references to the Weald and to Selwood, little is said in the records of the great forests themselves. Nothing comparable with the forest laws of later times is known from the Anglo-Saxon period. The clearance of forest was a long and slow process which had begun before the Romans left and was by no means complete when the

Normans came. By marking on a map of a small area the dwelling-sites known to have existed early in the Anglo-Saxon period and comparing their distribution with those recorded in the Domesday Survey, it is possible to see how great was the Anglo-Saxon contribution to this work whose principal memorials are now to be seen in the open face of the English countryside and in its place-names. Although there is little direct reference to the great forests by name, references to woodland in documents relating to farms and estates are innumerable, the antithetical phrase *be wuda and be felda* recurring again and again among the formulae used in wills and landcharters.

Woodland was much valued not only for its game, but also as swine pasture and as the source of building materials and fuel. A record has survived of a lawsuit over swine pasture which was heard before Beornwulf, king of Mercia, at a meeting of his council in 825. The dispute concerned woodland at Sinton, in Worcestershire, where the king's reeve who had charge of the swineherds sought to extend their pastures beyond the limits permitted by ancient custom. He was opposed by the bishop of Worcester and his community who owned the wood in question and who were able to show that since Æthelbald's time they had been entitled to two-thirds of the wood and of the mast and were liable only to provide mast for 300 swine. Several references occur in other documents to the rights of cutting and carting wood. Late in the tenth century an estate at Hatfield in Hertfordshire was given by Edgar to the monks of Ely 'because, since the country is wooded the brethren can find timber for the fabric of their church and wood sufficient for other purposes'.[1] The metaphor of wood-cutting was adopted by Alfred in the preface to his translation of Augustine's *Soliloquies* and here perhaps better than anywhere else in the records of the time the Anglo-Saxon woodlands come vividly to life:

Then I gathered for myself staves and props and bars, and handles for all the tools I knew how to use, and crossbars and beams for all the structures which I knew how to build, the fairest pieces of timber, as many as I could carry. I neither came home with a single load,

---

[1] *Liber Eliensis*, II, 7, ed. D. J. Stewart (London, 1848), p. 115.

nor did it suit me to bring home all the wood, even if I could have carried it. In each tree I saw something that I required at home. For I advise each of those who is strong and has many wagons, to plan to go to the same wood where I cut these props, and fetch for himself more there, and load his wagons with fair rods, so that he can plait many a fine wall, and put up many a peerless building, and build a fair enclosure with them.[1]

Fen, no less than forest, was a dominant feature in parts of the Anglo-Saxon landscape. The fens of Somerset played a decisive part in the history of England late in the ninth century because, with the additional protection given by Selwood, they provided Alfred with a secure stronghold during the third Danish attack against the kingdom of Wessex, but they were too small in extent and too remote in position to affect the distribution of settlement in early times or the course of political boundaries in later. In the east, however, from beyond York in the north to Cambridge in the south, fenland was a controlling factor even more potent than forest. York itself lay near the northern end of a belt of fenland which stretched southwards for 60 miles to the Trent west of Lincoln. Widening to a depth of 25 miles, this fenland, with the Humber estuary, formed part of the most important political boundary of Anglo-Saxon England, the division between the northern and southern kingdoms. The uplands of Lincolnshire, bounded on the west by the Trent valley, were limited on the east by the coastal fens which formed the northern outlier of the great East Anglian fens. These stretched from close by Lincoln itself southwards for nearly 80 miles to their southern tip near Cambridge. At their greatest width they were 40 miles across from Peterborough to Brandon. Round the Wash and varying in depth from 5 to 20 miles lay the silt lands and beyond that the great peat fen punctuated here and there by small areas of upland. No Anglo-Saxon cemeteries of the pagan period have been found within either the Humber or the East Anglian fens.

So far as we know the Humber fens were as barren of population in Roman times as they were in Anglo-Saxon, but this was

[1] The translation is from *English Historical Documents*, ed. D. C. Douglas, vol. I, ed. D. Whitelock (London, 1955), p. 844.

not so with the East Anglian fens. Aerial photography supplemented by excavation at a number of sites, indicates that during the Roman occupation large-scale drainage and engineering works were carried out in the East Anglian fens and that, particularly in the silt lands, they carried a relatively large population during much of the Roman period. They seem, indeed, to have formed one of the principal corn-growing areas of Roman Britain. The Cambridgeshire Car Dyke whose origin early in the Roman period has been demonstrated by excavation, formed one link in a series of similar works, including the Car and Foss Dykes of Lincolnshire, which enabled barge traffic to ply on inland waters from Cambridge as far north as York itself. We have yet to learn how long this system of inland waterways continued in use, but it seems certain that the neglect of Roman engineering works, perhaps combined with a slight fall in land levels and with the breaching of the silt barriers near the margins of the Wash, had resulted by the middle of the fifth century in the general abandonment of the East Anglian fens and the creation of conditions which remained unchanged until the drainage works of modern times.

The eighth-century monk who wrote an account of the life of Guthlac, has left a vivid description of the watery waste in the midst of which the hermit chose to make his home and though the evils of the place may have been exaggerated for the greater glory of the saint who was able to overcome them, there can be no doubt that the Fens were not then as they had been in Roman times. Today the East Anglian fens are the richest agricultural area in the whole of England. In this respect the contrast with Anglo-Saxon times is obvious enough, but there have been other and less obvious changes. Modern drainage has resulted in a great shrinkage of the peat and has led also to major changes in the courses of some of the rivers. Over much of their length the existing fenland rivers run between massive banks high above the level of the neighbouring land, but this is a result of peat shrinkage in modern times and the consequent lowering of land levels in relation to river beds. Embanked rivers formed no part of the Anglo-Saxon landscape.

Today the major outfall of the fenland rivers is at King's Lynn through which flow the waters of the Great Ouse, the Cam, the Little Ouse, the Wissey and the smaller streams which drain the western uplands of Norfolk, but in Romano-British times, as also in Anglo-Saxon, the Cam and the Great Ouse took a more westerly course. Below their junction they formed the Wellstream and combining with the Nene they passed through Wisbech beyond which the major outfall lay. It is probable that in the fifth century the Wellstream was the main channel of entry from the North Sea giving access to the fenland rivers and ultimately to the gravel terraces along the river banks beyond the Fens themselves. The story of the goading of Guthlac by soldiers who chattered in the Welsh language has been held to indicate the late survival of a Welsh population in the East Anglian fens, but there is little evidence in support of this view. The incident does not refer to the East Anglian Fens at all, but to a Welsh raid into Mercia early in the eighth century.[1]

The evidence of place-names indicates that the English settlements in Fenland were mainly on marginal or insular sites where conditions of livelihood were perhaps not unlike those of the Frisian *terpen*. The names of several Anglo-Saxon fenland peoples are preserved in a document known as the Tribal Hidage and in some instances these names survive in modern place-names, the *Spalde* preserved in the name Spalding, the *Wisse* who lived along the lower reaches of the Wissey and the Nene, and the *Hyrstingas* whose name survives in the hundred of Hurstingstone in Huntingdonshire. The most prominent of the fenland peoples were the *Gyrwe* (whose name means 'fen-dwellers', from O.E. *gyr* 'fen'). Bede knew something about them from the fact that Æthelthryth, wife of Ecgfrith, king of Northumbria, and foundress of the earliest monastic community at Ely, had at one time been married to one of their rulers. Too much has sometimes been made of the difficulties of earning a living from the Fens in their undrained state. No doubt there were many hazards but perhaps they were no greater than those which faced Anglo-Saxon farmers on other kinds of land. In the tenth century and later, marginal or insular

[1] See Sir Frank Stenton in Sir Cyril Fox, *Offa's Dyke* (London, 1955), pp. xx–xxi.

sites such as Peterborough, Ely, Crowland, Ramsey and Thorney supported large monastic communities which accumulated great wealth and it may well be that the monk who could count upon unlimited supplies of fowl, fish and eels was envied by his brother who had to put his whole trust in sheep and corn.

The Anglo-Saxons were not themselves road-builders as the Romans had been, but they came to a country in which the natural lines of communication had been more sharply defined by a large number of well-built roads, and anyone who examines stretches of these roads in areas remote from present-day traffic will be easily convinced of their prominence in the Anglo-Saxon landscape. At times within the Anglo-Saxon period they continued to serve the primary purpose for which they had been built, the rapid movement of armies. Two of the major battles between the northern and the southern English, at the Idle in 616 and in Hatfield Chase in 632, were fought near the Roman road from Lincoln to York by Doncaster. When the Gododdin came from Lothian to Catterick in the sixth century, when Æthelfrith went from Bernicia to Chester early in the seventh, when Cadwallon went from north Wales to the Roman Wall near Hexham, when the Danish invading army rode from East Anglia to York and when Harold Godwineson went from York to Hastings, on all these occasions the Roman roads, we can hardly doubt, played their part in promoting ease of movement.

The Anglo-Saxons themselves made a clear distinction between the road made artificially and the road made by the mere passage of traffic along it, a distinction still represented in the contrast between Watling *Street* and Icknield *Way*, the one Roman and the other prehistoric. In Old English documents the term *stræt* is almost invariably used of an artificially made road and it is almost always the case that the making was of Roman origin. The term *stræt* should not of course be taken to imply that the road to which it referred was paved. A passage in the so-called Laws of William I, a Norman-French compilation consisting partly of Norman innovation and partly of a restatement of ancient custom, names four roads in England which were privileged, in that anyone slaying or assaulting another who was travelling along one of them was held to have committed a breach of the king's peace. Three of the four, Watling Street, Ermine Street and the Fosse Way, were of Roman origin, and the fourth was the prehistoric Icknield Way.

Watling Street (O.E. *Wæclinga stræt*) derives its name from a people called *Wæclingas* who gave their name to what the Romans knew as *Verulamium, Uæclinga cæstir* in Bede and now St Albans. Nothing is known of the *Wæclingas* or of the circumstances which caused their name to be given to the road. Ermine Street also derived its name from an otherwise unknown people of the east midlands, the *Earningas*, whose name is also preserved in Arrington and in Armington Hundred in Cambridgeshire. The Fosse Way derives its name from the Latin *fossa*, perhaps with reference to the drainage ditches with which a Roman road was normally bounded. The etymology of the name Icknield is obscure. It has frequently been noticed that these four road names repeat themselves in widely separated parts of the country. For example, the Roman road from York to Corbridge has long been called Watling Street, although the more familiar usage is of the road from London to Chester. The explanation is no doubt to be found in the specific reference to these four in the Laws of William I and the subsequent application of their names to other roads so that they too might enjoy the same privileged status.

Names such as these reflect the terminology of clerks, though they must have been local in origin. Colloquial usage, reflected in definitions of estate boundaries and in place-names, is of a different order. The term *hrycgweg* is commonly used in Old English documents, sometimes of roads of a considerable length, as with the great Berkshire Ridgeway or the Ridgeway running north from Lincoln to the Humber. As its name suggests, this was a road which followed the line of a watershed, seeking to avoid the crossing of even small streams and thereby to avoid land which might become waterlogged. Accompanying a Ridgeway proper there is sometimes found what is called a Summer Way, that is to say a road following a parallel course below the summit of the ridge in question. Other names which seem generally to have been applied to through roads are *ðeodweg*, sometimes rendered *via publica* in Latin charters, *herepæð*, meaning 'army road' and *portweg*, commonly indicating a road which led to a town. No doubt it was very often the case that several different names were used locally of a through road. This was so with the Roman road which leaves Ermine Street at Arrington and passes through Cambridge and Ely to Denver and which, perhaps under the influence of late antiquarianism, has come to be called Akeman Street, a name which properly belongs to a road leading to Bath (O.E. *Acemannes ceaster*). This road was formerly known by a great variety of names along its course, such as Cow Street Way, Soldier's Way, Port Way, Landbeach Way, Mere Way, that is 'boundary way' (from O.E. *gemære weg*) and so forth.

2. THE COUNTRYSIDE

The people of Anglo-Saxon England were mainly an agricultural people who lived in villages, farms and hamlets. With few exceptions towns did not play an important part in the life of the country until the tenth century. So much may be said with confidence, but beyond this, and despite all that has been written about it, the agrarian organization of the Anglo-Saxon community remains a topic full of hazards, controversies and uncertainties. The shortage of evidence and the unevenness of its distribution both in time and place are difficulties which face the student of Anglo-Saxon England at every turn, but in seeking to understand the land and those who worked it, this problem is greatly aggravated both by the present lack of adequate texts of one of the major sources of evidence, the land charters,[1] and by the difficulty of penetrating beyond the technical jargon of recording clerks to the realities of farms and fields. The value of the great Domesday Survey as a source of information about the state of England on the day when Edward the Confessor was alive and dead is obvious enough, but there is no source which raises in more acute form the problem of relating what is there recorded to the realities of the time, particularly where we are concerned with the relation of individuals towards other individuals or to the land on which they

---

[1] For an introduction to the study of the charters see F. M. Stenton, *The Latin Charters of the Anglo-Saxon Period* (Oxford, 1955), in which, esp. pp. 1–9, will be found references to editions and to works on the principles of charter-criticism.

worked. The approach to Domesday of the geographer concerned with the physical distribution of woodland, meadows, fisheries, saltpans and the like, and their relation to geological formations and soil types, has now begun to yield valuable information of a kind different from that sought by the social or legal historian.[1]

Hitherto archaeological sources of evidence have been almost wholly neglected, though the results achieved in recent years by the application of methods devised by archaeologists in Denmark show how much they may have to give.[2] No Anglo-Saxon farm building can be described because none has yet been excavated and little work has yet been done on the study of cereal or animal remains of the Anglo-Saxon period. In these circumstances it is all too easy by applying universally evidence which should be applied only to a particular time and place, by drawing upon Continental analogy and even upon nineteenth-century English practice, to write in sweeping terms which bear little or no relation to reality. Wherever it is possible to learn something about an individual estate of the Anglo-Saxon period and about the individuals who worked upon it, the picture which emerges is one of great confusion and infinite variation.

Several terms were used in the Anglo-Saxon period to signify what is meant today by farm, village or hamlet, but the word 'farm' itself was not among them, not at least as meaning a tract of land held for purposes of cultivation. Old English *feorm* (Lat. *firma*) meant a fixed payment, sometimes in money but more commonly in kind, made as rent, tax or the like. The commonest suffix in English place-names is *tun*. In seventh-century West Saxon laws a fenced meadow could be called *gærs-tun* (cf. O.E. *ontynan* 'to enclose'), one of a number of compounds which suggest that the primary meaning of *tun* was 'enclosed piece of ground', but the word also meant a community of people such as might live on a farm or in a village and hence the farm or village

[1] See H. C. Darby, *The Domesday Geography of Eastern England* (Cambridge, 1952); also H. C. Darby and I. B. Terrett, *The Domesday Geography of Midland England* (Cambridge, 1954). These are the first two of a series of volumes intended to cover the whole of Domesday England.

[2] A. Steensberg, *Bondehuse og Vandmøller i Danmark gennem 2000 År* (København, 1952). The many illustrations have captions in English and there is an English summary of 38 pages.

itself. It is so used in seventh-century Kentish laws which convey the notion of subordination to higher authority in such phrases as *cyninges tun* (hence the many Kingstons), *eorles tun* and *mannes tun*. The word is most commonly rendered in Latin by *villa*. It was never used in early times with the sense 'town'. *Ham*, often confused in Anglo-Saxon times with *hamm*, 'enclosed possession, fold', is likewise commonly used of a farm, particularly in the eastern counties. Its meaning cannot be precisely distinguished from that of *tun*, though there is a little evidence to suggest that a *ham* may have been regarded as something smaller than a *tun*. The compounds *hamsteall*, *hamstede* seem to refer to the principal house on a farm.

Another word signifying a place where men lived was *wic*, a loan-word from the Latin *vicus*, which developed the meaning 'village', but retained the sense 'farm' in such compounds as *berewic*, *heordwic*, *sceapwic*. Something smaller than *ham*, *tun* or *wic* seems to be indicated by *worð* and the related *worðig* (the *-worthy* of many west country place-names), and *worðign* (yielding *-wardine*). In seventh-century Wessex a ceorl was required to maintain a hedge or fence round his *worðig* and if he did not do so he would have no claim to compensation for damage done by the straying beasts of his neighbours. *Tun* is widely distributed over the country, but other terms are found commonly in those parts of it which were extensively settled by Scandinavians. The commonest of these is the late Old English *by* (O.N. *býr*, *bær*; Swed. Dan. *by*) which commonly meant 'farm', but also meant 'village' or 'town'. It is this word from which the modern 'by-law' derives its first element. Another word denoting a farm or a group of homesteads is Old Norse *þorp* which is particularly common in the North Riding of Yorkshire and is specifically Danish rather than Norwegian.

The two major elements in Anglo-Saxon society are comprehended in a jingling phrase which is found in seventh-century Kentish laws—*ge eorle ge ceorle*, 'noblemen and commoners'. The word *ceorl* which at least for much of the Anglo-Saxon period did not convey the condition of servility which is implied by the modern 'churl', has been variously rendered peasant, freeman, commoner or husbandman. Most ceorls were farmers, but some followed other crafts, as jewellers, blacksmiths, merchants or the like, and perhaps it is best to retain the word ceorl itself. A ceorl can be described as a free man in the sense that, in contrast with serfs, he was recognized to have certain rights and obligations at law, that he could inherit, bequeath, rent or sell land and that it was not in the nature of his condition for him to be bound to the soil. Seventh-century Kentish laws recognized the right of a ceorl to defend himself against an accusation by an oath supported by three others of his own class, and recognized also the sanctity of his home by imposing penalties on anyone who broke into it. In seventh-century Wessex, and also in other parts of the country and at other times, a ceorl was liable for military service and for the payment of taxes. This latter obligation is one of the criteria by which a 'free man' can be distinguished from a serf, though such a man might be anything but free in his daily life. In certain circumstances, by the acquisition of land or by prospering in trade, a ceorl might raise himself to a higher social status which would bring him into the lower ranks of the nobility.

The status of a ceorl in relation to the nobility above him and the serfs beneath him can best be seen in the amount of his wergild, the sum payable to his kinsmen by a man who slew him. In seventh-century Wessex this sum was 200 shillings, a sixth part of the wergild of a nobleman, and it was similar both in amount and in proportion in Mercia and Northumbria, but not in Kent. In early times the wergild of a Kentish ceorl was reckoned at 100 shillings and of a Kentish nobleman at 300 shillings, but because of the difference in value between the Kentish and West Saxon shillings, the wergild of the Kentish ceorl was not, as it appears to be, lower, but very much higher, than that of the West Saxon ceorl. A wergild of 200 West Saxon shillings of 5 pennies each amounted to 1,000 silver coins, whereas a wergild of 100 Kentish shillings, a gold coin of 20 pennies, amounted to 2,000 silver coins. The greater wergild of the Kentish ceorl accords with other evidence which suggests that he was a man of higher economic standing than his counterpart in the other Anglo-Saxon kingdoms. On the other hand, the wergild of the Kentish nobleman was the same as that of the West Saxon nobleman, both at 6,000 silver coins. A list of wergilds prevailing in Northumbria at a time which seems not to be earlier than the tenth century uses a different unit of account, the thrymsa,[1] seemingly of 3 pennies. The Northumbrian ceorl's wergild reckoned at 266 thrymsas of 3 pennies each was close to the Mercian's at 200 shillings of 4 pennies each. For purposes of comparative value it may be noted that the same Northumbrian document gives the wergild of a thegn as 2,000 thrymsas and that of an ealdorman or a bishop as 8,000. If strict regard is had for identity of time and place, it seems not to be possible to equate these sums with values other than those of money. A code of law relating to London in the first half of the tenth century, and thus corresponding broadly in time though not of course in place with the list of Northumbrian wergilds, values an ox at a mancus (thirty pence), a cow at 20 pence, a pig at 10 pence and a sheep at a shilling, that is 5 pence. If the equation is permissible, the wergild of a West Saxon ceorl in the tenth century seems to have been equivalent in value to about 33 oxen or 200 sheep.

The one generalization about the Anglo-Saxon agrarian community upon which all seem to be agreed is that the condition of the peasantry was markedly worse in the later part of the period than it had been in the earlier. Even so it should be recognized that the position of the seventh-century ceorl as an independent freeman of some substance is mainly derived from the position which he held in law. It is not until the end of the eleventh century that anything can be learnt in detail about the ceorl's working life and even then the information is slight. We are told something about the extent of the landed endowments of seventh-century monasteries, but nothing at all, for example, about the way in which the 600 monks of Monkwearmouth and Jarrow obtained their daily food or about the life of the ceorls on their estates. Nevertheless, it may well have been the case that the original Anglo-Saxon settlement resulted in a measure of independence for the individual comparable with that enjoyed by the

[1] O.E. *þrymsa* derives from the Latin *tremissis*, meaning originally the third part of a *solidus*.

descendants of Danish settlers in much of eastern England in later times. Even in early times many ceorls must have been driven by circumstance into surrendering a greater or smaller part of their freedom to others who could at least provide them with the means of mere existence which their own resources perhaps did not always afford. Misfortune with stock or crops befalls all farmers, and in times when reserves were slight, if they existed at all, such misfortunes must have overwhelmed many households.

In seventh-century England, with as many as a dozen independent kingdoms, it was still possible for taxes to be paid direct to the royal household without opportunity for exploitation by intermediate collectors, but as political unity grew the king and his household became more remote and the business of government increasingly complex. During the Danish wars many crops were destroyed and many farms were burnt. Service in the militia and garrison duty in the new military strongholds were heavy burdens which took men away from their fields. Large sums of money had to be raised as tribute to the Danes. These and other factors, including the growth of powerful families among the nobility, tended towards the depression of many of the less fortunate, especially in the latter part of the period. We cannot follow these changes in detail, but there can be no doubt of the general sharpening of distinctions between peasantry and nobility which by the end of the eleventh century had produced semi-servile communities in many parts of the country. Even though the general trend in Anglo-Saxon society was towards the greater dependence of those who worked the land upon their masters and even though such evidence as we have compels us to refer to categories of dependents, ceorls, villeins, bordars, cottars and the like, it would be wrong to regard such categories as implying uniformity of obligation or of economic status within themselves. Sometimes the only surviving mark of freedom may be that obligation to pay taxes which had always lain on all free men.

In 1066 the Danelaw contained large numbers of men called sokemen (*sochemanni*) or freemen (*liberi homines*). Such men, though by no means free from obligations of one kind and another, enjoyed rights with regard to their land and to their own personal status which admit of their being called a peasant aristocracy in contrast with the villeins of Domesday, a category which in Domesday terminology undoubtedly included many men who would have been called ceorls in Old English terminology. Such a distinction, however, does not mean that the sokeman of the northern Danelaw or the freeman of East Anglia was economically more prosperous than his neighbouring villeins.[1]

Turning from the general to the particular, four documents may be quoted in illustration of conditions on different estates late in the Anglo-Saxon period. They are an account of the services rendered by ceorls on an estate at Hurstbourne Priors in Hampshire, a survey of an estate at Tiddenham in Gloucestershire, a treatise on estate management called *Rectitudines Singularum Personarum*, and one on the duties of a bailiff, called *Be Gesceadwisan Gerefan*. The ceorls of Hustbourne Priors, apparently holding hides, were required to pay to their lord forty pence a year from every hide, specified but now uncertain quantities of ale, wheat and barley, to plough three acres of their lord's land in their own time and sow them with their own seed, to mow half an acre of meadow, to supply specified amounts of wood and fencing, to wash and shear their lord's sheep in their own time and to work on their lord's land as they were bidden every week in the year except three, one at midwinter, the second at Easter and the third at the Rogation Days. The men thus closely involved in an agricultural routine are called ceorls in the document which records what was due from them, but in 1086 the Domesday surveyors mentioned only *villani* and *bordarii* in this estate.

The estate at Tiddenham in Gloucestershire lay in the triangle formed by the Wye and the Severn. It consisted of 30 hides made up of 9 hides of demesne land (*inland*) and 21 hides of land held by tenants (*gesette land*). Its basket weirs and hackle weirs on the two rivers produced a considerable part of its income. Every alternate fish, and all rare fishes, belonged to the lord of the estate. The survey does not mention ceorls, but refers to two other groups

---

[1] The view, held by many scholars, that the freemen and sokemen of East Anglia were descended from the rank-and-file of the ninth-century Danish armies is rejected by R. H. C. Davis, 'East Anglia and the Danelaw', *Trans. Roy. Hist. Soc.*, 5th series, 5 (1955), pp. 23–39.

who owed service, the *geneat* and the *gebur*. The *geneat* had to work on or off the estate as he was bidden, to ride, furnish carrying service, supply transport, drive herds and 'do many other things'. The *gebur* had to plough half an acre of the lord's land as week work, fetching the seed from the lord's barn, and a whole acre for church dues, supplying the seed himself. He had to supply materials for building the fish weirs and for fifteen poles of field fencing and also to fence and dig one pole of the bank surrounding the lord's house. He also had reaping and mowing duties. After Easter he rendered six pence and half a sester of honey, at Lammas six sesters of malt and at Martinmas a ball of net yarn. On the same estate whoever had seven swine had to render three and thereafter every tenth, and he still had to pay for mast.

The *Rectitudines Singularum Personarum* and the *Gerefa* are thought to be parts of a single work dealing with the management of an estate in the abstract rather than with one particular farm. After referring briefly to some of the duties of the lord of the estate, the *Rectitudines* describes the service due from various groups of people who worked on it. We have met with two of these groups, the *geneat* and *gebur*, in the survey of the estate at Tiddenham. The third group is represented by the term *cotsetla*. The *geneat* paid his lord a rent, though the amount is not specified, and also one swine each year for pasture rights. He did no week work, but had many other services to perform. These included escort duties for men visiting his lord, guarding his lord's person, riding services, carrying goods and leading loads, reaping and mowing on his lord's land at harvest and hay time, going on errands 'far or near wherever he is directed', and cutting and maintaining the deer fence and the fence round his lord's dwelling. He paid the taxes due to the church and took his share in alms-giving. The services of the *geneat*, though many, were by no means wholly agricultural in kind. Several of them might have been regarded as honourable duties and his position in the hierarchy of the ideal estate was substantially higher than that of the *gebur*.

The *gebur* held a yardland, a quarter of a hide, and when he received this holding from his lord, he also received two oxen, one cow, six sheep, seven of his acres already sown, farming implements and furniture for his house. On his death his lord inherited all that he left. The services which he gave in return are described as being heavy in some places, moderate in others. On some estates he gave two days' work of whatever kind was required every week in the year and three days in the week at harvest time and from Candlemas to Easter. He also ploughed an acre each week from the end of harvest time to Martinmas and fetched the seed for it from his lord's barn. In addition he ploughed three acres each year as boon work, two acres for his pasture rights and another three acres as rent for his land. He shared with another of his kind the duty of keeping one of his lord's hounds. Beyond all these services, he paid his lord ten pence each year at Michaelmas, twenty-three sesters of barley and two hens at Martinmas and a young sheep or two pence at Easter.

From the many services which were required of the *gebur*, it seems clear that such a man played a major part in the work of an agricultural estate and it seems equally clear that his life was nearer to serfdom than the life of the ceorls at Hurstbourne Priors, but even lower in the social scale was the *cotsetla*. It was considered that he ought to have a holding of five acres, more if it was the custom of the land, but not less because so much was required of him. He paid no rent for his land. His services varied, but in some places he was required to work every Monday of the year on his lord's land and on three days a week in August or sometimes every day of that month. It was reckoned that as a day's work he should reap an acre of oats and half an acre of other corn. If required he must help his lord to meet his obligations of coastguard duty and of maintaining the king's deer fence. Despite his low status he was regarded as a free man and as such he was liable for church taxes and for the payment of 'hearth-penny' on Holy Thursday.

Apart from the men who bore the main burden of work on an estate, there are other individuals, the bee-keeper whose post must have been one of great importance, the oxherd, the shepherd, the swineherd and others whose services are set out in the *Rectitu-*

dines. Controlling this varied force of workers and supervising the daily round on the estate in all its aspects was a bailiff or reeve, the man whose duties are described in *Be Gesceadwisan Gerefan*. Much was expected of a man who would have himself regarded as 'a wise reeve'. He ought to be well informed about the customary rights both of his lord and of the workers under his control. He must know the seasons of the different crops and know too that the seasons for different activities varied on different estates. He must not be too lax nor too overbearing and he must be ready to attend to small matters as well as great, for if he were too proud or too negligent to attend to cattle stalls or threshing floors, the result would 'soon show itself in the barn'. Throughout the year there were endless things for him to do. In May, June and July there was harrowing, carrying out manure, sheep-shearing, repairing hedges and attending to fish weir or mill. At harvest time there was reaping, carrying home and thatching the crops, and later cleaning out the folds and preparing the shelters for the cattle against the onset of winter. In winter there was ploughing, and if severe frost set in there was timber to be cut, there was the orchard to make, the cattle to be attended to in their stalls and the pigs in their styes. A stove should be set up on the threshing floor for oven or kiln. In spring there was still ploughing to be done, and grafting, setting the vineyard, sowing beans, madder, flax and woad, planting the garden and other things too many to be enumerated. The treatise makes no reference to the sowing of cereal crops. Whenever other work fell short there was the house to be cleaned and set in order, tables and benches to be made and floors to be scoured, ditches to be cleaned and hedges to be repaired. In addition it was the duty of the reeve to see that there were supplies of the many implements that were needed on the estate. These included all the tools of carpentry, the tools needed by the miller and the shoemaker, spinning and weaving implements, share coulter, scythe, sickle, rake, shovel, shears, flail, scales for weighing and every other kind of implement. He was responsible as well for the implements used in house or barn, pots and pans, beer-barrels, honey-bins, money-box, candle-sticks, salt-cellar, pepper-horn, as well as buckets, churn, cheese

vat and sieves, both of wire and of hair. In all, the author of
Gerefa enumerates more than a hundred different sorts of implement and although we may feel with him that 'it is tedious to
recount all that he who holds this office ought to think of', the list
repays reading for the substance which it gives to the picture of an
Anglo-Saxon farm, a substance which is not easily recaptured
from other sources.

The document describing what was due from the ceorls at
Hurstbourne Priors seems to imply that the holding of the ceorl
on this estate was the hide. This is one of the fundamental units
of Anglo-Saxon measurement, but it is often difficult to say
precisely what it was that the hide measured. Taxation in some
form or other was present throughout the Anglo-Saxon period
and even if there were no evidence of the fact we should have to
suppose the existence of some means of apportioning what was
due among the householders who were required to pay it. As far
back as records go we find it supposed that there was a unit, a
common measure, which could be used to convey an indication
of the number of households living in a particular area or of the
nature of a gift of land to a church.

There are many references to this unit in Bede's *Ecclesiastical
History*. He describes how after the defeat of Penda at the battle
at the *Winwæd*, Osuiu gave a thank-offering to the church of
twelve estates (*possessiunculae*), six of them in Bernicia and six in
Deira. Each of these estates was of ten households—*singulae uero
possessiones X erant familiarum, id est simul omnes CXX*. It will
be noticed that the unit here is the household, presumably of the
ceorl, and not a specific measurement of area. Describing the gift
of Iona to Columba, Bede says that it was not big, but about the
size of five households according to the reckoning of the English—
iuxta aestimationem Anglorum. This last phrase is of interest
because it shows that Bede was translating into Latin a customary
English method of reckoning and not inventing a method of his
own. Moreover, he was not saying in this instance that there were
in fact five households in Iona, but only that there was room for
them, which seems to indicate that there was something which
could be regarded as the normal holding of a household and that.

an expression such as *terra unius familiae* could be used to give some indication of physical area. In other words, Bede here seems to be saying that Iona was of a certain size. Elsewhere he applies the same method of reckoning to Man and Anglesey. The former had room for something over 300 families and the latter for 960. In this case Bede was not describing the actual acreage of the two islands because the two are much the same in physical area. That Anglesey could support more than three times as many households as Man is explained by Bede's remark that it was the more fertile of the two and produced a great abundance of crops. His reference to the number of households in these two islands follows his statement that they had been made subject to the English by Edwin, king of Northumbria. Subjection to a foreign overlord meant the payment of tribute by the conquered and we may guess that Bede based his reckoning of households on the amount of tribute which had been exacted. Other reckonings given by Bede are 600 households for the Isle of Thanet, about 600 for the Isle of Ely, 1,200 for the Isle of Wight, 7,000 for the South Saxons and 12,000 for the North and South Mercians together.

When Bede's *History* was translated into Old English his *familia* was rendered by *hid* or the related *hiwisc* and there seems to be no doubt that what Bede represented by *terra unius familiae* is what we now call the hide. When, however, we seek to penetrate beyond the hides of the documents and to translate them into terms of actual physical acreage, we meet with difficulties which seem to be insuperable. So far from assuming that the amount of land which would support a ceorl's household would be much the same all over the country, we can be sure that it would vary greatly according to the fertility of the soil, the nature of the holding and the standard of living of the household in question. No one would suppose, for example, that nowadays the same kind of livelihood, and therefore the same receipt to the Exchequer, would arise from a hundred acres of Cheviot sheep run as from a hundred acres of fenland arable. Moreover, we cannot be certain that a West Saxon, Mercian or East Anglian historian would have reckoned the same number of households in Anglesey, Sussex and Mercia as Bede did. Indeed, there is some evidence to the contrary, for the Tribal Hidage which refers to times earlier than the Danish invasion of 865 reckons the hidage of Mercia at 30,000 against the 12,000 of Bede. The actual size of Mercia was probably much the same at both times in question and since it seems unlikely that the number of tax-paying households would have increased two and a half times in what cannot have been a very long interval, it is difficult to avoid suspecting that different systems of reckoning were in use.

It is not until we reach the times of Domesday that we find there and in related documents a correlation of hides, virgates and acres which allows an equation to be made. In several instances in Cambridgeshire proper, in the Isle of Ely and in Essex it is possible to say that the reckoning then was 120 acres to the hide. In parts of Wessex on the other hand the hide seems to have contained no more than 40 acres. The fourth part of the hide was the yardland, the holding of the *gebur* of the *Rectitudines*, but care must be taken in translating the Old English *gierd*, *gyrd* because it had more than one meaning. Basically a *gierd* was simply a wooden rod which could be used for linear measurement and in this sense it corresponds with the modern rod, pole or perch which has a statutory length today of 16·5 ft. but which varied within wide limits in medieval times. This aspect of the *gierd* is emphasized in the compound *metgyrd*. Like the modern rod, pole or perch, *gierd* could and commonly did represent a measure of area, but it might be one of two very different areas. It might be no more than the fourth part of a single acre or it might be a much larger tenement composed of one such quarter-acre strip taken from every acre in the hide. In areas where the hide contained 120 acres this would yield a 30-acre tenement and this is what is normally meant by the 'yardland' or its equivalent the 'virgate'.

The home of hides and yardlands is mainly in the midlands and south. A well-known passage in the laws of Ine (c. 42) refers to the farming practices of ceorls in such a way as to indicate that in seventh-century Wessex, wherever local conditions were suitable, the open-field system of agriculture was in use. 'If ceorls have a common meadow or other shareland to enclose, and some have enclosed their share while others have not, and cattle eat up their common crops or their grass, then let those who are responsible for the gap go to the others who have enclosed their share and pay compensation to them.' The term here translated 'shareland' is O.E. *gedalland*, a term which is also found in land charters of a later period. In the open-field system of agriculture the arable holding of an individual was not held in a single compact block, but in a large number of small strips scattered about the arable belonging to the particular community. It is this practice to which the term *gedalland* refers, though it should not be interpreted further as implying that the arable so worked was communally owned. In Latin documents a corresponding phrase *segetibus mixtis* is sometimes found. Early investigators believed that the open-field system of agriculture was once all but universal in Anglo-Saxon England, but it is now clear that this was far from being the case. Its home lay principally in the midlands and south, but it was not practised in Kent, East Anglia or the northern parts of Northumbria.

The hide was never in regular use in Kent as a measure of the householder's land. The word used here was *sulung*, a term related to an Old English word for plough. There is no doubt that the acreage of the sulung was much greater than that of the hide. On occasion it could be regarded as containing twice as much land as the hide, a difference which accords with the higher status of the Kentish ceorl represented by the amount of his wergild. The fourth part of the sulung was the yoke (O.E. *geoc*). Very little is known about the agrarian structure of East Anglia in the Anglo-Saxon period and it is difficult to discover any standard holding. North of the Welland the unit of arable in times later than the Danish invasions was the ploughland (*plogesland*) which was divided into eight oxgangs, the bovates of Latin records. No documents relating to individual estates in the Anglo-Saxon period survive from Bernicia.

It has often been maintained that the Anglo-Saxons brought with them to Britain a type of plough which was larger and more efficient than any previously in use there. This plough, it has been said, was a wheel-plough with broad share and fixed mouldboard of such weight and cutting such a great furrow that it required eight oxen to draw it. There is at present no evidence for the existence of any such plough in Anglo-Saxon England. The modern word 'plough' derives from O.E. *ploh*, *plog*. In Anglo-Saxon times this word was used of a stretch of land which was worked by the plough, as in the compound *plogesland*, but not of the implement itself. The regular Old English word for the implement was *sulh* (var. *sylh*, *suluh*), cognate with Latin *sulcus*, 'furrow'. The plowman in Ælfric's *Colloquy* thus describes his work—'I go out at dawn, driving the oxen to the field and I yoke them to the plough...and when the oxen are yoked and the share and coulter fastened to the plough, every day I have to plough a full acre or more.' Apart from the implement itself, *sulh*, the terms here used are *iukian* for the act of attaching the oxen to the plough, *scear* for the blade which cut the ground horizontally at the bottom of the furrow, and *culter* for the knife which was attached to the plough-beam and made a vertical cut in the soil in front of the share.

The work from which these terms are drawn probably belongs to the eleventh century. The Old English Plough Riddle in the *Exeter Book* refers to tail, coulter, share-beam and share, though it is in its nature to do so in enigmatic terms. The riddle also makes plain that the plough left a clearly defined furrow, but this does not necessarily imply the use of the mould-board since the furrow could be turned by the mere tilting of the plough itself. Neither here nor anywhere else in written Anglo-Saxon sources is there any reference to mould-board or wheels, though it is possible that the use of a ground-wrest to clear the furrow was known in Anglo-Saxon times, as it seems to have been in Romano-British. There are drawings of ploughs in Anglo-Saxon manuscripts dating from the second half of the tenth century and later, and in such drawings a wheel-plough is represented, but not the mould-board. Some of these drawings show a plough drawn by four oxen and others by a pair, but in any event the drawings themselves are not admissible as evidence for the appearance of the Anglo-Saxon plough even in the eleventh century, let alone the sixth. Although the drawings may have been done by Anglo-Saxon monks, it is well established that a great many of the book illustrations of the late

Anglo-Saxon period were copied from others rather than drawn from life and further that many of the prototypes were of Continental origin. So far archaeological evidence has contributed nothing to the problem. No Anglo-Saxon plough has been found. From the evidence at present available there is nothing to show that the Anglo-Saxons introduced into Britain a better plough than had been in use there during the Roman occupation.

Indications of any major and immediate changes in the cultivation of cereals are equally slight, though no doubt changes of method occurred during the Anglo-Saxon period as a whole. This is a topic on which at present we are not very fully informed, though much has been learnt in recent years by the application of methods devised mainly by Danish archaeologists.[1] Apart from written records there are two main sources of evidence, the microscopic examination of carbonized grains of cereal recovered from dwelling-places and the study of grain impressions found on domestic pottery. Throughout most of the prehistoric period in Britain domestic pottery was fashioned from lumps of clay thrown on the floor of a dwelling place and then baked on the hearth. The clay from which such pottery was made tended to gather in grain and seeds from the floor on which it lay. Where such objects adhered to the outer surface of a pot they perished in the baking and left small cavities from which positive impressions can now be obtained by the use of suitable plastic material and the seeds which made them be thereby identified. This method can be applied to most, though not all, Anglo-Saxon pottery, but it cannot be used in the Roman period when most pottery was wheel-made, presenting a hard and smooth exterior surface to which grains could not adhere.

Custom changes slowly in the cultivation of cereals and a wide view must be taken. It is now established that wheat, mostly Emmer, was the principal cereal crop in the Neolithic Age of both Denmark and Britain. On Danish Neolithic pottery 87% of the grain impressions have been found to be of wheat and only 13%

---

[1] The comments which follow are based on K. Jessen and H. Helbæk, *Cereals in Great Britain and Ireland in Prehistoric and Early Historic Times* (Copenhagen, 1944), and H. Helbæk, 'Early Crops in Southern England', *Proceedings of the Prehistoric Society*, XVIII (1952), pp. 194–233.

barley. Evidence from the neolithic settlement at Windmill Hill, near Avebury in Wiltshire, shows that wheat formed nine-tenths of the cereals cultivated by its inhabitants, with Emmer by far the commonest variety, and barley less than one-tenth. Although the proportion of wheat to barley may not have been so high in other parts of Britain as it was at Windmill Hill, where the settlement was on chalk, there is enough evidence from other sites to show that wheat predominated in most of neolithic Britain as it did in Denmark. During the succeeding Bronze Age in Denmark and also in the Roman Iron Age the proportion of wheat to barley was almost exactly reversed. The material available from Denmark for the Roman Iron Age (A.D. 1–500) is large enough in quantity to have allowed the estimate that of all the cereals grown there at that time 81% was barley. What is true of Denmark is likely to have been true of the neighbouring parts of north-western Germany and the Low Countries, and it may accordingly be thought that barley was the principal cereal cultivated by the Anglo-Saxons before they invaded Britain.

The trend away from wheat to barley was not, however, peculiar to Denmark. A similar trend took place in Britain where 75% of the recorded grain impressions on pottery of the Early Bronze Age were of barley. Naked barley was then the commonest variety, but it was giving way to the hulled variety in the Late Bronze and Early Iron Ages. Until *c.* 1000 B.C. there seems to have been fairly close similarity between the cereals of Britain and Denmark, but there are some indications of divergence after that time. Spelt seems to have come to both countries in the Early Iron Age, though probably not from the same source. Oats came to Denmark at about the same time, though apparently not to Britain. Carbonized grains of oats have been found on Iron Age sites in Britain but mixed with larger quantities of wheat and barley, as though to suggest that the oats had been growing by chance rather than as a cultivated crop. On the other hand rye reached Britain, but not Denmark, *c.* 500 B.C., though it seems not to have become an established crop in Britain until the Roman period, when oats also were grown as a crop in Britain. Grain impressions are not available for the Roman period in Britain and the proportion of the different cereals grown at that time must depend on the microscopical examination of carbonized grains. Very little of this has yet been done and in some ways it is perhaps the less valuable of the two sources of evidence because of the accidental circumstances attending carbonization. The rough texture of Anglo-Saxon pottery in the pagan period is well suited for the preservation of grain impressions, but here again very little work has been done. The total of grain impressions so far recorded on Anglo-Saxon pottery is only 101. Of these eighty-three were of barley, all but three of them being of the hulled variety. Of the remainder, fourteen were of oats, one of wild oats and three of the seeds of flax and woad. Almost all the oat impressions are from the Cambridge region, but no significance can be attached to this unless a similar preponderance remains after the examination of much larger quantities of Anglo-Saxon pottery.

During the seventh century pagan burial customs went out of use and in consequence the supply of domestic pottery on which grain impressions might be found is no longer available. Linguistic evidence points to barley as the most widely cultivated of the cereals in the Anglo-Saxon period. The Old English name *bere* is common in itself and is also found in numerous compounds. A building for storing grain was called *bere-ærn*, whether the grain stored in it was barley or not, and a threshing-floor *bere-flor*. Two other compounds survive in many place-names, *bere-wic* (yielding Berwick) which, as early as the tenth century, had come to be used of a grange on an outlying part of a farm, and *bere-tun* or *bær-tun* (the latter form yielding Barton). *Bere* is also found compounded with *-croft*, *-land* and other terms relating to the countryside. The Old English name for oats, *ate*, is not very common, though it is found in medico-magical recipes. In glossaries it is sometimes equated with Latin *lollium*, *zizania*, 'weed', 'tares'. References to the Old English name for rye, *ryge*, are not common, but it is found in a number of place-names. The importance of the crop to the Anglo-Saxons is indicated by the fact that an assembly of the Kentish royal council which met in 695 to draw up laws for the kingdom of Kent, recorded in the preamble to the laws which it promulgated that the meeting had been held on the sixth day of the month of *Rugern*, that is the month of the rye harvest.

There can be little doubt that wheat was an important crop in Anglo-Saxon England. It may be recalled that Cuthbert tried to grow wheat on Farne, but knowing well enough that it was not an easy crop to grow, he providently asked the brethren of Lindisfarne to bring him some barley, and it was the barley which he eventually succeeded in growing. References to the Old English name *hwæte* are very common and it is significant that the name is compounded with a variety of words not compounded with *bere*. Such compounds are *hlaf-hwæte*, 'bread-wheat', *hwætte-gryttan*, 'wheaten groats', *hwæte-mealu*, 'wheat-meal' and *hwæte-medma*, 'wheat flour'. The Anglo-Saxons also adopted the word *spelt* (Lat. *spelta*) which they may have used indiscriminately of both Emmer and Einkorn. It is difficult to say how much of the true bread-wheat was grown by them, but probably very little.

The importance of the barley crop to the Anglo-Saxons consisted partly in its use by the brewer, but no doubt much of their bread was made from barley or rye. Wheat was also used for baking and some degree of skill seems to have been achieved in the process of refining flour. The O.E. *melu*, 'meal', could be used of any ground corn whether or not it had been sifted from the bran. More highly refined flour was called *smedma*. A distinction was made between the wheaten loaf, *hwæten hlaf*, presumably made from coarse flour, and the 'clean loaf', *clæne hlaf*, evidently made from sifted flour. Reference is also made to a third kind of loaf called *gesufel hlaf*, but the exact significance of this term is uncertain. Raised bread, *gehafen hlaf*, was known from very early times and there were several different Old English terms to express the idea of yeast. Most bread was probably hearth-baked in separate households, but oven baking was also practised. The importance of bread in the Anglo-Saxon diet is sufficiently indicated by the modern 'lord' and 'lady', deriving respectively from O.E. *hlaford*, formerly *hlafweard*, and *hlæfdige*, and meaning originally 'the keeper of the bread' and 'the kneader of the bread'.

It is probable that the household corn was normally ground by a hand-quern, O.E. *hand-cweorn*. The upper stone of this apparatus was called *cweorn-stan*. Many fragments of such querns, some of them made of Niedermendig lava, have been found at Thetford and other places. No doubt the hand-quern was the instrument used by the grinding servant to whom reference is made in early Kentish laws. There is no evidence that windmills were known in Anglo-Saxon times, but water-mills had come to be of major importance before the Norman Conquest. It is uncertain when they were first used by the Anglo-Saxons, but documentary evidence of them goes back to the eighth century. References to O.E. *mylen*, 'mill' and its various compounds, such as *mylen-pul*, 'mill pool', *mylen-broc*, 'mill stream', and *mylen-steall*, 'mill site', are very common in late documents.

The Domesday Survey refers to more than 5,600 mills, outside the northern counties which were not covered by the survey. Although the distribution of mills at that time was widely spread over the country as a whole, they seem to have been most numerous in the eastern counties south of Humber, especially in Lincolnshire and Suffolk, and on Salisbury Plain and its environments. The ratio of mills to households was possibly highest in this latter area. Recent analysis of the evidence relating to the shires of Lincoln, Norfolk, Suffolk, Essex, Cambridge and Huntingdon, has shown that Domesday refers to 964 mills in connexion with 2,784 settlements. In most of these counties there had been more mills in 1066 than there were in 1087. Rather more than half of these settlements had only one mill each or perhaps only a fraction of a mill shared with another community. There were eighty settlements which had four or five mills each, and some, particularly in Lincolnshire, had more. There were nine at Nettleton, thirteen at Louth and fourteen at Tealby. In Norfolk there were seven at Norwich and eight at Thetford. There were also eight at Meldreth in Cambridgeshire. No Anglo-Saxon water-mills have survived and nothing can be known of their design except by analogy from those which have remained in use in other parts of Britain until modern times.

3. TOWNS AND TRADE

There were three words in common use in Old English to describe a community larger than a *tun* or a *ham*, to indicate, that is, a town, though in using this word the sense to be conveyed is that of market town, not the urban agglomeration arising from the industrial revolution of modern times. The three words are *burh*, *port* and *ceaster*. Old English *burh* is cognate with Gothic *baurgs* which is used in the fourth-century Gothic Gospels to translate the Greek πόλις. The modern 'borough' represents a particular aspect of the O.E. *burh* whose basic meaning was 'a fortified place'. It is the word which is commonly used of prehistoric fortifications and where so used it generally survives as '-bury' from the dative *byrig*, but it was also used of the premises of an individual with reference to the fence or ditch protecting such premises. A passage in the laws of Alfred which sets out the penalties for breaking into the premises of a nobleman or other distinguished person calls such an offence *burhbryce*. It is evident from this passage that the residence of a king, bishop, ealdorman or nobleman might be called a *burh*, though it may be noted that a different term, *edorbryce*, is used of a like offence against a ceorl's premises. An early occurrence of *burh* in the sense 'town' may be noted in *Cantwaraburg* which is found in the *Anglo-Saxon Chronicle* under the year 754. Later in the *Chronicle*, *burh* is the word which is regularly used of the fortifications which were built by Alfred to secure his hold on Wessex and by Edward the Elder and Æthelflæd for the same purpose in the midlands.

The word *port* was used in Old English of a seaport, but it was also commonly used of a town and especially of a town which possessed market rights and rights of minting. The use of the word *port* by no means implies that the place to which it refers was situated on the coast. In the tenth century *port* and *burh* are equivalent in the sense 'town', but *port* was never used of the premises of an individual. O.E. *ceaster*, a loanword from Lat. *castra*, is the term commonly used of places which had been well known as towns in Roman Britain, such as Gloucester, Chester, Leicester and so forth. It does not, however, imply that there had been continuity of occupation on such sites, nor was it used exclusively of sites which had been Roman towns. Indeed, it is by no means safe to assume that a place of which it is used had been occupied during the Roman period. Particularly in northern England and south-eastern Scotland the element 'chester' is often found in places where no Roman remains are known to exist.

The Germanic invaders of Britain were individualists, not dwellers in towns. The point needs no elaboration because the contrast between the material civilization of north-west Europe in the fifth century and the cities of Italy and Greece is obvious enough. On the other hand, the invaders came to a country in which much capital had been invested in an attempt to force upon a reluctant tribal society Mediterranean conceptions of the city-state. Tribal capitals had been supplied with streets of regular chess-board plan and lavishly equipped with public buildings, not only market-place and town hall, but also public baths, temples and theatre or amphitheatre. This artificial cultivation took place mainly in the second century and although it must be remembered that many of the towns of Roman Britain are now so thickly covered by modern buildings that they cannot be completely excavated, the picture which emerges from others is one of towns which rarely achieved a degree of industrial strength great enough to enable them to survive the withdrawal from their midst of the Roman civilian administration. The prosperity of Roman Britain in its latter days lay in the countryside rather than in the towns and the attempt to impose the city state upon its society may be accounted, in contrast with Gaul, to have been a failure. Yet in saying so much, it should not be assumed that all the towns of Roman Britain had been abandoned before the end of the Roman period, or that there were none which survived the Anglo-Saxon invasions.

Almost all the Romano-British towns were on sites where there are still towns today, though one may note such exceptions as Silchester and Aldborough, and on almost all of them some form of town life can be shown to have existed during the Anglo-Saxon period. The investigator thus needs to ask not only which towns, if any, survived without any break of continuity, but also when and why town life began afresh on the other sites. It need hardly be said that a complete answer cannot be given to any of these questions and in many instances no answer can be given at all. If by town life we mean that kind of corporate existence which confers upon those who share it rights and duties in the way of government, law-giving, taxation and the like, it may be said at once that there is no evidence that this sort of town life survived the Anglo-Saxon invasions. If, on the other hand, we mean no more than the existence of communities larger than villages or hamlets, it may well be that something survived. Opinions expressed by modern writers have varied widely and there is abundant room for such difference of opinion on a matter for which proof is lacking. Earlier in the century, at a time when the prejudice against 'the barbarians' who overthrew the civilization of Imperial Rome was perhaps greater than it is now, there was a tendency to believe that the recorded slaughter of the British inhabitants of Pevensey in the fifth century was typical of what happened in the country as a whole and to accept as literal truth the testimony of Gildas that the cities of Roman Britain lay waste and uninhabited in his own day. More recently the matter has seemed to be one of degree rather than of choosing between wholesale destruction or universal survival.

Archaeological proof of the continuous occupation of any town site between *c.* 410 and 550 will always be difficult to establish, partly because the accurate dating of material remains of habitation depends in the last resort upon their being found in a context to which written records refer and these are lacking from the time in question, and partly because excavation would need to be undertaken on a very big scale before the continuing existence of a large community could be established. Work has recently been done on war-damaged sites in Canterbury and London and in both places evidence for some form of occupation between 400 and 600 has come to light, but not on a scale large enough to establish general conclusions. Excavations on the site of St Bride's Church in London, a site which lay outside the walls of the Roman town, disclosed an area which had been occupied in the Roman period and also in the Anglo-Saxon period. The evidence provided a hint, though no more, that occupation had been continuous and at least it may be said that there was no evidence of any clearly defined break.[1]

In other parts of the country Anglo-Saxon cemeteries have been found in significant relationship to Romano-British centres of occupation, such as Great Chesterford in Essex, Caistor by Norwich, Lincoln and York. Whether or not some of these cemeteries are to be regarded as representing communities of *foederati*, they offer a warning against setting too much store by the poetic fancy which viewed Roman buildings as the work of giants to be regarded from a distance with superstitious awe. This was not the attitude of Cuthbert who, on a visit to Carlisle in 685, was taken by his hosts to see the Roman walls and the Roman fountain. The city reeve who conducted this party of sightseers knew well enough that the buildings were of Roman construction. Carlisle of course was remote from the areas of invasion in the fifth century and though even here the point cannot be proved or disproved, there is no positive ground for thinking that the continuity of its occupation was broken between Romano-British and Anglo-Saxon times. Carlisle was known to Bede as *Lugubalia*, a form which is very close to the *Luguvall(i)um* of the Antonine Itineraries and the *Notitia Dignitatum* and in this point Carlisle is by no means exceptional. The Romano-British names of both London and York have survived, though *Eburacum* is so heavily disguised in the Anglo-Saxon adaptation *Eoforwic* that it would not have been recognized if the earlier name had not been known. Again one may compare Bede's *Lindocolina* with *Lindon Colonia* or his *Uerlamacaestir* with *Verulamium*. All in all, more than three-fourths of the recorded town names of Roman Britain have survived in a modified form to the present day, but it is by no means sure that this fact can be regarded as evidence for the unbroken continuity of community life on the sites in question.[2] It has been remarked that the buildings of a Roman town would have formed a prominent feature of the landscape whether they

---

[1] Information from Mr W. F. Grimes who directed the excavations. No detailed report has yet been published.
[2] K. Jackson, *Language and History in Early Britain* (Edinburgh, 1953), pp. 227–33.

were inhabited or not and that their names might have survived just as the Celtic names of hills and rivers survived. Yet, when the large proportion of surviving Romano-British town names is considered, together with other evidence, they seem to point towards at least some degree of continuing occupation rather than towards complete abandonment.

Even if continuity of occupation, or equally in some instances the lack of it, is difficult to establish, there is no evidence for the existence of Anglo-Saxon towns earlier than the ninth century in or near places which had not been centres of population in the Roman period, and thus it may at least be said that the sites of the earliest Anglo-Saxon towns were a legacy from Roman Britain. There is no means of knowing whether Gregory advised Augustine to establish the two metropolitan sees which he envisaged for the English Church, in London and York because he knew that they had been respectively the civil and military capitals of Roman Britain or because he believed them to be places of importance in his own day. Nor can we tell whether Augustine preferred Canterbury to London merely because he could find in Canterbury the royal patronage which he would not have had in London. It is noticeable, save in those parts of Northumbria which lay beyond the old Roman frontier, that the activities of bishops and lesser missionaries in the seventh century were frequently associated with Roman sites. Canterbury, Rochester, London, Winchester, Dorchester-on-Thames, Leicester and York were all episcopal seats before the ninth century and all save Leicester before the eighth. Paulinus baptized at Catterick, Lincoln and Littleborough (R.B. *Segelocum*, O.E. *Tiouulfingacæstir*), and there were missionaries in three of the Roman forts of the Saxon shore in the seventh century—Reculver, Bradwell-on-Sea and Burgh Castle. Remains of seventh-century churches still exist at Reculver and Bradwell. James the Deacon, renowned for his skill in the Gregorian chant, lived near Catterick after the flight of Paulinus. The influence of the Church, and in particular the need for centres from which its diocesan organization could be administered, may well have been a factor of some importance in stimulating the growth of town life in England before the Danish invasions. It is perhaps significant that the two East Anglian bishoprics, Dunwich and Elmham, were not on Roman sites, for indications of the destruction of British settlements are more marked in this area than in any other part of the country.

Since at least the time of Shakespeare the Channel and the neighbouring waters of the North Sea have been the Englishman's bulwark against the foreigner, and the conception of insularity has become so ingrained that it is now difficult to regard these waters in any other light. To the modern eye it is cause for wonder that the burial chamber of a seventh-century East Anglian king whose very identity is uncertain, should have contained treasures from Gaul, the Rhineland, the eastern Mediterranean and Sweden. It is very easy to think of Anglo-Saxon trade as something which expanded after the fashion of nineteenth-century English trade, as it were a movement away from isolation, but it is by no means easy to grasp that the reality was quite the reverse, that at no time in its subsequent history has England been more closely united with the maritime countries of north-western Europe than it was in the second half of the fifth and in the sixth centuries. The difficulty is made the greater by the fact that the modern historian has no choice but to use as terms of reference the names of countries and nations which did not then exist. His readers may well overlook the anachronisms involved.

During the Roman occupation Britain and Gaul were united not only by the bond of government but also by the bond of language. The political barrier was the Hadrianic Wall, not the Channel. Later in the Romano-British period, and particularly in the fourth century, the Channel coasts were fortified not against one another, but against an enemy from the north-east who threatened the southern shores of the Channel no less than the northern. Britain did indeed become isolated as a result of the withdrawal of the Roman forces, but isolated only from Rome, not from north-western Europe and not even from Gaul. During the fifth and sixth centuries Germanic settlements were established on both sides of the Channel, near Boulogne and Bayeux, as well as in Kent, Sussex and Wessex, and further west new links of a different kind were formed by the British movement into

Armorica. Where formerly the North Sea had marked the racial and linguistic boundary between the Celtic and Germanic peoples, by the end of the fifth century that boundary had crossed the sea and come to lie across Britain itself, with the result that the Narrow Seas ceased to be a barrier and became instead a bond closely uniting eastern Britain with the opposite Continental shores. The breakdown of the primitive Germanic language into its various branches and the slow growth of nationalism were factors tending to make this bond progressively weaker, but it was never completely broken in the Anglo-Saxon period and the conception of insularity has no place in that period.

Goods and men crossed the Channel and the North Sea in both directions in quantities which seem surprising to the modern eye too familiar with the sight of customs barriers and what they imply. Undoubtedly travel was attended by great physical hardship and danger, but these were not so much greater than the normal accompaniments of life at home. Objects recovered from pagan graves bear ample witness to this traffic. Bede relates that Benedict Biscop sent to Gaul for glass-makers to make the windows for his new monastery at Monkwearmouth because the art of making glass was not then known in Britain. In 756 the abbot of Monkwearmouth wrote to the archbishop of Mainz asking for a good glass-maker to be sent to him because the English had no skill in this art. Yet the number of glass vessels recovered from Anglo-Saxon graves is not far short of three hundred, a quantity which testifies to a very considerable traffic in this fragile substance. Almost all this glass was made in northern Gaul or the Rhineland, though one remarkable goblet, found in Sussex and bearing a Greek inscription, evidently came from the eastern Mediterranean.

Swords also came from the Rhineland with blades fashioned in the technique known to archaeologists as pattern-welding. The sword from Sutton Hoo was so rusted into its scabbard that the two parts had corroded into a single mass of metal, but X-ray photography has shown that its blade was of the pattern-welded Rhenish type. The jewels which decorated its sword-knot were of East Anglian workmanship and the jewelled pommel has been claimed as Swedish. There could scarcely be a more striking example than this single object provides of cultural fusion among the maritime peoples of that time. Cowry shells, amethyst beads and bronze vessels from Coptic Egypt show how wide were the contacts of pagan England in the sixth century. A valuable source of evidence is lost with the abandonment of pagan burial rites. It may be that in the seventh century Christianity imposed some slight barrier between Christian England and pagan Germany, but before that century was over new strength was given to the old bonds by the beginnings of the movement which took Anglo-Saxon missionaries to the Continent in large numbers. The pilgrimage overseas, on occasion as far as Syria, was a phenomenon of Anglo-Saxon religious life which can be observed throughout the period.

The evidence of coinage and currency has much to tell about the economic aspects of the change from Roman Britain to Anglo-Saxon England. During the Roman occupation Britain received large and regular supplies of imperial currency, some of it gold, much of it silver, but most of it bronze. Although bronze coins were struck in Britain itself in considerable quantities during the Roman occupation, the great bulk of its currency came from Gaul. In 395, at least fifteen and perhaps as many as thirty-five years before the Roman withdrawal, the Gallic mints were closed and thereafter regular supplies of new currency no longer reached Britain. Early in the fifth century gold and silver coinage went completely out of use in Britain and bronze could only circulate to the extent allowed by the existing stock of metal. In many parts of Britain hoards have been found containing large numbers of minutely small bronze coins, ranging in size from 7·5 mm. to as little as 1·5 mm. Although these coins, known to numismatists as *minimi* or *minimissimi*, are often so small and so poorly made that the designs on individual specimens can only be recognized by reference to others of the type, they can be seen to be based, not on the pattern of contemporary imperial coins of which no examples were available, but on types which had been circulating widely in Britain in earlier times. In some instances hoards containing *minimi* also contain clipped or broken coins of the fourth century. The view has recently been gaining ground that the *minimi* represent a much debased currency which was being struck locally in several parts of Britain in the fifth century and which, at least in native hands, may have continued in circulation long after the onset of the Anglo-Saxon invasions.[1] No more striking illustration of the economic disaster which had befallen Britain can be gained than by comparison of these wretched coins with the earlier currency of Roman Britain.

Roman coins have been found in small numbers in Anglo-Saxon graves, but in several instances they had been adapted for use as ornaments and it was for this purpose rather than as currency that they were prized. Although Roman coins reached Scandinavia in considerable numbers at an early date, there is no ground for thinking that coined money was in regular use among the Anglo-Saxons while they were still on the Continent, nor does it seem likely that they used such money in England before the middle of the sixth century at the earliest. At about this time there are signs that the disturbed conditions incident to the migrations themselves were beginning to give way to a more settled state. Shortly after 550 Merovingian gold coins, struck mainly in the mints of north-eastern Gaul, began to find their way into south-eastern England, particularly into Kent. These were gold coins, known as *tremisses*, each struck to a weight of about 1½ gm., one-third part of the gold *solidus*. Merovingian *tremisses* continued to reach England for at least a century from *c.* 550, although from the distribution of the surviving examples they seem not to have spread far outside the south-eastern districts. These coins provided the models upon which were based the earliest Anglo-Saxon coins to be struck in England. The hoard of forty gold coins which was deposited in a purse in the Sutton Hoo burial and whose composition is dated by numismatists to *c.* 650 or a little later, consisted entirely of Merovingian *tremisses*. A second hoard of similar date and containing originally 101 gold coins of which

---

[1] This is highly controversial matter. Numismatists incline to the view that some form of currency was used in parts of Britain from the end of the Roman period until the introduction of the Merovingian *tremissis*, *c.* 560, but archaeologists seem less ready to follow this view. See C. H. V. Sutherland, *Coinage and Currency in Roman Britain* (Oxford, 1937), pp. 98–125; also B. H. St J. O'Neill, *Num. Chron.*, 6th ser., VIII (1948), pp. 226–9; C. H. V. Sutherland, *ibid.* IX (1949), pp. 242–4; and P. V. Hill, *Brit. Num. Journ.* XXVI, 3rd ser., VI (1952), pp. 1–27.

ninety-seven survive, was found at Crondall in Hampshire in 1828. Dr Sutherland's exhaustive study of this hoard and of all the other Anglo-Saxon gold coins known to him leads to striking conclusions.[1] He finds evidence for thinking that from *c*. 575 gold coins began to be struck in south-eastern England in imitation of the Merovingian *tremisses* and generally by Merovingian moneyers.

A group of seven coins from the Crondall hoard, bearing a form of the name London and seeming to be ecclesiastical rather than regal in character, establish the existence of a London mint in the first half of the seventh century, probably in the period *c*. 610–30. The identity of other mints at which similar gold coins were being struck cannot be established with certainty, but there is a strong case for thinking that such mints existed in Kent at an equally early date. Among other gold coins bearing Anglo-Saxon names which suggest that they were regal issues, there is only one series which can be ascribed to one or other of two particular kings. These are the coins which bear the name *Pada* inscribed in runic characters. Some authorities identify *Pada* with Penda, king of Mercia, and others with his son Peada who ruled first over the Middle Angles and after his father's death over the whole of Mercia until his own death a year later. Unlike the London *tremisses* which were based on Merovingian types, the *Pada* coins were based on a Roman design and bear the remains of a Roman legend. The discovery of three gold coins of a different type at York suggests that there may have been a mint there also, but this is by no means certain.

It is now established that a gold currency was in circulation at least in south-eastern England during the latter part of the sixth and much of the seventh centuries, and further that this currency, whatever its later development may have owed to the Church, preceded the arrival of Augustine's mission in 597. These facts point to increasing wealth arising from trade through the Channel ports with Merovingian Gaul. They lend substance to Bede's description of London, in a passage referring to the early years of the seventh century, as a market for people of many nations who came to it by sea and land. Gold, however, never became the

[1] C. H. V. Sutherland, *Anglo-Saxon Gold Coinage* (Oxford, 1948).

standard currency of Anglo-Saxon England as a whole. Perhaps even as early as *c*. 600 silver coins of the type known to numismatists as *sceattas* began to be struck and in the second half of the century they displaced the gold. In appearance the *sceattas*, usually of a high degree of purity, are somewhat thicker than the silver pennies which were introduced in the second half of the eighth century by Offa. A few are inscribed, but normally they do not bear the name of mint, moneyer or king. Indeed, they seem to be commercial rather than regal issues. They show a rich variety of design, sometimes of great artistic merit, and they draw their patterns sometimes from Roman designs and sometimes from Germanic motifs. Because of their anonymity it is difficult to establish their chronology and they have not yet received that degree of detailed study which could extract from them much valuable evidence about internal trade and about relations between England, the Low Countries and Gaul in the seventh century.[1]

Although some *sceattas* have been found north of Humber, their distribution in England lies mainly on the south-eastern side of the Fosse Way which crosses the midlands from Lincoln to the Devon coast. Within this area they are most heavily concentrated in Kent and the area of the Thames estuary, with lesser groups near Cambridge and Southampton. Some of the English *sceattas*, abnormal in that their silver content is so debased that they are little better than bronze, bear a form of the London mint name, but no other mint can be identified in this way. The name *Pada* is again found on some examples, and also the name of Æthelred, Penda's son. Others bear the name *Epa*, possibly a hypocoristic form for Eorpwald, a seventh-century king of East Anglia.[2] It is certain that *sceattas* were being struck in England in considerable numbers in the seventh century and in much of the eighth. In the second half of the eighth century they were driven out by Offa's new coinage, but in a debased form known to numismatists as

---

[1] For recent papers on the *sceatta* coinage see *Num. Chron.*, 6th ser., II (1942), pp. 42–70; *Brit. Num. Journ.*, 3rd ser., IV, pt. iii (1945), pp. 195–210; *ibid.* VI, pt. ii (1952), pp. 129–54, and pt. iii, pp. 251–79.

[2] Suggested by B. Dickins, *Leeds Studies in English and Kindred Languages*, I (1932), pp. 20–1, but not accepted by C. H. V. Sutherland, *Anglo-Saxon Gold Coinage*, p. 43, n. 1.

stycas they continued in use in Northumbria until the Danish invasions.

Sceattas are by no means confined to England. They have been found in large numbers at points along the Frisian coast between the Scheldt and the Eider. Some of these Frisian coins bear the so-called *Sigillum Davidis* device of two interlocked triangles, and the fact that this device does not occur on *sceattas* found in England suggests that this particular type was struck in Frisia itself. *Sceattas* have also been found in France, not merely in its north-eastern parts but as far afield as Aquitaine and Provence, with more than a suggestion that some of them were locally struck. The *sceatta* coinage presents many difficult problems to those who study it and these problems are by no means confined to England. The existence of a prolific coinage common to both sides of the North Sea as far north as northern Frisia and Whitby and reaching southwards almost to Marseilles bears witness to an aspect of seventh-century Anglo-Saxon history which receives little notice in the predominantly ecclesiastical sources from which that history must be studied.

The legislation of tenth-century English kings refers to many measures aimed, not without success, at securing the purity and uniformity of the coinage, but no such uniformity is to be expected in the earlier part of the Anglo-Saxon period and it is therefore not surprising that difficulties should be encountered in seeking to correlate the coins themselves with the terms for currency used in early sources. The Latin *tremissis*, the third part of the *solidus*, passed into Old English in the form *tryms* or *þrymsa* (pl. *trymsas*, *þrymsas*). In the early glossaries *trimsas* is used as a translation of the Latin *asses*. It is also used as the unit in which the amounts of the Northumbrian wergilds are expressed. In this latter case the *tryms* was certainly not used of a coin corresponding with the Merovingian gold *tremissis* and perhaps it was no more than a unit of account. The earliest Kentish laws, those of Æthelberht which belong to the early part of the seventh century (before 617), use two terms for money, *scilling* and *sceatt*. These terms are certainly old, since both occur in poetry and in the other early Germanic languages. Several passages in Æthelberht's laws show that the *sceatt* was a twentieth part of the *scilling*. The Gothic equivalents *skatts* and *skilliggs* are used to translate δηνάριον and *solidus* respectively. Since the existence of a gold coinage in Kent in the sixth century is now established, it may be taken as highly probable that the *scilling* of Æthelberht's laws refers to a gold coin of a type deriving from the Merovingian *tremissis* and that the *sceatt* refers to a silver coin of the type still called *sceatt* by numismatists. The Kentish laws exist only in a single late manuscript and it has sometimes been thought that their monetary terms may be later interpolations, but in view of what is now known about the extent to which currency circulated in seventh-century England this supposition does not seem to be necessary.

The earliest code of West Saxon law belongs to the reign of Ine and dates from *c.* 690. Here the larger sums of money are again expressed in shillings, but for the smaller sums a form of the word 'penny' is used. It is certain that the West Saxon shilling of Ine's laws was not the same as the Kentish shilling of Æthelberht's laws. The former was the equivalent of four or five silver pennies against the twenty of the Kentish shilling. Moreover, gold was no longer in circulation by the time of Ine's laws and Ine's shilling is not to be regarded as more than a unit of account. The word 'penny' does not occur in the earliest poetic records and although it is found in the Continental Germanic languages it does not occur there before the eighth century. Its oldest form in Old English is *pending*. It has been suggested that this form derives from the name of Penda, king of Mercia, and that it was applied to coins first struck by his authority. A parallel formation is found in Old Irish *Oiffing* which may mean a coin struck by Offa.[1] The occurrence of the name *Pada* in runic characters on both gold and silver coins lends some support to this view. Unfortunately, no Mercian laws survive from seventh-century Mercia. If this derivation is accepted, the term 'penny', representing a silver coin, must have come into use in England soon after the middle of the seventh century to be subsequently carried by traders both to Frisia and to Merovingian Gaul.

---

[1] B. Dickins, *Leeds Studies*, I, pp. 20–1. Professor Dickins reminds me of O.E. *casering*, meaning a coin bearing the image of a Caesar.

Soon after the middle of the eighth century the *sceatt* coinage was replaced throughout the whole of England save Northumbria by the new silver penny introduced by Offa. This currency reform which took place by more than accidental coincidence at about the same time as a similar reform of the Frankish currency, is a strong indication of commercial activity. Offa's pennies, which seem mostly to have been struck in Canterbury, bore his own name and a portrait head on the obverse and the name of the moneyer on the reverse. For the remainder of the Anglo-Saxon period, and long afterwards, the English currency continued to be based on a silver penny of this type, although there was much variation of design and weight. There is no doubt that England's external and internal trade was of considerable bulk in the eighth century. A short-lived quarrel between Offa and Charlemagne resulted in the banning of English merchants from the ports in Gaul and a corresponding ban against Frankish merchants was imposed by Offa. After friendly relations had been restored, Charlemagne wrote to Offa telling him that he would look to Offa's request for certain black stones, perhaps Tournai stone for fonts, and asking in his turn if Offa would see that the English cloaks sent to his kingdom were of the same length as those which had been sent in earlier times. One of the oldest trades was the export of slaves to the Continent. Writing *c.* 450 to the soldiers of Coroticus, Patrick assumed that the newly-baptized converts carried off from Ireland by them would be sent to the slave markets and he contrasted their behaviour with that of the Christian Gauls whose custom it was to redeem those who had been sold into slavery. We may recall Gregory's meeting in Rome with the young Englishmen who are represented in Bede's version of the story as slaves, and also his instruction that some of the Church revenues in Gaul should be used to redeem young English slaves. Late in the seventh century the laws of Wihtred, king of Kent, permitted the sale overseas of a freeman caught in the act of theft, though this practice was forbidden in the laws of Ine king of Wessex. Bede tells of a young Northumbrian nobleman who had been taken prisoner by Mercians and then sold to a Frisian in London.

Bede's brief description of London is paralleled by a somewhat similar description of York written by Alcuin and there can be no doubt that these two places at least can properly be regarded as towns before the Danish invasions. There is a reference to a colony of Frisian merchants in York and a glimpse of London's sea-borne trade is revealed in a charter in which Æthelbald, king of Mercia, undertook that two ships belonging to the bishop of Worcester and his community should be exempt from the dues levied by the tax-gatherers in London's harbour. Southampton, too, whose market is mentioned as early as 720, developed into a place of considerable importance. The market at Canterbury is mentioned in a charter of 786 and no doubt its nearness to the Continent as well as the prominence which it won as the seat of the archbishops had led to its growth as a town of some importance at an earlier date. Charters relating to both Canterbury and Rochester indicate that urban development reached an advanced stage in both places before the Danish invasions. At least by the early part of the ninth century these two towns were divided into a number of enclosed tenements to some of which shares in the fields, woods and pastures lying outside the town were attached. Such an enclosed tenement was known as a *haga*, the 'haw' of modern writers, or as a *tun* in the simple sense of enclosure. At Canterbury it was customary law in the ninth century that a space of two feet should be left empty between houses to serve as eavesdrip.

Canterbury was evidently so populous by the middle of the ninth century that its houses had come to be closely packed together and we may be sure that Offa would not have preferred it as the minting place for his new coinage soon after the middle of the eighth if the work could have been done equally well in his own capital at Tamworth or at Lichfield, but Canterbury, like London, though for different reasons, enjoyed special advantages. Nothing is known of the size or appearance of Offa's Tamworth, but it may be thought that the development of urban life on a site so remote from sea or estuary would take place more slowly than at the seaports where the crafts of shipwright, sailmaker and rope-maker were a necessary accompaniment of the merchandise which passed through them. It is significant that the Old English *port* was used both of a seaport and of an inland market town. In the seventh century the men of Kent who traded in London were required to do their business in the presence of two or three trustworthy men so that if the ownership of goods was later disputed witnesses could be produced. A precaution such as this was the more necessary as London was no part of the kingdom of Kent. The more widespread control of merchants depended on the existence of recognized markets and there is not much evidence for the existence of such markets away from the seaports. Over most of the inland parts of the country trade in the seventh and eighth centuries is likely to have been in the hands of pedlars and travelling caravans to whom the lack of established markets and of secure warehouses for the storage of goods would present great difficulties. Merchants in seventh-century Wessex, like the Kentishmen in London, were required to transact their business before witnesses, and in the ninth century Alfred enacted that merchants setting out on a trading expedition were first to present to the king's reeve at a public meeting the men they were taking with them. They were to declare their numbers and to take with them only such men as could be brought to justice. In time the needs of such merchants would no doubt have led to the development of many inland markets, but in the event this slower process was greatly stimulated by the military need for providing defensible centres in the disturbed conditions arising from the Viking attacks in the ninth century.

The systematic fortification of southern England seems first to have been put in hand by Alfred as a means of securing Wessex and Kent against further Danish attack. The *Burghal Hidage*, a document which dates from the reign of his successor, Edward the Elder, contains valuable evidence about the places so fortified, about the way in which they were to be defended and about their size. The basis of the system was that a specified area of land was allotted to each stronghold such that if one man was sent in time of need from each hide, every pole of defence work could be defended by four men. The *Burghal Hidage* does not itself give the overall length of the defences at individual places, but it states the number of hides assigned to each centre and from this figure it is possible to calculate at least the theoretical length of the defences in question. Thirty places are named and all save one of the twenty-eight which can now be identified lie on or south of the Thames. The exception is Buckingham. They include a number of places which had been towns of some importance in the Roman period—Chichester, Porchester, Southampton, Winchester, Exeter and Bath—and at such places the old Roman defences would serve as the basis of the new stronghold. Winchester, Alfred's capital, and Wallingford, guarding a crossing of the Thames of great strategic importance in the circumstances of the times, were much the largest, each being allotted 2,400 hides. This allotment implies at least in theory that each of these places could in time of need be defended by 2,400 men and further, since each pole of the defences was to be manned by four men, that the circuit of the defences was 600 poles, that is 3,300 yards or a little less than two miles. These theoretical figures coincide almost exactly with the length of the medieval wall of Winchester, about 3,280 yards, which in turn is thought to follow the line of the Roman wall. In other words, the *burh* of Winchester in the time of Edward the Elder appears to have coincided in area with Roman Winchester. The theoretical length of the defences at Wallingford likewise corresponds with existing remains. Fortifications enclose three sides of a rectangle, and the sum of their length, added to the length of river which forms the fourth side, amounts to 3,030 yards, against a theoretical length of 3,300. These and similar correspondences at other places where fortifications remain suggest that in general the figures of the *Burghal Hidage* are a reliable guide to the size of the places to which they refer.

Next in order of size come Southwark with 1,800 hides, Wareham and Buckingham with 1,600 each, Oxford and Chichester with 1,500, Cricklade and Wilton with 1,400, and Lewes and Malmesbury with 1,200. Of these places the theoretical circuit of the defences can be checked at Wareham where a massive earthen bank and ditch enclose three sides of an area which is bounded on the fourth by the river. The actual length of the circuit, 2,180 yards, corresponds almost exactly with the theoretical length, 2,200 yards, which can be calculated from the data in the *Burghal Hidage*. Several of the places named in the document were very much smaller. Porchester, Hastings and Tisbury were allotted only 500 hides each, giving a defence circuit of 625 yards, and Lydford and Lyng, with only 150 hides each must have been very small indeed. Neither of these two last is today more than a village. The scheme outlined in the *Burghal Hidage* represents a strategic plan designed to ensure the defence of England south of Thames against military attack. It was not concerned with the business of administration which continued to be served by the shire system. There is no comparable document relating to England north of Thames, but the records of Edward the Elder's campaigns suggest that in English Mercia and in the Danelaw, as it came progressively under English control, a scheme similar to that which had been successful in the south was carried through in the midlands also. Here, however, the change was perhaps more radical, since the earlier territorial divisions seem to have been overlaid by the burghal system out of which the midland shires grew as units of administration.

It was envisaged in the treaty between Alfred and Guthrum that there were likely to be times when Englishmen and Danes would wish to trade with one another and it was agreed that on such occasions hostages should be exchanged so that peace might be preserved. The fortified strongholds of Wessex and the midlands had been created primarily to meet military needs. War or the threat of war was seldom absent from tenth-century England and in such conditions there would be profit to the merchant in the form of recognized markets and to the king in the form of greater tolls if trade could be directed to particular centres and thereby brought under some measure of control, directed in other words to the *burh* or, to use a term which emphasizes the mercantile rather than the military aspect of what may have been one and the same place, to the *port*. Early in the tenth century it was enacted by Edward the Elder that no one should buy or sell goods except in a market town (*port*) and in the presence of the town reeve (*port-gerefa*). No doubt the main purpose of this enactment was to bring money to the king's treasury, but in any case such an ambitious attempt at regulation could hardly have been effective outside the bounds of Wessex itself. Athelstan tried to follow Edward's policy, but he had first to except goods worth less than twenty pence and later to permit general buying and selling outside the *port* provided that it was done before witnesses. Edgar's laws, distinguishing between larger and smaller boroughs, enacted that there should be a body of thirty-six persons in each of the former and twelve in each of the latter. These men were required to take an oath that neither for money, favour nor fear would they deny what they had witnessed or witness what they had not seen. Two or three of those who had taken the oath were then required to be present as witnesses at every business transaction. A similar method of control was to be applied in rural hundreds where the body of sworn witnesses was to be the same as that for the smaller boroughs.

In addition to recognized markets there was need for uniformity of currency. The silver penny of the type introduced by Offa in the second half of the eighth century had become universally current in England south of Humber, but by the tenth century the situation had been complicated through the introduction into much of England by the Danish settlers, not of their own Scandinavian currency since they had none, but of their own system of weights and measures. The settlers were, however, quick to see the advantages of a circulating currency and we find them striking coins in London before the end of the ninth century and also in York in the first half of the tenth. From the time of Alfred onwards there are frequent references, alongside the English pound, shilling and penny, to the Scandinavian mark (O.E. *marc*, *mearc*, O.N. *mǫrk*) and its eighth part, the ore (O.E. *ora*, O.N. *eyrir*, pl. *aurar*). In the time of Æthelred the Unready when the pound contained 240 pence, the ore was reckoned at 16 pence, but in earlier times there was probably much variation. Athelstan sought to diminish confusion by enacting that there should be only one currency throughout his realm. If a moneyer was found guilty of issuing base coin, the hand with which he committed the crime was to be struck off and fastened to the mint.

The most remarkable feature in the monetary practice of the

tenth century was the high degree of decentralization in the striking of the coins themselves. Athelstan's laws specify the number of authorized moneyers in several towns, thereby giving some indication of the relative commercial importance of the towns in question. London, as might have been expected, heads the list with eight. Next comes Canterbury with seven of whom four were for the king, two for the archbishop and one for the abbot of St Augustine's, and then Winchester with six. There were to be two each in Lewes, Southampton, Wareham, Shaftesbury and Exeter, and one each in Hastings and Chichester. It will be noticed that all these places save London lay either in Kent or in Wessex. There is no reference by name to any town outside these areas, but the passage concludes, as though the list of individual places was too long to give, with the statement that there was to be one moneyer in each other *burh*.

Such widespread coining of money might have been expected to lead to a corresponding degree of variety in the coins struck and to unevenness of standard, but though the moneyers themselves were thus widely distributed, the dies from which they worked were cut in London and in this way effective control was maintained, the more so as minor variations of design were made at frequent intervals and whenever this was done individual moneyers, whose coins bore their own names, had to fetch the new dies from London. Nevertheless, the attention given in one of Æthelred's codes to the coinage and to means of maintaining its purity, suggests that the need for coined money with which to pay the tribute exacted by the Vikings had led to some deterioration of standards. Æthelred ruled that in the larger boroughs there were not to be more than three moneyers and in the others not more than one, though this regulation can hardly have applied to the largest of all, such as London, Winchester and York. The evidence of the coins themselves shows that there were at least twenty moneyers at work simultaneously in London in Edward the Confessor's reign, at least ten in York and at least nine in Winchester.

London and Winchester supplied the standards for the system of weights and measures which Edgar sought to establish throughout his kingdom, London undoubtedly because of its commercial pre-eminence and Winchester perhaps because it was the seat of the treasury. Unfortunately, neither of these two places was included in the Domesday Survey and we lack even the uncertain means provided by this document of reckoning their population at the time of the Norman Conquest. It has been reckoned that the population of York at the end of the Anglo-Saxon period was over, and perhaps greatly over, 8,000. Saving London, York was probably the most populous town in the country at this time. Elsewhere, as examples for comparison, the evidence suggests a figure of 5,000 each for Norwich and Lincoln, 4,000 for Thetford, 3,500 for Oxford, 2,000 for Colchester, 1,600 for Cambridge and 1,300 for Ipswich.[1] Even though these figures are no more than approximate, they are enough to show that at the end of the Anglo-Saxon period there were many centres of population large enough to be called towns, though it is seldom possible to learn much about the way in which their inhabitants earned their livelihood or about the way in which they were governed.

In some towns gilds existed. A gild of knights (*cnihtas*) existed in Canterbury at about the middle of the ninth century and others are recorded later at Dover, Winchester (both knights' gilds) and Cambridge (thegns' gild). A document from the reign of Athelstan gives a detailed account of a 'peace gild' which was established under the leadership of the bishops and reeves belonging to London for the purpose of carrying out royal decrees which had been issued previously. Its members were divided into groups of ten, each with a headman, and the groups of ten were combined into groups of a hundred. The headman of each group of ten, together with the headman of the hundred, formed a committee which administered the common fund to which each member of the gild contributed. Once a month the committee met together to take account of the affairs of the gild and thereafter to feast. This was not a merchant gild but a voluntary association which was intended to maintain peace and security in daily life by the apprehension of thieves and the recovery of stolen goods and which also provided spiritual benefits for its members.

[1] Save for Oxford these figures are derived from H. C. Darby, *The Domesday Geography of Eastern England* (Cambridge, 1952).

Casual references to the 'pound of the London husting' (*pondus hustingiae Londoniensis*) and the 'husting weight' (*hustinges gewiht*) suggest the existence in the tenth century of a court which may, among other things, have been concerned with the regulation of trade. Its name suggests that the husting court was of Scandinavian origin and perhaps it arose from the need for some means of negotiation between Scandinavians and Englishmen trading in London. Evidence referring to times after the Norman Conquest shows that it then met once every week. There was also a larger court which met in the open air three times a year. According to the laws of Edgar the courts of other boroughs were also to meet three times a year. A document from the reign of Æthelred the Unready sets out in some detail the dues to be paid by foreign merchants bringing goods to London. Tolls were levied on visiting ships according to their size and among the merchants who were then visiting the port were men from Rouen, Normandy, Ponthieu and Flanders. Their cargoes included wine, fish, planks of wood and pepper.

The evidence is just enough to establish that London in the eleventh century was an important centre of commerce with a large population. More than once during the second phase of the Viking attack its citizens stoutly and successfully defended it against those who sought to destroy it and such experiences encouraged the growth of communal feeling. London was undoubtedly pre-eminent among the towns of England in size and wealth, but it was hardly yet a national capital save in a commercial sense. It could not become the capital in a wider sense so long as the royal court and the business of government associated with it lacked any fixed and established centre, and such remained the case until the end of the Anglo-Saxon period. Even if London and Winchester had been included in Domesday Book it is doubtful whether much more would have been learnt about the houses in which their population lived or about the way in which they earned their living. Domesday Book contains a survey of some seventy boroughs, but the information there recorded about them is quite inadequate to give any picture of the various trades and industries or of their relative importance. Danish merchants were frequent visitors to York which may be presumed to have had an important share in the trade with Scandinavia.

Not all the Anglo-Saxon coins found in the Scandinavian countries can be presumed to represent the tribute exacted by the Viking armies. Some must have found their way across the North Sea in the hands of traders and it is significant that the earliest moneyers known to have worked in Scandinavia were men with English names. Some of the houses recently excavated at Thetford show constructional techniques which find their closest parallels in Sweden and Denmark. Glazed pottery and numerous fragments of querns made of Niedermendig lava testify to Thetford's connexions with the Low Countries and the Rhine-land.[1] Cheese was being exported from England to Flanders in the eleventh century. English merchants had at least some share in Mediterranean trade. On his visit to Rome in 1027 Cnut sought to secure from the Emperor Conrad and from the pope some ease-ment of the barriers and tolls which hindered English traders passing through their dominions. An Italian document[2] of the early eleventh century gives some details of the dues to be paid to the customs posts at the outlets of the Alpine passes and to the treasury at Pavia. English traders in particular had caused diffi-culties and as a result an agreement was reached whereby in place of the normal dues, they were to pay a specified amount every three years. The bulk of this payment consisted of fifty pounds of pure silver. The inclusion among the other items of two grey-hounds and two fur coats, the latter for the official in charge of the customs house, may suggest that such things coming from England were highly prized in Italy. Irish marten skins were among the products imported into Chester from Ireland. The manufacture of textiles and metal-working were two skills in which the English acquired a high reputation. Both Dunstan and Æthelwold were famed as metalworkers and some ecclesiastics of later times were renowned goldsmiths. Fragments of a stole and

---

[1] G. M. Knocker and R. G. Hughes, *Archaeol. News Letter*, vol. II, n. 8 (Jan. 1950), pp. 117–22. G. C. Dunning, *Archaeol. Journ.* CVI (1949), pp. 72–3, rejects the views advanced by T. C. Lethbridge, *Proc. Camb. Ant. Soc.* XLIII (1950), pp. 2–6, about the Byzantine origin of the Thetford glazed pottery.

[2] Cited by R. W. Southern, *The Making of the Middle Ages* (London, 1953), p. 43.

a maniple recovered from St Cuthbert's tomb in the nineteenth century represent West Saxon work of the tenth. It is all but certain that the Bayeux tapestry was made in England. A similar tapestry recording the deeds of Byrhtnoth who was killed in the battle of Maldon in 991 once belonged to Ely. Shortly after the Norman Conquest textiles of outstanding quality were commonly called *opus Anglicanum*, a tribute which suggests considerable development of cloth manufacture in England. Salt was among the necessities of life and its production was widely distributed wherever conditions were suitable. Salt-making was an important industry round the shores of the Wash, as also along the coast of Sussex and in Cheshire. Droitwich in particular developed into a major source of supply for much of the western midlands. Of other minerals, iron was produced in the Forest of Dean and on a smaller scale in other parts of the country, and lead in Derbyshire. There is no evidence for the use of coal in the Anglo-Saxon period. Fisheries, notably the East Anglian herring fisheries, played an important part in the economy of many coastal towns, particularly Dunwich, Southwold and Yarmouth.

CHAPTER VI

LETTERS

I. LANGUAGE

ALFRED THE GREAT called the language which he spoke *Englisc*. Anglo-Saxon authors who wrote in Latin called it *lingua Anglica* or *lingua Saxonica*. Two names for this language have come into general use in modern times, Anglo-Saxon and Old English. Since both refer to the same language and to the same period of time, either may be used, but grammarians usually prefer the latter because it distinguishes one stage in the development of the language from two later stages, called respectively Middle English and Modern English. The distinguishing characteristics of Middle English first began to appear in the first half of the eleventh century and they developed rapidly late in that century and at the beginning of the twelfth. They came first into the spoken language and Old English continued in use for the written word after the spoken word had made the transition from Old to Middle English. The characteristic sounds of Modern English began to appear in the first half of the fifteenth century.

Old English belongs to the Indo-Germanic family of languages in which it is a member of the West-Germanic division of the Germanic branch. Besides Old English there are four other members of the West-Germanic branch: (1) Old High German, (2) Old Low German, commonly called Old Saxon, (3) Frankish, (4) Old Frisian. These five form a group intermediate between the Scandinavian dialects on the one hand and the south-west Germanic dialects on the other. Within the group the most closely related to Old English was Old Frisian which shared with Old English most of the changes distinguishing these two from the other members of the group. So close was their relationship that some have claimed the existence of a common Anglo-Frisian language, but most grammarians do not admit this claim and it is perhaps enough to recall, in explanation of their resemblance, the literary and archaeological evidence mentioned above (pp. 10, 15). Within Old English, divisions of two kinds are recognized, chronological, which must be more or less arbitrary, and dialectal. The chronological divisions are threefold: (1) Primitive Old English to *c.* 700, (2) Early Old English *c.* 700 to *c.* 900, (3) Late Old English *c.* 900 to *c.* 1100. The major dialectal divisions are also threefold: (1) Saxon, especially West Saxon, (2) Kentish, (3) Anglian. Anglian is subdivided into Mercian and Northumbrian, and the latter is further subdivided into North and South Northumbrian. The Kentish and Anglian dialects are sometimes grouped together under the name Non-West Saxon.

Knowledge of the different dialects of Old English varies greatly in both place and time. The materials are most plentiful for West Saxon by which is meant the language of the kingdom of Wessex, but even here very little remains before the middle of the ninth century. The best examples of pure Early West Saxon are found in the contemporary manuscripts of Alfred's translations of Latin works, such as the Cotton and Hatton manuscripts of the *Cura Pastoralis* and the Lauderdale manuscript of the *Orosius*. The Parker manuscript of the *Anglo-Saxon Chronicle* is a particularly valuable source of information about the development of West Saxon because it was written by a variety of hands over a long period. Its earlier part, from the beginning till 891, was written by a single scribe *c.* 900 and represents Early West Saxon. Although there are many gaps, it was continued at intervals, first at Winchester and later at Canterbury, by various hands during most of the tenth and eleventh centuries. This one manuscript offers unequalled opportunities for studying the development both of linguistic forms and of handwriting over a long period. Late West Saxon can be further studied in the numerous works of Ælfric, abbot of Eynsham in Oxfordshire, who wrote mainly in the last decade of the tenth century. In the latter part of the Anglo-Saxon period there developed alongside the spoken dialects a literary language which was used in all the cultural centres of

England. This language was basically West Saxon, but it contained some admixture of forms from other dialects, principally Anglian. It is the language of the four great codices which contain the bulk of Anglo-Saxon poetry, the *Beowulf* manuscript, the Junius manuscript, sometimes called the Cædmon manuscript, the *Exeter Book* and the *Vercelli Book*.

Most Anglo-Saxon literature, both prose and verse, is preserved in the West Saxon dialect or in the literary language which was based upon it, and for this reason it is customary to regard West Saxon as the 'classical' form of Old English and to use it as the norm by which to measure dialectal variations elsewhere. The materials for studying the non-West Saxon dialects are in no way comparable in bulk or in form with those in West Saxon. Specimens of Kentish are mainly confined to charters of which the earliest date from the late seventh century and to glosses in the British Museum Cotton manuscript, Vespasian D VI. In contrast with Kentish, which was confined to a rather small area, both Mercian and Northumbrian covered very large areas and there was naturally some variation between their different parts. Apart from runic inscriptions Early Northumbrian is found in three short poems called *Cædmon's Hymn*, *Bede's Death-Song* and *The Leiden Riddle*, in the Old English names of people and places in Bede's *Ecclesiastical History* and in the Durham *Liber Vitae*, a book containing the names of those who were remembered by the monks of Lindisfarne in their prayers. Late Northumbrian is represented by the gloss to the *Lindisfarne Gospels*, by the gloss to part of the Gospel of St Mark and to those of Luke and John in the Rushworth manuscript (known as *Rushworth²*), and by the Durham *Ritual*. Several of these Northumbrian works can be located with more or less exactness by their known association with particular parts of Northumbria at particular times and they can therefore be regarded as being *a priori* in the Northumbrian dialect, but this is not the case with Mercia whose literary history is largely unknown. Since there are very few documents which can be shown on historical grounds to have been written at a particular time in a particular part of Mercia, there has been a tendency to apply the term 'Mercian' rather loosely to all those documents which could not be recognized as belonging to other dialects. There is, however, general consent that the gloss to the Psalms in the British Museum Cotton manuscript, Vespasian A 1, commonly called the *Vespasian Psalter*, represents the south-west midland dialect of a time considerably earlier than Alfred. Among other works which have been ascribed to various parts of Mercia are the Epinal and Corpus glossaries, the gloss to the Gospel of St Matthew and to a small part of that of St Mark in the Rushworth manuscript (known as *Rushworth*[1]), a tenth-century life of the Mercian Saint Chad (*Ceadda*) which survives only in a twelfth-century manuscript and a small number of charters from the south-west midlands. It is likely in an area so large as Mercia that there were several different dialects.

The Celtic language, in its various forms, continued to be spoken in the remoter parts of Britain throughout the Anglo-Saxon period. A third language was introduced in the second half of the ninth century. This was Old Norse, the name given to the language spoken by all the inhabitants of Scandinavia at the beginning of the Viking Age. Like Old English to which it was closely related, Old Norse belongs to the Indo-Germanic group of languages. Its dialectal differences were not great when the Viking Age began, but they began to develop rapidly shortly before the year 1000. Two main divisions of Old Norse are recognized: (1) West Norse which was spoken in Norway and in the Norwegian settlements overseas, (2) East Norse which was spoken in Sweden and Denmark and in their colonies. Almost all Old Norse literature was written in Old Icelandic which belongs to the West Norse division. Where Scandinavians settled in the remoter islands of Britain their language, gradually modified by time, continued to be spoken for several centuries. That those who settled in England, both Danes and Norwegians, continued to speak their own language for a considerable time after the settlements is sufficiently proved by the very large number of surviving Scandinavian place-names and by the influence of Old Norse upon Old English, but Old Norse never became a literary language in England and it is difficult to say how long it continued to be spoken there.

Many Scandinavian runic inscriptions found in the Isle of Man attest that it was widely spoken there in the eleventh and twelfth centuries, but only a few such inscriptions are known from England and some of these are obscure or wholly illegible. A tympanum over the door of Pennington church in Lancashire which is held to date from *c.* 1100 bears an inscription which is Scandinavian both in its language and in its runes. There is another inscription in Scandinavian runes of about the same date in Carlisle Cathedral. These are indications that at least in north-western England a Scandinavian language was still being spoken in the twelfth century. Scandinavian runes on a bone comb from Lincoln and on a stone from St Paul's churchyard, London, are less sure evidence, since the one may not have been made in England and the other may have been associated with a recently arrived follower of Cnut. On the other hand, the rebuilding of the church at Kirkdale in the East Riding of Yorkshire during the latter part of Edward the Confessor's reign was commemorated by an inscription in Old English, though it contains Scandinavian personal names and one Scandinavian loanword (see Pl. XII, p. 192).

Over much of England in the tenth and eleventh centuries there is likely to have been considerable linguistic diversity, especially in the north-west where many of the Scandinavian settlers were descendants of a generation which had lived in Ireland. The Gospatric writ which was issued between 1041 and 1064, though now found only in a thirteenth-century transcript, contains a mixture of literary West Saxon, Anglian, Scandinavian and Celtic.[1]

2. ORTHOGRAPHY

The Anglo-Saxons were acquainted with two alphabets, the runic which they themselves introduced into Britain, and the Latin which, as may be seen from the form in which they wrote it, they learnt from the Irish. The use of runes was very limited and it was the Latin alphabet which was used as the universal instrument of written Old English. The Latin alphabet was capable of representing most of the sounds of Old English, but it could not express all its finer nuances. The chief inconsistencies in the

[1] Facsimile, E.P.N.S. XXII, opp. p. xxvi.

writing of Old English were in the use of the letters *c* and *g* which between them served for several different sounds. The letter *g* was used in early times as both a back and a front spirant, sounds approximating to those heard respectively in Modern High German *sagen* and Modern English *yonder*. It was later used as a back stop as in Modern English *good*. The letter *c* was used as both a back and a front stop, corresponding broadly with Modern English *could* and *kid*. In the runic alphabet symbols were created to distinguish between the back and front sounds of *c* and *g* in a way in which the Latin alphabet did not. The letter *b* was originally used in Old English as a spirant and in early manuscripts *b* is often found where a later manuscript would have *f*. Two letters were borrowed from the runic alphabet, þ, which was called *þorn* and represented *th*, and p which was called *wynn* and represented *w*. A third letter, ð, also representing *th*, was developed by a modification of the Latin uncial *d*. The resemblance of the Old English p (*wynn*) to the Latin *p* has been responsible for many misreadings in texts, and care must be taken to distinguish between them. þ and ð were used indiscriminately for the voiceless spirant (Modern English *think*) and the voiced spirant (Modern English *then*). Four letters of the Latin alphabet were commonly written in forms with which familiarity must be acquired. They were $f = \digamma, g = 3, r = p, s = r$. Vowel length is not usually marked in Old English manuscripts, but it is sometimes shown by duplication of the vowel in question or by an acute accent. Scribes writing in Latin used an elaborate system of abbreviations, but such abbreviations are much less common in Old English manuscripts. The most frequently used was 7 for O.E. *and*.

The oldest runic inscriptions found in circumstances which allow them to be dated archaeologically come from Denmark and are generally ascribed to the period *c*. A.D. 300. At that date a common series of runes was being used in Scandinavia and by the Goths near the lower Danube. The same series came into use among the western Germanic peoples, but not until about 150 years later. No general agreement has yet been reached about the origin of the runic alphabet which is sometimes called the *fuþorc* after its first six letters. It used to be thought that it was derived in part from the Latin alphabet and in part from the Greek, but some scholars are now inclined to associate it more particularly with a north Italic alphabet and to attribute some part in its development to the *Eruli* (called *Heruli* by Latin writers), a people of prominence in Denmark from A.D. *c.* 250 to *c.* 450. The oldest Germanic series of runes consisted of twenty-four symbols which were ordered in three groups of eight. In its later Scandinavian form these symbols were reduced to sixteen, but the form used in England was increased to over thirty by the addition of several new symbols. The method of forming runic letters by vertical and diagonal strokes, but without horizontal or strongly curved strokes, suggests that it was intended primarily for use on wood. Individual runes were often thought to have magical properties.

The old Germanic rune series spread southwards from Scandinavia into western Europe where two distinct series developed. One spread across Europe from Westphalia in the north-west to Hungary in the south-east and the other moved along the North Sea coast whence the Anglo-Saxons brought it to Britain. The runes of this latter series are called the Anglo-Frisian runes. About forty runic inscriptions are known in England on coins, household objects, weapons and stone burial monuments.[1] Among the earliest of these are the inscriptions on a gold coin of unknown provenance struck in imitation of a *solidus* of Honorius and on a scabbard mount from Chessell Down in the Isle of Wight. Runic inscriptions are also found on a number of silver coins, some of them associated with kings of Mercia and Northumbria in the seventh and eighth centuries. There are about twenty memorial stones, mostly from the north of England, inscribed with runes. Among them are two from Hartlepool, each bearing a woman's name, and one from Lindisfarne, also with a woman's name. Longer runic inscriptions are found on three stones from Thornhill in Yorkshire, on a stone from Falstone in Northumberland whose Old English inscription is written both in the Latin and in the runic alphabet, and on the Bewcastle cross in Cumber-

---

[1] The Old English inscriptions, whether in the runic or the Latin alphabet, have never been adequately presented as a whole. I am greatly indebted to Professor Bruce Dickins for help on this topic, particularly for allowing me to reproduce his system of transliteration, see Fig. 5.

PLATE XIV

FRONT PANEL OF THE FRANKS CASKET

The Franks Casket is made of whalebone and measures 9 in. by 7½ in. Its original height is uncertain. Belonging at one time to a French family, it was later bought by Sir Augustus Franks who presented it to the British Museum in 1867. It is held to be Northumbrian work of *c.* 700.

The sinister compartment represents the adoration of the Magi. The dexter scene shows Weland the Smith after taking vengeance on king Niðhad by killing his sons. He holds one of the skulls in a pair of tongs and with the other hand offers a cup made from the second skull to Beaduhild, the king's daughter, who is accompanied by an attendant. A headless body lies below. The remaining figure may be that of Weland's brother catching birds with which to make magic wings to aid their escape.

The inscription begins at the dexter side and reads clockwise. The runes in the bottom panel are in retrograde.

TRANSCRIPTION

ᚻᚱᚩᚾᚫᛋ ᛒᚫᚾ᛬ᚠᛁᛋᛚ ᚠᛚᚩᛞᚢᚨᚻᚩᚠ ᚩᚾ ᚠᛖᚱᚷᛁᛗᛖᛒᛖᚱᛁᚷ᛬

(r. to l.) ᚹᚪᚱᚦ ᚷᚪᛋᚱᛁᚳ ᚷᚱᚩᚱᚾ ᚦᚫᚱ ᚻᛖ ᚩᚾ ᚷᚱᛖᚢᛏ ᚷᛁᛋᚹᚩᛗ

(*sinister panel*) ᛗᚫᚷᛁ (mægi)

TRANSLITERATION

hronæs ban | fisc flodu | ahof on ferg|enberig | warþ gasric grorn þær he on greut giswom |

TRANSLATION

'This is whale's bone. The sea cast up the fish on the rocky shore. The ocean became turbid where he swam aground on the shingle.'

Its first two words apart, the inscription forms an alliterative couplet. There is room for argument about parts of the translation. See E. van K. Dobbie, *The Anglo-Saxon Minor Poems* (New York,

PLATE XIV

1   2   3   4   5   6   7   8   9 10 11 12   13 14   15 16

ᚠ ᚢ ᚦ ᚨ ᚱ ᚺ ᚷ ᚹ   ᚺ ᛏ ᛁ ᚷ ᛋ ᛢ ᚥ ᚼ

f   u   þ   o   r   c   g   w   h   n   i   j   ȝ   p (x) s

17 18 19 20 21 22 23 24   25 26 27 28 29 30 31

ᛏ ᛒ ᛖ ᛗ ᛚ ᛝ ᛟ ᚼ   ᚨ ᚫ ᚣ ᛠ ᛣ ᛤ ᛤ

t   b   e   m   l   ŋ   œ   d   a   æ   y êa k   ǩ   ḡ

Fig. 5. The Runes used in Old English Inscriptions.

The system of transliteration is that devised by B. Dickins, *Leeds Studies in Old English*, no. 1 (1932), pp. 15–19.

land. The most notable English runic inscriptions are those found on the Ruthwell Cross in Dumfriesshire upon which some extracts from an Old English poem called *The Dream of the Rood* are carved, and upon the Franks Casket, a small box of whalebone which is held to have been made in Northumbria *c.* 700 (see Pl. XIV). Inscriptions in the Mercian dialect are found on a bone plate from Derbyshire now in the British Museum, on a stone at Overchurch in Cheshire and upon the metal chrismale now preserved at Mortain in Normandy. Kentish runic inscriptions are found on a gravestone from Sandwich, a cross slab from Dover and a single-edged knife of the kind called scramasax. This last, now in the British Museum, was found in the Thames and has inscribed upon it a runic alphabet of twenty-eight characters and a man's name. The latest English runic inscriptions belong to the early part of the tenth century. The runic alphabet seems not to have been used much in England for monumental purposes after the Danish invasion of 865. Runic poems are preserved from Norway, Iceland and England. These consist of a series of short stanzas one of which was devoted to each of the letters of the alphabet. It has been remarked that these poems are exactly parallel to nursery rhymes of the type—

A was an Archer who shot at a frog;
B was a Butcher who had a big dog.[1]

[1] B. Dickins, *Runic and Heroic Poems* (Cambridge, 1915), v.

There is some variation in the shape of individual runes, but those shown above (Fig. 5) may be regarded as the normal form of the runes found in Old English inscriptions.

In Latin, as in Greek, palaeography, upper-case or capital letters are called majuscules, and lower-case or small letters are called minuscules. Two forms of majuscules are recognized. Those in which the letters are formed by strokes meeting at angles and in which curves are avoided as far as possible are called square capitals or, in a slightly modified form, rustic capitals. Letters fashioned in this way were particularly suited for carving on hard surfaces such as stone or metal. Those in which curves are freely used (cf. E with Є) are called uncials and they were more suitable for writing with a pen on a smooth, soft surface such as vellum. From a mixture of uncials and minuscules there developed a hand which is known as the half-uncial and it is this which formed the basis of the national book hand in both England and Ireland during the Anglo-Saxon period. It is to be supposed that the earliest Roman missionaries in south-eastern England were trained in the contemporary Italian hand, but this hand did not become established in England, and it had no influence upon the development of the native English hand which was originally based entirely upon the half-uncial hand of Irish scribes. This hand is found in both Ireland and England in majuscule and minuscule forms. The *Lindisfarne Gospels* represent the English half-uncial hand in its perfection. A good example of the pointed minuscule hand is found in the Moore manuscript of Bede's *Ecclesiastical History* which was written in 737, perhaps in an Anglo-Saxon foundation on the Continent but certainly by a scribe trained in Northumbria (see Pl. XVI, facing p. 324).

Although with the passage of time there were naturally small changes in letter forms, there was only one major change in the book hand used in England during the Anglo-Saxon period. This was due to the introduction of the Carolingian minuscule hand which was developed to a high degree of perfection as the book hand of the Frankish Empire whence it spread to most of the countries of western Europe to become the basis of most European forms of handwriting in modern times. In England these foreign minuscules began to displace the native form for Latin texts during the tenth century, but for writings in the vernacular the old native form continued in use though it was slightly modified by the influence of the new forms. A specimen from the A text of the *Anglo-Saxon Chronicle* illustrates a southern English hand at about the middle of the tenth century (Pl. IV, p. 88). This may be compared with the hands shown on Plate III (facing p. 34 above) and Plate XVI (facing p. 324 below), the former a Southern English hand of *c*. 900 and the latter the work of a Northumbrian scribe writing in 737.

3. THE GROWTH OF SCHOLARSHIP

If literacy may be regarded as a major criterion of civilization, the Anglo-Saxons can be called a barbaric people when they began to settle in Britain at about the middle of the fifth century, since they knew nothing of books and virtually nothing of letters. Their transition from barbarism to literacy is marked by three stages: first, by making contact with those who could teach them; secondly, by assembling books, necessarily foreign, which could be read and copied; and thirdly, by the creation of original works. Even before any Roman mission set foot in Britain Gregory had used some of the Church's revenues in Gaul for training English boys who had found their way there as slaves and it may be taken for granted that schools for training young men for the ministry were set up in England as soon as the Roman Church had established a foothold. There will have been such schools at Canterbury, Rochester and London in the early years of the seventh century. After his conversion in Gaul Sigeberht, king of East Anglia, established a school in his own kingdom after the manner he had seen in Gaul. His bishop, Felix, sent him masters and teachers 'according to the custom of the people of Kent'.[1] The instruction given in such schools was designed to educate men for the priesthood. Much of it will have been devoted to the teaching of Latin, so that the pupils could learn to read the Bible and the liturgy.

Music was important for services, and so also was a knowledge

[1] Bede, *H.E.* iii, c. 18.

of the Church calendar and of the means by which it was computed. Bede has left a vivid picture of Augustine and his companions advancing to their first meeting with Æthelberht of Kent, not armed with cunning sorceries as Æthelberht feared, but carrying a silver cross and chanting the litany. James the Deacon taught the Roman chant in Canterbury and went later with Paulinus to teach it in Northumbria. A generation after, Eddius Stephanus, Wilfrid's biographer, went from Canterbury to Northumbria where he became famous as a teacher of singing. A little later Putta, bishop of Rochester, became renowned for his skill in the Roman chant and in 678 Benedict Biscop was able to bring to England John, arch-cantor of St Peter's in Rome. John not only taught the Roman chant to the cantors of Monkwearmouth and Jarrow and to those of other Northumbrian monasteries, but he also left behind him after his visit many manuscripts which were still preserved in Bede's time. From the earliest days of the Roman mission in England the teaching of music which involved not only the art of reading musical notation, but also increasing familiarity with the Latin tongue, became an important factor in the progress towards more difficult forms of reading and writing.

Augustine and his successors in Kent, as well as Paulinus in Northumbria, would have with them such books as were necessary for holding services and for giving instruction. Alfred believed that among Augustine's books was a copy of Gregory's *Pastoral Care*, a work which Alfred himself translated late in the ninth century, and in the library of Corpus Christi College, Cambridge, there is a copy of the Gospels, written in a sixth-century Italian hand, which according to Canterbury tradition once belonged to Augustine and may well have been his. It is likely that soon after their arrival the Roman missionaries in Kent began to keep a few historical records and in later times when Bede came to write his *Ecclesiastical History* he was able to get copies of various documents relating to the early days of the mission in Kent, but these were mostly of foreign origin. There are no native English records from these times and it may indeed be supposed that during the first half of the seventh century the Roman missionaries in south-eastern England were so heavily engaged in their fight against deeply rooted paganism that the teaching of letters to their converts was beyond their power. Anglo-Saxon handwriting of the eighth century plainly reveals its descent from the Irish form of the Latin alphabet, not from the seventh-century Italian hand, and it is to the Irish monks who came to England in large numbers, beginning with the settlement of Aidan at Lindisfarne in 635, that much of the credit for teaching letters to the English must be ascribed. Lindisfarne was only one of several monasteries founded in Northumbria at this time and as the century passed Irish monks found their way into most of the English kingdoms. The reputation of Irish learning stood high in England and in the second half of the seventh century many Englishmen, especially from Northumbria, went to study in Irish monasteries. The zeal of the Irish for learning and teaching was undoubtedly great, but it should not be forgotten that the Englishmen whom they attracted to their schools were men whose fathers had been ignorant of the very existence of the Latin alphabet. Towards the end of the seventh century Aldhelm remarked that many Englishmen were still going to Ireland though they could then receive just as good an education in England.

The collecting of books, which may be held to mark the second stage in the advance towards literacy, seems to have begun soon after the conversion and the work proceeded at a great pace during the second half of the seventh century. Among the most ardent collectors was Benedict Biscop who in the course of several journeys to Rome and a sojourn of two years in Lérins acquired many books which he brought back to England and which he housed in the libraries at Monkwearmouth and Jarrow. On his return from one of his visits to Rome he accompanied Theodore, the newly appointed archbishop of Canterbury, and his companion Hadrian, formerly abbot of a monastery near Naples. For two years (669–71) he remained in Canterbury with Theodore, a man whom Bede described as 'deep in all secular and ecclesiastical learning, whether Greek or Latin'.[1] During these years he must have learnt much which he would later be able to impart to his fellow Northumbrians. Shortly before his death in 689 he

---

[1] *Historia Abbatum*, c. 3.

commanded the brethren of Monkwearmouth and Jarrow to keep the libraries intact, and Ceolfrith who presided over the two monasteries for close on thirty years before his death in *c.* 716 added many more books.

Bede was about forty years old when Ceolfrith died and he had already written a number of works. From the information which he gave his readers about the authorities he used in these and in his later works it is possible to learn something about the content of the library upon whose resources he drew. Some eighty different authorities were represented. His acquaintance with classical authors was not large, but he knew some of the works of Virgil and Pliny at first hand. He was well read in the Christian poets, among them Juvencus, Prudentius, Paulinus of Nola, Sedulius, Prosper, Fortunatus, Cyprianus Gallus and Arator. Among the historical works which he used were those of Josephus, Eusebius (but only in Latin translations from the Greek), Orosius, Cassiodorus and Gregory of Tours. Most of Bede's library was undoubtedly composed of theological works. He was of course deeply familiar with the Bible and he made great use of the writings of the Christian Fathers, especially Ambrose, Jerome, Augustine and Gregory. It is thought that there was a Greek text of the Acts at Jarrow in Bede's time,[1] but it is doubtful whether the other parts of the Greek New Testament were there. Bede occasionally used Greek authorities, but he seems only to have done so in Latin translations. Greek was certainly taught in the school established at Canterbury by Theodore and Hadrian, and according to Bede there were some pupils of the school still alive in his own day who were as familiar with both Latin and Greek as they were with their own tongue. There were certainly other well equipped libraries in England by *c.* 700 or a little later, but we have not the means of learning in such detail what books they contained. One such was at Hexham, collected mainly by Acca to whom Bede dedicated many of his works. From the books at Malmesbury, many of them of Irish origin, and at Canterbury, Aldhelm acquired a range of learning hardly less than that of his great contemporary Bede, and indeed his use of the works of Lucan, Ovid, Cicero and

---

[1] Now Bodleian MS. Cod. Laudianus Graecus 35.

Sallust, as well as of Virgil and Pliny, suggests that his knowledge of the classical writers was greater than Bede's.

Books were being copied by English monks in their own scriptoria before 700. Not later than 678 Wilfrid ordered for his newly dedicated church at Ripon a copy of the four Gospels to be written in letters of gold on parchment dyed with purple. He also ordered jewellers to make gold cases set with precious stones to hold them. Wilfrid's biographer remarks that these Gospels were of a beauty hitherto unheard of in England. There were certainly jewellers of outstanding skill in seventh-century England but the reference to purple parchment and to the use of gold suggests that the book itself may have been written abroad. A jewelled cover was made for the famous *Lindisfarne Gospels*, though it no longer survives.[1]

Only one Anglo-Saxon book thought to be of the seventh century now survives in its original binding. This book, now preserved in the Library of Stonyhurst College, Lancashire, and known as the *Stonyhurst Gospels*, though in fact it contains only the Gospel of St John, is recorded to have been found lying on the lid of the inner coffin of St Cuthbert's tomb when the tomb was opened in 1104. Its binding is dark red leather made of African goat. It bears on the front an embossed vine-scroll pattern and on the back a linear pattern representing a double cruciform ornament. About the year 700 Ceolfrith ordered three copies to be made of a Bible with the Vulgate text which Benedict Biscop had brought back from Rome. Two of the copies were intended respectively for the libraries of Monkwearmouth and Jarrow. One of these two has perished entirely and only some small fragments of a second are preserved in the British Museum and at Durham. The third copy was intended as a gift to the pope, as witness no doubt of the progress of Christianity in a remote corner of the world. It was to be taken to Rome by Ceolfrith himself, but as he was passing through Gaul in 716 he died and the book was taken the rest of the way by his companions. In modern times this same

---

[1] Professor B. Dickins draws my attention to a note in a sixteenth-century hand in a Canterbury Psalter attributed to the tenth century, MS. C.C.C.C. 411, f. 140*v*: *Hoc psalterium laminis argenteis deauratis et gemmis ornatum, quodam fuit .N. Cantuar. Archiepiscopi, tandem venit in manus Thomæ Becket quondam Cant. archiepiscopi quod testatum est in veteri scripto.*

book was discovered in the convent at Monte Amiato near Sienna. It is now preserved in the Laurentian library at Florence and is known as the *Codex Amiatinus*. Apart from some initial folios which possibly do not form part of the original volume, the text itself is largely free from ornament, having only one decorative initial and one full-page miniature representing Christ in glory within a circular medallion accompanied by attendant angels and with one of the evangelists, together with his appropriate symbol, in each of the four corners.

One of the first aims of every Anglo-Saxon religious foundation must have been to acquire a copy of the Gospels and no doubt the larger houses came to possess more than one, but apart from the copies which were in daily use, many foundations employed the varied skills of calligrapher, artist and jeweller to produce a copy of the Gospels worthy of special veneration as the most precious possession of the house. To the reverent care with which such books were guarded is due the survival today of several Gospel books which are among the greatest achievements in manuscript illumination of any age. Such are the *Lindisfarne Gospels* now in the British Museum, the *Book of Durrow* and the *Book of Kells*, both in the library of Trinity College, Dublin, the *Gospels of St Chad*, perhaps better called the *Lichfield Gospels* after their present home in the library of Lichfield Cathedral, and the *Echternach Gospels* now in the Bibliothèque Nationale at Paris. There is no direct evidence about the place or date at which these Gospels were written, but all are agreed that in their text and in their illuminations they represent a common tradition which is part Mediterranean, part Germanic and part Celtic.

The best evidence of date and locality comes from the *Lindisfarne Gospels* and the *Echternach Gospels*. On a blank space on folio 259 of the former there was written at about the middle of the tenth century a brief note in Old English stating that Eadfrith, bishop of Lindisfarne, wrote the book, that Æthelwald, bishop of Lindisfarne, bound it and that Billfrith made the ornaments upon its outside and adorned it with precious metals and gems. Although the exact meaning of this note is not everywhere clear, it seems likely that Billfrith's work consisted in making a separate outer case for the book such as was made for the Gospels ordered by Wilfrid for his church at Ripon. Some, reluctant to believe that so fine a work could be produced at an English monastery in the seventh century, have attacked the authenticity of this note, but there is no rational basis for such an attack. We need not find it difficult to believe that those who made a work of such splendour were remembered by name two or three centuries later and in the ascription of the work to men of whom very little else is known, we may find an additional reason for believing in the authenticity of that ascription. Had the work been attributed to Cuthbert himself the case would have been different. Eadfrith became bishop of Lindisfarne in 698 and died in office in 721. Æthelwald held the same see from 724 to 740. We may believe that the *Lindisfarne Gospels* were written at Lindisfarne about the year 700 or perhaps a little earlier if Eadfrith wrote the book before he was cumbered with episcopal duties in 698 (Pl. XV overleaf).

The evidence for dating the *Echternach Gospels* is of a different kind. Among the missionaries who went to the Continent near the end of the seventh century was the Northumbrian Willibrord. Early in the eighth century he founded a monastery at Echternach in what is now Luxembourg. Echternach became one of the main centres of Anglo-Saxon missionary activities on the Continent and became also the centre of a small school of illuminators. The most famous of their products is the manuscript which we now know as the *Echternach Gospels*. It yields no direct evidence of date in itself, but it is closely related to another of the group, a calendar which can be dated on internal evidence between 703 and 721 and which in all probability was made for Willibrord himself at the time of Echternach's foundation. The *Echternach Gospels*, though perhaps a little later, thus seem to coincide roughly with the date of the *Lindisfarne Gospels* and they undoubtedly spring from the same Northumbrian background. In their turn the *Echternach Gospels* show a style of art which is very similar to that of the *Book of Durrow*. The latter has often been claimed as an Irish work, but some of the zoomorphic patterns on the jewellery from Sutton Hoo bear so close a resemblance to patterns found in the *Book of Durrow* that it becomes difficult to dissociate it from the

PLATE XV

THE LINDISFARNE GOSPELS
British Museum Cotton MS Nero D, iv, f. 29.

The plate shows St Matthew's Gospel at chapter 1, verse 18. The opening words of this verse—"Now the birth of Jesus Christ was on this wise..."—coming after seventeen verses of genealogical material were held to mark the real beginning of the Gospel and for this reason the passage was richly illuminated, especially the great monogram.

It would be difficult to find a more striking portrayal of the different influences which met in Bede's Northumbria. The spiral pattern came from the Celtic world, the convoluted birds and beasts from the Germanic and the Vulgate text from the Mediterranean.

The rubric above the monogram is written in uncials and the four lines of text below, of which the first seems to be unfinished, in ornamental capitals with elaborate ligatures designed to make the best use of the space available. Between the lines and in the margins is the gloss written by a Northumbrian scribe in the tenth century.

RUBRIC

onginneð	godspell	æft	matheus
Incipit	euangelium	secundum	mattheu*m*

TEXT

Cristes	soðlice	cynnreccenise ꝺ cneuresū suæ ꝺ ðus	
Christi	autem	generatio	sic

wæs	mið ðy	wæs	biwoedded ꝺ beboden ꝺ befeastnad ꝺ betaht
erat	cvm	esset	desbonsata

	moder	his		
	mater	eius	Maria	Iosebh

The glossator sometimes uses two or three Old English words, separated by the abbreviation for the Latin *uel*, to render one of the Latin.

Top left (outside the monogram)
uutedlice (*emended to* uutodlice) suæ wæs cristes cneureso

Bottom right (in margin)
togemanne nalles to habbanne f̃ wif

abiathar ðe aldormon wæs in ðæm tid in hierusalem fore biscob. he bebeod maria iosephe to gemenne 7 to begoeong (*emended* to begeong) anne mið claennisse.

PLATE XV

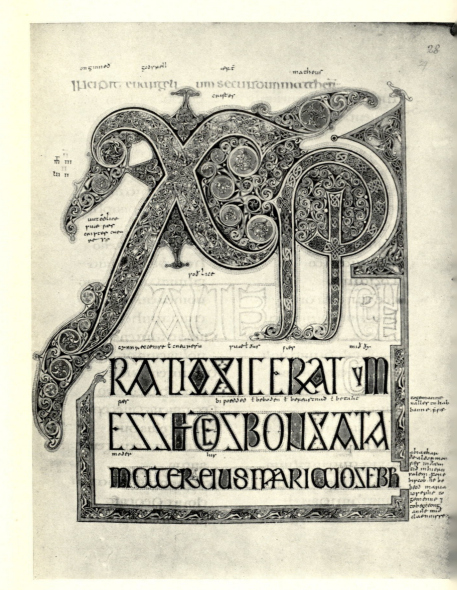

school of illuminators which flourished in Northumbria late in the seventh and early in the eighth centuries, the more so as the *Book of Durrow*, like the *Lindisfarne Gospels*, uses a good Vulgate text which is not likely to have been in Ireland at this time. To regard any one of these illuminated Gospels as being particularly English or particularly Irish is to misunderstand the peculiar nature of that Northumbrian civilization which resulted from the impact of Mediterranean and Celtic teaching upon a people governed by Germanic kings and speaking a Germanic language. Lindisfarne was originally an Irish foundation in an English kingdom. Cuthbert, its greatest son, was an Englishman, but the way of his life was Celtic. Jarrow and Monkwearmouth acquired most of their books from Rome, but Bede found many works there which were of Irish origin. The world into which Bede was born knew nothing of nationalism, but was one whose many strands were no less closely interwoven than the twisting limbs of those birds and beasts which adorn the pages of the *Lindisfarne Gospels* themselves.[1]

The oldest surviving written record from Northumbria which can be precisely dated is the dedication slab of Benedict Biscop's church at Jarrow. This slab (see Pl. VI, opp. p. 156), now placed in the wall over the western arch of the tower of Jarrow church, records that the building was dedicated on the 9th of the Kalends of May in the fifteenth year of the reign of Ecgfrith and the fourth of the abbacy of Ceolfrith. By modern reckoning the day of dedication was 23 April 685. From the shape of some of its letters it may be held as certain that this inscription was cut by an English stonemason and not by one of the Gaulish masons brought by Benedict Biscop to help in the building of the church. It is significant that this inscription should be concerned with chronology because the study of chronology was one of the principal starting-points of Anglo-Saxon historiography. The computation of the Church calendar and above all the controversy between the Roman and Celtic Churches about the right way of calculating the date of Easter created in those concerned a sense for the passage of

[1] Much that has been written on this topic is tinged with nationalist prejudice. The views of the historian of art must be supported by those of the palaeographer and the philologist before sure conclusions can be reached.

historical time which laid the foundations of the annalistic form of historical records in Anglo-Saxon England. No one concerned in the arguments advanced at the synod of Whitby could have failed to acquire some understanding of chronological matters. The construction of Easter tables from which could be calculated the date of Easter in years to come involved the setting out in parallel columns of a variety of data and in particular it required the adoption of an era by which individual years might be identified in a long series. For many years the Mediterranean and Western Churches identified individual years by the number which had elapsed since the persecutions of Diocletian, but when it came to be thought inappropriate that a persecutor of the Christian Church should thus be so prominently remembered, the era of Diocletian was replaced by an era which numbered the years from the birth of Christ. In this way the era *anno Domini* came into being. It is one measure of Bede's greatness that he was the first writer to adopt it as the regular chronological basis of a major historical work. Easter tables were primarily intended for forecasting the date of an event in the future, but once that purpose had been served they could be used for another purpose, the recording of an event which was passed. It is likely that in many places, by no means in England alone, where Easter tables were in use, once the data of each year had been used for their primary purpose, the margin opposite came to be used as a place on which brief historical memoranda were recorded. The tables were certainly used in this way in Canterbury and in Northumbria and from these beginnings, with the later separation of the marginal notes from the table itself, there grew the regular annalistic chronicle which lies at the foundation of English historiography.

If chronology was one starting-point of historiography, the other was hagiography. A necessary companion to the Easter tables was the Julian calendar which provided a place on which might be recorded the anniversaries of the saints. Anniversaries might be observed not merely by prayers for those concerned, but also by homilies or commemorative sermons. Such a homily lies behind the *Life of Ceolfrith*, and Bede's *History of the Abbots of Wearmouth and Jarrow* may likewise be based in some part on homiletic material. To judge from the number of surviving examples the writing of saints' *Lives* became a popular form of literary composition in the first half of the eighth century. An unknown monk of Lindisfarne wrote a *Life of Cuthbert* about the year 700. A little later Bede himself wrote two *Lives* of Cuthbert, one in verse and the other in prose, using the anonymous Lindisfarne *Life* as the basis of both. A *Life of Gregory* was written at Whitby and Eddius Stephanus wrote a *Life of Wilfrid*. There is no reason to suppose that the writing of hagiography was peculiar to Northumbria. Somewhere in the east midlands Felix wrote a *Life of Guthlac*, dedicating it to Ælfwald, king of East Anglia. This work still survives, but the *Life of Æthelburh* of Barking which was used by Bede, has since been lost.

These early saints' *Lives*, all of them written in Latin, provide valuable material for the early history of the English Church, but they must be used with care, partly because they were written for the greater glory of the house to which the subject belonged and partly because there was much in their content that was highly conventional. When we find Eddius Stephanus protesting that he has neither the understanding nor the eloquence to undertake such a task, but that he is constrained to do so by the command of his superior, and protesting further that he will not write of anything which he has not received on good authority from trustworthy witnesses, we should not draw conclusions either about the inadequacy of his education or about the veracity of what he relates. The identical words are to be found in the preface to the anonymous *Life of Cuthbert*, and even here they are not original. The anonymous author described his inadequacy to fulfil the task allotted to him in words which he borrowed verbatim from the introduction to Victorius of Aquitaine's work on the Paschal Cycle, and vouched for the veracity of his authorities in words similarly borrowed from Sulpicius Severus' *Life of Martin*. Later in the *Life of Cuthbert* the virtues which the saint displayed as bishop are described in words borrowed from the same source and when Eddius Stephanus wished to describe the virtues of Wilfrid he could not do better than borrow the relevant phrase from the *Life of Cuthbert*. Those who use such works as sources of history must first learn to recognize what was conventional in the writing of hagiography in those times, yet when the conventional is set aside much of value remains.

Even when full allowance has been made for the loss of manuscripts, there can be little doubt of the pre-eminence of the twin monasteries of Monkwearmouth and Jarrow in the intellectual life of England during the early part of the eighth century, and none at all of the intellectual sovereignty of their greatest son whose mental stature is to be measured against the greatest minds of the Middle Ages over the whole field of letters in western Europe. Very little is known about Bede's life, save what he himself appended to his *Ecclesiastical History*. He was born *c.* 671, traditionally at Monkton in County Durham, within the territory which later belonged to Jarrow. Nothing is known of his parents who entrusted him at the age of seven to the care of Benedict Biscop. His first monastic home was at Monkwearmouth but he later moved to Jarrow where he remained until his death in 735. He was admitted to the diaconate in his nineteenth year which was below the canonical age, and to the priesthood in his thirtieth. Apart from a visit to Lindisfarne and another to York, there is no evidence that he travelled far beyond the bounds of the two monasteries. His life was that of a scholar, spent in the religious duties of his Order and in the study of books. In his own eyes and to his contemporaries he was first and foremost a teacher. To posterity he is known chiefly as the author of the *Ecclesiastical History of the English Nation*, but this was almost the last in the long series of works which he produced over thirty years or so. Most of his works were concerned with expounding the Scriptures and since his Biblical commentaries have not yet been critically examined as a whole, his place as a theologian is still to be determined. His earliest works *On Metre*, *On the Figures and Tropes of Holy Scripture*, *On Orthography* and *On Times*, all of which were written in or before 703, were manuals for use by pupils in the monastic school. The last of these, which was prompted by the Easter controversy, was one of two main works devoted to chronology. Twenty-two years later he wrote a greatly enlarged chronological treatise *On the Reckoning of Times*. In the interval between these two he wrote more than a dozen other works of which most were Biblical commentaries on books of both the Old and the New Testaments. To this period of his life there belongs also a scientific work *On the Nature of Things* which was derived largely from Pliny's *Natural History* and from Isidore's *Etymologies*, as well as two hagiographical works, the prose and verse lives of Cuthbert, and a work which is more strictly biographical, the *History of the Abbots of Wearmouth and Jarrow*. This latter is replete with precise factual information of the greatest interest and is wholly free from the miraculous.

Bede seems to have recognized by appending to his *Ecclesiastical History* a short survey of his life and works that this was the culmination of all his literary endeavours, even though the long list of his works was not yet quite complete. It is certain that there are few books whose influence upon later generations has been more widespread or more lasting. It was designed to relate in narrative form the history of Christianity among the English people from its antecedent days during the Roman occupation of Britain until the year 731 on the basis of all that Bede could learn from former writings, from the traditions of his elders or from his own direct experience. For the earlier part of the work he had to draw upon older written authorities, principally Orosius, Gildas and Constantius. It was not his practice to refer to his authorities when using written works of history, but in a Preface which directly or indirectly has served as the model for successive generations of historians even to the present day, he named with care and gratitude those who had helped him either by sending him written documents or by telling him orally all that they thought worthy of his attention. Prominent among his helpers were Albinus, abbot of St Augustine's, Canterbury, who had benefited from the teaching of Theodore and Hadrian, Nothhelm, a priest of London, who acted as intermediary between Canterbury and Jarrow and who even travelled to Rome to search the papal archives for letters of Gregory and other popes, and Daniel, bishop of the West Saxons, who wrote to him about the ecclesiastical history of Wessex, Sussex and the Isle of Wight. The monks of Lastingham told him

PLATE XVI

THE MOORE MANUSCRIPT OF BEDE'S
ECCLESIASTICAL HISTORY

This manuscript, now in the University Library, Cambridge, class-mark Kk. v. 16, is the oldest of the five eighth-century manuscripts of Bede's *Ecclesiastical History*. Written almost certainly in 737, that is two years after Bede's death, it is an outstanding example of the eighth-century Hiberno-Saxon minuscule hand. Marginalia suggest that it was on the continent in the tenth century, but whether it was originally written there at some Anglo-Saxon monastic centre or whether it was written in Northumbria and subsequently taken abroad remains uncertain. The page illustrated is f. 44 *b*, the opening page of the third book of the *History*. There follows a text and translation of the first ten lines. Contractions have been expanded, punctuation modernized and capitals supplied.

At interfecto in pugna Ęduino, suscepit pro illo regnum Deirorum, de qua / prouincia ille generis prosapiam et primordia regni habuerat, / filius patrui eius Aelfrici uocabulo Osric, qui ad prædicationem Pau/lini fidei erat sacramentis inbutus. Porro regnum Berniciorum, nam in / has duas prouincias gens Nordanhymbrorum antiquitus diuisa erat, sus/cepit filius Aedilfridi qui de illa prouincia generis et regni originem / duxerat, nomine Eanfrid. Siquidem tempore toto quo regnauit Ęduini, / filii praefati regis Aedilfridi qui ante illum regnauerat, cum magna / nobilium iuuentute apud Scottos siue Pictos exulabant ibique ad / doctrinam Scottorum cathecizati et baptismatis sunt gratia recreati.

Translation

After Edwin had been killed in battle he was succeeded in the kingdom of Deira, the province to which his family belonged and where he had first begun to reign, by a son of Ælfric, his father's brother. The name of this son was Osric, a man who had been instructed in the mysteries of the faith through the preaching of Paulinus. But in the kingdom of Bernicia—for the Northumbrians had of old been divided into two provinces—Eanfrith began to reign. He was a son of Æthelfrith whose family had come from that province and who had first reigned there. During the whole of Edwin's reign the sons of this king Æthelfrith who had reigned before Edwin, and many of the young noblemen, were in exile among the Scots or the Picts and there they were instructed according to the teaching of the Scots and were reborn by the grace of baptism.

PLATE XVI

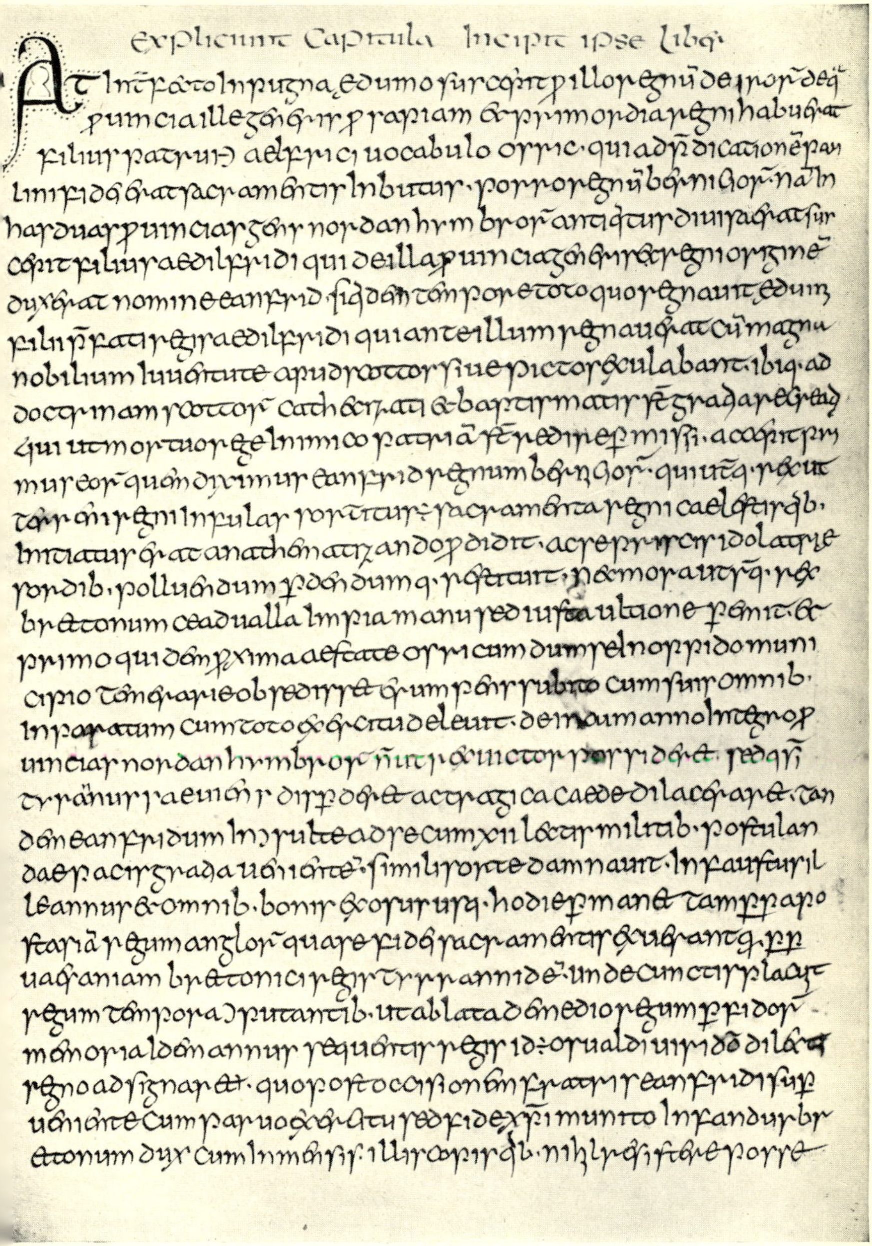
Explicivnt capitula incipit ipse liber
At interfecto in pugna aeduino suscepit pro illo regnum deirorum in qua
prouincia ille generis prosapiam et primordia regni habuerat
filius patrui eius aelfrici uocabulo osric qui ad praedicationem pau
lini fidei erat sacramentis inbutus porro regnum berniciorum nam in
has duas prouincias gens nordanhymbrorum antiquitus diuisa erat sus
cepit filius aedilfridi qui de illa prouincia generis et regni originem
duxerat nomine eanfrid siquidem tempore toto quo regnauit eduini
filii fratris regis aedilfridi qui ante illum regnauerat cum magna
nobilium iuuentute apud scottos siue pictos exulabant ibique ad
doctrinam scottorum cathecizati et baptismatis sunt gratia recreati
qui ut mortuo rege inimico patriam sunt redire permissi accepit pri
mus eorum quem diximus eanfrid regnum berniciorum qui uterque rex ut
terrenis regni infulas sortitus est sacramenta regni caelestis quibus
initiatus erat anathematizando prodidit ac se priscis idolatriae
sordibus polluendum perdendumque restituit nec mora utrumque rex
brettonum caedualla impia manu sed iusta ultione peremit et
primo quidem proxima aestate osricum dum se in oppido muni
cipio temerarie obsideret erumpens subito cum suis omnibus
inparatum cum toto exercitu deleuit deinde cum anno integro pro
uincias nordanhymbrorum non ut rex uictor possideret sed quasi
tyrannus saeuiens disperderet ac tragica caede dilaceraret tan
dem eanfridum inconsulte ad se cum xii lectis militibus postulan
dae pacis gratia uenientem simili sorte damnauit infaustus il
le annus et omnibus bonis exosus usque hodie permanet tam propter apo
stasiam regum anglorum qua se fidei sacramentis exuerant quam propter
uesaniam brettonici regis tyrannidem unde cunctis placuit
regum tempora computantibus ut ablata de medio regum perfidorum
memoria idem annus sequentis regis id est osualdi uiri deo dilecti
regno adsignaretur quo post occisionem fratris eanfridi super
ueniente cum paruo exercitu sed fide christi munito infandus br
ettonum dux cum inmensis illis copiis quibus nihil resistere posse

what they knew of Mercia and Essex and from other sources he learnt about Lindsey and East Anglia. For his native Northumbria he drew, not upon any particular authority, but partly upon the rich body of oral tradition which was current in his own time and partly upon his own direct knowledge. If today's reader of this Preface is led by its very modernity to expect a work which in its fundamental approach to history differs little from modern works of narrative history, he will not be disappointed. So familiar will seem its form that he will rather find it difficult to realize how great an achievement it was in Bede's day. To take one point alone, the chronological framework resting upon the era of the Incarnation has become so fundamental a part of modern historiography that we cannot now grasp how great was the innovation made by Bede. Yet the Preface does much more than convey acknowledgements for help received. It shows, as indeed does other evidence, that we must not be misled by the very greatness of Bede into supposing that Northumbria was the only kingdom in which intellectual interests flourished in his lifetime. In almost every kingdom in the land there were men who, if individually of smaller stature, were at least able to understand the kind of information which was likely to interest him. They could send him documents or write letters or travel the length of the country to talk with him.

The *Ecclesiastical History* is pre-eminent among all the materials of Anglo-Saxon history as a masterpiece of historical narrative and as a source of accurate information. Few are likely to underestimate its value. Perhaps the danger is rather in forgetting that almost all we know about the history of the Church in England from 597 to 731 is drawn from this one book, the product of a single mind. It would be folly to believe either that Bede was acquainted with all that happened in that period or that in expressing what he knew he was wholly free from prejudice. He wrote, as he himself clearly stated, in order that those who heard his work read might be encouraged to imitate what was good in their past history and to shun what was hurtful and perverse, and some of those who listened may have been left with the impression that in Bede's sight few things were more hurtful and perverse than the British Church. He was a man of about sixty when he wrote the *History* and he had then passed all but the days of his infancy in one of the principal strongholds of Benedictine monasticism in England. Although the decisions of the synod of Whitby were taken before his birth, his lifetime (*c.* 671–735) coincided with the real triumph of the Roman Church in England and the complete discomfiture of its Celtic adversaries. He had played no small part in that triumph by his earlier writings on the Easter controversy, but in the *History* he struck a blow for Rome whose effect was felt throughout the Middle Ages. It is a measure of its force that the first modern English translation of the work, published at Antwerp in 1565, was made by Thomas Stapleton whose purpose in making it was to influence Elizabeth I against the Reformation by showing how wide was the gap between the 'pretended reformers' and the Church of Augustine of Canterbury.

Much of Bede's greatness lay in those powers of synthesis and detachment which enabled him to distil a living work from a great variety of information drawn from widely scattered sources. In the mind of his older contemporary, Aldhelm, learning of equal depth produced little more than an extravagant form of intellectual virtuosity. Aldhelm, who was born *c.* 640, was educated partly at Malmesbury, an Irish foundation whose abbot he later became, and partly at Canterbury. In 705 he became the first bishop of Sherborne and he died in office four years later. Like Bede he drank deeply from the streams of Irish and Mediterranean scholarship, but their waters produced in him a state of intellectual intoxication which delighted its beholders, but which left little to posterity. His most popular works were a poem on virginity and a prose treatise on the same subject. His poem began with an elaborate double acrostic in which the initial and final letters of the lines formed one and the same hexameter verse, reading the initial letters downwards and the final letters upwards. In such mental gymnastics lay his chief delight and we may be sure that in this present world he would have enjoyed both *Finnegans Wake* and the more elaborate forms of crossword puzzle. There is more of interest and value to be found in his letters. In one of these, addressed to Geraint of Cornwall on the errors of the British Church in the south-west, he showed that he could write straightforward Latin prose, but in another, in which he sought to demonstrate the excellence of English teaching, he used such a wealth of vocabulary and such an overwhelming weight of metaphor, simile and alliteration that the letter itself is scarcely intelligible. It is possible that this letter was addressed to Aldfrith, king of Northumbria, who was certainly the recipient of another of Aldhelm's letters which, apart from a treatise on the number seven and on the hexameter as a verse form, contained a collection of a hundred metrical riddles. These are now the most attractive of Aldhelm's literary remains and also the earliest surviving examples of a type of light mental exercise which enjoyed great popularity among scholarly men in Anglo-Saxon England. Aldfrith, though a secular ruler, was a man whose learning was great enough to allow him to enjoy Aldhelm's writings. His mother may have been Irish and during the reign of his brother, Ecgfrith, he lived in exile partly in Ireland and partly in Iona. None of his writings survives, but he acquired a high reputation as a scholar and a poet among the Irish by whom he was known as Flann Fina. Some scholars have suggested that the Old English poem *Beowulf* was composed at his court, but this suggestion has not found general favour.

The names of Theodore, Aldhelm and Bede are representative of deep learning in three widely separated parts of England—Canterbury, Malmesbury and Jarrow. There is a danger that the quality of Northumbrian scholarship in the age of Bede may overshadow the steady growth of letters in other parts of England. It is hard to combat this danger because so little now survives from south of Humber, yet from evidence scattered here and there, it is difficult to escape the impression that there were in the eighth century many monasteries both in the midlands and in Wessex where good learning was to be found. Tatwine, who became archbishop of Canterbury in 731, the year in which Bede finished his *Ecclesiastical History*, was a Mercian educated at Breedon-on-the-Hill in Leicestershire. The great basilican church at Brixworth in Northamptonshire surely housed men of learning and we dare not suppose, merely because there is no written evidence, that there were no scholars at *Medeshamstede* (Peterborough), the parent house of these two midland foundations. In Wessex the monasteries at Exeter and Nursling produced the greatest of the Anglo-Saxon missionaries, Boniface, who was able to turn to a place so remote as Whithorn where he found a pupil of Aldhelm's to advise him on a difficult point of canon law. The letters of Boniface and his successor Lullus are good evidence that there were many people in eighth-century England, women as well as men, who could write fluently in Latin, and good evidence too that educated men in all parts of England corresponded freely with one another and with their countrymen engaged in missionary work across the sea. In the year of Bede's death (735) his former pupil, Egbert, whose brother was king of Northumbria, became archbishop of York and unless we are greatly deceived by the surviving evidence York succeeded to the position of intellectual distinction formerly held by Jarrow. Egbert established a school to which the sons of noblemen were attracted and as the century passed several of the nobility, including even the king himself, abandoned their secular lives to become monks at York.

The greatest of Egbert's pupils was Alcuin who, towards the end of the eighth century, carried the tradition of learning which he had inherited through Egbert from Bede to the court of Charlemagne. Alcuin himself wrote a long poem called *Verses on the Saints of the Church of York* in which he traced the history of York and its great men, telling something of the methods of teaching which he had experienced there and of the great library which was gathered by Egbert's kinsman and successor in the archbishopric, Æthelberht. From this work and from the work of Alcuin's biographer much can be learnt about the great school at York whose fame attracted scholars both from the Continent and from Ireland. Alcuin himself succeeded Æthelberht as master of the school shortly before he left Northumbria in 782 to spend most of his remaining years abroad, where his greatest work was done and where he played a major part in the revival of learning in the Carolingian Empire. Eleven years later he heard of the sack of Lindisfarne. As late as *c.* 850 a scholar could still write from abroad asking for books from the York library, but in 866 York itself passed into the hands of the Danes and its library was destroyed.

4. VERNACULAR POETRY

Latin continued to serve as the main vehicle of Anglo-Saxon prose literature until the time of Alfred. Particular circumstances occasionally led to the use of the vernacular for prose writings at an earlier date, but in general it is only to be expected that a literature which both in its form and in its content sprang from a Latin parentage should itself have been written in the Latin language. The earliest surviving Anglo-Saxon document written in the vernacular is the code of laws which was issued between 597 and 616 by Æthelberht of Kent. The date of this document falls a generation or so before the first mission of the Roman Church to Northumbria and a century before the earliest of Bede's works. There are two other surviving Kentish law codes in the vernacular, the one issued *c*. 685 and the other *c*. 694, but all three of these codes survive only in a twelfth-century manuscript in which the language has been modernized. Nearly contemporary with the latest of the three is a West Saxon code issued by King Ine. Law codes, however, were not literary compositions designed either for the instruction or the entertainment of a limited number of educated people, but were of universal application within the bounds of the particular kingdom to which they referred. Furthermore, at least the earlier Anglo-Saxon codes were, save for the impact of Christianity, little more than the embodiment in writing of primitive Germanic custom whose roots lay deep in the past. Customary law employed a highly specialized vocabulary and the task of rendering this vocabulary accurately in Latin would have been difficult and perhaps impossible in a society whose knowledge of Latin was as yet very slight.

Bede and his contemporaries undoubtedly looked upon Latin as the language of scholarship, but he himself realized that the use of the vernacular might be an effective means of furthering the teaching of Christianity. Writing to Egbert, bishop of York, in 734 he urged him to ensure that there were enough priests and teachers to instruct the people in the fundamentals of the

Christian faith, especially in the Apostles' Creed and in the Lord's Prayer. It was not enough, he wrote, that they should be familiar to those who knew Latin. They should be constantly repeated in the language of the people, and to this end he had often given translations to monks who were ignorant of Latin. In addition, as we learn from the account of his last days written by one of his disciples, Bede translated some extracts from the works of Isidore and was at the time of his death engaged on a translation of the Gospel of St John. He did not live to complete this work and no part of it or of his other translations has survived.

Bede is said to have been skilled in vernacular poetry and there were certainly others in the seventh century who realized that the popular love of minstrelsy which the Anglo-Saxons shared in common with other Germanic peoples, might prove the most effective ally in teaching men who could not read and who knew no Latin. If Latin remained the language of scholarship, vernacular poetry became the means by which scholars imparted the fruits of their learning to those who were in need not of learning but of salvation. The student of Old English poetry, inevitably confining himself to a small selection of texts, seeking to understand this or that allusion or to re-create the image of a remote past, may easily overlook one salient fact, that far the greater part of this poetry as it survives today is religious in kind and was fashioned as the instrument of the teacher. Even in *Beowulf* itself, where a heroic tale is set against a pagan background, Christian principles are of its very essence. The student often seeks in vain to understand the allusion which needed no explanation to an Anglo-Saxon audience and takes for granted the familiar Christian teaching which to that audience was largely new.

The Germanic love of minstrelsy was deeply rooted in the past and was old even when the Romans first came to Britain. The Roman historian Tacitus refers to the ancient songs (*carmina antiqua*) of the *Germani* and adds that they were the only kind of historical tradition which they possessed. Elsewhere he refers to the Germanic chieftain Arminius who, no longer alive himself, was remembered in poetic lays. Although the Anglo-Saxon invaders of the fifth century were illiterate in the sense that they could neither read nor write, it is probable that they brought to Britain with them a store of songs and poems of many kinds which provided them with their chief means of entertainment. We cannot tell how much has been lost, but we can be certain that the surviving fragments represent only a very small part of the whole. Much would have been lost through the normal hazards to which manuscripts are exposed by the mere passage of time, but in a society whose intellectual life was dominated by a Church which vigorously condemned the recitation of heathen poetry, the odds against the transmission of such poetry in writing were very great indeed. There were certainly ecclesiastics in the eighth century who enjoyed listening to old stories of heathen times, but they were severely censured by the Church for doing so. Priests who prated in church like secular bards were condemned at the synod of *Clofeshoh* in 747, as also were monasteries which had become the haunts of versifiers and harpists. Near the end of the century Alcuin wrote to Hygebald, bishop of Lindisfarne, denouncing the monks who invited harpists to entertain them while they dined. 'When priests dine together let the words of God be read. It is fitting on such occasions to listen to a reader, not to a harpist, to the discourses of the fathers, not to the poems of the heathen. What has Ingeld to do with Christ? Strait is the house; it will not be able to hold them both.'[1] Remembering this forthright attitude of churchmen towards the recitation of heathen poetry, we should remember also that churchmen alone knew how to write and that they were therefore the arbiters of what might be handed down to posterity. When so much that has survived of Anglo-Saxon poetry is devoted to the Christian God, we may guess that much of what has perished by deliberate condemnation was devoted to the pagan gods of the Germanic world and therein we may see one reason why so little is known of Anglo-Saxon paganism.

The important place which minstrelsy held in Anglo-Saxon court life in the seventh century is indicated by the discovery of a harp among the objects in the Sutton Hoo ship burial. In *Beowulf* the recitation of lays, some of them represented as ancient compositions and some of them as newly made for the occasion,

[1] *M.G.H., Epist. Karol. Aevi*, II, p. 183.

formed a major part in the celebrations which followed the hero's victory over the monster Grendel, and in this respect it may be inferred that the poem reflects the customs of the age in which it was written, the eighth century as some scholars are inclined to believe. It is a safe inference that court poets and wandering minstrels of the kind portrayed in *Widsið* and *Deor* formed an important element in Anglo-Saxon society in the early Christian period, but it would not have suited the purpose of Bede or of any other monastic historian to refer to such men, and still less to the songs which they sang. We know the story of the heathen high priest Coifi only because he helped to overthrow the temple in which he had formerly served. Similarly the two earliest literary references to Anglo-Saxon secular minstrelsy owe their preservation to their association with two men who were prominent as teachers of Christianity.

The first is the familiar tale of the poet Cædmon which testifies to the popularity of minstrelsy among villagers in the seventh century. Bede relates that when Cædmon's fellow villagers were gathered in the evening to eat and drink, it was the custom for each of them in turn to entertain his companions with a song to the accompaniment of the harp. When the unhappy Cædmon, not yet visited by the inspiration which later made him a famous poet, saw the harp approaching, he would leave the table and make his way home. At this time he was a cowherd and his companions at table were probably of similar station. Cædmon then received divine inspiration, and his first poem, a brief hymn in praise of the Creator, composed in his sleep and remembered later when he awoke, attracted the attention of the abbess of Whitby who persuaded him to abandon his secular life and become a monk. Bede gave a Latin paraphrase of this hymn in the *Ecclesiastical History*, but in several manuscripts of this work, one of which was written two years after Bede's death, the hymn is found written in the vernacular as an addition to the text of the *History* itself. Later in his life, according to Bede, Cædmon composed many other poems on topics drawn from the Old and New Testaments, thus seeking to familiarize the unlearned with the more important parts of the Bible by presenting them in the familiar language of entertainment. Bede's list of Cædmon's poetical works led in comparatively modern times to the ascription to him of a number of religious poems which survive in the Junius manuscript, sometimes called the Cædmon manuscript, but most modern scholars, although recognizing certain poems to be in the Cædmonian tradition, are reluctant to accept more than the nine-line *Hymn* as being undoubtedly the work of Cædmon himself.

The second early reference to minstrels is found in a tale told by William of Malmesbury who derived it from the now lost *Handboc* of King Alfred. It tells how the learned Aldhelm, who became the first bishop of Sherborne in 705, used to take his stand on a bridge, in the manner of a professional minstrel, and sing to the people passing by, hoping in this way to attract them to come and listen to him in church. We know nothing of the songs which Aldhelm sang, but we may surmise that they were of a popular kind and we may infer from the story as a whole that in seventh-century England minstrels were accustomed to play the harp and sing to its accompaniment wherever there were men to listen.

Those who handle the materials of history wish to know in the case of each document by whom its content was composed, at what place, at what time and for what purpose. They also wish to know whether the document survives in an original manuscript or only in later copies. So far as Anglo-Saxon prose writings are concerned, whether the language in which they are written is Latin or Old English, it is usually possible to give at least an approximate answer to all these questions. In the case of poetic records, however, they are almost all anonymous and it is rarely possible to establish either the time or place of their composition with any certainty. Before the age of Alfred only three names emerge from this general anonymity, those of Cædmon of whose works only the *Hymn* of nine lines certainly survives, of Bede from whom we have the *Death Song*, a poem of five lines which he composed on his deathbed and which was taken down by his disciple Cuthbert, and of Cynewulf of whose works some 2,600 lines survive. Despite the comparative bulk of his poetry, Cynewulf himself is little more than a name disguised in runic letters

and ingeniously woven into the closing lines of the poems themselves. Two of his poems, *Juliana* which tells the legend of a saint
who suffered martyrdom at Nicomedia in the reign of Galerius
Maximianus, and the *Ascension* which was based on a Latin
homily on this topic by Gregory the Great, are found in the
Exeter Book. The other two, *Elene* and *The Fates of the Apostles*,
are found in the *Vercelli Book*. The former describes the vision of
the Cross that came to Constantine the Great and the finding of
the Cross itself by Helena Augusta, and the latter is a short piece
based on a Latin work which depended ultimately on the Greek
Acts. Each of these poems bears the signature *Cynewulf* or *Cynwulf* so contrived as to suggest that its owner was seeking to
reconcile a tradition of anonymity with a desire to be remembered
in the prayers of his readers. The signature to *Juliana*, which is
thus interpreted by Sisam,[1] may serve as an example of the
methods:

> I must go hence to seek another place according to my deeds in the
> past. Sadly will journey *Cēn*, *Ȳr* and *Nēd*; the King of Heaven, the
> Giver of Victory, will be stern when *Eoh*, *Wyn* and *Ūr*, sin-stained and
> trembling, await what will be adjudged them according to their deeds,
> as the earning of life on earth. *Lagu*, *Feoh* shall stand and quake in
> misery.

The letters represented by their names in this translation are
represented in the manuscript by the appropriate runic symbols.
Since each runic symbol had its own name and since the sound
represented by it corresponded with the initial letter of that name,
it will be seen that the letters in this passage—*cēn*, *ȳr*, *nēd*, *eoh*,
wyn, *ūr*, *lagu* and *feoh*—represent in thin disguise the name
Cynewulf. The same signature, twice in the form *Cynwulf*, is
similarly incorporated in the three other poems. There are other
works which can be recognized as being in the manner of Cynewulf, but none that can be ascribed to him with certainty. It may
be inferred from the content of the four signed poems that
Cynewulf was an ecclesiastic and that he was well read in Latin
works on religious matters, but he is not otherwise known to

---

[1] K. Sisam, *Studies in the History of Old English Literature* (Oxford, 1953),
p. 21.

history. Cædmon's poetry, according to Bede's list of the topics upon which he wrote, seems to belong to an age in which the greatest need was that the contents of the Bible itself should be made more widely known, whereas Cynewulf's, it may be thought, seems to reflect a society which already knew something of the Bible and which might therefore be nourished on such meat as the legendary lives of saints could provide. The content of Cynewulf's poems, certain linguistic evidence and the technique of his verse combine to suggest that he wrote in the Anglian dialect and that he lived late in the eighth or in the ninth century before the great Danish invasion of 865.

The great bulk of the anonymous Old English poetry is preserved in four large volumes, all of which are thought to belong to the great age of Anglo-Saxon book production which fell shortly before and shortly after the year 1000. These four volumes are the Junius manuscript, the *Vercelli Book*, the *Beowulf* manuscript and the *Exeter Book*. The first of these four, the Junius manuscript, may at one time have belonged to St Augustine's, Canterbury, but there is no direct evidence that it was written there and nothing certain is known about its history until its acquisition by James Ussher, archbishop of Armagh, in the seventeenth century. Ussher gave it to Francis Dujon, a distinguished Dutch scholar, who was long resident in England and who is known in literature as Junius. Together with other manuscripts belonging to Junius, it was bequeathed to the Bodleian Library where it is now numbered Junius XI. The manuscript consists of 116 folios which have been paginated in modern times from 1 to 229. It is not a mere miscellany brought together haphazardly as time and opportunity served, but a carefully prepared volume of religious poetry evidently intended to mark an occasion of some importance, but it yields no evidence of what that occasion was. A single scribe wrote the whole book as far as p. 212, but from there to the end the work of three other scribes can be discerned. As with other collections of Old English verse, the poems were written in continuous lines as though they were prose compositions. At frequent intervals spaces were left for the subsequent addition of drawings to illustrate the text, but this part of the work was never completed.

The manuscript now contains forty-nine illustrations, variously half, three-quarter and full page, from pp. 1–96, and in the remainder of it there are somewhat more than eighty blank spaces left for drawings to be added. It will thus be seen that if the original design had been completed it would rarely have been possible to open the book at any point without being confronted by at least one drawing on the two pages exposed to view. In addition to the illustrative drawings which are done in outline, mostly in brown ink, but with occasional use of red, green and black, there are a number of ornamental capitals.

The book contains the text of four poems on religious themes drawn from the Old Testament and amounting in all to a little more than 5,000 lines of verse. These four poems are now known as *Genesis, Exodus, Daniel* and *Christ and Satan*. Because of a superficial resemblance between the themes of these poems and the subjects upon which, according to Bede, Cædmon himself wrote and because of a further resemblance between Cædmon's *Hymn* and some of the lines in *Genesis*, Junius supposed that the manuscript did in fact contain the long lost poetry of Cædmon. For this reason the book is sometimes called the Cædmon manuscript, but since most scholars are now reluctant to believe that any part of its content can be ascribed to Cædmon, the name Junius manuscript is to be preferred. *Genesis*, which is substantially more than a mere poetic paraphrase of the Old Testament book, is not in its present form a homogeneous work. Lines 235–851, known as *Genesis* B to distinguish them from the remainder of the work, called *Genesis* A, can be recognized as being basically Old Saxon both in their vocabulary and in their grammatical structure rather than Old English. A fragment of an Old Saxon poem which corresponds with twenty-five lines of *Genesis* B is preserved in the Vatican Library. The second poem, *Exodus*, which contains a narrative of the flight of the Israelites and the crossing of the Red Sea, draws only to a small extent on the Book of Exodus. Much of its material seems to be closely related to the liturgy of the services for Holy Saturday, a day whose services were devoted to the baptism of catechumens. *Daniel*, the third poem, follows closely the first five chapters of the Book of Daniel, but the narrative is interrupted by a defect in the manuscript in the middle of Belshazzar's Feast. The last of the four poems, *Christ and Satan*, falls into three distinct sections, the *Lamentations of the Fallen Angels*, deriving from the body of tradition which grew around the story of the six days of Creation as told in the Book of Genesis, the *Harrowing of Hell* which depends ultimately on the apocryphal Gospel of Nicodemus, and a fragment on the *Temptation of Christ* which is based on Matt. iv. 1–11.

The Junius manuscript, though not comparable in splendour either with the *Lindisfarne Gospels* or with the *Benedictional* of Æthelwold, is a sumptuous volume carefully prepared and richly illustrated after the fashion of its time. The *Vercelli Book*, of 136 folios, is of a different order. It has no illuminations and it differs further from the Junius manuscript in being a miscellany which is part prose and part verse. Both in its form and in its content, it is a book such as might have been, and evidently was, taken on a journey to provide entertainment and instruction for those who travelled with it. Vercelli, where the book now rests, lies on the pilgrim route to Rome for those who travelled by the Great St Bernard Pass. Several attempts have been made to account for its presence there, but none of these attempts advances beyond unconvincing conjecture. A small number of marginalia seem to indicate that it was still in England for a part of the eleventh century, but that it was taken to Italy during the first half of that century. Apart from some homilies which form its prose element, the book contains five poems on religious themes, amounting in all to some 3,500 lines of verse, and a fragmentary verse rendering of Psalm xxviii. Among the five poems are two of the works which incorporate the signature of Cynewulf, *The Fates of the Apostles* and *Elene*. The longest of the other three is *Andreas*. This represents an attempt to fashion an epic tale from the materials of a saint's life. Its ultimate source was probably a Greek text of the Acts of St Andrew and St Matthew, but it is likely that the poet worked from an intermediate Latin translation of this work. The remaining two are an *Address of the Soul to the Body* and *The Dream of the Rood*. Two versions of the former are found in Old English, the other being in the *Exeter Book*. The

Vercelli version consists of an address by a condemned soul to the body which it had previously inhabited and of a further address to its body by a blessed soul. This latter part is not found in the Exeter version of the poem. In the *Dream of the Rood* which many hold to be the most beautiful of all Old English poems, the poet tells first of a vision in which he beheld the Cross raised on high, ablaze with light and shining with gold and jewels. In his vision the Cross itself comes to life and tells its story, how it was once a forest tree on the edge of a wood until evil men fashioned it into a means of punishment for sinners.

> Long years ago   (well yet I remember)
> They hewed me down   on the edge of the holt,
> Severed my trunk;   strong foemen took me,
> For a spectacle wrought me,   a gallows for rogues.
> High on their shoulders   they bore me to hilltop,
> Fastened me firmly,   an army of foes.[1]

Though trembling with horror the Cross stood firm as Almighty God embraced it for the redemption of mankind. Later it was thrown down all stained with the blood of Christ, but finally it was recovered from the trench in which it had been buried and became honoured above all other trees.

> Now may you learn,   O man beloved,
> The bitter sorrows   that I have borne,
> The work of caitiffs.   But the time is come
> That men upon earth   and through all creation
> Show me honour   and bow to this sign.
> On me a while   God's son once suffered;
> Now I tower under heaven   in glory attired
> With healing for all   that hold me in awe.

The poem ends with some personal reflections by the poet himself upon the joys of the life to come. In its every line this work is inspired with intense personal emotion and we need hardly look further for its source. Some passages from it, carved in runes, find a worthy setting on the shaft of the great cross at Ruthwell in Dumfriesshire.

The British Museum manuscript Cotton Vitellius A xv con-

---

[1] This and the other quotations which follow are from translations by C. W. Kennedy.

sists now of two originally distinct works which were bound as one in the sixteenth or seventeenth century. The name '*Beowulf* manuscript' is here used to designate the second of these two works, that is folios 94–209, the name being understood to refer to the whole of their content and not merely to those folios which contain the poem *Beowulf*. Upon its first page (fo. 94 *a*) the *Beowulf* manuscript bears the signature, dated 1563, of Lawrence Nowell who was at that time dean of Lichfield. It is not known how or whence Nowell acquired the manuscript, but such is the uncertainty about the place at which the poem *Beowulf* was composed that even a sixteenth-century association with Lichfield may not be without some bearing on the problem. The manuscript passed into the collection of Sir Robert Cotton who died in 1631. A hundred years later it was badly scorched in the great fire which destroyed or damaged much of the Cotton collection when it was housed at Westminster. Its pages became so brittle through their scorching that they gradually crumbled away with the result that many words at the edges and corners are now missing. In 1787, half a century or so after the fire, an Icelander, Grímur Jónsson Thorkelin, who knew some Anglo-Saxon, himself made one transcript of the manuscript and caused another to be made by a professional copyist who was entirely ignorant of the language. Many words which have now entirely vanished were then visible and these transcripts, though neither of them is strictly accurate, are now indispensable for restoring the manuscript text. The *Beowulf* manuscript contains five pieces of which the first three, *The Passion of St Christopher*, *The Wonders of the East* and *The Letter of Alexander to Aristotle*, are in prose. The second of these is illustrated by some rather poor drawings. The last two pieces in the book are *Beowulf* itself, an heroic poem of 3,182 lines, and *Judith*, a fragment of 350 lines which is all that survives of a much longer work based on the apocryphal Book of Judith. This collection of prose and verse pieces makes an odd assortment. All are copies from earlier manuscripts and it is probable that, save for *Judith*, they owe their presence in a single book to the fact that they are all concerned in one way or another with monsters.

Beowulf holds a unique place in European literature. Its story is a simple one in essence. Hrothgar, a rich and powerful king of the Danes, ruled long in peace and prosperity, but after a time horror descended upon his kingdom in the shape of a ferocious monster called Grendel who attacked Heorot, the hall in which Hrothgar lived,

> Storming the building   he burst the portal
> Though fashioned of iron,   with fiendish strength;
> Forced open the entrance   in savage fury
> And rushed in rage   o'er the shining floor.
> A baleful glare   from his eyes was gleaming
> Most like to a flame.

News of this calamity reached the Geats, a people who lived in southern Sweden, and Beowulf, a nephew of Hygelac, king of the Geats, set out with a band of followers to attack the monster. As they slept in the hall, Grendel burst in upon them and seized one of the band, tearing him limb from limb, but Beowulf grappled with the monster and by wrenching one of his arms from its socket, he inflicted a mortal wound upon him. There was great rejoicing on the morrow as Hrothgar and the Danes followed the track of the monster to the dark mere in which he lived and died, but on the next night Grendel's mother came to Heorot to avenge her offspring. She slew one of Hrothgar's retainers and carried off his body to the mere.

> Wild and lonely   the land they live in,
> Wind-swept ridges   and wolf-retreats,
> Dread tracts of fen   where the falling torrent
> Downward dips   into gloom and shadow,
> Under the dusk   of the darkening cliff...
> 'Tis an eerie spot!   Its tossing spray
> Mounts dark to heaven   when high winds stir
> The driving storm,   and the sky is murky,
> And with foul weather   the heavens weep.

The Danes and the Geats followed the monster to her lair and Beowulf, fully armed, plunged into the mere. After swimming downwards for a whole day he came at last to a great cave in which the monster lived and there, when almost at the point of death himself, he slew her with an ancient sword which he found in the cave. There was again great rejoicing, after which Beowulf set sail for his home in Götland where he related his adventures and was richly rewarded for his prowess. He took part in wars between the Geats and the Swedes and in time he became king of the Geats himself. After a prosperous reign of fifty years his own land was attacked by a dragon which had been roused to fury by the plundering of a treasure which it had guarded for three hundred years. The aged Beowulf set out to attack the dragon and slew it with the help of one of his retainers, but Beowulf himself received fatal wounds in the combat, and the poem ends with an account of the building of his funeral pyre and the chanting of praises by his warriors as they rode around it.

Thus told the tale seems slight, the stuff of folk mythology the world over, but it is a tale told on an epic scale, the only one of its kind surviving in an old Germanic language, for recitation to an aristocratic audience which was assumed by the poet to be familiar with a multitude of stories about the heroes of the past. By digressing from his main theme, sometimes at length and sometimes by the seemingly casual introduction of a mere name or phrase, the poet could call to the minds of his listeners memories of other heroic tales which were familiar enough to them, but which are now at best only half known to modern readers of the poem. The value of the poem which is indeed immeasurable, lies less in its tales of monsters and dragons than in its wealth of allusion and in its power to recapture something of the atmosphere, and perhaps also something of the history, of a distant age. There is no evidence to show whether Beowulf himself, the hero of the poem, is a character from history or from fiction, but there can be no doubting the historical reality of the various peoples, Swedes (*Sweon*), Geats (*Geatas*), Danes (*Dene*) and others, among whom he experienced his many adventures. One particular incident, the death of Hygelac, king of the Geats and uncle of Beowulf, in a raid against a tribe who lived near the coast north of the lower Rhine, is confirmed by independent evidence in the *Historia Francorum* of Gregory of Tours. Gregory, who was writing towards the end of the sixth century, ascribes the incident to *c.* 521. An anonymous Gaulish history written in the first half of the eighth century also refers to Hygelac's death and gives some information additional to that found in Gregory's *Historia Francorum*. A third work, the *Liber Monstrorum*, thought by some to have been composed in England in the eighth century, records that Hygelac's bones were then preserved on an island off the mouth of the Rhine where they were shown to travellers for their wondrous size. Such abundance of corroborative evidence establishes the fact of the raid and of Hygelac's death in it beyond all doubt. Although this is the only incident in the poem for which such evidence exists, its mere existence in this one case at least increases the probability that historical fact lies behind other episodes.

The opening lines of the poem contain a celebrated description of the funeral rites of Scyld, the mythical founder of the royal house to which Hrothgar belonged. After his death Scyld's body was laid in a ship together with weapons of war, raiment of battle and a great wealth of treasure, and the whole ship with its rich cargo was then set adrift on the sea. Such extravagant expenditure of national wealth on the burial of a king might well be regarded as no more than the fiction of an imaginative poet, but in the light of the discoveries made at Sutton Hoo this seeming fiction has become instead a part of social history. In several other matters of lesser import archaeological evidence indicates that the poet of *Beowulf* drew upon the realities of his age for the setting of his work. Most scholars now believe that the poem is in its present form the creation of a single poet who wrote in an Anglian dialect, and there is further agreement that the date of its composition must lie between the time of Cædmon, who was alive in the second half of the seventh century, and the beginning of sustained Viking attacks against England in the first half of the ninth century, between *c.* 670 and *c.* 830. For many years scholars have tended to ascribe the poem to the earlier part of this period, to *c.* 700, but the possibility of a later date cannot be excluded.

The place of its composition seems to be even more open to doubt than its date. If the poem is thought to have been composed *c.* 700, then it may be argued, as it has been, that the Northumbrian court provided the only cultural environment in which such a work could have been produced at that time. If a date late in the eighth century can be accepted, it may similarly be argued, as again it has been, that the court of Offa, king of Mercia, provides the most likely environment. Arguments of this kind, however, are dangerous because the materials of history for the earlier half of the Anglo-Saxon period are so unevenly distributed. To say that only the Northumbrian court or only the Mercian court yielded the background necessary for the production of such a poem as *Beowulf* is to forget that the history of East Anglia before the Danish invasions is unknown not because it had no history but because its records have been destroyed. In the end it is perhaps well to recall that the *Beowulf* manuscript bears the name of Lawrence Nowell, a sixteenth-century dean of Lichfield, and in so doing to remark that the fourth of the great collections of Anglo-Saxon poetry, the *Exeter Book*, has remained in the Chapter Library of Exeter cathedral from the eleventh century to the present day.

The *Exeter Book* is a manuscript of 131 leaves. The first seven leaves do not properly belong to it, but once formed part of another manuscript which is now preserved in Cambridge University Library (MS. Ii, ii, 11). In two late eleventh-century lists of the benefactions of Leofric, bishop of Exeter (d. 1072), one in the *Exeter Book* itself and the other in a copy of the Gospels now in the Bodleian Library, there is mention of *.i. mycel englisc boc be gehwilcum þingum on leoðwisan geworht*, 'a large English book on various subjects composed in verse'. Although there is no other evidence, it is inferred by all scholars that this 'large English book' and the manuscript which we now call the *Exeter Book* are one and the same. The *Exeter Book* has no illustrations, but it is the largest and most varied in content of all the four poetical codices. Apart from a collection of ninety-five riddles whose length varies from as few as 5 lines to as many as 100, it contains some thirty other poetical pieces whose content amounts in all to more than 6,000 lines of verse. The first two poems, *Christ* and *Guthlac*, are also by far the longest. The use of double spacing, punctuation and capitals in the manuscript presents the *Christ* in three main divisions which have sometimes been distinguished by modern editors as *Christ I, II and III*, and sometimes as *The Nativity, The*

343

Ascension and *The Day of Judgement*. Whether these three parts are the work of the same author or of different authors has long been discussed. The second of the three alone bears the runic signature of Cynewulf and the most recent authoritative opinion admits only this one of the three to be Cynewulf's work. *The Nativity* consists of a series of short lyrical pieces based upon antiphons borrowed from the liturgy, *The Ascension* is drawn largely from a homily by Gregory the Great on this topic and *The Day of Judgement* which is a powerful descriptive piece, seems to derive partly from a variety of Latin sources and partly from the poet's own inventive powers. *Guthlac* is a verse legend of the English saint whose cell in the fens of Middle Anglia later became the abbey of Crowland. The poem falls into two distinct parts. The first of these, *Guthlac A*, tells of the saint's struggles with the demons who haunted the lonely fens in which he established his hermitage, and the second, *Guthlac B*, gives a short summary of *Guthlac A* and an account of the saint's last illness and death. Next in length is *Juliana*, another of the poems bearing the signature of Cynewulf.

Among a number of other poems handling Christian themes, some of them quite short, are four, *Phoenix*, *Panther*, *Whale* and *Partridge*, which are in the form of Christian allegory. Rather more than half of the *Phoenix* is a paraphrase of the Latin poem *De Ave Phoenice* which is ascribed to Lactantius. Its latter part is devoted to an elaborate interpretation of the fiery death and re-birth of the Phoenix such as to make the whole work an allegory of the doctrine of the Resurrection. The other three allegorical poems are found as consecutive pieces in another part of the manuscript and are undoubtedly related to the Christian *Physiologus*, though whether they represent the whole or only a part of the Anglo-Saxon *Physiologus* is uncertain. The *Panther* (Christ) is represented, strangely to modern readers, as kindly, gracious and gentle to all save his one foe, the dragon (Satan). After eating his fill, he sleeps for three nights and on the third day he rises glorified from his sleep (the Resurrection). The *Whale* (the Devil) is portrayed as a monstrous beast of the sea who beguiles unwary fish so that they swim into his open jaws which then close around them. Owing to the loss of a leaf from the manuscript, the *Partridge* survives only as a fragment of 16 lines, too little to yield any information about the nature of the fable or of its interpretation. Among the other minor poems in the *Exeter Book* are a number which are variously didactic, homiletic or aphoristic in purpose. Such are the *Gifts of Men*, describing the various endowments of the human race, the *Fates of Men*, recounting the different kinds of good or ill fortune which may befall mankind, the *Advice of a Father to his Son*, a poem of religious exhortation, and the *Gnomic Verses*, or *Maxims* as they are sometimes called. These last are in the form of brief, aphoristic sayings sometimes setting forth the proverbial wisdom of folklore, sometimes defining the properties of things ('frost must freeze; fire must melt wood') and sometimes defining virtues or vices. The influence of this gnomic or aphoristic tradition is strong throughout Old English poetry and is by no means confined to specific collections of gnomic verses.

There remain three other groups of poems in the *Exeter Book*, a small group of five poems in the elegiac mood, two whose background is of Continental heroic tradition and finally the *Riddles*. The elegies, in their treatment of timeless, universal themes, have lost none of their power in the centuries which have elapsed since they were composed. The *Wanderer* is a vivid and emotional reflection on the tragedy of a man without a country who recalls his former joys as he faces the storms of winter and the terrors of night, lordless and with no friend to help him. All earthly things are transient, only the mercy of God is everlasting—the theme is one which must be all too bitterly vivid to many homeless wanderers of the present age. So also with the *Seafarer* which tells of the sailor's struggles against the elements, the bitter night watches, the numbing cold, the wild calls of the seabirds, and yet through all the spirit within, which urges him on again and again to face all the perils and hardships which are the sailor's lot.

> In my ears no sound   but the roar of the sea,
> The icy combers,   the cry of the swan;
> In place of the mead-hall   and laughter of men
> My only singing   the sea-mew's call,

> The scream of the gannet, the shriek of the gull:
> Through the wail of the wild gale beating the bluffs...
> Yet still, even now, my spirit within me
> Drives me seaward to sail the deep,
> To ride the long swell of the salt sea-wave.

Two others, the *Wife's Lament* and the *Husband's Message*, tell of the grief of a wife who has been separated from her husband by the cruelty of his kinsmen and of a lover's message, carved in runes on a wooden tablet, summoning his wife to renew her old pledges and join him in his new home across the sea. The last of the elegiac group, the *Ruin*, no more than a fragment, has for its theme the poet's reflections as he gazes at the ruins of some abandoned city, probably Bath, and recalls its vanished glories. The two poems whose scene is laid on the Continent are *Widsið* and *Deor*. The former is a composite fiction presented as the song of a far-travelled minstrel who has passed his life wandering from one royal court to another, practising his art and receiving its rewards. Much of the poem consists of a mere versified catalogue of famous men and races. More than any other surviving work, this poem establishes the prominence of the place held by the minstrel in the primitive Germanic world. *Deor* is the lament of a minstrel who has been displaced in his lord's favour by another. He seeks consolation in his sorrow by reciting the misfortunes which had befallen others famous in legend or history.

The Old English *Riddles*, like their counterparts in Latin from which many of them are derived, are short poems, commonly about a dozen lines in length, in which a great variety of the ordinary, everyday objects of life are described in enigmatic terms calculated to rouse the interest of their hearers. The range of subjects which they represent is extremely wide. Some are concerned with the greater aspects of nature—sun, moon, sky, wind, sea—but most deal with man's more immediate environment; the cuckoo [9][1] whose kindly foster-mother was left with the fewer of her own sons and daughters for her kindness, the bullock [38] who breaks the ground when alive (as he draws the plough) and binds

---

[1] The references are to the enumeration in *The Exeter Book*, ed. G. P. Krapp and E. van K. Dobbie (New York, 1936).

the living when he is dead (with thongs made from his hide), the bellows [37] whose swollen belly is at its back and whose fullness flies out through its eye. The humour of some of these brief and often delicate poems comes as a welcome counterpoise to the sense of tragedy which impregnates so much Old English poetry. The bookworm [47] comes as a thievish visitor to devour the famous utterance of a great man, but no whit the wiser is he for the words which he swallows. Others have valuable information for the historian, such as the *Book Riddle* [26] which gives an interesting account of the preparation of parchment. And others again achieve great poetic beauty, as in the *Riddle of the Song Thrush* [8].[1]

> I carol my song   in many a cadence,
> With modulation   and change of note.
> Clearly I call,   keeping the melody,
> An old evening-singer   unceasing in song.
> To earls in their houses   I bring great bliss;
> When I chant my carols   in varying strains,
> Men sit in their dwellings   silent and still.
> Say what I'm called   who mimic so clearly
> The songs of a jester,   and sing to the world
> Many a melody   welcome to men.

Nothing is known of the men who caused these four books to be compiled, of the motives which prompted them or even of the places at which the books were written. In general terms it may be said that they were produced in southern England and that with the exception of only a very few pieces their contents are very much older than the manuscripts which contain them. In the revival of learning which was set on foot by Alfred and brought to its full stature late in the tenth and early in the eleventh centuries, only a very small place is held by the composition of vernacular poetry, in comparison at least with the surviving prose works of that age. It has almost become part of the canon of Anglo-Saxon poetical studies to believe that although the early poetry has been transmitted to posterity through the medium of southern English, and predominantly West Saxon religious

---

[1] So interpreted by J. Young, *Review of English Studies* (1942), pp. 308–12.

houses, most of the poems themselves were originally composed in places where an Anglian dialect was spoken, and predominantly in Northumbria. Such a belief, however, can hardly rest on secure foundations when so much of the unknown lies between the original composition and the surviving manuscript, the more so as it is very rare indeed for any Anglo-Saxon poem to survive in more than a single manuscript. We cannot tell how often, where or by whom that manuscript was copied before it reached its present form. Nothing is known about the history of individual scribes or about the frequency with which scribes worked in places to which they did not belong by birth. In these circumstances it becomes impossible to ascribe the composition of a particular poem to any particular part of the country by linguistic criteria alone. Anyone seeking to take a comprehensive view of Anglo-Saxon poetry as a whole from the contents of these four codices will observe that most of it is religious in kind, but he must not forget that poetry which did not concern Christian themes was vigorously condemned by the Church and that what survives was perhaps no more than the fanciful choice of three or four unknown individuals. If he finds the note of gloom and tragedy at times a little oppressive, he should recall that the religious poem was in some sense the companion of the sermon and that wholly secular poetry survives in appreciable bulk only in the *Riddles* whose lightness and humour may well surprise him.

In addition to the works in the four great poetical collections, there are in various scattered places a number of other poems, some of them mere fragments, some of them minor works on religious themes and some of them composed in commemoration of particular historical events. Among the fragmentary pieces are two, *Waldere* and the *Fight at Finnsburg*, whose action like that of *Widsið*, *Deor* and *Beowulf* is set against a Continental background and whose content provides at least a hint of how much secular poetry has been lost. Two sheets of parchment which came to be used as fly-leaves for a book of sermons in the Royal Library at Copenhagen, contain what remains of *Waldere*, 63 lines in all. The fragments of text which they preserve concern the legend of Walter of Aquitaine and from their spirit and design they may well have belonged to an epic narrative comparable in scale with *Beowulf* itself. The *Fight at Finnsburg*, a fragment of 48 lines, is now known only from a text printed by George Hickes in 1705 from a leaf of parchment which was then in the library at Lambeth Palace, but which has since been lost. Something has been said above of its contents and of its relation to the *Finn Episode* in *Beowulf*. Among the minor religious poems may be noted two dialogues called *Solomon and Saturn* in which Saturn, the upholder of pagan wisdom, is presented in debate with Solomon, the champion of Christian teaching.

The commemorative poems are found mainly in the *Anglo-Saxon Chronicle*, marking such events as the capture of the Five Boroughs by Edmund in 942, the coronation and death of Edgar, the death of Alfred the Ætheling and the death of Edward the Confessor. Among the poems of this kind are two notable battle pieces, the one celebrating the battle of *Brunanburh* in 937, found in five of the seven extant texts of the *Chronicle*, and the other describing the heroic fight of Byrhtnoth, the ealdorman of Essex, against the Danes in the battle of Maldon in 991. The only recorded manuscript of this latter was almost wholly destroyed in the fire of 1731 and the text is now derived from a transcript made shortly before the fire. Both these pieces yield signs that they were composed soon after the events which they commemorate, and in their metrical form, as well as in the conventions of their terminology, they recall the heroic poetry of earlier times. *Brunanburh* is less a descriptive piece than a song of triumph, marking an event which was recognized even then as a great occasion in the movement towards national unity. *Maldon*, on the other hand, though concerned with an event which seems not to have been of any major importance in itself, describes a battle in which the contestants displayed the ideals of the ancient Germanic heroic code. It is a stirring poem which witnesses the enduring strength of the older poetic form and also of the qualities for which Tacitus praised the *Germani* nearly nine centuries earlier.

5. ALFRED AND THE 'ANGLO-SAXON CHRONICLE'

Alfred became king in 871. Rather more than twenty years later, in 894, as most believe, he translated into English the *Pastoral Care* of Gregory the Great. He sent a copy of his translation to each of his bishops, together with a prefatory letter in which he described the state of learning in England at the time of his accession and suggested ways in which improvement might be made. Looking back to earlier times, he recalled how once men had crossed the seas to England in search of learning and wisdom, but when he became king Englishmen who had wanted such things had had to seek them abroad. The decay of English learning had been so great that he could not then recall a single clerk south of Thames who could understand his service books in English or translate a letter from Latin into English. There were very few south of Humber and not many beyond it. He recalled also how the churches throughout the country had been filled with treasures and books before their destruction by the Danes, but even then, despite the numbers of clergy, they could make little use of these books because they were not written in their own language. The remedy, as it seemed to him, was to do as other peoples had done, translate into their own language such books as it was most needful for all men to know and further to set the free-born youth of the country to learning their letters at least until they could read English well. Those who were intended for Holy orders should be further instructed in Latin.

Though every student of Old English reads this letter which rightly finds a place in every selection of Old English texts, no degree of familiarity with it can lessen the strength of its testimony to the greatness of its author. It may well be that as Alfred looked back over a generation of destructive warfare, he somewhat exaggerated both the splendours of earlier ages and the extent of decay in his own time. When he wrote, there were again learned bishops in the land and though some of those whom he brought to his court to assist him in his educational plans were foreigners, there were others whom he had been able to find in England. The archbishop of Rheims sent him a Frankish scholar called Grimbald, Asser came from Wales, and John from the Old Saxons, but there were four others who are known by name and all of them were Mercians, Plegmund who became archbishop of Canterbury, Werferth bishop of Worcester, and two Mercian priests, Athelstan and Werwulf. Much of Mercia, particularly its south-western part, had escaped the attacks of the Danes and it is probable that Alfred's Mercian helpers brought with them a tradition of learning which had suffered no interruption since the times of Irish influence at Malmesbury. A curious entry in the *Anglo-Saxon Chronicle*[1] seems at least to hint that men of learning at Alfred's court and perhaps even Alfred himself were in touch with Irish scholars. Three men, it records, crossed from Ireland in a boat without any steering gear. After seven days they landed in Cornwall whence they went straight to Alfred's court—'thus were they named, Dubslane, Maccbethu and Mælinmun. And Swifneh the best teacher among the Irish died.' The annalist seems to have regarded these men as pilgrims trusting the sea to carry them they cared not where, but we may wonder why they went straight to Alfred's court, unless it was to tell him the news of Swifneh's death.

Alfred's plans for increasing the number of books which could be read in English must have seemed to his contemporaries difficult to fulfil, but in fact the translation of several major works was completed. The first of them, the *Dialogues* of Gregory the Great, concerning the lives of early Italian saints, was made by Bishop Werferth. Four others, the *Pastoral Care* of Gregory, the *Universal History Against the Pagans* of Orosius, Boethius' *On the Consolation of Philosophy* and part of St Augustine's *Soliloquies*, were all the work wholly or in part of Alfred himself. A translation was made of Bede's *Ecclesiastical History* and this too is commonly ascribed to Alfred though the ascription is not wholly free from doubt. This latter work is a fairly close rendering of the Latin original and one of its main interests now perhaps lies in the equation it provides of ninth-century Old English with eighth-century Latin. In the other translations Alfred was much freer in his methods, at times introducing his own reflections on the matter before him and at times adding fresh information. The

[1] 891 A.

most interesting and historically valuable of his additions are found in his version of the *History* of Orosius. The author of this work being a Spaniard naturally concerned himself mainly with the Mediterranean world. To correct the balance of the work for English readers, Alfred added to it information which he derived from two travellers who visited his court, Ohthere and Wulfstan. They told him much about the voyages they had made and the people they had visited, and their evidence, as recorded by Alfred, is now of the highest value for information about the lands and peoples of north-western Europe in the ninth century.

During the reign of Alfred the *Anglo-Saxon Chronicle*, itself the greatest single source of information about the narrative of Anglo-Saxon times, ceases for a while at least to be a mere catalogue of isolated events and becomes instead a detailed account of contemporary history. To describe this work as a single source is indeed both inaccurate and misleading, since the name is not used of any one work, but of a group of texts which differ from one another in their date and place of origin and often in their content as well. There is no evidence that Alfred himself was at any time directly concerned in the compilation of what is comprehensively called the *Anglo-Saxon Chronicle*, but it seems probable that the growth of interest during his reign in the recording of contemporary history owed something to his general encouragement of learning. A little has already been said of the growth of the annalistic form of recorded history out of the tables used by the Church for calculating the date of Easter. In its essence the form resembles a diary whose entries were made year by year instead of day by day. It could serve as a repository of the simplest statements of fact, demanding of the compilers no more than a knowledge of writing and of the facts to be recorded, yet at the same time it offered ample scope for a writer who wished to give a detailed account of the events of his day and perhaps even to make his own comments upon them. It could be neglected for years on end and again taken up as opportunity served. It could be easily copied in its place of origin and widely distributed to other centres where fresh material could be added to it. With all these advantages it is not surprising that the annalistic chronicle came to be the most popular and widespread means of recording history in the Middle Ages.

In most of western Europe such chronicles were kept in Latin, and Latin was also used for this purpose in England. There are indications that Latin annals were being kept in or near York in the eighth century and it is likely enough that they were being kept in other parts of England at this time. Several of the histories and chronicles ascribed to named authors, such as Symeon of Durham, Florence of Worcester and Henry of Huntingdon, who lived after the Norman Conquest, are not histories written by those authors themselves in the sense that the *Ecclesiastical History* was written by Bede, but are in much of their content mere compilations derived from earlier annals which do not now survive in independent form. Some of these earlier annals were in Latin and some in Old English. The particular value of the *Anglo-Saxon Chronicle* lies partly in the wide span of time covered by its several texts, but mainly in the use of the vernacular in preference to Latin. In addition to being a historical source of the highest importance, it supplies invaluable evidence for the development of the Old English language.

There are extant seven chronicles of which six are written wholly in Old English and the seventh partly in Old English and partly in Latin. Their relationship to one another is very complex and as yet by no means fully determined. The oldest of them, called A or more exactly A¹, is now MS. 173 in the library of Corpus Christi College, Cambridge. It formerly belonged to Matthew Parker, archbishop of Canterbury, and it is often known as the Parker Chronicle, occasionally as the Winchester Chronicle. It extends from the year A.D. 1 to 1070. That part of it which covers the tenth century, as far as 1001, was written at Winchester and thereafter it was transferred to Canterbury where a number of Kentish interpolations were made in its earlier part. From its beginning to 891 it is written in a single hand, to be dated *c.* 900, and thereafter in a variety of hands about contemporary with the events which they record. Apart from its factual content, it thus affords valuable evidence of changing fashions in language and handwriting for close on two centuries. It is certain that the earlier part of this text as far as the closing years of the tenth century was written in the kingdom of Wessex, but whether its birthplace was Winchester or some centre farther to the west is doubtful. Although it is now the oldest surviving version of the *Chronicle*, it is not in itself a wholly original work, but a copy removed from that original by more than one stage.

The second text, known as A² (Brit. Mus. MS. Cotton, Otho B xi), now consists only of a few charred fragments, all that survived the fire of 1731. Its former content is known from a sixteenth-century transcript now in the British Museum (Add. MS. 43703) and from the printed edition which Wheloc prepared as an appendix to his edition of Bede's *History*, published at Cambridge in 1643. These sources show that A² was a copy of A¹ and was probably made at Winchester in the eleventh century. Towards the end of Alfred's reign it appears that copies of a West Saxon chronicle resembling A¹ were distributed to several religious centres in various parts of the country. Two of the other five surviving texts are thought to derive ultimately from a West Saxon chronicle which had been sent perhaps to Abingdon in this way. These are B (Brit. Mus. MS. Cotton, Tiberius A vi) which extends as far as 977 and is written in a hand of *c*. 1000, and C (Brit. Mus. MS. Cotton, Tiberius B i) which is written in various eleventh-century hands and continues as far as 1066. Two others, D (Brit. Mus. MS. Cotton, Tiberius B iv) and E (Bodleian MS. Laud 636), are related to a text which was at some time in the north, probably at York. D, written in various hands not earlier than the eleventh century, was continued as far as 1079. It has been attributed at different times both to Worcester and Evesham, but neither attribution is firmly grounded and D may yet prove to be itself a northern manuscript. E, written in a single hand as far as 1121 and continued by other hands till as late as 1154, later than any of the other surviving texts, was written at Peterborough on the foundation of a Canterbury chronicle. The last of the seven, F (Brit. Mus. MS. Cotton, Domitian A viii), is a bilingual text, part Latin and part English, which was written at St Augustine's, Canterbury, *c*. 1100. Its value as a source of independent historical information is slight.

It is impossible to set too high a value upon these seven manu-scripts which comprise the *Anglo-Saxon Chronicle*. But for them and for the *Ecclesiastical History* of Bede it would have been impossible to write the narrative of English history for six hundred years before the Norman Conquest. Much of their content is common to some or all of them, particularly in the earlier centuries, since all depend ultimately on a common source, but their wide geographical diffusion gave opportunity for the interpolation of existing local records and for the continuing addition of divergent matter in later times. There are many years for which no entries were made at all, and there are long stretches for which they record no more than the barest details of battles and of the succession of kings and bishops. But at other times, particularly in the reigns of Alfred, Æthelred the Unready and Edward the Confessor (and in the case of text E till as late as the accession of Henry II), the *Chronicle* expands into a full and detailed narrative of enthralling interest and of the highest historical value.

Alfred's own court was the main centre of his educational reforms. He made some attempt to establish monastic foundations in his own kingdom of Wessex, but the great monastic revival and the widespread resurgence of learning which it bred belong to a later generation. During the reigns of his two successors, Edward the Elder and Athelstan, the country was too much occupied with military matters for many men to be able to devote themselves to the study of books. Even so there are indications that some books were being written during the early decades of the tenth century. On his progress northwards to invade Scotland in 934 Athelstan visited Beverley, Ripon and Chester-le-Street, making them generous gifts of vestments, jewelled plate and books. To the monks of Chester-le-Street he gave two copies of the Gospels, ornamented with gold and silver, as well as a volume containing Bede's prose and verse lives of St Cuthbert. This latter may still be seen in the library of Corpus Christi College, Cambridge (MS. 183). It is written in a fine hand, probably at some monastery in the south-west, and on the reverse of its first folio, it bears a full-page illumination said to represent Athelstan himself presenting the book to St Cuthbert.

6. LEARNING IN THE NEW MONASTICISM

It was not until the second half of the century, when new and reformed monasteries began to prosper in large numbers, that there came opportunity for a more widespread revival of learning. From the first the leaders of the reform movement, particularly Dunstan and Æthelwold, concerned themselves closely with education. The future prosperity of the movement depended upon the recruitment of monks from the children who were trained in the monastic schools. These children, collectively called the *schola*, were placed in the care of a professed monk, the *magister scholae* or *custos*, from whom they received elementary instruction. They were taught to read, using the Psalter as their reading book, to repeat the *Credo* and the *Paternoster* as well as the Psalms by heart, and to write. Since Latin was the language of the cloister, they were necessarily given some acquaintance with its grammar and syntax. Although they lived together as a separate body within the community as a whole, they were required to take a full part in the normal observances of monastic life and to enable them to do this much of their schooling must have been devoted to instruction in the chant. In the more advanced stages of education teaching was given in grammar, rhetoric and dialectic —the *trivium*—and in music, arithmetic, geometry and astronomy —the *quadrivium*.

The emphasis which the reformed monasticism laid upon education bore fruit towards the end of the eleventh century, as the generation following the great reformers reached maturity of intellect and strove to meet the greatly increased demand for books resulting from the rapid multiplication of monasteries and churches. The monks themselves needed service-books and books of instruction to assist them in their educational work, as well as books with which to stock their libraries, and for this last the new learning of the Carolingian revival on the Continent provided an abundant supply of works for copying. In addition the parish clergy needed books to instruct them in the proper fulfilment of their duties. The result of these varying demands was the production of a very large body of religious literature late in the tenth and early in the eleventh centuries. Some of it, intended for use in the monasteries where it was written, was in Latin, but much of it, meant rather for the instruction and guidance of village priests, was written in the vernacular. Almost all of it was in prose. Foremost among several distinguished scholars who contributed to this work was Ælfric, a man comparable both in the volume of his writings and in the quality of his mind even with Bede himself. Nothing is known of the family to which he belonged and even the date of his birth is uncertain, though it was probably *c*. 955 or a little earlier. He became a pupil in the monastic school at Winchester under Æthelwold and there he remained until *c*. 987 when he was sent to instruct the monks of a house lately founded at Cerne Abbas in Dorset. In 1005 he became the first abbot of another new foundation, at Eynsham near Oxford, and here he spent the rest of his life. The date of his death is unknown.

Much of Ælfric's literary work seems to have been done while he was at Cerne. Between 990 and 994 he issued his *Catholic Homilies*, two series of sermons dedicated to the archbishop of Canterbury and planned as a collection, partly doctrinal and partly historical in character, such as might be of service to priests throughout the whole of the Church year. They were mainly derived, as Ælfric himself acknowledged, from the works of Augustine, Jerome, Gregory the Great and Bede. His greatest debt seems to have been to Gregory. He explained that he had chosen to issue the homilies in English because he had found that unlearned men, not knowing Latin, had been misled by the errors contained in other English books, excepting always those which had been translated by Alfred. A few years later he issued his *Lives of the Saints*, a collection of about forty compositions concerning in particular the saints whose festivals were observed by monks. In much of its content this work does not differ greatly from the *Catholic Homilies*. Both were didactic in purpose and both used the narrative of saints' lives as the text for homiletic discourse. No doubt drawing upon his own memories of the time when he was a pupil in the monastic school at Winchester, Ælfric wrote two or three works designed to assist the pupils of this and other schools in learning Latin. One of these was his Latin

Grammar which he based upon a work of the grammarian Priscian. He also compiled a Latin-English *Vocabulary* in which he arranged according to their subject a selection of words most likely to be in daily use in the conversation of the monastic schools. The most celebrated of his instructional works is the *Colloquy*, representing a conversation between a teacher, a novice and a variety of other persons engaged in the common occupations of life, a ploughman, a shepherd, a hunter, a merchant and so forth. Each answers questions put to him by the teacher about his trade, though it is not of course to be supposed that representatives of each of these callings were in fact present at the schools in which the *Colloquy* was used. The piece is as it were a play intended to give practice at conversing in Latin to the pupils who would no doubt play the various parts in turn. The dialogue is very realistic and contains information which is now of great historical value.

Much of Ælfric's work reveals his concern with the well-being of the Church as a whole, not merely with that of the monastic body alone, and it is perhaps in this respect that the Church which was brought into being by the great reformers of the tenth century seems to differ most markedly from its counterpart in the age of Bede. Ælfric was able to find patrons even among the lay nobility and it was in response to a request from Æthelweard, a nobleman who held office as an ealdorman in the western parts of Wessex, that he undertook a translation of the Old Testament. Æthelweard was himself the author of a Latin chronicle which was based on a text of the *Anglo-Saxon Chronicle* no longer surviving. His Latin is difficult and at times unintelligible, but that he was able to write Latin at all and that he gave his patronage to a monastic writer such as Ælfric are signs that the revived interest in learning at this time was not confined to the cloister.

Nor does the example of Æthelweard stand alone. Later in his life Ælfric wrote a treatise on the Old and New Testaments designed to serve as a layman's introduction to the Bible. It was prefaced with a long address to a thane who lived not far from Eynsham and for whom Ælfric had undertaken the work in response to his repeated requests for English books. This same thane was also the recipient of a letter from Ælfric urging the celibacy of the clergy. Ælfric's plan for a translation of the Old Testament, not in fact carried to completion, was less for a close translation than for a work which should be part translation, part paraphrase and part commentary, a work such as might be used more by the preacher in church than by the solitary reader. In these and in his other works, such as the pastoral letters which he wrote for Wulfsige, bishop of Sherborne, and for Wulfstan, bishop of Worcester and archbishop of York, and in a Latin life of his former teacher Æthelwold, Ælfric strove with great success to pass on to his own and to later generations the Christian ideals of the age into which he had been born. It is not always easy to realize that his life largely coincided with the reign of Æthelred the Unready and that in a political sense the age to which he belonged reached its climax with the conquest of England by Cnut.

Ælfric was by far the most prolific writer of his age, but there were many others at work as well. His contemporary, Wulfstan, bishop of London and later of Worcester, a see which he held in plurality with the archbishopric of York, wrote a number of homilies and played a considerable part in drafting the law codes of his times. In the most powerful of his sermons, the *Sermo Lupi ad Anglos*, he denounced the social evils of his age in language whose force and passion recall the *De Excidio* of Gildas. Wulfstan was as much statesman as ecclesiastic, and his style was that of the preacher and rhetorician rather than of the cloistered teacher such as Ælfric.

Another of Ælfric's contemporaries and a representative of the new learning in the fenland monasteries was Byrhtferth, a monk of Ramsey[1] and at one time a pupil of the learned Abbo who had been brought from Fleury by Oswald to teach in the monastic school at Ramsey. He was the author of a number of sermons and of Latin commentaries on four of the writings of Bede for whose works he had the highest admiration. Like Ælfric he was concerned to see that the parish clergy were properly instructed in their duties and it was to this end that he wrote his *Manual* or

---

[1] It should not be necessary to state that this is Ramsey in Huntingdonshire, but in the most recent general text-book on its subject G. K. Anderson, *The Literature of the Anglo-Saxons* (Princeton, 1949), p. 384, places Byrhtferth at Ramsay (*sic*) in the Isle of Man.

Enchiridion, as he variously called it. In this work he set out in simple terms the elements of astronomy and mathematics, discoursing on the signs of the zodiac, describing the courses of the sun and moon and relating all to the calculation of the calendar. Although Byrhtferth asked the indulgence of scholars and educated men who knew these things perfectly, we may guess that the rustic priests and young boys for whom he was writing found his work difficult enough and that his exposition of the mysteries of regulars, concurrents and intercalations was not always as successful as he hoped in distracting young clerks from their dice-playing. Here, nevertheless, they could find multiplication tables and tables of weights and measures, they could learn how to avoid solecisms of speech both in their own language and in Latin, they could learn also something about the meaning of grammatical terms, as syllepsis, paronomasia, polysyndeton and suchlike. They could also, to help them in their reading, acquire familiarity with the different signs used by grammarians for accents and with a variety of other symbols which in a modern textual edition might be comprehended in the term *sigla*. They could learn too, as we may with interest ourselves, that 240 pence and 20 shillings were then reckoned to the pound, and for the elucidation of more difficult matters they would be helped, if we may infer as much from the only surviving manuscript of the *Manual*, by a series of diagrams, some of them of great intricacy. In brief, Byrhtferth's *Manual* is a handbook to the elementary science of the day and as such it is, next to Bede's scientific works to which it is greatly indebted, the most important work of its kind in the Anglo-Saxon period.

Several other manuscripts containing pseudo-scientific material survive from the later part of the Anglo-Saxon period. A *Leech Book* sometimes known as the *Leech Book of Bald* from an Anglo-Saxon leech of that name who once owned it, contains descriptions of a large number of diseases as well as prescriptions for their cure. The *Herbarium* and the *Medicina de Quadrupedibus* describe the healing virtues of plants and animals respectively. The earliest manuscript of the former contains numerous coloured drawings of plants, but the figures were derived from other sources and the manuscript itself was badly damaged in the fire of 1731. Another work of the same kind, conventionally called *Lacnunga*, contains a collection of some 200 prescriptions, remedies, charms and prayers against all manner of afflictions, real and imaginary, and deriving from a great variety of sources, much of it ultimately Greek, Roman and Byzantine in origin, some of it Celtic and some of it from pagan Teutonic magic. This pseudo-medical and magical medley represents a world apart from the scientific writings of Bede and Byrhtferth. So far from containing any rational element which might have marked the beginnings of scientific advance, 'it is the last stage of a process that has left no legitimate successor, a final pathological disintegration of the great system of Greek medical thought'.[1]

The richly illuminated Gospel books which belong to the age of Bede have long been held among the most precious relics of the Anglo-Saxon period, but it is only in recent years that the drawings and paintings to be found in so many of the manuscripts associated with the reformed monasticism of the tenth and eleventh centuries have begun to find their proper place in the history of English art. Before the Danish invasions the art of manuscript illumination was predominantly, though not exclusively, a Northumbrian creation which grew from the intertwining of Celtic, Germanic and Mediterranean roots. This art was carried to the Continent in the eighth century by the Anglo-Saxon missionaries and there in due time it came to form one element in the art of the Carolingian revival. Transformed there by fusion with other elements, it crossed back again to England on the pages of Bibles, psalters and other works to inspire the artists of the new English monasticism. Transformed again in England, it grew into something which can no longer be called Anglo-Saxon but which is, as more than one writer has remarked, something peculiarly English, the beginnings of a tradition to which William Blake was heir. The new monasticism did not spread beyond the midlands and this new art was predominantly southern. Its ancestry is not wholly unrecognizable, but in

[1] J. H. G. Grattan and C. Singer, *Anglo-Saxon Magic and Medicine* (Oxford, 1952), p. 94.

general the old decorative motifs had given way to new. Even though something of the native interlace remained it was thrust wholly into the background by the ultimately classical acanthus, but the change was not merely, or even chiefly, in the adoption of different motifs. One of the most notable changes and one which does not appear to those who know manuscripts only in the dull flatness of monochrome reproduction, is in brilliance of colour and the lavish use of gold.

Outstanding among the many works which display this brilliance is the *Benedictional of Æthelwold* which is owned by the Duke of Devonshire and preserved at Chatsworth. This work consists of a collection of episcopal benedictions arranged for use on different days in the Church year, but the interest of its text is wholly subordinate to that of its many splendid illuminations, illustrating such scenes as the Nativity, the Entry into Jerusalem, the Women at the Sepulchre and so forth. This work is the most notable example of what is commonly called the Winchester School of Art. We know that Winchester played an important part in the Benedictine revival and also that some illuminated manuscripts were produced there. But in speaking of a Winchester School of Art, it must be remembered that close contact was maintained between the various new and reformed houses of southern England and East Anglia, and that in consequence there is some danger in associating a manuscript with Winchester in particular solely because its style of art resembles that found in other manuscripts which can be ascribed to Winchester on direct evidence. Until recently the part played by Winchester artists has perhaps been over-emphasized at the expense of the East Anglian monasteries. There are some, for example, who think that the *Benedictional of Æthelwold* was produced at Thorney, itself a house founded by Æthelwold who belonged to Winchester. The *Benedictional of Æthelwold* is the outstanding example of the technique of painting in full colour.

Alongside this technique English artists developed another, one which had found no place in the art of earlier times in England, the technique of drawing in outline (see Pls. V, IX, pp. 98, 174 above). There still survive about sixty manuscripts which contain drawings of this kind, sometimes in large numbers. The Junius manuscript has forty-nine outline drawings and was designed to contain about 130. The popularity of outline drawings was perhaps due in part to economic causes. They could be produced more quickly and they required less costly materials than paintings in full colour. Canterbury artists made an important contribution in this field of drawing, most notably in the Canterbury copy of the Utrecht Psalter. Of the manuscripts containing outline drawings which can be attributed with confidence to particular monasteries, about twelve belong to the two Canterbury houses, Christchurch and St Augustine's, but there are others from Winchester, Exeter, Worcester, Glastonbury, Sherborne and Bury St Edmunds. Anyone who wishes to understand something of the emotional force which inspired the new monasticism would do well to study these drawings. He will be impressed at once by their strength and vitality, and, if he has previously studied the movement only through its written memorials, he may well be astonished by their gaiety. Here it may seem is the echo of a sentence which recurs in the *Regularis Concordia* almost as a refrain—'then all the bells shall peal'.

SELECT BIBLIOGRAPHY

The pages which follow are intended to guide the interested reader towards authoritative modern works on different aspects of the Anglo-Saxon period and also towards the more important of the original sources.

1. GENERAL AND POLITICAL HISTORY

The most authoritative work is Sir Frank Stenton's *Anglo-Saxon England* (Oxford History of England, vol. II, 2nd ed. 1947). It includes a full bibliography. The period *c.* 400–600 is treated more fully by J. N. L. Myres in R. G. Collingwood and J. N. L. Myres, *Roman Britain and the English Settlements* (Oxford History of England, vol. I, 2nd ed. 1937) and also by R. H. Hodgkin, *A History of the Anglo-Saxons*, 2 vols. (3rd ed., Oxford, 1952). This latter, which is very richly illustrated, continues as far as the death of Alfred. Other general works written by scholars are D. Whitelock, *The Beginnings of English Society* (Pelican History of England, vol. 2, London, 1952) and G. O. Sayles, *The Medieval Foundations of England* (2nd ed. London, 1950). F. Barlow. *The Feudal Kingdom of England 1042–1216* (London, 1955). For the Celtic world contemporary with Anglo-Saxon England see J. E. Lloyd, *A History of Wales*, 2 vols. (3rd ed., London, 1939), A. H. Williams, *Introduction to the History of Wales*, 2 vols. (Cardiff, 1941–8), W. F. Skene, *Celtic Scotland*, 3 vols. (Edinburgh, 1876–80), H. M. Chadwick, *Early Scotland* (Cambridge, 1949), E. MacNeill, *Phases of Irish History* (Dublin, 1919), *Celtic Ireland* (Dublin, 1921), K. Jackson, *Language and History in Early Britain* (Edinburgh, 1953) and N. K. Chadwick (ed.), *Studies in Early British History* (Cambridge, 1954).

2. BRITAIN AND THE VIKINGS

The most recent general survey is T. D. Kendrick's *A History of the Vikings* (London, 1930), but it now needs revision in many points. Among older books which still have value are A. Mawer, *The Vikings* (Cambridge Manuals of Science and Literature, 1913), and C. F. Keary, *The Vikings in Western Christendom* (London, 1891). G. Turville-Petre gives a good introduction to Scandinavian history in *The Heroic*

Age of Scandinavia (Hutchinson's University Library; London, 1951). Among books written by Scandinavians, but available in English, are A. W. Brøgger, *Ancient Emigrants* (Oxford, 1929) and A. Olrik, *Viking Civilisation* (London, 1930). Books dealing with Scandinavian antiquities in the Viking Age are A. W. Brøgger and H. Shetelig, *The Viking Ships, Their Ancestry and Evolution* (Oslo, 1953), H. Shetelig and H. Falk, *Scandinavian Archaeology* (Oxford, 1937) and H. Shetelig (ed.), *Viking Antiquities in Great Britain and Ireland* (Oslo, pts. I–V 1940, pt. VI 1954).

3. ECCLESIASTICAL HISTORY

Books which will be found helpful on Celtic Christianity in Britain are H. Williams, *Christianity in Early Britain* (Oxford, 1912) and J. A. Duke, *The Columban Church* (Oxford, 1932). For the transition from the classical to the western Christian world N. K. Chadwick's *Poetry and Letters in Early Christian Gaul* (London, 1955) is valuable. No history of the Anglo-Saxon Church has been written since that by W. Hunt, *The English Church from its Foundation to the Norman Conquest* (London, 1907). An older but excellent book which is in danger of being forgotten is W. Bright, *Chapters of Early English Church History* (3rd ed., Oxford, 1897). The monastic history of the later Anglo-Saxon church is discussed by D. Knowles, *The Monastic Order in England* (Cambridge, 1949) and there are studies of other times and people by A. Hamilton Thompson (ed.), *Bede: his Life, Times and Writings* (Oxford, 1935), J. Armitage Robinson, *The Times of St Dunstan* (Oxford, 1923) and E. S. Duckett, *Anglo-Saxon Saints and Scholars* (New York, 1947), *Alcuin, Friend of Charlemagne* (New York, 1951),*Saint Dunstan of Canterbury* (New York, 1955) The most detailed study of the Anglo-Saxon mission to the Continent is that by W. Levison, *England and the Continent in the Eighth Century* (Oxford, 1946). S. J. Crawford's, *Anglo-Saxon Influence on Western Christendom* (Oxford, 1933) gives a shorter account of the same subject. For sources in translation see C. H. Talbot, *The Anglo-Saxon Missionaries in Germany* (London and New York, 1954). The best survey of Anglo-Saxon architecture is by A. W. Clapham, *English Romanesque Architecture*, vol. I, *Before the Conquest* (Oxford, 1930). There is an exellent regional study by A. R. and P. M. Green, *Saxon Architecture and Sculpture in Hampshire* (Winchester, 1951).

4. INSTITUTIONS

Recent works which embrace the Anglo-Saxon period but also extend beyond it are J. E. A. Jolliffe, *The Constitutional History of England* (2nd ed., London, 1947), S. B. Chrimes, *An Introduction to the Administrative History of Medieval England* (Studies in Medieval History, vol. VII; Oxford, 1952) and W. A. Morris, *The Medieval English Sheriff to 1300* (Manchester, 1927). There is still much of value to be found in W. Stubbs, *A Constitutional History of England*, vol. I (Oxford, 1897). Works whose contents are confined to the Anglo-Saxon period include H. M. Chadwick, *Studies on Anglo-Saxon Institutions* (Cambridge, 1905), L. M. Larson, *The King's Household in England before the Norman Conquest* (Madison, 1904), F. Liebermann, The *National Assembly in the Anglo-Saxon Period* (Halle, 1913) and T. J. Oleson, *The Witenagemot in the Reign of Edward the Confessor* (London and Toronto, 1955).

5. SOCIETY AND ECONOMY

The best account of early Germanic society is that of H. M. Chadwick, *The Heroic Age* (Cambridge, 1912). The best introduction to the relation of physical geography to historical problems in early Britain is Sir Cyril Fox's essay *The Personality of Britain* (4th ed., Cardiff, 1952). Similar matters are discussed in greater detail in H. C. Darby (ed.), *An Historical Geography of England before A.D. 1800* (Cambridge, 1936). See also H. C. Darby, *The Domesday Geography of Eastern England* (Cambridge, 1952) and H. C. Darby and I. B. Terrett (edd.), *The Domesday Geography of Midland England* (Cambridge, 1954). These are the first two volumes of a series intended to cover the whole of Domesday England. Among the more important books dealing with agriculture are H. L. Gray, *English Field Systems* (Cambridge, Mass., 1915) and C. S. and C. S. Orwin, *The Open Fields* (Oxford, 2nd ed., 1954). Older works include F. W. Maitland, *Domesday Book and Beyond* (Cambridge, 1897), F. Seebohm, *The English Village Community* (London, 1896) and *Tribal Custom in Anglo-Saxon Law* (Cambridge, 1911), also P. Vinogradoff, *English Society in the Eleventh Century* (Oxford, 1908), and *The Growth of the Manor* (2nd ed., London, 1911). These works contain much of value although their conclusions cannot always be followed. J. E. A. Jolliffe, *Pre-Feudal England: The Jutes* (Oxford, 1933) contains a detailed study of the social organization of Kent and neighbouring parts. The growth of town life in Anglo-Saxon England is studied in the earlier part of J. Tait, *The Medieval English Borough* (Manchester, 1936).

Select Bibliography

6. LETTERS

General surveys of Anglo-Saxon literature will be found in *The Cambridge History of English Literature*, vol. 1 (Cambridge, 1907), W. L. Renwick and H. Orton, *The Beginnings of English Literature to Skelton, 1509* (2nd ed., London, 1952), G. K. Anderson, *The Literature of the Anglo-Saxons* (Princeton, 1949) and by K. Malone in A. C. Baugh, *A Literary History of England*, bk. 1, pt. i (New York, 1948). Particular studies are almost without number. Among those which may be specially recommended are R. W. Chambers, *Beowulf, an Introduction to the Study of the Poem* (Cambridge, 1932), C. W. Kennedy, *The Earliest English Poetry* (Oxford, 1943), B. S. Phillpotts, *Edda and Saga*, Home University Library (London, 1931), K. Sisam, *Studies in the History of Old English Literature* (Oxford, 1953), G. Turville-Petre, *Origins of Icelandic Literature* (Oxford, 1953), D. Whitelock, *The Audience of Beowulf* (Oxford, 1951), R. M. Wilson, *The Lost Literature of Medieval England* (Methuen's Old English Library, London, 1952) and C. E. Wright, *The Cultivation of Saga in Anglo-Saxon England* (Edinburgh, 1939). Latin scholarship among the Anglo-Saxons is discussed by M. L. W. Laistner, *Thought and Letters in Western Europe, A.D. 500–900* (London, 1931), and J. D. A. Ogilvy, *Books Known to Anglo-Latin Writers from Aldhelm to Alcuin* (670–804) (Cambridge, Mass., 1936).

7. ART AND ARCHAEOLOGY

A great deal has been written about Anglo-Saxon antiquities in the last thirty years. There are general surveys, some of them extending beyond the Anglo-Saxon period, by T. D. Kendrick, *Anglo-Saxon Art to A.D. 900* (London, 1938) and *Late Saxon and Viking Art* (London, 1949), E. Kitzinger, *Early Medieval Art in the British Museum* (British Museum, 1940), W. Oakeshott, *The Sequence of English Medieval Art* (London, 1950), A. Stone, *Sculpture in England: The Middle Ages* (London 1955) and D. Talbot Rice, *English Art 871–1100* (Oxford, 1952). This last forms vol. 11 in the Oxford History of English Art. Vol. 1 is in preparation. J. Brøndsted's *Early English Ornament* (Copenhagen, 1924) is valuable because of its author's knowledge of Scandinavian antiquities, and the relations between Anglo-Saxon and Irish art are examined by F. Henry, *Irish Art in the Early Christian Period* (London, 1940). G. Baldwin Brown, *The Arts in Early England*, 6 vols. (London, 1903–37) deals with ecclesiastical architecture, pagan antiquities, Christian sculpture, the *Lindisfarne Gospels* and other matters. Much that has been written about Anglo-Saxon pagan anti-quities is contained in periodicals, but among separate studies may be noted R. Jessup, *Anglo-Saxon Jewellery* (London, 1950), E. T. Leeds, *The Archaeology of the Anglo-Saxon Settlements* (Oxford, 1913), *Early Anglo-Saxon Art and Archaeology* (Oxford, 1936), *A Corpus of Early Anglo-Saxon Great Square-Headed Brooches* (Oxford, 1949). G. J. Copley, *The Conquest of Wessex in the Sixth Century* (London, 1954) makes good use of archaeological and place-name evidence. Numerous papers have been written about the material from Sutton Hoo which awaits publication as a whole by the British Museum. Meanwhile preliminary accounts can be read in R. L. S. Bruce Mitford's *The Sutton Hoo Ship Burial, A Provisional Guide* (British Museum, 1947) and in the same writer's appendix to the third edition of R. H. Hodg-kin's *A History of the Anglo-Saxons* (Oxford, 1952). Among other specialist studies may be noted Sir Cyril Fox, *Offa's Dyke* (London, 1955), W. G. Collingwood, *Northumbrian Crosses of the Pre-Norman Age* (London, 1927), D. McIntyre, *The Coffin of Saint Cuthbert* (introd. by E. Kitzinger; Oxford, 1950), J. R. Kirk, *The Alfred and Minster Lovel Jewels* (Ashmolean Museum, 1948) and E. Maclagan, *The Bayeux Tapestry* (King Penguin Book, London, 1943). There are facsimiles of many important manuscripts of the Anglo-Saxon period. These include the four poetical codices, the Thorkelin transcripts of *Beowulf*, the *Lindisfarne Gospels* (in part), the *Book of Kells*, the *Benedictional* of Æthelwold, the Leningrad Manuscript of Bede, the Parker and Peter-borough texts of the *Anglo-Saxon Chronicle*, the Tollemache *Orosius* and others, but these are costly works which are not likely to be found outside the more important libraries. The general surveys noted above contain many reproductions from illuminated manuscripts and among other works dealing with this topic particularly may be mentioned F. Masai, *Essai sur les Origines de la Miniature Dite Irlandaise* (Brussels, 1947) and F. Wormald, *English Drawings of the Tenth and Eleventh Centuries* (London, 1952). A. Fairbank, *A Book of Scripts* (King Penguin Book, London, 1949) offers a cheap and handy introduction to calligraphy.

8. ORIGINAL SOURCES

The two outstanding sources for the Anglo-Saxon period are Bede's *Ecclesiastical History of the English Nation* and the *Anglo-Saxon Chronicle*. The standard text of Bede's *History* is that by C. Plummer (Oxford, 1896). There are translations by J. E. King (Loeb Classical Library, London, 1930), V. D. Scudder (Everyman's Library, London,

1910), L. C. Jane (Temple Classics, 1903), A. M. Sellar (London, 1907) and L. Sherley-Price (Penguin Books, 1955). The A and E texts of the *Anglo-Saxon Chronicle*, with passages from other versions, are found in C. Plummer, *Two of the Saxon Chronicles Parallel* (Oxford, 1892). There is an accurate translation by G. N. Garmonsway, *The Anglo-Saxon Chronicle translated with Introduction and Notes* (Everyman's Library, London, 1953). This translation follows Plummer's text page for page and there is a good bibliography. Latin sources which are available with text and translation in the same volume include B. Colgrave, *The Life of Bishop Wilfrid by Eddius Stephanus* (Cambridge, 1927) and *Two Lives of Saint Cuthbert* (Cambridge, 1940), T. Symons, *Regularis Concordia* (Nelson's Medieval Classics, London, 1953) and A. Campbell *Encomium Emmae Reginae* (Camden Third Series, LXXII; London, 1949). A new edition of *The Life of Guthlac* by B. Colgrave is now in the press. Among the documentary sources are F. L. Attenborough, *The Laws of the Earliest English Kings* (Cambridge, 1922), A. J. Robertson, *The Laws of the Kings of England from Edmund to Henry I* (Cambridge, 1925), D. Whitelock, *Anglo-Saxon Wills* (Cambridge, 1930), A. J. Robertson, *Anglo-Saxon Charters* (Cambridge, 1939), F. E. Harmer, *Anglo-Saxon Writs* (Manchester, 1952). All these contain texts, translations and notes. An introduction to the study of the Anglo-Saxon charters, with references to editions and works on charter criticism, will be found in F. M. Stenton, *The Latin Charters of the Anglo-Saxon Period* (Oxford, 1955). For advanced study of the laws F. Liebermann, *Die Gesetze der Angelsachsen*, 3 vols. (Halle, 1903–16) is indispensable. Among documentary collections are R. W. Chambers, *England before the Norman Conquest* (London, 1928, with extracts in translation from many sources), M. Ashdown, *English and Norse Documents Relating to the Reign of Ethelred the Unready* (Cambridge, 1930, texts with translation) and F. E. Harmer, *Select English Historical Documents of the Ninth and Tenth Centuries* (Cambridge, 1914, texts with translation). The latest and most comprehensive collection of documents, all in translation, is *English Historical Documents*, gen. ed. D. C. Douglas, vol. I, *c.* 500–1042, ed. D. Whitelock (London, 1955), vol. II, 1042–1189 (containing a reproduction of the Bayeux Tapestry), ed. D. C. Douglas and G. W. Greenaway (London, 1953).

There is no complete collective edition of the Old English prose texts, but the more important texts have been published by the Early English Text Society or in C. W. M. Grein and R. P. Wülker, *Bibliothek der angelsächsischen Prosa*, 11 vols. (1872–1922, incomplete). A new edition of the first series of Ælfric's homilies is being prepared by P. A. M.

Clemoes for the Early English Text Society. The poetic texts exist in a collective edition published by Columbia University, *The Anglo-Saxon Poetic Records*, ed. G. P. Krapp and E. van K. Dobbie, 6 vols. (1931–53). The novice will normally make his first acquaintance with Anglo-Saxon prose and poetry through a Primer or Reader and will later use editions of separate works or extracts from them. The most recent editions of *Beowulf* are those by C. L. Wrenn (Oxford, 1953) and E. van K. Dobbie (Columbia, 1953). Earlier editions are by Fr. Klaeber (3rd ed. 1951), W. J. Sedgefield (3rd ed. 1935), and R. W. Chambers and A. J. Wyatt (1914). Cheap and reliable texts of several Old English works are available in Methuen's Old English Library. The poetic texts available in this series are *Cædmon's Hymn*, *Bede's Death Song*, *The Leiden Riddle*, *Deor*, *Waldere*, *The Dream of the Rood*, *Widsith*, *The Battle of Maldon* and *Judith*. The prose texts are *The Parker Chronicle: 832–900*, *Ælfric's Colloquy* and the *Sermo Lupi ad Anglos*. All these texts have detailed notes and a glossary, but no translation. Among other editions of poetic texts are A. Campbell, *The Battle of Brunanburh* (London, 1938), B. Dickins, *Runic and Heroic Poems of the Old Teutonic Peoples* (Cambridge, 1915, with translation), and N. Kershaw, *Anglo-Saxon and Norse Poems* (Cambridge, 1922, with translation). Among translations of poetic texts are J. R. Clark Hall, *Beowulf and The Finnesburg Fragment* (new ed., revised by C. L. Wrenn; London, 1950, in prose), A. S. Cook and C. B. Tinker, *Select Translations from Old English Poetry* (Cambridge, 1926, in prose and verse), R. K. Gordon, *Anglo-Saxon Poetry* (Everyman's Library, London, 1954, in prose and including a translation of *Beowulf*), C. W. Kennedy, *The Poems of Cynewulf* (London, 1910, in prose), *The Cædmon Poems* (London, 1916, in prose), *Old English Elegies* (Princeton, 1936, in alliterative verse), *Early English Christian Poetry* (London, 1952, in alliterative verse) and K. Malone, *Ten Old English Poems* (Baltimore, 1941, in alliterative verse).

The novice should take his first steps in Old English with the aid of H. Sweet, *Anglo-Saxon Primer* (9th ed., revised throughout by N. Davis; Oxford, 1953). He would be well advised not to use the earlier editions. From there he may progress to G. L. Brook, *An Introduction to Old English* (Manchester, 1955) and thence to a Reader such as A. J. Wyatt, *An Anglo-Saxon Reader* (Cambridge, 1925), H. Sweet, *An Anglo-Saxon Reader* (revised by C. T. Onions, 12th ed., Oxford, 1950) or P. S. Ardern, *First Readings in Old English* (2nd ed., Wellington, N.Z., 1951). For dictionary he may use J. R. C. Hall, *A Concise Anglo-Saxon Dictionary* (3rd ed., Cambridge, 1931) or H. Sweet, *The Student's Anglo-Saxon Dictionary* (Oxford, 1897). If he persevere he may ultimately progress to R. Girvan, *Angelsaksisch Handboek, in het Nederlandisch Bewerkt door E. L. Deuschle, Oudgermaansche Handboeken IV* (Haarlem, 1931), or to E. Sievers and K. Brunner, *Altenglische Grammatik, nach der Angelsächsischen Grammatik von Eduard Sievers neubearbeitet von Karl Brunner; zweite revidierte Auflage der Neubearbeitung* (Halle, 1951). The most comprehensive dictionary is J. Bosworth and T. N. Toller, *An Anglo-Saxon Dictionary* (Oxford, 1882–98), *Supplements*, Parts I–III (Oxford, 1908–21).

INDEX

Index